Performing Religion in Public

Performing Religion in Public

Edited by

Claire Maria Chambers, Simon W. du Toit
and Joshua Edelman

First published 2013 by
PALGRAVE MACMILLAN

Palgrave Macmillan in the UK is an imprint of Macmillan Publishers Limited, registered in England, company number 785998, of Houndmills, Basingstoke, Hampshire RG21 6XS.

Palgrave Macmillan in the US is a division of St Martin's Press LLC, 175 Fifth Avenue, New York, NY 10010.

Palgrave Macmillan is the global academic imprint of the above companies and has companies and representatives throughout the world.

Palgrave® and Macmillan® are registered trademarks in the United States, the United Kingdom, Europe and other countries.

ISBN 978–1–137–33862–4

This book is printed on paper suitable for recycling and made from fully managed and sustained forest sources. Logging, pulping and manufacturing processes are expected to conform to the environmental regulations of the country of origin.

A catalogue record for this book is available from the British Library.

A catalog record for this book is available from the Library of Congress.

Typeset by MPS Limited, Chennai, India.

Contents

List of Figures   vii

Acknowledgements   viii

Notes on Contributors   ix

Introduction: The Public Problem of Religious Doings   1
Claire Maria Chambers, Simon W. du Toit, and Joshua Edelman

Part I   Publics and the Non-Democratic State

1   The Market for Argument   27
     Simon W. du Toit

2   Public Acts of Private Devotion: From Silent Prayer to
     Ceremonies in France's Early Seminaries   49
     Joy Palacios

3   The Durban Passion Play: Religious Performance,
     Power and Difference   71
     Michael Lambert and Tamantha Hammerschlag

Part I Discussion   87

Part II   Visceral Publics

4   Church on/as Stage: Stewart Headlam's Rhetorical Theology   97
     Tom Grimwood and Peter Yeandle

5   The Intolerable, Intimate Public of Contemporary
     American Street Preaching   117
     Joshua Edelman

6   Faith, Fright, and Excessive Feeling   134
     Kris Messer

Part II Discussion   153

Part III   Publics and Commodification

7   Congregations, Audiences, Actors: Religious Performance
     and the Individual in Mid-Nineteenth-Century Nottingham   163
     Jo Robinson and Lucie Sutherland

8   Sufi Ceremonies in Private and Public   179
     Esra Çizmeci

9   From Religion to Culture: The Performative *Pūjā* and
    Spectacular Religion in India   194
    Saayan Chattopadhyay

Part III Discussion   209

Part IV   Ephemeral Publics

10 Coming Out of the (Confessional) Closet: Christian
    Performatives, Queer Performativities   219
    Stephen D. Seely

11 Performing Jewish Sexuality: *Mikveh* Spaces in Orthodox
    Jewish Publics   237
    Shira Schwartz

12 Busking and the Performance of Generosity: A Political
    Economy of the Spiritual Gift   256
    Claire Maria Chambers

Part IV Discussion   278

Index   286

List of Figures

1.1	Paul's Cross Churchyard in 1600	34
7.1	*Nottingham Journal,* 17 July 1865	171
9.1	*Durga Puja* street scene	198
9.2	*Durga Puja* – tourist consumers inside a *pandal*	200
12.1	One of the numbered music notes painted on the Market sidewalk to indicate an official busking spot, December 2010	270
12.2	Blues musician Reggie Miles plays his saw and sings for an audience of one, December 2010	273

Acknowledgements

Work for this project has been aided and supported by a great number of people as well as some institutions. In particular, we would like to thank members of the Performance and Religion Working Group of the International Federation for Theatre Research; members of the Religion and Theatre Focus Group of the Association for Theatre in Higher Education; the Sogang University Office of Faculty Research for its 2012 Research Support grant; T.H.P. Haynes and B. Matthews of the Tonbridge School in Tonbridge, Kent, UK; Amy Champ; Sacha Lake; Edmund B. Lingan; Lea Mühlstein; Kate Newey; Jeffrey Richards; Carolyn Roark; Kim Skjoldager-Nielsen; Rabbi Debbie Young-Somers; and Paula Kennedy. Permission to reprint images has come from Peter Blayney and the Nottingham Local Studies Library, Nottingham City Council. Our cover image is by Chris Schwalm, whose website is www.cjschwalm.com.

As editors, we are very grateful to our contributors for their scholarship, wisdom, work and insights. We acknowledge how much this project has benefited from our collaborators, partners and interlocutors. Responsibility for mistakes, however, remains our own.

Notes on Contributors

Claire Maria Chambers is Assistant Professor of Drama in the Department of English and Linguistics at Sogang University in Seoul, South Korea, where she teaches modern American and British drama. Her research investigates the influence of apophatic spiritualities (for example, negative theology, Christian mysticism and Orthodox iconography) on theories of presence and representation, but she is interested in how these practices refute transcendence. She analyses the performance of religion in contemporary culture and politics through the enacted rhetorics of liturgy and ritual, and approaches the playwright as performance theorist. Her articles can be found in *Performance Research, Performance and Spirituality, Liturgy* and *Ecumenica*.

Saayan Chattopadhyay is Assistant Professor and Head of the Department of Journalism and Mass Communication at Baruipur College, Calcutta University, India. After a stint as a journalist, he is currently engaged in research in media, ethnicity and gender. He has published articles and book chapters in *Studies in South Asian Film and Media, The Journal of Contemporary Literature, Sarai Reader, Senses of Cinema, Proteus: A Journal of Ideas*, and chapters for books published by IGI 11 Global, Sussex Academic Press, and VDM Publishing, among others. His research interests include postcolonial journalism, popular culture, performative theory, and masculinity studies.

Esra Çizmeci, holder of the Sacred Heart Scholarship, pursues her research on Sufi ritual performance as a PhD student at Roehampton University, UK. She holds an MFA in Acting and an MA in Theatre History and Criticism from CUNY Brooklyn College. Esra also received a Buchwald Fellowship from CUNY to research Tiyatro Boyali Kus, a Turkish theatre company, focusing on their use of Theatre of the Oppressed techniques. She worked with LOTOS Collective of UK to collaborate on *Triangulated City*, a Live Art performance project in Beirut with Zoukak Theatre Company & Cultural Association of Lebanon. Currently, Esra works as a lecturer at Istanbul Aydın University.

Simon W. du Toit works in theatre as an actor, director, teacher and scholar. Currently he is an Outstanding Scholars Advisor and also a Sessional Instructor in the School of Dramatic Art at the University of Windsor, Canada. His research interests focus on the intersections between cultural performance, religion and the theatre; and he is also a member of the peer review board of *Ecumenica*. His work has been published in *Ecumenica, Liturgy*, and the *Journal of Dramatic Theory and Criticism*.

x *Notes on Contributors*

Joshua Edelman is Fellow in Research and Enterprise at the Royal Central School of Speech and Drama, University of London, UK. His research focuses on the functions of theatre and performance in the religious and political systems of the contemporary West. He is a member of the Project on European Theatre Systems, works with the Institute for Theology, Imagination and the Arts at the University of St Andrews, and currently serves as co-convenor of the Performance and Religion Working Group of the International Federation for Theatre Research. His research has appeared in a range of journals from *Nordic Theatre Studies* to *Liturgy*.

Tom Grimwood is a Senior Lecturer in Ethics and Cultural Theory at the University of Cumbria, UK. His research focuses on cultural hermeneutics and, in particular, the formative role of ambiguity within acts of interpretation. He has applied this to a range of subjects, from the work of irony in Nietzsche and Kierkegaard, to the paradoxes of embodiment in Simone de Beauvoir and Catherine of Siena. His work has appeared in journals such as *Angelaki, The Journal for Cultural Research, Feminist Theology* and *The British Journal for the History of Philosophy*. His book *Irony, Misogyny and Interpretation* was published in 2012.

Tamantha Hammerschlag is a lecturer in the School of The Arts (Drama and Performance Studies) at the University of KwaZulu-Natal in Pietermaritzburg, South Africa. She has written articles on the body and performance and theatre aesthetics. In addition to her academic work, she is a playwright, theatre director and designer.

Michael Lambert was a Senior Lecturer in the School of Religious Studies, Philosophy and Classics (Classics) at the University of KwaZulu-Natal in Pietermaritzburg, South Africa. He is presently lecturing at the University of Cape Town. He is the author of *The Classics and South African Identities* (2011) and of book chapters and articles on comparative ancient Greek and traditional Zulu religion. Other research interests include gender and sexuality in antiquity, and Greek and Roman literature. General interests include music, languages and travel: he is director of the University Madrigal Singers, teaches Spanish and has led many overseas Classics tours to countries such as Greece, Italy and Turkey.

Kris Messer holds an MFA in playwriting from Brown University and a PhD in Theatre History and Performance Studies from the University of Maryland, College Park. She is an Instructor in the Department of Humanistic Studies at the Maryland Institute College of Art, USA and a Visiting Lecturer in the Graduate Program at the University of Maryland, College Park, USA. She has done research on Christian Community-based performance in North

America, and she is interested in the field of community-based performance as it intersects spirituality, the body, and gender.

Joy Palacios holds a PhD in Performance Studies from the University of California, Berkeley. Her research investigates the political impact of religious practice in its public, embodied and organized forms, with special attention to patterns of disavowal and overlap between religious expression and the performing arts. Her book project, with the current title 'Preaching for the Eyes: Priests, Actors, and Ceremonial Splendor in Early Modern France', examines the link between the reform of Catholic worship through seminary education during the Counter-Reformation and the rise of clerical animosity toward actors in seventeenth- and eighteenth-century France. Palacios is presently a visiting scholar at Vanderbilt University's Divinity School, USA.

Jo Robinson is Associate Professor in Drama and Performance in the School of English, University of Nottingham, UK. She led the Arts and Humanities Research Council funded interdisciplinary project, 'Mapping Performance Culture', which created an innovative map interface to enable exploration of nineteenth-century performance history in Nottingham. Her research focuses on theatre historiography, methodologies of mapping and understanding the role of community in the creation and reception of performance. Her work has been published in a number of journals, including *Nineteenth Century Theatre and Film*, *New Theatre Quarterly* and *Performance Research*.

Shira Schwartz is currently completing her fourth year of doctoral study in theatre and performance at York University in Toronto, Canada. After finishing her BA in 2007 with a specialization in collective creation, she lived in Jerusalem for six months and studied in an orthodox Jewish seminary for women. Upon her return she began her MA, which she completed in 2009. Her current area of research is Performing Jewishness and Sexuality. She is also interested in ethnography, dramaturgy and new play development.

Stephen D. Seely is a PhD candidate in the Department of Women's and Gender Studies at Rutgers University, USA. His project looks at notions of 'other worlds' and 'other lives' in philosophy, literature, revolutionary movements, and art. He has published work on affect theory, queer theory and becoming. He also has two co-edited special editions currently in progress: 'Derrida and the Material Turn' and 'Revolutionary/Queer/Desire: The Afterlives of Guy Hocquenghem'.

Lucie Sutherland teaches drama and performance at the University of Nottingham, UK. Her research is primarily concerned with the theatre industry from the mid-nineteenth century to the present day, most particularly in relations to developments in professional infrastructure over that period of time relating to commercial management and actor training. In addition, as part of the Arts and Humanities Research Council funded 'Mapping Performance Culture' project she has published on civic identity and performance culture in nineteenth-century Nottingham, work extended through the co-authored contribution to this volume. Interest in current performance practice is also reflected in regular contributions, as a theatre critic, to the *Times Literary Supplement*.

Peter Yeandle is Lecturer in Economic History at the University of Manchester, UK. His current research project focuses on performance histories of protest and social activism. Recent publications include essays on the Occupy movement in historical context, John Ruskin's influence on the late-Victorian Christian Socialist movement, and West End dramatizations of Ruskinian political economy. He is currently co-editing a forthcoming volume of essays provisionally entitled 'Politics, Performance and Popular Culture: Theatre and Society in Nineteenth-century Britain'. He retains an interest in the politics of history teaching, which is the subject of a forthcoming monograph, *Rethinking 'Our Island Story'*.

Introduction: The Public Problem of Religious Doings

Claire Maria Chambers, Simon W. du Toit, and Joshua Edelman

As lived practice, religion troubles many of our common understandings of contemporary public life. It refuses confinement to a segregated sphere, whether intellectual, domestic, or personal; it holds extraordinary political and cultural influence without necessarily respecting modern, secular norms of reasonable argument or human equality. It seeps across boundaries between the public and the private, the political and the personal, the representative, the ontological, and the performative. As such, there has been considerable debate over the appropriate relationship between religion and the public life we have come to share as citizens of the post-Enlightenment West. In political theory that shared life has often been conceptualized as the 'public sphere': a deliberative space with agreed-upon rules for rational argumentation in which equal citizens meet to build communities, identities, and political opinions.

The public sphere is often understood to be a secular and rationalist space, from which religion is to be excluded. But this separation cannot be maintained. Certain issues continue to trouble and transgress the borders that have been drawn between the public sphere and religion: arguments about the visibility of mosques and minarets in some European cities, the display of overt signs of religious affiliation such as a hijab in public schools and workplaces, the struggle for same-sex couples for both civil and religious marriage, debates about the teaching of evolution, Creationism, or Yoga in public schools, the 'war on terror' and its relationship to a crusade, the role of theocracy in global politics, and so on. We face a timely need to re-conceive the relationship between religion and the public sphere.

German political theorist Jürgen Habermas, the intellectual source of most contemporary discussion of the public sphere, has himself noted an increasingly urgent need to address the role of religion in public affairs, brought on by cultural and political divisions in the West 'prompted by the Iraq War'.[1] In response to that need, this book argues that we can better understand religion's relationship to the public sphere by conceiving religion *performatively*, rather than normatively. That is, religion is not (just) a set

1

of ethical, ontological or theological assertions, but a dynamic, lived, and fluidly embodied set of actions, practices, gestures and speech acts at specific points in time and space. Its meaning comes not (only) through theological argument, but (also) through ritual, liturgy, prayer, meditation, et cetera. In short, religions exist because they are performed. The theoretical position of this volume is that, like religion, the public sphere is performatively constituted in this way. The meeting of these two epistemologies of practice – the public sphere and religion – undermines any effort either makes to contain the other. In particular, it contests dichotomies such as the sacred versus the secular, the private versus the public, and the rational versus the revealed.

Let us tease this out through an example. In 1931, the newspaper baron William Randolph Hearst bought the thirteenth-century monastery of Santa María de Óvila in La Mancha, Spain, and had much of its beautiful stonework dismantled and shipped to his hometown of San Francisco, California, in order to build himself a private castle. Unlike the Hollywood version of this story,[2] however, Hearst never built his Xanadu. His failing fortunes and the Depression scuttled the project, and Hearst donated the stones to the city, which eventually used them to adorn the paths of Golden Gate Park. At some point in the late 1980s or early 1990s – the record does not specify – a city park worker apparently placed an unremarkable, four-foot granite traffic bollard amidst the stones. A few years later, a spiritual devotee named Baba Kali Das (or Michael Bowen) saw the bollard and recognized it as a *lingam,* a representation of the god Shiva often used as a focus for devotion, and began to worship it appropriately, chanting prayers and offerings of flowers and incense. Soon, Hindu and New Age worshippers began gathering up the Óvila stones to build a devotional circle around the *lingam.* Their actions caused problems for the city's need to keep its park safe, ordered, and open to all. A spontaneously emerging site of neo-Hindu worship was not a part of their plans for the use of this public space.[3]

These stones make a useful illustration of ways in which religion can wrestle with the secular public sphere (and the governmentality that supports it) for a space of its own. Throughout their years, the Óvila stones (as well as the anonymous bollard) served as spatial markers, defining different sorts of spaces as appropriate for different sorts of religious and secular practices. The Óvila stones originally marked out a place intentionally distinct and removed from 'worldly' civic life, one designed to facilitate the daily rituals of the austere, self-sufficient religious life of Cistercian monks. Centuries later, these stones were turned into a commodity and transported half a world away to contribute to a secular space for civic tranquillity, but they were appropriated to frame a surreptitious, unauthorized performance of neo-Hindu devotion, alongside a traffic bollard chosen for its shape and location. All these stones are now located in a public space that civic authorities constructed as secular and inclusive, but they have been used, reused, and misused to facilitate or inhibit religious practices of all sorts for most of their history.

Importantly, these stones did all this work without proclamation – they remained stones, not placards. They were silent; they did not assert a religious (or secular) argument to which members of the public or governing authorities could give assent or take issue. Instead, they worked practically, as props, making possible performances that could hail a group as a public, either religiously (as monks, as worshippers) or secularly (as citizens of the city of San Francisco). The stones had no *inherent* religious or secular identity; rather, their identity came from their participation in a set of discursive, gestural acts that both inscribed and described them with one.

The stones are thus an excellent example of the performative. They exist as stones, but their meaning comes from how they are used; they become either *lingam* or bollard according to the context in which they participate. Caught up in the production of community and identity of Baba Kali Das and his fellow worshippers, as well as the performance of the city of San Francisco itself in its role as keeper of the peace and arbiter of the use of public space, the stones are the medium through which these communities and identities perform their entrance into and dialogue within the public sphere. A medium is a vehicle; it only expresses when it is actively deployed, when it performs. Like the stones, religion itself is one of the many mediums through which the construction of the public sphere takes place. And like the traffic of worshippers and citizens through the park and across these stones, the public sphere itself is not a distinct and static zone, but an intersection.

In La Mancha, the stones marked out a space set aside for a quite demanding form of religious devotion, one open only to those who were willing to live under those particular religious strictures. In San Francisco, the same stones, appropriated and repurposed by market forces, eventually were used to mark out a public space, open to all, and governed by democratically established principles of what was and was not an appropriate use of public space. Neither act of marking-out posed a problem in itself; the monastery worked perfectly well as a monastery as did the park as a park. These acts only became transgressive – and thus interesting for our purposes here – when a religious act irrupted into a space designated as secular and public; when, that is, someone began performing devotional actions appropriate to a monastery in a public space such as a park.

This volume explores such acts of disjunction because they have an extraordinary potential to reveal the function that religion can serve in contemporary democratic societies. In many ways, contemporary publics thrive on such disjunctions: religious festivals that get caught up in a secular party scene, or prayers around school flagpoles that assert both religious affiliation and constitutional rights, are actions that demonstrate the imbrication of religiosity and the secular in contemporary civic life. Nevertheless, these disjunctions raise difficult and fascinating questions about the nature of the intellectual, social, and physical space that we share as members of a democratic polity and about the role that religion plays within it.

Rather than becoming mired in a polemical debate about the appropriate public role of religion, this volume hopes to reframe the discussion. We seek to explore the different territories between the two seemingly irreconcilable stances of secularity and religiosity. These are grounds that shift and slip, like sand dunes, keeping shape but always moving, because they uncover relationships between different aspects of public life that are in process and constantly performed. 'Religion' is not one stable foundation to be unearthed as a genealogical imperative, nor is 'secularity' to be constructed as a future evolutionary necessity. Talal Asad suggests that what is new about secularism is that it presupposes 'new concepts of 'religion', 'ethics', and 'politics,' and new imperatives associated with them'; if that is so, then also on this list must be a new concept of the public sphere's relation to religion and religious expression.[4]

We recognize religion as a lived social and political reality, and thus we necessarily recognize that there are limits to normative arguments for social formation from either religious or secular perspectives.[5] From this perspective, the question of whether or not religious interventions in the public sphere (which can be clearly observed) are legitimate or illegitimate, allowable or impermissible, is simply not the most interesting or helpful one. The narrow focus on that question reduces our interest in religion's role in public life down to the theological or political *claims* made by religion, and the degree to which they are valid, authoritative, or compelling. That reduction is a product of the familiar binary between religion and reason; but religion functions not only, or even primarily, through claims, but through organized, meaningful practices (such as rituals and ethical systems), actions, and displays of belonging, all of which inform public life, cultural identity, and political deliberation.

In short, we understand religion's public power not in terms of the arguments it makes, but in terms of its performative presence. That presence has a potency and fluidity with which any adequate explanation of public religiosity must come to terms. We hope to show that the methods developed by the academic field of performance studies are particularly useful for this task.

The chapters below describe a number of performative irruptions of religion into the secular public sphere, as well as the use of 'publicness' to inform an understanding of the religious aspects of social identity. In their various ways, they all engage with the methods of performance studies. These methods can articulate the means by which religious action can be socially effective in ways other than the assertion of a compelling claim. Performance studies often regards cultural, linguistic, and political structures as sites for historical or critical excavation, but not as sources for a hidden, normative point of origin. Rather, performance studies looks to trace out the repeated interventions of power in the construction of that history – the power of the wealthy and the ruling as well as the power of the masses, of particular communities, or of the subaltern in one form or another.

Such an approach is useful because religious expression in public life often 'reasons' in ways that challenge an assumed normative primacy of logical abstraction. The bodies and voices that perform religiously often belong to those excluded from the privileged spheres of public rational debate, thus exposing the disjunctions of power and subjectivity, sovereignty and agency that allow the public sphere to function in the first place.

This volume asserts that the public is felt and performed as much as it is deliberated, and it is acted upon by those whose lives and bodies make up a democracy as much as it is enacted through speech, gesture, text, or image. That *aesthetic* and *affective* expression of the public sphere – which sits necessarily but uncomfortably alongside its political and philosophical construction – is an important aspect of the space religion occupies in the public sphere, and it is a prime site for performative analysis.

Habermas and the bourgeois public sphere

The central voice around which discussion of the public sphere is organized is that of the German political philosopher Jürgen Habermas, one of Europe's leading contemporary public intellectuals. His defining the notion of the public sphere in *The Structural Transformation of the Public Sphere* (1962) excluded religious discourse from public life, and he and his interlocutors have been debating and revising that relationship ever since. As this debate, to which we hope to contribute with this book, is structured by Habermasian concepts, an outline of them is useful here.

Habermas' model of the public sphere is both a historical explanation and a normative proposal. He traces the emergence of the public sphere to the salon culture and coffeehouses of France, England, and Germany in the late seventeenth and early eighteenth centuries, a period during which the increasing market circulation of print permitted the exchange of opinion across social boundaries. By means of the circulation of public opinion, sovereign authority was effectively democratized, undermining the imperial power of monarchs across Europe.[6] The force of public debate gradually displaced the legitimizing power of religion, until 'public opinion' itself became a legitimizing force for sovereign authority.

Habermas advanced this view of the social role of communicative action as a key component of the social conditions of a democracy. Ken Hirschkop suggests that, in doing so, Habermas was responding directly to the emerging power of the welfare state in Germany in the early 1960s,[7] which Habermas perceived as threatening to democracy for two reasons: it viewed citizens as clients, compromising the differentiation between public and private; and it professionalized policy-making, taking it out of the purview of public criticism. Habermas has also consistently framed his ideas to counterbalance the nationalist, populist view of sovereignty supported by Carl Schmitt and others, which Habermas finds is exemplified in the Nazi regime.

In this early work Habermas objected to the sectarian and anti-egalitarian nature of religious arguments, as they exclude nonbelievers (and believers of different traditions) from the publics they seek to address. Rational deliberation was viewed as providing legitimation to political authority, whereas the return of religious authority to politics threatened a return to more primitive conditions that, for centuries, produced 'bloody religious wars.'[8] He viewed religious traditions as having a similar social function as the family or the education system; they are 'general reproductive functions of the lifeworld,'[9] and are concerned with social reproduction and integration. Habermas emphasized the importance of differentiating the public sphere from both private life and official power. In his view, religions are inescapably tied to private life, and the meanings available in religious discourses are therefore not always susceptible to generalization. Only the mutual understanding produced by reason can serve as the unifying force that gives coherence to democratic societies.

The coffeehouses of early modern England served an important, though idealized, role in what was a particularly twentieth-century western struggle. Although the public sphere itself has no real political power, its capacity for independently influencing politics must be protected, Habermas feels, as a bulwark against the increasing disenfranchisement of citizens in democratic nations. As influential as the idea of the public sphere has been, it is only one important element in Habermas's broader project. For Habermas, communicative action is the social force that sustains democratic polity. Reason communicated in debate is the compelling force that alone provides common ground across lines of religious and cultural difference.[10]

Perhaps because Habermas's concept of the bourgeois public sphere remains such a durable framework for political theorists of democracy, it has been engaged with, challenged, and reimagined from several critical perspectives. Habermas himself has been remarkably open to this engagement and has often revised his views in response to it. He has grappled with Rawls's initial insistence that rational debate must be the only basis for communication in the public sphere. For both, democracy depends upon equality of access to public argument, and a mutually comprehensible language of discussion. Both Rawls and Habermas have modified their early positions on the role of reason, allowing for the public articulation of a religious voice but still insisting that religious arguments must enter the public sphere 'in translation' to a reasonable, generally accessible language.[11]

To be sure, both reason and religion create closed circles of discourse; only rational arguments will work in a rational debate; only religious reasoning can argue with religious conviction. This is the problem that Habermas tries to untie in the quest for a global democratic order in which the notion of a common public good empowered by the public sphere has begun to fracture. Religion is an undeniable political reality – one that holds a particular potency in our pluralist, multicultural society.

This is Habermas's challenge. On the one hand, he suggests that religion must be excluded from the public sphere because it is anti-democratic: it threatens to create and reproduce irrational and indefensible identifications with subcommunities that undermine the inclusivity and egalitarianism necessary for all citizens to take part in the deliberative governance of their society. On the other hand, modern social life is alienating and fractious, and religious identifications offer an enormously potent sense of belonging and purpose that would be extremely valuable to the contemporary democratic project. Habermas wonders how the social power of religion can be harnessed without succumbing to an anti-rationalist, anti-democratic logic. In this book, we suggest one path to an answer: that we should understand religion's public power not in terms of the arguments it makes, but in terms of the performative acts it generates.

The bourgeois public sphere is not an ideal that ever came to full fruition, but it can be turned to as a model for 'unremitting self-critique of modern society that simultaneously called forth greater scrutiny of the "public sphere" itself.'[12] This is exactly the kind of self-scrutiny this volume proposes, one where the deliberative functions and identificatory processes of public religious performances open up the public sphere as a performative event itself.

Responses to Habermas

Nancy Fraser was one of the first to point out in an influential essay that the Habermasian bourgeois public sphere was 'constituted by a number of significant exclusions',[13] such as gender and class. On the basis of inequalities of access, Fraser, citing Geoff Eley, suggests that in fact from its inception, the public sphere was constructed in conflict. Fraser asks whether it is even possible for speakers to 'bracket status differentials' and social inequalities when they are engaged in public discussion. Fraser's provocation gives rise to a series of questions that this collection proposes to explore. To what extent do religious cultures produce social inequalities, and in fact succeed by creating them? Does religious life require exclusionary discourses and practices to maintain its stability? Conversely, to what extent, and in what contexts, are religious voices marginalized, contained, or oppressed, either simply because they are religious or because their religiousness has not been rationally authorized? If status differentials cannot, in fact, be bracketed off in public discussion, in what ways are they marked, or in what ways do they make their presence felt?

Another critical issue Fraser raises is that for her, 'public spheres are not only arenas for the formation of discursive opinion; in addition, they are arenas for the formation and enactment of social identities.'[14] Michael Warner similarly has criticized Habermas's construction of the bourgeois public sphere as a space that 'claimed to have no relation to the body image at all'.[15] This abstraction serves to privilege unmarked identities: 'the male, the white, the middle-class, the normal'.[16] The critical role of embodiment in discourse, its disavowal in the public sphere, and the elision of the historically and culturally particular in public argument open further key points of entry for examining the public sphere as performed. Religious performances often offer up spatial, temporal, and social orders on the basis of bodily markers, including the denial of the body implicit in both much rationalist modern philosophy and the theological positions of many religious traditions. A performative view of religion can help us ask once again whether it is either possible or desirable to 'bracket off' embodiment from reasoned debate, as the Habermasian public sphere seems to do. When Cornel West announces himself as 'a blues man in the life of the mind, a jazzman in the world of ideas', he is drawing attention to his own warmly embraced embodied stance as a 'Negro Christian' public intellectual, and he refuses any effort to normalize, conceal, and 'deodorize the funk' of his particular, historical, embodied humanity.[17]

Michael Warner's *Publics and Counterpublics* (2002) offers a significant development of Habermas's ideas. Warner draws attention to the possibility of multiple publics functioning within the same cultural environment, one general and dominant (unmarked) public and a number of counterpublics marked off as particular. For Warner, the existence of the counterpublic challenges boundaries between the public and the private. Warner observes that 'the public sphere is a principal instance of the forms of embodiment and social relations that are themselves at issue'.[18] For Warner, participation in a public cannot be reduced to rational communication because any public communication demands the embodied performance of the private. In Warner's model, participants in counterpublics are 'marked off from persons or citizens in general',[19] and play a resistant and subordinate role within a dominant culture. However, as in any other kind of public, discursive circulation among strangers remains a critical feature of counterpublics. In that respect, Warner, like Habermas, recognizes the centrality of communicative action in democracies. He regards 'stranger sociability' as one of the normative features of modernity.[20]

For Warner, publics are among the conditions of textuality. He often directly addresses the reader as a 'public' and performs the discursive reflexivity he posits. Perhaps because of that principle, Warner regards public religious speech as having a strictly private function. His argument is grounded in the Protestant Christian preaching tradition, and he develops it at some length. He suggests that sermons, for example, arise from a divine address to 'particular persons in their singularity,' and are thus not essentially circulating forms of discourse that could lead to the creation of either a public or a counterpublic.[21] The history of public preaching casts serious doubt on this claim. To what extent, and in what contexts is religious discourse private, or public? Clearly, Christian preaching in the West served a different social function in the nineteenth century than it did in the sixteenth or seventeenth centuries. What role do historical conditions have in the circulation of religious discourses? By what means, and in what manner, is the circulation of religious discourse effective in producing a public, or a counterpublic? Is religious discourse capable of 'reflexivity about its own circulation'[22] in a way that would mark it as constitutive of a public (or a counterpublic) to which agency could be attributed?

It is perhaps in his comments about poetic world-making that Warner opens the most salient theoretical door for our consideration. Within gay or queer counterpublics, the boundaries of discursive address are redrawn in such a way that speakers must inevitably take up a double consciousness 'between modes of publicness'.[23] Where dominant publics tend to assume a universal sphere of address, counterpublics take up a 'poesis of scene making' that may serve a transformative, rather than replicative, social function. Warner's theorizing marks the transition from embodiment to textuality as the scene for the performative production of a counterpublic.[24] Warner's work has been viewed as a generative intervention into queer theory, but it has consequences that far transcend these origins. Any model for social force has to account for the workings of power in a way that accords with history. Warner's proposal troubles the role of 'rational-critical reflection as the self-image of humanity', and opens a space for embodied practice to be considered as a constitutive part of how democratic publics are shaped.

Habermas's engagement with religions

Habermas has not only been committed to dialogue with his critics in the secular academy; he has maintained a conversation with his religious critics as well. Particularly in the face of the growing interculturalism in his native Germany and elsewhere, Habermas has consistently perceived the necessity for rethinking categories such as the public and the private, the nation-state and democracy, and secular and religious culture. As many have observed, he has moved away from his early position that assumed that western cultures were growing increasingly secular, and has shown an open-minded engagement with the question of how religions can constructively participate in political processes within democratic nation states.[25] More recently, he has participated in a number of public discussions concerning the role of religion in the public sphere.

Habermas's 2007 debate with philosophers at the Jesuit School for Philosophy in Munich, later published in English under the title *An Awareness of What is Missing*, acknowledges his growing recognition that reason may not offer the resources needed to underpin secular morality. In that debate, Habermas addresses the insufficiency of 'post-metaphysical thinking' to cope with the failure of modernism to sustain 'the precepts of its morality of justice', and suggests that religion may have a role to play in filling that void.[26] Both sides of this philosophical and theological debate, however, seem to assume that religion is reducible to its propositional content. Habermas has insisted elsewhere that religious citizens within democracies face an epistemic challenge to accommodate faith to the 'autonomous progress of secular knowledge'. That process will finally only succeed in the arena of 'the faith and practice of the religious community'.[27] This cognitive flow from secular knowledge into cultural practice, however, reverses the relations between reason and embodiment as they are understood in performance studies.

Although Habermas seems increasingly ready to consider the implications of religious practice, he also offers a stern warning. The root of the desire to exclude religion from the public sphere is the fear of its return as a proto-governmental voice, one that is unresponsive to the demand of Enlightened rationality that all human beings must be equal in dignity under the law. The demand for equality is framed as a rational principle, and therefore, there is a terrifying prospect that religiously-based forms of authority and government may not recognize it. 'Nothing is more threatening than the fundamentalist refusal to communicate', Habermas writes.[28]

And here the American critic Stanley Fish cries foul. Such an attitude demands that religion must reduce itself to an instrument serving the ends of democratic rationality. But religious discourse (especially fundamentalist discourse) has its own ends to serve. The only relationship that Habermas can establish with such religious voices, according to Fish, is to refuse them tolerance, which is simply ineffective. 'If you wish to strike a blow against beliefs you think pernicious, you will have to do something more than exclaim, "I exclude you from my community of mutual respect."'[29] Fish connects this inability to recognize and respond to genuine alterity with his fundamental objection to the Habermasian project: its 'linguistic utopianism' fears interpretative multiplicity, and craves a unanimity that is 'impossible because the multidirectional fecundity of "diversity" Habermas fears is a property of language, not a misuse of it'.[30] Fish notes Habermas's desire for communication untrammelled by private interests or whims, and traces it to the Platonic elevation of philosophy over rhetoric.[31] Our approach addresses Fish's concern by focusing on the public sphere not as an *assertion* of certain normative democratic values, but as a *performative* space that can contain multiple voices without resolving them into harmony or unison.

From an explicitly Christian perspective, Nicholas Wolterstorff similarly challenges the ability of Habermas's public sphere to come to terms with otherness. Wolterstorff argues that asking religious people to set aside the religious traditions that have shaped them in favour of an impersonal reason is to ask the impossible: 'we live *inside* our traditions, not alongside.'[32] Demands for exclusively rational argument are not in fact neutral. He argues that rational argument will privilege secular positions; whereas religious discourses are often clearly marked as such, 'comprehensive secular perspectives will go undetected'.[33] Habermas's reply resonates with Fish in its suggestion that religion ought, in fact, to be marked out as different and treated with particular scepticism. Conflicts between faith traditions, Habermas argues, 'cannot be solved by compromise', but can only be contained, because of their absolute claims.[34] Again, we suggest that a reconceptualization of religion in performative terms, rather than propositional ones, considerably complicates Habermas's response.

At a public event held at Cooper Union in New York City in 2009, Habermas joined Judith Butler, Charles Taylor, and Cornel West in a lively discussion on the topic of religion's role in public debate.[35] Among the many significant ideas raised, the necessity of reconsidering the boundaries between religiosity and secularity is perhaps the most consequential. Craig Calhoun, Mark Juergensmeyer, and Jonathan Vanantwerpen have since made a significant contribution to that effort. Their co-edited volume, *Rethinking Secularism* (2011), offers a collection of essays that consider the difficulties of maintaining the secular/religious divide in an increasingly transnational global context. Calhoun's essay, 'Secularism, Citizenship, and the Public Sphere', questions the insistence that religion must remain a private matter: 'Religion simply was never in every sense private, any more than it was always conservative.'[36]

The Cooper Union discussion offered a public performance of a long-standing difference of opinion between Habermas and Taylor. Taylor's *Sources of the Self* (1989) provides a critical analysis of Habermas's view of reason and ethics;[37] in 1991 Taylor responded directly to Habermas's view of communicative action, describing it as a 'purely proceduralist ethics'.[38] Although the two share a strong mutual respect and a deep-seated desire to promote a just and moral democratic society, Taylor differs from Habermas on the most basic elements of their social and moral theory, and this difference leads him to reject Habermas's discourse theory of morality. Taylor's more phenomenological approach has led him to call for a reappraisal of the idea of secularity, a project he undertook himself in *A Secular Age* (2007).

In their debate of 2009, Taylor returned to his framework for the three goods that modern secular democracies require: liberty, equality, and fraternity. Taylor used these ideas to undermine what he called the 'fetishization of the favored institutional arrangements',[39] the separation of church and state that is commonly supposed to define secularity. He also forcefully challenged the 'distinction in rational credibility between religious and nonreligious discourse', calling it 'utterly without foundation'.[40] Instead, Taylor's approach accounted for the unifying *experiences* that maintain communities, secular or religious. As Talal Asad reflects on Taylor's position, 'Secularism is not simply an intellectual answer to a question about enduring social peace and toleration. It is an enactment by which a political medium (representation of citizenship) redefines and transcends particular and differentiating practices of the self that are articulated through class, gender, and religion.'[41] The 'transcendence' of any social category such as class, gender, or religion toward an overarching 'universalizing concept'[42] is embedded in practice and discourse.

What is at stake in the struggle to accommodate reason and faith in the public sphere is nothing less than the nature of the polity that underlies the democratic state. Habermas continues to assert the necessity of non-religious speech in formal arenas of judicial and political practice, such as parliament. At that level, the language of religious truth has no place. However, he does not ignore the fact that religious language contains truth that may be accessible to those outside the religion, but these ideas 'can only enter into the institutionalized practice of deliberation and decision-making if the necessary translation already occurs in the pre-parliamentarian domain, i.e., in the political public sphere itself'.[43] It is precisely for this reason that reconsideration of the features and varieties of secularisms has become more urgent.[44] To insist that religious language be 'translated' into language readily accessible to all certainly implies a totalizing prejudice that favors the speech of rational western thought, which has its own religious history. Fish rejects this as a misrecognition of the essential otherness of religious claims. As Saba Mahmood recently pointed out, 'the secular liberal principles of freedom of religion and speech are not neutral mechanisms for the negotiation of religious difference and remain quite partial to certain normative conceptions of religion, subject, language, and injury'.[45] Mahmood's neat tie-in of the legal assertion of secularity to the perquisites of the nation is a challenge to the religious history and normative assertions of Habermas's argument.

While not often in direct conversation with Habermas, Talal Asad's engagement with the question of secularism as a new kind of social and political space importantly provides another means to look at the performative dimension of religion in public. What concerns Asad is *how* religion becomes public, in the 'worldwide explosion of politicized religion in modern and modernizing societies.' This explosive growth would seem to disprove the 'secularization thesis' that modernity separates religion from other social spaces, privatizes religion, and results in the decline of the social significance of religious belief.[46] Writes Asad, 'The public sphere is not an empty space for carrying out debates. It is constituted by the sensibilities – memories and aspirations, fears and hopes – of speakers and listeners. And also by the manner in which they exist (and are made to exist) for each other, and by their propensity to act or react in distinctive ways.'[47] Because of its performative constitution, religion's powerful suasion of public feeling will never be contained by or constrained to the moral and the rational, despite Habermas's injunction to 'translate' itself into 'universally accessible discourse.' In fact, religion challenges the authority of existing assumptions of rationality, accessibility, and universality.

Performance studies

Habermas maintains that in a necessary process of translating religious and secular ways of speaking, 'the religious side must accept the authority of "natural" reason as the fallible results of the institutionalized sciences and the basic principles of the universalistic egalitarianism in law and morality,' and 'secular reason may not set itself up as the judge concerning truths of faith, even though in the end it can accept as reasonable only what it can translate into its own, in principle universally accessible, discourses'.[48] What are the remains of this process of translation, when *untranslatability* structures encounter with political, cultural, and social others, rather than with agreement or compromise? This is a question that hones in on performance as a means to interpret religion in the public sphere. As Diana Taylor writes, '[T]he problem of untranslatability, as I see it, is actually a positive one, a necessary stumbling block that reminds us that "we" – whether in our various disciplines, or languages, or geographic locations throughout the Americas [or religious convictions or political affiliations] – do not simply or unproblematically understand each other.'[49]

How do we not understand each other? We turn to performance studies as a means to unpack this 'how.' This volume explicitly engages the public sphere not only as a performative event, but itself as a performative – something that is constructed in the process of its expression, something that resists representation, repetition and replication because it exists in the moment, in its own doing. As with the example of the Óvila stones, the public sphere is a medium for expression and an intersection of expressions. Since by asking readers to consider the public sphere a performative this volume already asks implicitly 'What is the public sphere?' it is then also helpful to take a mindful step back and ask, 'What is performance?' and briefly situate this volume within the history and methods of performance studies.

Performance is a way of knowing through doing. It is an active epistemology. This assertion is the organizing concept behind the various schools of performance studies that now span the English-speaking world. For scholars dedicated to this field, performance is 'not only a subject for study but also an interpretive grid laid upon the process of study itself, and indeed upon almost any sort of human activity, collective or individual'.[50] As a theoretical lens, performance encounters human expression and interaction as an activity that produces culture, identity, discourse, and the structures of power at play within such production. More concerned with relationships than definitions, the performative lens often focuses on intercultural traffic between worldviews, working comparatively 'between theatre and anthropology',[51] for example. As an epistemology, performance is necessarily self-reflexive; it tries to think through its own doing. In this way, performance studies challenges the traditional academic separation of theory and practice, arguing instead for their integration: 'Performance studies struggles to open the space between analysis and action, and to pull the pin on the binary opposition between theory and practice. This embrace of different ways of knowing is radical because it cuts to the root of how knowledge is organized in the academy.'[52]

Performance's introspection and reflexivity is also a challenge to itself. Sometimes its inward turn makes for convolution rather than clarity, and although the international perspective of performance studies seems to be widening, scholars should still heed the warning that 'there is a danger that performance studies, for all its radical notions of 'discipline' and critical practice', will become mired in 'having a conversation with itself'.[53] The criticism that performance studies is esoteric when it should be accessible marks the fact that this 'anti-' or 'inter-' or 'trans-discipline' tries to deconstruct itself at the same time that it aims to apply itself. These two tasks cannot be fully separated; its application *is* the process of self-reflection. We use performance to theorize the public sphere in relation to religion because the public sphere *is discursive* as much as it creates space for discourse; it *performs a public* as much as it *performs publicly*. This double movement holds the performative faces of the public sphere reflexively up to one another so that we may attempt to watch ourselves in the process of construction, aware of the limits, reaching across boundaries of untranslatability.

Performance resists categorization and definition, and as such, the politics of performance studies itself tend to focus on modes of resisting domination and hegemonic control – whether in academia, politics, culture, or religion. Performance is inherently political, just as our operative terms 'public', 'private', and 'religion' are inherently political because they describe the dynamics of community and difference. Performance creates difference and multiplicity because it is never exactly reproducible. Performance resists definition because it is always in process, engaged in repetitions that Judith Butler calls 'ritualized production',[54] building off Foucault's notion of iteration in language. *A* performance may be repeated, but the very process of restaging a performance necessarily alters and modifies it. Performances may cite one another, but they can never exactly replicate an absent original.[55] Since each performance is its own unique event, live performance resists economies of reproduction and circulation. This is an essential aspect of the nature of performance. In the technical terms of performance theorist Peggy Phelan, performance comes into being through disappearance.[56] Through this process, performance grasps the political power of representation while escaping the control of systems of reproduction.

Analyzing the public sphere together with religion as social and political constructions 'enables us to think of performance – whether it is theatre or sport – as something that forms part of the entire ensemble of social relations rather than as an autonomous viewpoint from which the culture of the society in question may be interpreted'. Performance has 'no position which might allow it to stand apart from the myths or ideologies which shape and sustain the society of which it is a part'.[57] By enjoining readers to encounter the performance of religion in the public sphere from within, we must let go of the insider/outsider binary, and let go of the Enlightenment notion of an objective viewer looking down from above. Such liberation resists, and attempts to dismantle, the hegemonic hierarchies that organize human relationship, which are most often applied as constraints to identity and behaviour.

As an academic field, performance studies grew out of the experimental theatre movement of the 1960s and 70s in Britain and the United States, and its intersection with ritual studies and anthropology. After the Second World War, the Korean War, and on the threshold of the Vietnam War, an important moment arose for re-evaluating the differences and relationships between bodies, objects, and practices, and between the imaginary and the real. 'Performance' emerges from this time as a theoretical term that asks how we translate experience, how someone can know an Other, especially when great differences in experiences and background seem to prohibit direct communication. The performative lens looks for attempts at translation – where sense can be made from what people do together when doctrinal differences would seem to block mutual understanding. But performance also offers ways to respect and engage with the ways in which these attempts manifest *un*translatabilty, where 'the cleavage between [for example] secular knowledge and revealed knowledge cannot be bridged'.[58] By not only *thinking* about religion in the public sphere, but by entering, doing, dancing, talking, touching, fighting, eating, smelling, and embracing the lived public reality of religion, the chapters in this volume performatively engage the intersection between untranslatables.

Acts of translation are possible and necessary because of the *failure* of direct translatability (one-to-one correspondence between languages), analogous to the way that performance can repeat, but never exactly replicate, itself. Phenomenology, another key performance studies methodology, analyzes this process as experience. Phenomenology does not posit the observer as separate *from* the world, but rather as *of* the world and *with* the world, even *as* the world. The horizon of perception is indeed a limitation, but also the point at which the 'frame' – such as the frame of the mind or the body, the delineation of the skin or the limited purview of sight – opens out as the means of inclusion and experience, rather than only exclusion and selection. Phenomenology questions the frame as a limitation altogether, instead seeing boundaries as permeable and flexible, or even soluble. When phenomenologically approached, the performance of religion in the public sphere questions the priority of rationality and debate. If there is no 'outside,' only an 'inside' of phenomenal experience, that fact disrupts the very idea of the possibility of a public sphere as entirely separate from a private, and especially a religious, interiority.

Much of the genesis of the performance studies approach can be traced back to the collaborative relationship between anthropologist Victor Turner and theatre director and scholar Richard Schechner, who together studied the patterns of religious ritual as a means to better understand cultural 'others' and to search for foundational patterns of universal human performance. Radical theatre groups like the Performance Group and the Living Theatre created events that disrupted the established roles of audience and performers, such as *Dionysus in '69* and *Paradise Now,* and combined ritual, spirituality, religion, art, protest, and the politics of peace; out of the same forge, performance studies emerged to propose epistemologies that linked reason, politics, community, and embodiment. 'Truth' came to be understood in terms of 'experience', and the opposition between the 'real' and the 'constructed' was questioned. This development opened up for exploration the simultaneity of the philosopher's propositional *is* and the actor's imaginative *as* of ontology, epistemology, and phenomenology. Understanding religion as both separate from but simultaneously constitutive of the public sphere can draw from this complex and perplexing conflation of *is* and *as* that lies at the heart of performance studies.

Performance studies is an attempt to make use of an analysis of performative events and practices as a means to gain access to the network of relations between dialectics such as public/private, politics/culture, and ideology/theology. It seeks both to separate out the threads and to look for parallels, nodes, tangles, and crossings. Marking or framing is perhaps the most identifiable part of any 'event' itself – such as when the curtain rises and the audience sees the theatre set beyond the proscenium arch for the first time, or such as the transplantation of the Óvila stones to San Francisco. Performance studies questions the workings of these frames, where they begin and end, and how easily their boundaries may be maintained. 'To say something is a performance amounts to an ontological affirmation, though a thoroughly localized one. What one society considers a performance might be considered a non-event elsewhere.'[59] What does our society consider a public, and how can we be sure of the stability of the frame that surrounds it? One society's public may very well be another society's private sphere.

This questioning has critical intent. When a performance studies scholar seeks to delineate the normative frame, she simultaneously deconstructs it. To expose the frame is to do the work of alternative history, to re-write the story of its genesis. We take up the challenge of dismantling the often-assumed a priori genesis *ex nihilo* of the normative exclusion of religion from the public sphere. We ask: How is religion itself a discourse participating in other discourses of power, politics, rationality, and debate? How do religious performances and practices constitute various public spheres, private realms, and the relationships between them? But, most importantly, how does the undeniable influence of religion in the public sphere unfold the performative dimension of publics themselves?

Approaching religion in the public sphere from the perspective of performance studies means both tracing and breaking apart the frames that both religion and secularism set up to cordon off one another's prohibited ground, a process of translation that exposes the untranslatable as well. It means seeking to understand when and how the two came to be so separated, and how these frames are inflected and shaped by the discourse of power and history that came to define them. Performance, because it is neither simply a process, an event, nor an object, but rather an 'essentially contested concept',[60] is like an untranslatable word about which one grasps the sense even though one knows that by trying to define it one would render it meaningless. Religion, too, finally resists any theoretical 'place' or definition. It, too, is an undefinable – a 'performance' par excellence, existing as the effects of performative processes, rather than a reality bound by ontological affirmations. To be sure, it demands spaces that are physically inhabited (the market, the public square, the café or coffeehouse), but also exists through the virtual spaces of performative processes such as dialogue, text circulation, image production, and ritual repetition. It is a constant negotiation between participants, their beliefs and desires, their traditions, and the social networks of which they are a part. But secular reason also just as easily fits these characteristics, which demonstrates that the public sphere, where the dialogue between reason and religion takes place, is also an active space of constant negotiation; a space of performative acts of translation.

Engaging the public; considering religion

Habermas and Warner both recognize that the public sphere is an imagined space as much as it is a real one – it lives and is performed between the *is* and the *as*. Today's global culture necessitates constant negotiation for creating solidarity and common means of will-formation in democratic dialogues that span our pluralistic world. We are not the first to suggest that an intervention from performance studies might facilitate this task: Baz Kershaw's *The Radical in Performance* celebrates the subversive power of performance to critically engage with dominant political structures; John McKenzie's *Perform or Else* details the performative means by which knowledge and power are exercised in postmodernity; and the collection *Performing Democracy,* edited by Susan Haedicke and Tobin Nellhaus, offers a broad range of examples of how performance can empower and define communities and help them to resist various forms of oppression. Nor are we the first to explore the relevance of religious action for theatre and performance studies. This interest has taken on a particularly political shade in recent years. In introducing his collection *Religion, Theatre, and Performance,* Lance Gharavi writes, 'I want to suggest a shift in perspective: religion should no longer be thought of as something that can be "safely" sequestered in the private sphere', as it is a 'public force'.[61]

To contribute to this developing discourse, this book takes on the specific task of focusing on a critical seam within a secular conception of the public sphere: moments in which religious acts break into the public sphere and, in so doing, interrogate its intellectual and social assumptions. Is disinterested reason or rational deliberation still a necessary precondition for the efficacy and legitimacy of the public sphere? As Habermas and others have noted, 'more than reason alone is needed'.[62] This collection proposes that reason's lack is supplied by performance. Amidst the mounting pressures produced by cultural and political division, the collisions between secularism, religion, multiculturalism, and commodification threaten global stability, and call for innovative approaches to theoretical understanding and to safeguarding the cultural goods Taylor calls for: liberty, equality, and fraternity. At the intersection between performance, religion, and the public sphere we hope to find fresh insight and inspiration.

The chapters that follow take up the public sphere as a model with which to think about the multifaceted surfaces of public cultures and the ongoing discussion about deliberative politics in plural settings. The chapters are grouped into four parts according to their central theoretical concerns, rather than any similarities between the religious performances they document. This arrangement also allows history and normativity to interrogate each other, as they engage in a variety of ways with the pillars of Habermas's public sphere theory. Each part closes with a short dialogue in which the authors reflect on the threads that draw their chapters together.

The tensions between emergent publics and sovereign control of public speech emerge clearly in the book's first part, *Publics and the Non-Democratic State*, in which two of the chapters focus on contexts set prior to the emergence of democracy, and the third examines the Republic of South Africa during and after apartheid. Each author marks the ways in which the circulation of religious discourses were both constrained and instigated under non-democratic conditions. Simon du Toit observes the role of antitheatricality in early modern England in generating an early counterpublic. In English puritan culture, performance played a central role in constructing a subversive public space and circulating political resistance in the uncertain, shifting territory between text and speech; protecting its efficacy was a defining act of resistance. In her study of the training of eighteenth-century Parisian seminarians, Joy Palacios historically positions shifting attitudes toward the role of public performance in the creation of private, devotional experience and religious identity. Palacios illustrates how, through methods like role-play and rehearsal, seminary training in early modern France infused private religious experience with new awareness of public performance. Finally, Michael Lambert and Tamantha Hammerschlag offer an intriguing view of the Durban Passion Play, which is modelled on the Oberammergau Passion Play, and its performance history under widely divergent South African regimes. Their chapter marks shifts in the public role of religious performance under changing political structures, from the proto-fascist apartheid government through the period of apartheid's collapse and into the current period of challenging economic and political upheaval.

The chapters in *Visceral Publics* analyze religious acts of devotion, exchange, and identity construction based on a visceral engagement with Christian notions of sociality which offer a challenge or alternative to a Habermasian construction of a public sphere based on discursive rationality. Tom Grimwood and Peter Yeandle offer an intriguing complication of nineteenth-century British religious culture, at a time when Habermas sees the bourgeois public sphere at its most effective. Their chapter suggests that British religious culture was often politically resistant, fragmentary, and far from monolithic. Reverend Stewart Headlam's rhetorical theology challenged boundaries between orthodox Anglicanism, performance, and the public sphere, with its emphasis on beauty as an experience of divine grace available to – and merited by – all people. Their analysis suggests the ways in which religious culture was already implicit in the idea of the British bourgeois public. Joshua Edelman examines a particularly anti-rationalist appropriation of the public sphere: the yell of the open-air street preacher. He argues that, in most cases, the street preacher's hail characterizes its (unwilling) public as ignorant and foolish, and that this characterization is intolerable: it cannot be reasonably accepted in the manner that Warner's counterpublic hails are. However, he notes the possibility that, if the preacher is willing to join himself to the public that he hails (and thus undermine his position of privilege), there is an intimacy possible in the form that may be no more convincing but is nevertheless hugely compelling. Kris Messer describes the American evangelical Christian practice of performing Judgment Houses – popular immersive performances where the consequences of sin and disbelief are graphically dramatized by and for small communities. Messer describes how these performances construct an alternative, nostalgic politics of spirituality based on a visceral, terrifying, even cathartic experience of the consequences of sin.

The third part of the book, *Publics and Commodification*, surveys the effects of high capitalism in eroding monolithic religious authority and democratic exchange in three different cultural contexts. Theatre historians Jo Robinson and Lucie Sutherland construct a spatially inflected view of market competition and the role of consumer choice in structuring 'overlap' in public space. Market circulation of religious performance created a complex fabric of nineteenth-century English religious publics in Nottingham; Robinson and Sutherland embrace critical insights from geography, performance, and theatre history to document that rich exchange. Esra Çizmeci describes how the Sema ceremony, commonly known as the whirling Sufi dance, has been both contained and commodified by the Turkish government in its effort to construct Turkey as a tourist cultural destination. However, some Sufi performers have resisted the secularizing force of these actions, and their work continues to circulate in the Turkish public sphere, where it makes a post-secular contribution to the Turkish imagined community. Saayan Chattopadhyay's examination of the Hindu *Dūrgā Pūjā* in India interrogates the boundaries between sacred and secular, arguing that market forces have produced and circulated a secular Hindu culture. Chattopadhyay proposes a postcolonial, post-deregulation reading of the Indian public sphere that implies a cultural turn in Hindu public religious performance, marking the public sphere as a site for the fetishizing of modernity.

Ephemeral Publics offers three views of the contemporary experience of publics in a postmodern world. In the historical exchange between scenarios of 'coming out,' Stephen Seely examines the analogous structures of identity formation within Christianity and queerness, where the confessional and the closet act as signifiers of and spaces for both Christian and queer counterpublics and identities. Seely argues that 'coming out' is indeed a religious performance, but rather than decry this, envisions the overlaps between Christianity and non-heteronormative performances as transforming the power of subalterns within the public sphere, from a position of privately acquiescing to oppression by confessing difference, to 'a public performance of faith in futures and relational modes to come.' Shira Shwartz offers a glimpse of the intimate public that is formed around the orthodox Jewish rituals of female sexuality and *mikveh*, or ritual immersion. Schwartz argues that the sum of the individual rituals and interactions of the *mikveh* creates a third space – neither the private home nor the public synagogue – that acts as a feminine counterpublic within the wider (if still narrow) public of Orthodox Judaism. Claire Chambers turns to the alternative communities and economies created by street artists, or 'buskers', to suggest that the art commodity itself, when it is approached not as an object of exchange but rather as a gift constantly being given, challenges an early Habermasian attitude toward the public sphere. In the performance of busking, a private act of charitable giving to a street artist also publicly enters into an alternative economy of gifting and being given, disrupting normative concepts of private, atomistic agency within a market economy and creating instead a ritual where everyone feels each tug in the web of exchange.

The chapters that follow represent a world of perspectives. As the wealth of scholarship on the performative religious dimensions of the public sphere demonstrates, the ideal public sphere that Habermas offers as a model for self-reflexive criticism creates ample room for re-imagining the role of religion in the enfolding of public, private, religious and secular that is a fact of global politics. By engaging the public sphere performatively, we can learn from it as both a metatopos (an imagined space performed between the 'is' and the 'as,' a process, an event, and an act of translation) and a phenomenal, local space, in which both imagination and experience come into play.

Notes

1. Jürgen Habermas, 'Religion in the Public Sphere', *European Journal of Philosophy* 14(1) (2006): 2.
2. *Citizen Kane*. Dir. Orson Welles, Mercury Productions, 1942, Film.

3. See Chris Arthur, 'Meaning, Media and Method in the Study of Religion', in *Religion: Empirical Studies* (London: Ashgate, 2004), 19.
4. Talal Asad, *Formations of the Secular: Christianity, Islam, Modernity* (Stanford, CA: Stanford University Press, 2003), 2.
5. If one demands a kind of Rawlsian secular legitimation of political values in order to justify a faithful person's religious motivations for political conduct, then secularists should also recognize that their assumption of neutral standing similarly needs the same application of a deliberative, democratic process. Both sides need self-reflexive, historical positioning. See Habermas, 'Religion in the Public Sphere', 20.
6. This view of Habermas's contribution is widely accepted and celebrated; see, for example, the editors' introduction to Jostein Gripsrud, Hallvard Moe, Anders Molander, and Graham Murdock (eds), *The Idea of the Public Sphere* (Plymouth, UK: Lexington Books, 2010), xiii–xiv.
7. Ken Hirschkop, 'Justice and Drama: on Bakhtin as a Complement to Habermas', in *After Habermas: New Perspectives on the Public Sphere* (London: Blackwell, 2004), 49.
8. Eduardo Mendieta and Jonathan Van Antwerpen (eds), *The Power of Religion in the Public Sphere* (New York: Columbia University Press, 2011), 19.
9. Jürgen Habermas, *Between Facts and Norms: Contributions to a Discourse Theory of Law and Democracy*, trans. William Rehg (Cambridge, MA: MIT Press, 1996), 360.
10. Habermas, 'Religion in the Public Sphere', 4.
11. Habermas has taken this position in a number of contexts. See 'Religion in the Public Sphere', 10; *An Awareness of What is Missing: Faith and Reason in a Post-Secular Age*, trans. Ciaran Cronin (Cambridge: Polity, 2010), 16; and '"The Political": The Rational Meaning of a Questionable Inheritance of Political Theology', in Mendieta and Van Antwerpen (eds), *Power of Religion*, 25.
12. Mendieta and Van Antwerpen (eds), *Power of Religion*, 2–3.
13. Nancy Fraser, 'Rethinking the Public Sphere: A Contribution to the Critique of Actually Existing Democracy', in Bruce Robbins (ed.), *The Phantom Public Sphere* (Minneapolis: University of Minnesota Press, 1993), 5.
14. Fraser, 'Rethinking the Public Sphere', 16.
15. Michael Warner, 'The Mass Public and the Mass Subject', in Craig Calhoun, *Habermas and the Public Sphere* (Cambridge, MA: MIT Press, 1992), 239.
16. Warner, 'Mass Public', 240.
17. Cornel West, 'Prophetic Religion and the Future of Capitalist Civilization', in Mendieta and Van Antwerpen, *Power of Religion*, 93, 97–8.
18. Michael Warner, *Publics and Counterpublics*, (New York: Zone Books, 2002), 54.
19. Warner, *Publics and Counterpublics*, 56.
20. Warner, *Publics and Counterpublics*, 299, n. 3.
21. Warner, *Publics and Counterpublics*, 85.
22. Warner, *Publics and Counterpublics*, 99.
23. Warner, *Publics and Counterpublics*, 120.
24. Warner, *Publics and Counterpublics*, 122–4.
25. See Austin Harrington, 'Habermas's Theological Turn?', *Journal for the Theory of Social Behaviour*, 37(1) (2007): 45–61.
26. Habermas, *An Awareness of What is Missing*, 18.
27. Habermas, 'Religion in the Public Sphere', 14.
28. Habermas, *An Awareness of What is Missing*, 10.
29. Stanley Fish, 'Boutique Multiculturalism', in *The Trouble with Principle* (Cambridge, MA: Harvard University Press, 1999), 69.
30. Fish, 'The Dance of Theory', in *The Trouble with Principle*, 132.

31. See Fish's essay 'Rhetoric', as reprinted in H. Aram Vesser (ed.), *The Stanley Fish Reader* (Oxford: Blackwell, 1999), 137ff.
32. Robert Audi and Nicholas Wolterstorff, *Religion in the Public Square: The Place of Religious Convictions in Political Debate*, (Lanham, MD: Rowman and Littlefield, 1997), 89 (original emphasis).
33. Audi and Wolterstorff, *Religion in the Public Square*, 105.
34. Habermas, 'Religion and the Public Sphere', 12.
35. Mendieta and Van Antwerpen, (eds), *The Power of Religion in the Public Sphere*.
36. Craig Calhoun, Mark Juergensmeyer, and Jonathan Van Antwerpen (eds), *Rethinking Secularism*, (New York: Oxford University Press, 2011), 79.
37. Charles Taylor, *Sources of the Self: The Making of Modern Identity* (Cambridge, MA: Harvard University Press, 1989), 85–8.
38. Charles Taylor, *Communicative Action: Essays on Jurgen Habermas's Theory of Communicative Action*, edited by Axel Honneth and Hans Joas, (Cambridge, MA: MIT Press, 1991), 31.
39. Mendieta and Van Antwerpen (eds), *The Power of Religion in the Public Sphere*, 41.
40. Mendieta and Van Antwerpen (eds), *The Power of Religion in the Public Sphere*, 53.
41. Asad, *Formations of the Secular* 5.
42. Those familiar with Asad's critical anthropology will remember his deconstruction of Clifford Geertz's concept that religion is a universal category of human experience in 'Religion as an Anthropological Category' in *Genealogies of Religion: Discipline and Reasons of Power in Christianity and Islam* (Baltimore and London: Johns Hopkins University Press, 1993).
43. Habermas, 'Religion in the Public Sphere', 11.
44. See, for example, Craig Calhoun, Mark Juergensmeyer, and Jonathan VanAntwerpen (eds), *Rethinking Secularism*, (Oxford: Oxford University Press, 2011).
45. Saba Mahmood, 'Religious Reason and Secular Affect: An Incommensurable Divide?', *Critical Inquiry*, 35(4), *The Fate of Disciplines*, edited byJames Chandler and Arnold I. Davidson (Summer 2009), 861.
46. Asad here summarizes and criticizes the work of José Casanova's *Public Religions in the Modern World* (Chicago: University of Chicago Press, 1994) in 'Secularism, Nation-State, Religion' in *Formations of the Secular*, 181–2.
47. Asad, *Formations of the Secular,* 185.
48. Habermas, "An Awareness of What is Missing" 16.
49. Diana Taylor, *The Archive and the Repertoire* (Durham and London: Duke University Press, 2003) 15.
50. Marvin Carlson, *Performance: a Critical Introduction* (London and New York: Routledge, 1996), 190.
51. Richard Schechner, *Between Theatre and Anthropology* (Philadelphia: University of Pennsylvania Press, 1985).
52. Dwight Conquergood, 'Performance Studies: Interventions and Radical Research', *TDR*, 46(2) (Summer 2002) 145–6.
53. Jools Gilson-Ellis, 'Say Just What You Mean', *TDR*, 39(4) (Autumn 1995), 176.
54. Judith Butler, *Bodies That Matter* (New York: Routledge, 1993), 95.
55. In *Gender Trouble*, Butler outlines gender as a performative, and a gendered subject as 'performatively constituted' by culturally inscribed acts that *signify* gender. Judith Butler, *Gender Trouble* (New York: Routledge, 1990), 25.
56. Peggy Phelan, 'The Ontology of Performance: Representation Without Reproduction', in *Unmarked: The Politics of Performance* (London and New York: Routledge, 1993), 146.

57. Nicholas Ridout, 'Performance and Democracy', in *The Cambridge Companion to Performance Studies*, edited by Tracy C. Davis (Cambridge and New York: Cambridge University Press, 2008), 17.
58. Habermas, *An Awareness of What is Missing*, 17.
59. Diana Taylor, *The Archive and the Repertoire: Performing Cultural Memory in the Americas*, (Durham, NC: Duke University Press, 2003), 3.
60. Dwight Conquergood, 'Of Caravans and Carnivals: Performance Studies in Motion', *TDR*, 39(4) (1995): 137.
61. Lance Gharavi, 'Introduction' to *Religion, Theatre, and Performance: Acts of Faith* (London: Routledge, 2012).
62. Lukas Kaelin, 'Habermas, the Jesuits and Religion: Notes on a Discussion about the Role of Religion in Society', *Prajna Vihara: Journal of Philosophy and Religion*, 9(2) (2008): 20.

Works cited

Arthur, Chris. 'Meaning, Media and Method in the Study of Religion', in *Religion: Empirical Studies*. London: Ashgate, 2004.
Asad, Talal. *Genealogies of Religion: Discipline and Reasons of Power in Christianity and Islam*. Baltimore and London: Johns Hopkins University Press, 1993.
——. *Formations of the Secular: Christianity, Islam, Modernity*. Stanford, CA: Stanford University Press, 2003.
Audi, Robert and Nicholas Wolterstorff. *Religion in the Public Square: The Place of Religious Convictions in Political Debate*. Lanham, MD: Rowman and Littlefield, 1997.
Butler, Judith. *Gender Trouble*. New York: Routledge, 1990.
——. *Bodies That Matter*. New York: Routledge, 1993.
Calhoun, Craig, Mark Juergensmeyer, and Jonathan Van Antwerpen (eds). *Rethinking Secularism*. New York: Oxford University Press, 2011.
Carlson, Marvin. *Performance: a Critical Introduction*. London and New York: Routledge, 1996.
Casanova, José. *Public Religions in the Modern World*. Chicago: University of Chicago Press, 1994.
Conquergood, Dwight. 'Of Caravans and Carnivals: Performance Studies in Motion', *TDR*, 39:4 (1995).
——. 'Performance Studies: Interventions and Radical Research', *TDR*, 46:2 (2002).
Crossley, Nick, and John Michael Roberts (eds). *After Habermas: New Perspectives on the Public Sphere*. London: Blackwell, 2004.
Fish, Stanley. *The Trouble with Principle*. Cambridge, MA: Harvard University Press, 1999.
——. *The Stanley Fish Reader*, edited by H. Aram Vesser. Oxford: Blackwell, 1999.
Fraser, Nancy. 'Rethinking the Public Sphere: A Contribution to the Critique of Actually Existing Democracy', in Bruce Robbins (ed.), *The Phantom Public Sphere*. Minneapolis: University of Minnesota Press, 1993.
Gharavi, Lance (ed.). *Religion, Theatre, and Performance: Acts of Faith*. London: Routledge, 2012.
Gilson-Ellis, Jools. 'Say Just What You Mean', *TDR*, 39:4 (1995).
Gripsrud, Jostein, Hallvard Moe, Anders Molander, and Graham Murdock (eds). *The Idea of the Public Sphere*. Plymouth, UK: Lexington Books, 2010.
Habermas, Jürgen. *Between Facts and Norms: Contributions to a Discourse Theory of Law and Democracy*, trans. William Rehg. Cambridge, MA: MIT Press, 1996.

——. 'Religion in the Public Sphere', *European Journal of Philosophy*, 14(1) (2006).

——. *An Awareness of What is Missing: Faith and Reason in a Post-Secular Age*, trans. Ciaran Cronin. Cambridge: Polity, 2010.

——. '"The Political": The Rational Meaning of a Questionable Inheritance of Political Theology', in Mendieta and Van Antwerpen eds., 2011, *q.v.*

Harrington, Austin. 'Habermas's Theological Turn?', *Journal for the Theory of Social Behaviour*, 37(1) (2007): 45–61.

Hirschkop, Ken. 'Justice and Drama: on Bakhtin as a Complement to Habermas', in *After Habermas: New Perspectives on the Public Sphere*. London: Blackwell, 2004.

Kaelin, Lukas. 'Habermas, the Jesuits and Religion: Notes on a Discussion about the Role of Religion in Society', *Prajna Vihara :Journal of Philosophy and Religion*, 9(2) (2008): 1–30.

Mahmood, Saba. 'Religious Reason and Secular Affect: An Incommensurable Divide?', *Critical Inquiry*, 35(4) (2009), *The Fate of Disciplines*, edited by James Chandler and Arnold I. Davidson.

Mendieta, Eduardo and Jonathan Van Antwerpen (eds). *The Power of Religion in the Public Sphere*. New York: Columbia University Press, 2011.

Phelan, Peggy. *Unmarked: The Politics of Performance*. New York: Routledge, 1993.

Ridout, Nicholas. 'Performance and Democracy', in *The Cambridge Companion to Performance Studies*, edited by Tracy C. Davis. Cambridge and New York: Cambridge University Press, 2008.

Schechner, Richard. *Between Theatre and Anthropology*. Philadelphia: University of Pennsylvania Press, 1985.

Taylor, Charles. 'Challenging Issues About the Secular Age', *Modern Theology*, 26(3) (July 2010): 404–15.

——. *Sources of the Self: The Making of Modern Identity* Cambridge, MA: Harvard University Press, 1989.

——. *Communicative Action: Essays on Jürgen Habermas's Theory of Communicative Action*, edited by Axel Honneth and Hans Joas. Cambridge, MA: MIT Press, 1991.

Taylor, Diana. *The Archive and the Repertoire*. Durham, NC: Duke University Press, 2003.

Warner, Michael. 'The Mass Public and the Mass Subject', in Craig Calhoun, *Habermas and the Public Sphere*. Cambridge, MA: MIT Press, 1992.

——. *Publics and Counterpublics*. New York: Zone Books, 2002.

Welles, Orson, dir. *Citizen Kane*. Mercury Productions, 1942, Film.

West, Cornell. 'Prophetic Religion and the Future of Capitalist Civilization', in Mendieta and Van Antwerpen (eds), 2011, *q.v.*

Part I
Publics and the Non-Democratic State

1
The Market for Argument

Simon W. du Toit

Significant cultural changes in England in the early modern period produced what Victor Turner calls a 'social drama'[1] that endured for centuries. Those changes created the conditions for the emergence of publics long before the print culture associated with eighteenth-century coffeehouses contributed to the construction of democratic nations. In this chapter I want to trace how the performance of religion in public became a crucial aspect of the struggle to control the politics and religious culture of early modern England. The public performance of private religious identity was the crux of a struggle between radical puritan[2] reformers and supporters of Queen Elizabeth's *via media*, the middle road between Catholic and Protestant that seemed necessary to avoid civil war. The increasing political and social significance of performance in shaping civic order in early modern England emerges clearly in the puritan determination to assert its religious efficacy. That determination was expressed, in part, as antitheatricality. As puritans developed performance strategies as the central means of constructing a puritan counterpublic,[3] antitheatricality emerged in the 1570s as a marker of their effort to shape a reformed, *new* England. This struggle between kinds of performance demonstrates the power of performance to reciprocally order both interiority and social space in early modern England.

The recent, ambitious *Making Publics* project[4] has offered a rich reading of those cultural changes. Among them were the growth in power of a centralized government, a new understanding of publicity and privacy, the increasing commodification of theatre performance, and a religious revolution. Torrance Kirby's contribution to *Making Publics* weaves those threads into a fabric he calls the 'culture of persuasion' that developed out of the newly Protestant national church in England. As a person's private convictions were increasingly at stake in religious practices, Kirby suggests, the locus of faith shifted from a sacramental tradition towards an evangelical interiority.[5] Paul Yachnin's analysis of *Hamlet*, for example, points out that Shakespeare's play includes both Catholic and Protestant elements. Hamlet has returned from Wittenberg, which many in the early modern audience would have recognized as the site of Luther's Protestant university; and Hamlet's ghostly father has returned from purgatory, a distinctively Catholic space, to charge the young prince with a new task. The play, and Shakespeare's theatre, therefore contributed by means of performance to the production of a new English public, by providing a space in which the decisive issue dividing the nation could be approached in a less threatening, fictional space. As Yachnin points out, that space is 'attenuated' by its fictional nature.[6] And there lies the rub: it was precisely the theatrical attenuation of the authority of public speech to which puritans, beginning in the late 1570s, vociferously objected. The Vestiarian Controversy of 1566, the first significant public conflict involving the puritan movement, seemed on the surface to have been about whether or not ministers had to wear a surplice during services. It was in fact a struggle over the limits of the authority and efficacy of religious speech; the puritans were unwilling to concede that any aspect of worship could be described as *adiaphora*, or 'thinges indifferent'. The puritan body revealed in early modern religious politics is, above all, a body that performs a resistant refusal to be silenced. It claims the right to speak about any matter it views as having ritual significance, and to circulate that speech in public.[7] This chapter will explore puritan performance through a brief glance at the work of Rev. Richard Greenham, and a more careful reading of a sermon performed by Rev. John Stockwood. Greenham was a pioneering practitioner of puritan 'practical divinity'[8] whose ministry in Dry Drayton, Cambridgeshire in the 1570s and 1580s offered leadership to the puritan movement. Stockwood's sermons have been most widely known as antitheatrical pamphlets. Through a discussion of Greenham and Stockwood's performance methods, I hope to show the contribution of public religious performance to the emergence of a counterpublic in early modern England.

Rev. John Stockwood delivered two sermons at Paul's Cross, London, on 24 August 1578 and 10 May 1579. Later antitheatrical pamphlets used the Paul's Cross sermons of Stockwood and Thomas White as authority and precedent; the sermons circulated and re-circulated in print. I will suggest, however, that Stockwood's sermons can be read as resistant political action whose embodied performance, delivered with the fire of passionate preaching for which many puritans were notorious, produced his social status. Stockwood's preaching contributed to the construction of a puritan counterpublic, and the circulation of a resistant order of both private interiority and public space. Consumption, digestion, and circulation of discourse that shaped bodily order produced performances such as Stockwood's, and contributed significantly to the market value of prophetic performative speech.[9] The evidence presented below suggests that the performative authority puritans accorded to ritual speech placed ritual performance into circulation in distinctive ways in early modern London. Consumers sought it out because of its perceived efficacy, and therefore protecting its efficacy was of paramount importance.

To attend to Stockwood's deployment of performance strategies I will examine three important aspects of place in performance: the bodily, the geographic, and the textual. Paul's Cross blended church, state, and discursive authority in early modern London, as it was at once the seat of the Bishop of London, the pulpit from which official state policy was often announced, and the centre of London's bookselling trade. I will anatomize the role of embodiment in Stockwood's assertion of a proper social order, in both its public and its private aspect. The proper order of the affections in the humoral body emerges, in Stockwood's view, as a crucial aspect of preaching efficacy. Finally, I will trace the patterns of circulation that enabled Stockwood to participate in the construction of the resistant power constituted in the puritan poetic world.

Performance in puritan culture

In early modern English puritan culture, preaching was connected to many other practices structured around the consumption and performance of prophetic speech. As Michael Warner notes, 'embodied sociability' often troubles or displaces the 'ideology of reading' that marks a public.[10] Prophetic speech was a marker of puritan social status, and was intended to circulate across parish and other social boundaries into the marketplace. Puritan ritual practices such as the establishment of lectureships, outdoor fasts, and regional 'prophesyings'[11] offered varieties of preaching, differing from sermons in that they were held on market day and were open to a general public, and their focus was more overtly educational than hortatory. Domestic practices – conferring with others, Sabbath exercises, daily devotions in the home, and repetition (the practice of repeating back the key points of sermons) – were constructed by means of prophetic speech.[12] Puritan speech practices were so distinctive and effective as social markers that playwrights of the day were able to caricature puritans on the stage by only slightly exaggerating their idiom, as is shown perhaps most famously in Ben Jonson's *Bartholomew Fair*. Patrick Collinson has even suggested that what has come to be thought of as puritanism was in fact an invention of the early modern theatre.[13]

The connection between embodiment, performance, and social order in puritan culture is evident in the privileging of speech as an aspect of the interiorization of religious authority to which Kirby alludes. The social order of the family was central to the uptake of prophetic speech in puritan culture, as was suggested, for example, by the puritan preacher Richard Greenham: 'If ever wee would have the church of god to continue long among us, wee must bring it into our housholds, and nourish it in our families.'[14] The male head of the puritan family took up and reiterated the edifying authority of the preaching minister, and included everyone in the household, including children and servants, in daily devotions, repetitions after church, and catechism training.[15]

The ordering action of prophetic speech was perceived as a physiological aspect of interiority. The performance of prophetic speech had to be sustained continuously if it was to maintain order and efficacy. For example, the citation below from Greenham's 'Treatise of the Sabboth', which is given the marginal note 'Preparation to the Sabboth', warns of the consequences of failing to pray properly before worship:

> For what is the cause why in the prayers of the Church wee so little profit? what causeth the word to be of so small power with us? whereof commeth it that the Sacraments are of such slender account with us? Is it not because we draw neere to the Lord with uncatechised hearts, and uncircumcised eares, without prepared affections, and unschooled senses: so that we come unto and depart from the house of God with no more profit, then wee get at stage-playes, where delighting our eyes and eares for a while with the view of the pageants, afterward we vainly depart?[16]

For Greenham, the inability of 'stage-playes' to produce any 'profit' has little to do with any inherent quality of their own, but rather has to do with the proper ordering of the body. If 'wee' are to profit from preaching, if the 'Sacraments' and the prayers of the faithful are to have any authority and efficacy, the place for them within the interiority of the ordered humoral body must be prepared. Greenham carefully anatomizes the *loci* of interior order in this passage: hearts, affections, and the senses particularly of eye and ear. These must be 'schooled' and 'circumcised' in preparatory prayer if the Word is to resound in our mouths; and the responsibility for any failure of its efficacy is therefore human rather than divine. Greenham's statement locates the authority of acceptable ritual in the full process of prophetic performance exercised upon puritan interiority. He distinguishes that process from unacceptable ritual in which the process of interior ordering is incomplete. Vain church attendance is just as empty as the vanity of 'stage-playes'. Although they might delight the eyes and ears for a while, 'stage-playes' lack the authority to rightly order the ritualized godly body. Delight of the unschooled senses and affections occurs in a place from which we vainly depart. Interior order, expressed in the humoral vocabulary of the body, gave authority to puritan speech; understanding, affection, and memory replaced statues, chalices, and stained glass windows as the places that marked ritual practice. By means of a distinctive cultural disposition to produce, market, and consume prophetic performance, Greenham's view of puritan speech strove to map interiority among the faithful. In the antitheatrical sermons of John Stockwood, the reciprocal correspondence between interiority and public space may be clearly seen.

The sermon performances of John Stockwood

Stockwood's preaching performance was an effort to re-inscribe the civic space of the city – a performance that resisted the force of sovereign authority in order to make and market what Warner calls an 'alternative poetic world'. The public preaching of the English Reformation initiated a genealogy of preaching performance, surrogated in future Protestant Christian preaching performances, within which puritans used preaching to construct a counterpublic. Puritan preaching challenged the boundaries between public and private, and by doing so effectively politicized interiority. I will suggest that the mapping of the body performed in puritan public preaching functioned by means of a 'market for argument', a reflexively circulating body of public discourse that had consequences for the emerging idea of the English public.

In early modern England the idea of argument was complex. What Shakespeare's Rosencrantz calls 'argument'[17] is a notion that captures both the rhetorical and the performative aspects of Stockwood's sermon: an argument is the premise for a plot, and therefore constructs character and action on the stage; but it also proposes rhetorical structure and, with it, social action. Like a play, a Paul's Cross sermon is caught between text and utterance; where does its performative force lie? It is produced to engage with and construct a public. However, like a map, Stockwood's sermon at Paul's Cross also constitutes an embodied image of social space that is determined by performance, in which the citation of bodily order plays a central role. It performs relations of power by resisting sovereign authority and proposing an alternative world.

Jean-Christophe Agnew's *Worlds Apart* connects the idea of the market to the theatre in early modern England by observing the early modern shift of the market 'from a place to a process to a principle to a power'.[18] Agnew brings 'market as place' together with 'market as action': 'thus confronting the conditions of its own performance, [the theatre] invoked the same problematic of exchange – the same questions of authenticity, accountability, and intentionality – at issue in the 'idea of [the] market'.[19] The new theatres were markets for a model of performative speech that directly challenged the ritual authority of prophetic speech. The public theatre offered that challenge in part by appropriating the same civic places in which puritans had taken refuge from official persecution: on the margins of the city, in the Liberties and suburbs. The rise of the public theatre forced puritan culture to fight for its survival on two fronts: against the ecclesiastical authorities, and against what it viewed as the theatrical appropriation of the authority of public performative speech. In the market for argument, godly text and godly speech circulated by offering in the marketplace the religious value that had previously been accorded to the relics treasured in Catholic worship.[20] Consumption and production of godly performance marked the consumer's social status, permitting identification across social boundaries. I hope to suggest below how the placelessness of the early modern market for argument permitted and constructed the stranger sociability required as the cornerstone of any enduring public.

Early modern conditions of textuality

> [F]orasmuch as Christe himselfe preaching the Gospell of the kingdome
> from place to place, delivered the glad and ioyfull tidinges of salvation ...
> I also having offered me by my text very fit and iust occasion, have
> laboured to sette foorth the dignitie and worthines of this function ...[21]

This citation from the Epistle Dedicatory of Stockwood's sermon marks
the sermon's cycle of transitions from text into speech and back into text.
These are words written in reflection after the fact, in which Stockwood
marks the 'occasion' for performance given him by authority of Biblical
text. Stockwood's sermon was preached into a space of discourse marked
out also by sovereign and ecclesiastical authority. The print version of the
sermon, offered to the public as a pamphlet in the same location in the city
some months later, engaged with a public that existed by virtue of its being
addressed. Stockwood establishes both the sermon's topic and its central
performative action: the assertion of the rightful authority of preaching to
address the public 'from place to place'. Paul's Cross was not only the site
of the city's most prominent pulpit cross. It was also surrounded by the
city's heaviest concentration of booksellers and printers, and it was therefore among London's greatest centres of discursive and material exchange.
The cathedral and the immediately surrounding vicinity was the seat of the
Bishop of London but it was also a vigorous marketplace in which news and
goods changed hands, and in which 'a strange humming of buzze-mixt of
walking, tongues and feet' of voices might be heard.[22] At the centre of this
market stands the pulpit at Paul's Cross. The outward flow of circulation
from this intense discursive centre reached far into the English countryside
by means of the petty chapmen who carried and re-sold the books, pamphlets, and almanacs produced in London, as Margaret Spufford and Tessa
Watt have shown.[23] The power of this circulatory mechanism to shock the
English nation was demonstrated many times, perhaps most memorably in
the pamphlet war that surrounded the Martin Marprelate controversy. A little more than a decade after Stockwood preached this sermon, puritan writer
John Penry was executed, in part because he was believed to have written
the Marprelate pamphlets. Those scurrilous documents satirically attacked
church authorities; not only was Penry executed, but the means of their
production was destroyed. The press on which printer Robert Waldegrave
produced the Marprelate pamphlets was sawn in half.[24]

The obvious religious associations of St Paul's, which might seem to our
modern eyes to authoritatively condition the space, were naturalized and
submerged in early modern England. It was simply taken for granted that
England was a Christian nation. What was very much at stake was the *nature*
of its public faith. The notion of England as a Protestant state had been
made official by Henry VIII only 45 years before Stockwood's sermon, in

1534, and was, of course, a deeply contested matter.[25] As John Stockwood climbed the stairs into the Paul's Cross pulpit, he faced a crowd that was divided by class, religious allegiance, politics, and interest.

Stockwood was appointed schoolmaster at Tonbridge under the sponsorship of the Skinners Company.[26] Their sponsorship may have extended to underwriting Stockwood's appearance at Paul's Cross as well. Bishop John Aylmer, whose duty it was to invite Paul's Cross preachers, was a willing and eager opponent of puritanism;[27] he cannot have been pleased to offer an invitation to Stockwood, but in so doing he authorized Stockwood's preaching performance as a proper use of the Paul's Cross pulpit. By means of the mechanism of private sponsorship marginal voices were given access to the public pulpit as an expression of the national struggle to establish a clear and official religious voice. Within the social drama enacted between Protestant and Catholic, puritans occupied a radical minority position. Aylmer's invitation enabled Stockwood to 'pass' as an official speaker, but I hope to suggest how his reflexive resistance of that role risked flaunting his minority status. Months later, in January 1580, Aylmer began a more focused campaign against London puritans.[28] Stockwood was not asked back for a third visit.

While it seems highly unlikely that Queen Elizabeth and her court heard Stockwood preach in 1579, it is much more likely that puritans from across London did. 'Gadding to sermons' across parish boundaries, a practice that demonstrates the market value of puritan performance, had on occasion been sufficiently controversial that gadders to sermons had been arrested and jailed.[29] The practice was widespread among puritans, prompting concern on the part of ecclesiastical authorities, who saw sermon-gadding as an attempt to undermine church order. Those puritans who chose to come to Paul's Cross would not have done anything improper because of its status as a public venue, but Stockwood could not have been known to them personally as he lived in Tonbridge. The public he addressed was gathered for the occasion as a heterogeneous gathering of consumers, whose public civility performed stranger sociability.

Even as he spoke, some members of his auditory might well have read the Biblical text on which Stockwood preached.[30] Taking up the text of a sermon by referring to it in print was a common practice among puritans at worship. This layered manner of consumption sustains the blended force of print and speech, taking the authority of both text and performance into their bodies. Doing so allows them to cite and re-characterize the sermon in a way that is typical of the circulation of discourse among puritans in early modern England. Puritans were marked by that distinctive set of practices noted above, which were grounded in the uptake, citation and re-characterization of religious discourse. As Warner points out, the social uptake of discourse lies at the heart of the idea of the public sphere.[31] Although the exercise of rational debate was as dear to puritans as to anyone else, theoretical insistence on the primacy of reason, in puritan culture as later in the Enlightenment, masks the performance of social power and resistance through the uptake and citation of particular markers of bodily order.

As Peter Blayney's map of Paul's Churchyard shows (Figure 1.1),[32] book-sellers could stand and listen to the sermon of a given Sunday even as they sold the texts of past sermons. That layering of text and speech was particularly marked for Stockwood. His 1579 sermon was his second Paul's Cross appearance in less than a year. The print version of Stockwood's first Paul's Cross sermon, preached on 24 August 1578, was on sale less than two hundred feet away at George Bishop's bookshop, the Bell, as Stockwood preached in May 1579. His second performance was therefore unique among the antitheatrical sermons: the performative force of his speech was reinforced by the authoritative market presence of his earlier performance, reiterated as text.

Before, during, and after Stockwood's 1579 performance, Mr Bishop was able to offer potential customers the opportunity to purchase the Stockwood of 1578 in print. Customers might have been seen holding the earlier sermon, or perhaps tucking it into their pockets, even as Stockwood's voice and embodied presence filled the space. Stockwood's second sermon performance appropriated, conflated, and re-circulated the social powers of text and speech.

Puritan prophesyings were held on market day and during large fairs. Puritan pamphlets as a body announced the place of puritan speech in the

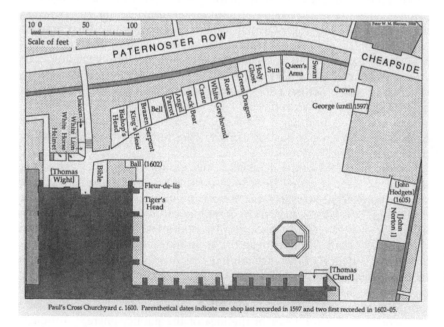

Paul's Cross Churchyard c. 1600. Parenthetical dates indicate one shop last recorded in 1597 and two first recorded in 1602–05.

Figure 1.1   Paul's Cross Churchyard in 1600

marketplace. As Peter Lake suggests, godly pamphlets formed part of an economy of print that included murder pamphlets and other sensational forms.[33] Godly pamphlets similarly were protected by, and extended, the deputized authority granted them by the prophetic voice: they claimed to speak for God. Market forces served to reinforce the value of reiteration: 'if one pamphlet awakens interest, several flame it, and the interest excited is both immediate (providing for quick sale) and transitory (providing for quick succession)'.[34] The transitory nature of the pamphlet echoes the transitory nature of speech; reiteration is necessary and, in fact, useful.

Godly cheap print originated in London but it circulated throughout England; its consumers often read it out loud, at which time it returned to the field of embodiment and performance. The market for argument therefore has a substantial range of circulation.[35] Stockwood's argument continues to circulate today through the good offices of Early English Books Online, where it is known as STC (2nd edn) 23285. Stockwood hails the reader with the puritan idea of embodiment, which today is often resisted and marked as obscene, 'puritanical.' I must beg your indulgence, then, as I propose to hear him speak once more. Read aloud, if you will, the following selection from his sermon.

Puritan flaunting: the puritan counterpublic

> Shall sinne therefore be left unrebuked, because naughtie men, to excuse themselves, whose consciences accuse them, will goe about too perswade men of great countenaunce that we preach against them? Which now a dayes is a practise too common. What if for hatred of him that rebuketh in the gate, and through abhorring him that speaketh uprightly, we be tearmed by the odious names of Puritans, Precisians, unspotted brethren, as nothing is more usuall in companies, ... where swearing and blaspheming the name God ...[36]

This passage taken from early in Stockwood's sermon marks his performance as reflexively political in nature. Stockwood casts himself in a resistant role, and directly attributes the repression of puritan speech to the court intrigues of 'naughtie men'. He thereby avoids directly attacking Queen Elizabeth and the episcopate, a subtle move that he will develop further. Since Christ himself took on the office of preacher when he might have claimed any more noble office, preaching is 'not so meane or base a thing, that anie man ought to be ashamed or thinke scorne of the same'.[37] And yet, incredibly enough to Stockwood, that is exactly what has happened. Stockwood avoids attributing to the Crown the suppression of puritan prophetic speech by laying the problem at the door of the Catholics, but his awareness of his marked public status as an 'odious ... Puritan' is quite clear. He claims the freedom to speak in public on the grounds of a common Christian discourse, but in doing so he performs the very action he knows is marked as transgressive; he will be hated for rebuking at the gate, but he turns once again to official religious discourse to authorize his claim:

> Secondly, in that Christ so diligently, frequenteth, & resorteth unto open assemblies and publike meetinges of the Churche there teaching and preaching unto the people, hee doeth by this example confirme the use of the common comming together of Christians in one publick place, for the hearing of the word which is indeede very commendable, and in no case to be contemned or despised.[38]

The puritans of early modern England were increasingly cast in the social imaginary as 'Monsters of Impudence',[39] marked off from the English public most particularly by their pious speech, but also by their consumption of religious print. The process of stigmatizing puritan speech was initiated at the very highest levels of government, emerging from sovereign proclamation. Puritan preaching was a resistant form of public address, under official attack from the court and the episcopate. The need for the Tudor regime to control public speech in order to maintain its sovereign authority predates Elizabeth's accession,[40] but during her regime several injunctions were issued that specifically aimed at suppressing puritan cultural practices. On 7 May 1577, for example, Elizabeth sent a letter to John Whitgift, who was at that point still Bishop of Winchester, instructing him to suppress all 'assemblees' or 'prophesyenges' in his diocese. She describes such meetings as 'unmeete for vulgar people', and suggests they caused the people to be 'schismatically divided', 'to the breach of common ordre'.[41] Rather than describing preaching in church, Stockwood alludes above to 'open assemblies and publike meetinges' in language that strikingly parallels Elizabeth's letter to Whitgift. Puritan public speech was distinct from, and critical of, the power of the sovereign performative.[42] Stockwood's sermon performance in May of 1579 was offered only two years after Elizabeth's letter to Whitgift, and responds in a timely way to the court's intensifying effort to contain puritan speech.

The printed material associated with those speech practices was sufficiently distinctive to mark puritans socially, and to constitute a performative hail that called out to others, addressing them as 'my fellow puritans'. This public performance was mutely transformative, and occasioned resistance from some unwilling spectators. In participating in the reshaping of public space, for example, puritan women also seemed to be transgressing gender boundaries, as in this vignette Collinson narrates:

> In Colchester, an innkeeper complained to two of his customers about the sermon-going habits of the good wives of the town: 'There be a sort of women of this town that go to the Sermons with the books under their arms . . .& when they come there the whores must be pewed & there they set & sleep & what they do we cannot see & then they come home to

their husbands & say he made a good & godly sermon, & yet they play the Whores before they come home...'[43]

The innkeeper sexualizes these puritan women, marking their transgression by categorizing their bodies as grotesque and suspicious. He associates their practice of going to 'Sermons' with the material props used in their performance, 'the books under their arms'. The social marker of the consumption of print is sufficient for him to identify them as 'good wives.' Perhaps he was illiterate; the consumption of godly print evidently provoked his anxiety.

Stockwood's sermon was a performance of resistant speech, and constructed his social persona as a speaker of what Judith Butler has called 'impossible speech'. Butler notes the operation of official censorship in deciding not only what is speakable, but also in performatively producing the speaker as a subject: 'To move outside of the domain of speakability is to risk one's status as a subject.'[44] Within ten years of Stockwood's sermon government agents were running sting operations at the booksellers' stalls, attempting to entrap clergy into seditious speech.[45] What Elizabeth's court construed as 'impossible speech', the puritans construed as an effort to criticize and reshape the governing rules of speech. It is inevitable, then, that such an effort should be taken up performatively into embodiment. Puritans were caricatured in early modern literature on the basis of their embodied performance, as grotesque, transgressive subjects, a phenomenon Kristen Poole has described. The caricatures represent puritans as indulging in bodily excess: 'In early modern literature, it is the drunken, gluttonous, and lascivious puritan who predominates.'[46] In fact, Poole suggests, the very term 'Puritan' often signifies 'the indeterminable, the unlocatable' social element. Puritan speech, in a curious paradox, was both the means by which puritans were caricatured and the act that erased them as social subjects.

Private and public bodies

. . . so that by the diligent hearing of the word of God truely preached in these assemblies, we learn to geve over the corrupt lusts of our olde man, we doe profite unto newnes and amendement of life . . . [47]

Stockwood here suggests that hearing the Word has the effect of ordering interiority. The 'assemblies' in question claim efficacy in producing 'amendement of life'. They produce 'profite' by properly ordering the affections, the 'lusts of our olde man'. Stockwood invokes the authority of sacred text, reiterates it as performative speech, and asserts its perlocutionary effect as a material ordering of the body. Stockwood's sermon makes the private, interior terrain of the body a matter of public argument; he politicizes the private. His address is therefore both personal and impersonal; his speech addresses both public affairs generally, and private perception. Where later puritan preaching insisted on a focus on interiority, as Warner points out,[48] that is not sufficient reason to propose its disavowal of public political efficacy. In Protestantism, as Kirby notes, the public nature of interiority is inescapably invoked; hence the Protestant eschewal of the confessional, that site of bodily disclosure of which Foucault makes so much.[49]

> Preaching requyreth an earnest and willing minde, a bolde spirite, a fervent desire, a glad and ioyfull affection from the very hearte, to extoll, advaunce, commend and set foorth openly before all men, the word of God, and glad tidinges of the kingdome, without all respect of filthie lucre, or vaine seeking to please men, for the which so doo are not the servauntes of God.[50]

Although today one can only approach Stockwood's sermon through textual analysis, it is important to remember that his performance of it was as passionately outspoken as its contents. 'Stockwood was famous for his fiery, uncompromising style of preaching.'[51] His sermon might in fact be viewed as a kind of manual for the performance of public sermons, one that predated William Perkins' famous *Art of Prophesying* by 13 years. Stockwood is explicit here in privileging the proper bodily order of Christ-like preaching, which constructs a unity between interiority and the social persona or office of the preacher. Stockwood emphasizes the efficacy of preaching that is 'set foorthe' from properly ordered interior spaces against the 'vaine' effort to please. The 'earnest' mind of such a preacher experiences the proper affections of joy and gladness, and speaks with a 'bolde' spirit. Just as Perkins was later to use the humoral imagery of fire to describe godly affection,[52] Stockwood uses the contrasting coldness of those whose 'colde sermons take as colde effect in the mindes of those before whom they speake'.[53] Stockwood's humoral figure is no mere conceit, but rather is an aspect of the humoral ordering of the body produced by properly prophetic speech: 'For this fervencie and earnestnes in the preacher, is it in deede which pearceth deepe into the conscience of the hearer, GOD his spirite woorking ...'.[54] Not the play, but the sermon, is the thing that catches consciences; but to do so it must speak with the fire of the Holy Spirit.

Stockwood juxtaposes 'this zealous and fervent manner of teaching' against 'this other kinde of teaching which mans brayne hath forged' in which the senses are not schooled, which 'pierceth not the hearte, delighteth the sense of the bodye, but moveth not the minde...'. Stockwood is marketing the efficacy of passionate performance to 'teach' because it embodies the presence of God. His performance refuses the silence imposed by the official *via media*, and simultaneously marks him as notorious. Stockwood claims status as a 'servaunt of God,' whose performance transforms his physiognomy as well as that of his audience. That Protean power, which prompted some to feel a superstitious fear of the stage actor's art,[55] was for Stockwood the force that produced 'newnes and amendement of life'.

Later in his performance Stockwood privileges the ordered, healthy body of puritan social order over a substantial list of civic ills, among them swearing, blasphemy, spousal abandonment, drunkenness, and 'filthie playes', all which go unpunished by the 'common wealth', and along with them the 'ignorant and unable ministers, idle shepheardes, dumbe dogges', who go uncorrected by the church authorities. All these are 'God his iuste plagues and scourges',[56] which beg for spiritual physic from God's word. Stockwood therefore places the theatre in the same category as 'unable ministers'; they are members of the class of 'vayne exercises'. As Stockwood's sermon draws to a close he calls for the leadership of the church to gather in a 'godly conference' to discuss 'in prayer and fasting' the 'defaultes of the Citie, and house of the Lord'.[57] When bodily order circulates and is taken up into speech in the form of prayer, civic order will result in the 'Citie'.

To be sure, the concluding aim of the speaker in traditional preaching is for the auditory to experience that 'now God speaks'.[58] But that individual experience of conviction or conversion is far from being the only social force produced by Stockwood's Paul's Cross sermon, which was reflexive about its public and political function. Not merely conversion, but the nature of that conversion, was the crux of the political struggle between the state and the dissenters. Puritans insisted on the primacy of preaching *as* the public circulation of private interiority. The efficacy of preaching in producing a proper interior order is a consistent thread in puritan argument, and the vanity of other kinds of performance is consistently attacked. When the episcopate offered a reading ministry that reiterated sovereign authority, supplying the *Book of Homilies* (1565) to read in church for the many ministers who were unable to preach, those reading preachers were repeatedly attacked as 'dumbe dogges'.[59] Where Elizabeth I had promised she would 'make no windows into men's souls,' puritans insisted that the window onto physiological interiority presented and mapped in public speech acts was precisely what was needed. If 'Mr. Clap ...told me the very secrets of my heart in his sermon', as Warner points out,[60] then one important consequence of his speaking them was to enter them into public circulation.

Poetic world-making

> Let us learne therefore by this example of Christe diligently preaching in the Synagogues of the Jewes ... diligently to make our repayre unto publike places of preaching the woorde at times appoynted; and let us not onely our selves resorte thither, but also see that our whole houses and families, and all those that belong unto our chardge come thither also, where they may be taught...[61]

Viewed in the context of the official suppression alluded to above, Stockwood's argument in defence of public preaching and the right of public assembly emerges as a resistant political action whose embodied performance, delivered with the fire of passionate preaching for which many puritans were notorious, signals his counterpublic status. Stockwood's preaching style, as much as the text, proposes the uptake of the domestic and civic Puritan social order noted above in Greenham's work, to which Stockwood here alludes.

Having ordered bodily and domestic space, Stockwood moves to suggest an order for the godly temporal and spatial environment. That ordering scheme begins, of course, with Sabbath observance:

> If God himselfe were so severe for the observation of his Sabboth, that hee willed him which on that day gathered stickes, to be stoned to death weene wee at his hande to escape unpunished whom all kinde of vayne exercises may on that day pul us from holy meetings . . . [62]

Stockwood suggests Sabbath observance is literally a matter of life and death. For the inhabitants of London participation in 'vayne exercises' is a product of the original sin, an overweening pride, and is a practice that should expect providential punishment. First among those practices is attendance at the theatre:

> And here I cannot but lament the great disorder of this honorable citie, wherin, in this cleare light of the Gospel, & in the often and vehement outcrying of God his Preachers against suche horrible abuses, there are notwithstanding suffered licentiously too reigne many detestable excercises and filthie stage playes, which on the Lordes day robbe him of halfe his service, and drawe thronges and heapes of wanton youthes unto the seeyng & hearing of Baudie Enterludes, to the poysoning and corrupting of their mindes and soules ...[63]

Stockwood privileges the authority of prophetic speech to order the civic environment. The 'often and vehement' performative action of preaching to order the 'honorable citie' has been abused. To borrow Austin's language, the sermons have been rendered 'unhappy'.[64] Instead, 'filthie stage playes' are 'suffered' to 'reigne'. The resultant social disorder is given a humoral reading, in that it disorders bodies that should be properly ordered, 'poysoning and corrupting' the interior places of their 'mindes and soules' by means of the unschooled senses of 'seeyng and hearing'. Such exercises are vain because they produce not 'amendement of life' but rather a disordered interior space. That interior disorder is reflected in the social calamity of rampant disease: the onset of plague. If God once lifts his providential hand, 'staying the plague among you', then once again godly time and place are abused, as 'on this Sunday, and that Sunday' Londoners go to 'suche a place, and such a place', in such numbers that they run 'thicke and threefolde'.

Instead of containing their consumption in a public fast to meet the threat of plague, these 'heapes of wanton youthes' consume 'Baudie Enterludes'. The consequences of such a practice of consumption extend to the marking of opposed public spaces: 'youre Churches [are] in moste places emptie, when as the Theaters of the Players are as ful as they can throng',[65] For Stockwood the city was a disordered social space in which both the puritan church and the 'filthie stage' were banished to the outskirts and the lawless 'liberties'.

Stockwood's sermon has been best known as an antitheatrical pamphlet. However, those who heard him preach it would have socially coded it as a performance of puritan persona. The site of its performance accorded to the sermon an official status and authority on which Stockwood and others drew. Preaching at Paul's Cross offered the preacher a powerful integration of social forces generated by official authority, civic geography, performance, and print. All of these elements were imbricated in the scenario of Stockwood's 'argument'. Later antitheatrical pamphlets cited the Paul's Cross sermons of Stockwood and Thomas White; the sermons circulated and re-circulated in print,[66] reiterating and extending both the authority of the site of their utterance and the performative, civic, and social mapping they instigated. The circulation of discourse, in print and in bodies, was the primary mechanism for the construction and proper order of the puritan poetic world.

Conclusion

Stockwood's sermon discloses a widespread anxiety about the diminishing efficacy of performative speech. History has not accorded to him a prominent role in the leadership of the puritan movement. Rather, his sermon provides an example of the adoption of performance strategies among an amorphous resistant group whose boundaries defy definition. Stockwood's sermon shows that puritan performance meets all the standards Warner asks of a counterpublic: puritans were marked off among English subjects, and aware of their subordinate status. Their prophetic speech enabled a horizon of exchange that was distinct from, and critical of, authority, and their argument circulated widely in a way that was outside their control. However, rather than resisting a dominant public, the puritan counterpublic directly resisted sovereign power by appropriating to individual speakers the same religious authority that was, at that time, allied to the throne.

As Stockwood left the Paul's Cross pulpit in May 1579, he was stepping back into relative obscurity. His journey to London seems to end in what Agnew has called the 'placeless church';[67] Stockwood's disappearance from the historical record leaves him in a kind of liminal state, in which his performance remains available in the market to be taken up, repeatedly re-characterized, and re-circulated. His sermons have become an easy target for critics seeking to characterize early modern antitheatricality. Implicit in such criticism is the assumption that the public sphere is a secular space. Just as Stockwood's body performed a 'placeless church' on the cultural margins, so his sermons have lost their sense of political and religious place, and have become, instead, exemplary of intolerant polemic.

The increasing importance of performance in early modern ritual practice displaces the priority of thought over action in the formation of publics.[68] This view accords with Warner's critique of Habermas's reduction of the public sphere to people's public use of their reason. As Warner suggests, 'The public sphere is a principal instance of the forms of embodiment and social relations that are themselves at issue'.[69] What is taken up, cited, and re-characterized in the circulation of religious practices is not only rational discourse but also bodily order. A religious public is an embodied public. A preaching body takes up, performs, and produces 'argument'.

Preaching as public religious speech is inevitably political. It performs (divine) power and shapes both individual interiority and social norms. It asks God to shape the social order. Warner is correct that preaching's 'intention' is to order interiority, but historical conditions have produced periods and contested civic spaces in which both the strategies for ordering interiority and the nature of interior order have been particularly politicized. Stockwood's antitheatrical sermon seems a useful marker of that kind of social struggle in early modern London.

Notes

1. Victor Turner, *From Ritual to Theatre: The Human Seriousness of Play* (New York: PAJ Publications, 1982), 9–12.
2. Granting the contested nature of the term, throughout this chapter I will describe radical Protestants as 'puritan' to distinguish them from stage representations of them as Puritan.
3. Michael Warner, *Publics and Counterpublics* (New York: Zone Books, 2002), 56–65. Warner defines a counterpublic as a public whose participants are marked off from the general public; who maintain an awareness of subordinate status; whose membership enables a horizon of opinion and exchange; whose exchanges remain distinct from authority and have a critical relation to power; and whose extent is in principle made indefinite by the public circulation of discourse. This paper intentionally takes up and re-circulates terms from Warner's work. Portions of this chapter were first presented at PSi16, *Performing Publics*, the sixteenth conference of Performance Studies International, at Toronto in June 2010. That conference was conceived as a focused discussion of the relations between performance and Warner's views of the public sphere.
4. *Making Publics* is a research project that took place over a five-year period between 2005 and 2010, hosted at McGill University in Montreal. *Making Publics* gathered dozens of scholars from around the world to investigate the ways in which developments in the early modern period created the social conditions for the emergence of publics. See http://www.makingpublics.org.

5. Torrance Kirby, Matthew Milner and Robert Tittler, 'The Reformation', *Ideas: The Origins of the Modern Public*, Episode 2, David Cayley, host. Canadian Broadcasting Corporation. 17 September 2009. mp3 file. Last accessed 7 February 2013. Available at http://www.cbc.ca/ideas/episodes/features/2010/04/26/the-origins-of-the-modern-public/.

6. Paul Yachnin, Steven Mullaney and Michael Bristol, 'Theatre and Publics', *Ideas: The Origins of the Modern Public*, Episode 7, David Cayley, host. Canadian Broadcasting Corporation. 22 October 2009. mp3 file. Last accessed 7 February 2013. Available at http://www.cbc.ca/ideas/episodes/features/2010/04/26/the-origins-of-the-modern-public/.

7. The puritan publication 'Fortress of Fathers' (1566) is a sustained attack on the theology of *adiaphora*, which are indifferent matters that do not theologically have salvific significance. The opening preamble of 'Fortress of Fathers' states its resistance 'Against such as wold bring in an Abuse of idol stouff, and of thinges indifferent...', The limits of *adiaphora* are here encroached upon by puritan speech, which immediately challenges 'th'Aucthoritie of Princes and prelates'.

8. Kenneth L. Parker and Eric J. Carlson, *'Practical Divinity': The Works and Life of Revd Richard Greenham* (Aldershot: Ashgate, 1998).

9. Prophetic speech had two effects in the period: to exhort its hearers to repentance, and to place both performer and auditory in the context of a Biblical view of time. See Mary Morrissey, 'Elect Nations and Prophetic Preaching: *Types and Examples* in the Paul's Cross Jeremiad', in Lori Anne Ferrell and Peter McCullough (eds), *The English Sermon Revised* (Manchester and New York: Manchester University Press, 2000).

10. Warner, *Publics and Counterpublics*, 123.

11. A prophesying was an open meeting of preachers at which a series of sermons were performed, attended by, and afterwards discussed amongst the godly public. Puritan prophesyings were held on market day, and during large fairs. Margaret Spufford notes a synod held at Stourbridge Fair in 1587. See her *Contrasting Communities: English Villagers in the Sixteenth and Seventeenth Centuries* (Cambridge: Cambridge University Press, 1974) 261. See also Patrick Collinson, *Godly People: Essays on English Protestantism and Puritanism* (London: Hambledon Press, 1983), 357.

12. The connections between puritan cultural practices and the antitheatrical pamphlets are explored at length in my unpublished dissertation, *The Antitheatrical Body: Puritans and Performance in Early Modern England, 1577–1620* (University of Maryland, 2008).

13. See Patrick Collinson, 'The Theatre Constructs Puritanism', in David L. Smith, Richard Strier, and David Bevington (eds), *The Theatrical City: Culture, Theatre and Politics in London, 1576–1649* (Cambridge: Cambridge University Press, 1995), 157–69. Collinson says, 'This argument arises from the interest of a historian of religion in the construction of religious identities partly, and in the case of Puritanism largely, by a process of negative stigmatisation, but also by a measure of reciprocal self-recognition in the stigmatized.'

14. REM524, Fol. 62v, in Parker and Carlson, *'Practical Divinity'*, 242.

15. Patrick Collinson, *The Elizabethan Puritan Movement* (hereafter *EPM*) (Berkeley: University of California Press, 1967), 375; and also Christopher Hill, *Society and Puritanism in Pre-Revolutionary England* (New York: Schocken Books, 1964), 461.

16. Richard Greenham, *Workes...collected into one volume* (London: T. Creede, 1599, 5th edn, 1612), 360.

17. *Hamlet* 2.2.355. Commenting on the struggle between the children's and adult companies, Rosencrantz suggests 'There was for a while no money bid for argument, unless the poet and the player went to cuffs in the question.'

18. Jean-Christophe Agnew, *Worlds Apart: The Market and the Theatre in Anglo-American Thought, 1550–1750* (Cambridge: Cambridge University Press, 1986), 56.

19. Agnew, *Worlds Apart*, 11. See also David Hawkes' *Idols of the Marketplace: Idolatry and Commodity Fetishism in English Literature, 1580–1680* (London: Palgrave, 2001), which connects puritan objections to the stage to the emergent market economy.

20. See Anne M. Myers, 'Father John Gerard's Object Lessons,' in . Ronald Corthell *et al.* (ed.), *Catholic Culture in Early Modern England* (Notre Dame, IN: University of Notre Dame, 2007), 216–34.

21. John Stockwood, *A very fruiteful Sermon preched at Paules Crosse the tenth of May last, being the first Sunday in Easter Terme: in which are conteined very necessary and profitable lessons and instructions for this time* (London: George Bishop, 1579) A4v–A5r.

22. John Earle, *Micro-Cosmographie* (London: William Stansby, 1628). Cited in Pamela Tudor-Craig, *'Old St Paul's': The Society of Antiquaries Diptych, 1616* (London: London Topographical Society, 2004), 29.

23. See Tessa Watt, *Cheap Print and Popular Piety, 1550–1640* (Cambridge: Cambridge University Press, 1991), and Margaret Spufford, *Small Books and Pleasant Histories: Popular Fiction and its Readership in Seventeenth Century England* (Athens, GA: University of Georgia Press, 1981).

24. Patrick Collinson, 'Ecclesiastical Vitriol: Religious Satire in the 1590's and the Invention of Puritanism', in John Guy (ed.), *The Reign of Elizabeth I: Court and Culture in the Last Decade* (Cambridge: Cambridge University Press, 1995), 157.

25. Torrance Kirby traces the public role of Paul's Cross in the period, noting the association of 'the royal claim to ecclesiastical jurisdiction' with 'the status of the sacrament'. See his paper 'The Public Sermon: Paul's Cross and the Culture of Persuasion in England, 1534–1570', *Renaissance and Reformation*, 31(1) (Winter 2008). Kirby ascribes authority to the force of rhetoric 'to persuade, to resolve the conscience through closely reasoned biblical exegesis, cogent argumentation ...'. This rhetorical framework suggests a priority of thought over action that Kirby later complicates, alluding to the 'human faculties of memory, understanding, and will' that were the focus of the 'Augustinian anthropology of the evangelical reformers'. I want to broaden Kirby's view by implicating bodily order and performance in puritan rhetoric.

26. Oxford Dictionary of National Biography, s.v. John Stockwood. Consulted March 3, 2010. Available at http://www.oxforddnb.com. John Field, one of the original leaders of the London puritan movement, was supported at Oxford by the Clothworkers' Company. See Collinson, *EPM*, 87.

27. Collinson describes Aylmer's role in suppressing prophesyings, a role that Aylmer assumed from Archbishop Grindal in 1576; Aylmer was later one of the main targets of the satirical Marprelate pamphlets. Collinson, *EPM*, 192–5, 391–3.

28. Collinson, *EPM*, 202.

29. Collinson notes the 1567 arrest of over a hundred people who had 'gadded' from all across London to hear two preachers. *EPM*, 88.

30. In John Gipkyn's diptych *Old St. Pauls* (1616), people are shown reading text during the preaching of a sermon at Paul's Cross. See Pamela Tudor-Craig, *'Old St Paul's'*, Plate 2.

31. Warner, *Publics and Counterpublics*, 144–5.
32. This is a revised version of the map of Paul's Cross published in Peter W.M. Blayney, *The Bookshops in Paul's Cross Churchyard* (London: The Bibliographical Society, 1990), 76. Reproduced by permission of Dr Blayney. The octagonal figure to the lower right is the pulpit from which Paul's Cross sermons were spoken. George Bishop's shop, The Bell, is to the northwest; Bishop commissioned Thomas Dawson to print Stockwood's Paul's Cross sermons.
33. Peter Lake with Michael Questier, *The Antichrist's Lewd Hat: Protestants, Papists, and Players in Post-Reformation England* (New Haven, CT: Yale University Press, 2002), xxii.
34. Lake, *Antichrist's Lewd Hat*, 33.
35. Warner, *Publics and Counterpublics*, 91.
36. Stockwood, *A very fruiteful Sermon*, B7r.
37. Stockwood, *A very fruiteful Sermon*, C5v–6r.
38. Stockwood, *A very fruiteful Sermon*, D6r–v.
39. Warner, *Publics and Counterpublics*, 13.
40. Edward VI issued one such proclamation 'Prohibiting Private Innovations in Ceremonies' in 1548; see Hampton Court, 6 February 1548, Edward VI, in Paul L. Hughes and James F. Larkin (eds), *Tudor Royal Proclamations: Volume 1, the Early Tudors (1485–1553)* (New Haven and London: Yale University Press, 1964), 416–17 and following. Mary's Catholic regime followed suit, suppressing Protestant preaching.
41. Laud-Selden-Fairhurst MS 2003, fols. 40–1, reprinted in Stanford E. Lehmberg, 'Archbishop Grindal and the Prophesyings', *Historical Magazine of the Protestant Episcopal Church* 34(2) (1965): 142.
42. Warner, *Publics and Counterpublics*, 56.
43. Patrick Collinson, 'Elizabethan and Jacobean Puritan Popular Culture', in Christopher Durston and Jacqueline Eales (eds), *The Culture of English Puritanism 1560–1700* (London: Macmillan, 1996), 48–9.
44. Judith Butler, *Excitable Speech: A Politics of the Performative* (New York: Routledge, 1997), 133.
45. Collinson, *EPM*, 405.
46. Kristen Poole, *Radical Religion from Shakespeare to Milton: Figures of Nonconformity in Early Modern England* (Cambridge: Cambridge University Press, 2000), 12.
47. Stockwood, *A very fruiteful Sermon*, D7r.
48. Warner, *Publics and Counterpublics*, 84.
49. Michel Foucault, *The History of Sexuality: An Introduction, Vol. 1* (New York: Vintage Books, 1990), 58–73. The 'medicalization of the effects of confession' Foucault traces resonates strongly with the puritan practices noted here, with this important distinction: where the ritual of the Catholic confessional was sequestered both physically and discursively, Protestant and particularly puritan confession was public.
50. Stockwood, *A very fruiteful Sermon*, H1v.
51. Oxford Dictionary of National Biography, s.v. John Stockwood. Consulted 3 March 2010. Available at http://www.oxforddnb.com.
52. Bryan Crockett, *The Play of Paradox – Stage and Sermon in Renaissance England* (Philadelphia: University of Pennsylvania Press, 1995), 11. Crockett connects Perkins' construction with Method acting, but does not engage with the passage's use of humoral physiology.
53. Stockwood, *A very fruiteful Sermon*, H3r.

54. Stockwood, *A very fruiteful Sermon*, H3v.
55. Joseph Roach, *The Player's Passion: Studies in the Science of Acting* (Ann Arbor, MI: University of Michigan Press, 1993), 27–8.
56. Stockwood, *A very fruiteful Sermon*, J7v, J5r–v. Peter Lake notes that Stockwood's fervency in preaching, while exemplary of puritan speech, should not be construed as being *exclusively* puritan: 'While it would be an error to see the mode of discourse and address identified above as the Paul's Cross jeremiad as a puritan monopoly, there can be no doubt that the first and most natural exponents of it, men like Stockwood and Thomas White, were puritans' (*Lewd Hat*, 561).
57. Stockwood, *A very fruiteful Sermon*, K3v.
58. Warner, *Publics and Counterpublics*, 83.
59. This characterization was found not only in Stockwood's sermon (J5r–v, noted above), but also in Edward Dering's infamous sermon before Queen Elizabeth I, preached in early 1569, in which he called the bulk of Elizabeth's churchmen 'dum dogs, and could not barcke'. Edward Dering, *A Sermon Preach'd Before the Quene's Maiestie* (London: John Awdely, 1569), E4r. Stockwood's reiteration of it here, ten years later, was another important marker of his political resistance; Dering had directly rebuked the Queen, and his career suffered because of it.
60. Warner, *Publics and Counterpublics*, 84.
61. Stockwood, *A very fruiteful Sermon*, D7v.
62. Stockwood, *A very fruiteful Sermon*, D8r–v.
63. Stockwood, *A very fruiteful Sermon*, E1r.
64. J.L. Austin, *How to Do Things With Words*, edited by J.O. Urmson (Cambridge, MA: Harvard University Press, 1962), 15.
65. Stockwood, *A very fruiteful Sermon*, E2r.
66. Lake and Questier, *Lewd Hat*, 426.
67. Agnew, *Worlds Apart*, 142.
68. Catherine Bell, *Ritual Theory, Ritual Practice* (New York: Oxford University Press, 1992), 98.
69. Warner, *Publics and Counterpublics*, 48–54.

Works Cited

Agnew, Jean-Christophe. *Worlds Apart: The Market and the Theatre in Anglo-American Thought, 1550–1750*. Cambridge: Cambridge University Press, 1986.
Austin, J.L. *How to Do Things With Words*, edited by J.O. Urmson. Cambridge, MA: Harvard University Press, 1962.
Bell, Catherine. *Ritual Theory, Ritual Practice*. New York: Oxford University Press, 1992.
Blayney, Peter W.M. *The Bookshops in Paul's Cross Churchyard*. London: The Bibliographical Society, 1990.
Butler, Judith. *Excitable Speech: A Politics of the Performative*. New York: Routledge, 1997.
Collinson, Patrick. *The Elizabethan Puritan Movement*. Berkeley: University of California Press, 1967.
———. *Godly People: Essays on English Protestantism and Puritanism*. London: Hambledon Press, 1983.
———. 'The Theatre Constructs Puritanism', in David L. Smith, Richard Strier, and David Bevington (eds), *The Theatrical City: Culture, Theatre and Politics in London, 1576–1649*. Cambridge: Cambridge University Press, 1995.

———. 'Ecclesiastical Vitriol: Religious Satire in the 1590's and the Invention of Puritanism', in John Guy (ed.), *The Reign of Elizabeth I: Court and Culture in the Last Decade*. Cambridge: Cambridge University Press, 1995.

———. 'Elizabethan and Jacobean Puritan Popular Culture', in Christopher Durston and Jacqueline Eales (eds), *The Culture of English Puritanism 1560–1700*. London: Macmillan, 1996.

Crockett, Bryan. *The Play of Paradox – Stage and Sermon in Renaissance England*. Philadelphia: University of Pennsylvania Press, 1995.

Dering, Edward. *A Sermon Preach'd Before the Quene's Maiestie*. London: John Awdely, 1569.

de Certeau, Michel. *The Practice of Everyday Life*. Translated by Steven Rendall. Berkeley: Univ. of California Press, 1984. Arts de Faire.

du Toit, Simon. *The Antitheatrical Body: Puritans and Performance in Early Modern England, 1577–1620*. PhD diss.. University of Maryland, College Park, 2008.

Foucault, Michel. *The History of Sexuality: An Introduction*, vol. 1. New York: Vintage Books, 1990.

Greenham, Richard. *Workes... collected into one volume*, 5th edn. London: T. Creede, 1599, 1612.

Hawkes, David. *Idols of the Marketplace: Idolatry and Commodity Fetishism in English Literature, 1580–1680*. London: Palgrave, 2001.

Hill, Christopher. *Society and Puritanism in Pre-Revolutionary England*. New York, Schocken Books, 1964.

Hughes, Paul L. and James F. Larkin (eds). *Tudor Royal Proclamations: Volume 1, the Early Tudors (1485–1553)*. New Haven and London: Yale University Press, 1964.

I.B. *The fortresse of fathers*. Emden: van der Erve, 1566. STC (2nd edn) 1040.

Kirby, Torrance. 'The Public Sermon: Paul's Cross and the culture of persuasion in England, 1534–1570', *Renaissance and Reformation*, 31(1) (Winter 2008).

Kirby, Torrance, Matthew Milner, and Robert Tittler. 'The Reformation', *Ideas: The Origins of the Modern Public*, Episode 2. David Cayley, host. Canadian Broadcasting Corporation. 17 September 2009. mp3 file. Last accessed 7 February 2013. Available at http://www.cbc.ca/ideas/episodes/features/2010/04/26/the-origins-of-the-modern-public/.

Lake, Peter, with Michael Questier. *The Antichrist's Lewd Hat: Protestants, Papists, and Players in Post-Reformation England*. New Haven, CT: Yale University Press, 2002.

Lehmberg, Stanford E. 'Archbishop Grindal and the Prophesyings.' *Historical Magazine of the Protestant Episcopal Church*, 34(2) (1965).

Morrissey, Mary. 'Elect Nations and Prophetic Preaching: *Types and Examples* in the Paul's Cross Jeremiad', in Lori Anne Ferrell and Peter McCullough (eds), *The English Sermon Revised*. Manchester and New York: Manchester University Press, 2000.

Myers, Anne M. 'Father John Gerard's Object Lessons', in Ronald Corthell et al. (eds), *Catholic Culture in Early Modern England*. Notre Dame, IN: University of Notre Dame, 2007.

Parker, Kenneth L., and Eric J. Carlson. *'Practical Divinity': The Works and Life of Revd Richard Greenham*. Aldershot: Ashgate, 1998.

Poole, Kristen. *Radical Religion from Shakespeare to Milton: Figures of Nonconformity in Early Modern England*. Cambridge: Cambridge University Press, 2000.

Roach, Joseph. *The Player's Passion: Studies in the Science of Acting*. Ann Arbor: University of Michigan Press, 1993.

Shakespeare, William. *Hamlet*, edited by David Bevington. New York: Longman, 2003.

Spufford, Margaret. *Contrasting Communities: English Villagers in the Sixteenth and Seventeenth Centuries*. Cambridge: Cambridge University Press, 1974.

————. *Small Books and Pleasant Histories: Popular Fiction and its Readership in Seventeenth Century England*. Athens, GA: University of Georgia Press, 1981.

Stockwood, John. *A very fruiteful Sermon preched at Paules Crosse the tenth of May last, being the first Sunday in Easter Terme: in which are conteined very necessary and profitable lessons and instructions for this time*. London: George Bishop, 1579.

Tudor-Craig, Pamela. *'Old St Paul's': The Society of Antiquaries Diptych, 1616*. London: London Topographical Society, 2004.

Turner, Victor. *From Ritual to Theatre: The Human Seriousness of Play*. New York: PAJ Publications, 1982.

Warner, Michael. *Publics and Counterpublics*. New York: Zone Books, 2002.

Watt, Tessa. *Cheap Print and Popular Piety, 1550–1640*. Cambridge: Cambridge University Press, 1991.

Yachnin, Paul, Steven Mullaney, and Michael Bristol. 'Theatre and Publics', *Ideas: The Origins of the Modern Public*, Episode 7. David Cayley, host. Canadian Broadcasting Corporation. 22 October 2009. mp3 file. Last accessed 7 February 2013. Available at http://www.cbc.ca/ideas/episodes/features/2010/04/26/the-origins-of-the-modern-public/.

2
Public Acts of Private Devotion: From Silent Prayer to Ceremonies in France's Early Seminaries

Joy Palacios

Clergymen at the Seminary of Saint-Sulpice during the seventeenth century conducted their devotional exercises in a group setting. Their devotional acts were consequently interior but not quite private. At four-thirty each summer morning and five o'clock in the winter in 1682, when the French sun had not quite risen over Paris, a young cleric went door to door at the seminary's dormitory, lighting lamps and knocking to awaken those of his fellow seminarians who had not jumped out of bed at the sound of the morning bells.[1] Private devotions practiced together began the day. At five-thirty, the seminarians filed into the *Salle des exercices*, or classroom, for an hour of 'silent prayer in common, partly kneeling and partly standing'.[2] After Mass, breakfast, classes, and lessons in plain chant, the seminarians gathered again for a second devotional exercise before lunch, this one called the *examen particulier*, or personal examination. The *examen particulier* had two parts. First, 'each person [read] silently, on bended knees and bare-headed, a chapter of the New Testament.'[3] Second, they listened to a short guided reflection on a vice or virtue, called the *examen* or 'examination,' upon which the group meditated quietly until lunch. Lunch gave way to an hour of recreation followed by an afternoon occupied by classes and the recitation of canonical hours, ending with dinner at seven o'clock and one final devotional exercise at eight-thirty in the evening when, as the house rules stated, 'we do in common the evening prayer and examination of conscience.'[4] Practiced in common, one could even describe the non-private nature of seminary devotions as public.

'Public' is the word that seemed fitting to Émile Goichot, author of a post-humously published dissertation about the devotional exercise conducted each day before lunch, the *examen particulier*. Goichot writes, 'The essential innovation of Saint-Sulpice was in effect to institutionalize as a public exercise the act of private devotion.'[5] Goichot did not use the word 'public' anachronistically. The *règlements*, or rules, from the Seminary of Saint-Nicolas-du-Chardonnet – whose students in the late seventeenth century also participated in group devotional exercises every morning, afternoon, and evening – referred to these activities as 'public exercise[s].'[6] The term 'public' in this context did not, however, mean that seminary directors thought that seminarians formed a public. Although early modern French speakers used 'public' as a noun to refer to an assembly or audience – like the 'public' that gathered physically in a playhouse or the virtual 'public' that read a book – seminary directors used 'public' as an adjective. As an adjective, the term meant exterior and exposed, accessible, open to all, common, or known, as opposed to something 'particular,' which concerned just one person, or something 'private,' which remained hidden or secret.[7] The seminary directors' usage reflected the fact that for most French speakers, the substantive form of the term 'public' blended in with its adjectival uses. It designated a formless crowd rather than a rational meeting of minds in a non-political, virtual space or sphere, as Habermas later uses it.[8] The slippage between the early modern meanings of 'public' as an adjective and a noun reveals the difference between the quality of being public and the constitution of a public, between circumstances that rendered religious life visible and the process by which a group of strangers might come to see themselves as participating in an abstract association that could be referred to as a noun, as 'a public'.

And yet, the quality of being public had implications for the formation of groupings that could classify as 'a public', however great or small. Changes in publicness could bring about new types of association, or what Bronwen Wilson and Paul Yachnin call 'publics'. While not Habermasian in nature, early modern publics 'allowed people to connect with others in ways not rooted in family, rank, or vocation, but rather founded in voluntary groupings built on the shared interests, tastes, commitments, and desires of individuals'.[9] These informal associations exhibited many of the key characteristics attributed to publics by Michael Warner. To list just three, they created relations among strangers, addressed these strangers in a mode that was both personal and impersonal, and were self-organizing.[10] However, both the Wilson and Yachnin volume and Warner alike question whether religious practices are intrinsically antithetical to the circulation of texts and ideas on which the formation of publics relies.[11] Religious practices can form a community, but can they provide the grounds for a public?

This essay investigates the publicness with which seminary training in early modern France infused priestly private devotion. By examining the pedagogical practices used to teach silent prayer at the seminaries of Saint-Sulpice and Saint-Nicolas-du-Chardonnet, I argue that the modes of assembly and exposure that characterized the practice of silent prayer in these institutions created conditions in which seminarians could form a public in the sense imagined by Wilson and Yachnin, as a noun. Religious practice and public-making were not mutually exclusive. However, so as to forge a community, seminary rules limited this potential public by curtailing modes of circulation within the seminary that would have otherwise enabled the associations created through silent prayer to be self-organizing, and thus take on a life of their own. In this particular context the demands of institution-building, not the nature of religious practice, prevented publicness from producing a public.

'Preaching to the eyes' by learning to pray

The impulse to institutionalize private devotional acts as public exercises arose from the same historical forces that prompted seventeenth-century French clergymen to start seeing the liturgy as an exercise directed not only toward God but also toward worshippers. The term liturgy, as Dom Gregory Dix explains, 'covers generally all that worship which is officially organised by the church, and which is open to and offered by, or in the name of, all who are members of the church.'[12] Although public in the sense that liturgical actions are open to and offered by, or in the name of, all the faithful, Catholic worship did not always place itself on display. Medieval churches enclosed the Mass in an inner area accessible only to churchmen. In large churches like cathedrals, this space, called the *chœur* or chancel, was entirely closed off from the part of the church where laypeople worshipped, called the nave.[13] At the beginning of the seventeenth century, French clergymen therefore considered liturgical ceremonies as gestures intended for God's eyes only; French laity 'heard' rather than saw the Mass. However, in order to valorize the Catholic Mass in the wake of Protestant critiques, Catholic churches began to open their chancels, and priests, now celebrating the sacraments in front of worshippers who watched and evaluated them, began to think of ceremonies as actions directed toward spectators. In the words of Jean-Jacques Olier, the founder of the Seminary of Saint-Sulpice, ceremonies in the seventeenth century needed to function as 'preaching for the eyes'.[14] Audience awareness restructured the early modern Mass.

France's first seminaries, founded in the 1640s, promoted the new audience-oriented transformations sweeping through the liturgy. In performance terms, they had two central aims: to train priests to skillfully conduct ceremonies, and to teach priests to embody a clerical persona. To accomplish these objectives, seminaries offered what we would now call vocational training. Seminaries housed young men preparing for the priesthood, required them to live in community and follow a rule, gave them lessons in the pastoral skills they would need on a daily basis as priests – how to conduct the ceremonies of the Mass, administer the sacraments, preach, teach, chant, and keep church records – and transmitted hands-on experience by making seminarians work in the local parish church. Seminary jargon referred to these outward-oriented pastoral skills as 'exterior dispositions'.[15] The same audience awareness that shaped the way seminaries taught the exterior aspects of priestly work also permeated the 'interior dispositions' required of seminarians. Olier referred to a priest's spiritual life as an 'interior garment ... that must be reflected on the outside'.[16] The spiritual formation imparted by seminary training linked devotional practice to liturgical responsibility, positioning prayer as a means to improve ceremonial performance as well as a way to obtain God's grace. A lesson on silent prayer given during the evening session of a pre-ordination retreat offered by the seminaries informed its participants:

> He who gives himself to Silent Prayer performs the functions of the Ecclesiastical State much better because, given that in prayer one conceives of their importance and dignity and one receives the feelings of affection and respect, you apply yourself afterward with more attention and modesty: Thus one preaches much better, one celebrates the Mass better...[17]

Devotional diligence enhanced ceremonial action. Seminarians learned to pray so as to better preach to parishioners' eyes.

Although seminary directors promoted prayer as much for its exterior as its interior benefits, silent prayer – referred to in seminary handbooks as *l'oraison mentale*, literally translated as 'mental prayer' – constituted a priest's principal inward occupation or *exercice*.[18] It indeed amounted to a form of interior exercise. The *oraison mentale* demanded inner gymnastics. The prayer had three parts, a beginning, middle, and end, or 'the preparation, the body of the prayer, and thanksgiving.'[19] Each part of *l'oraison mentale* involved a series of interior acts. The preparation involved 'putting oneself in God's presence', 'invoking His assistance', and 'presenting the subject of the prayer to oneself'.[20] The body of the prayer required seminarians to produce three more acts: 'considerations of the understanding', affections, and resolutions.[21] To produce considerations they reflected on the vice, virtue, maxim, or mystery designated by the prayer's topic, ascertained its truthfulness intellectually, and then evaluated their behaviour in light of their findings.[22] Next, the seminarian produced affections that corresponded to his considerations, like adoration or love for God, contrition for sins committed, hate for evil, or thankfulness for blessings.[23] Then, to complete the prayer's body, the seminarian made a resolution, defined by a seminary handbook as 'a specific point, and a plan that one forms during the prayer to police your morals, correct some fault, or practice some virtue'.[24] The prayer ended with 'three small acts', namely, the giving of thanks, an offering, and requests.[25] Devotion demanded tremendous inner work.

Seminarians learned to pray from conferences, rules, and handbooks, and through daily practice, instructor feedback, and self-correction. Very few documents survive that give an anecdotal glimpse or inside perspective of the ups, downs, nuances, and aberrations experienced by seminarians as they learned to pray. Instructors gave their feedback orally, to the benefit of their students but not to the archive. Students kept track of their self-corrections in notebooks, where they marked their goals and tallied their mistakes, but I have not yet found any examples of such notebooks at the archives of the Seminary of Saint-Sulpice, the French national archives, or the French national library, where the manuscripts consulted for this essay are conserved.[26] A picture of seminary devotions must therefore rely on normative sources – the rules and handbooks that told seminarians what they *should* do – rather than on sources that describe what they *did* do. This essay draws primarily on two normative sources: a manuscript copy of the general rules for the Seminary of Saint-Sulpice that dates from 1682 and is conserved at the French national library as manuscript Fr. 11760; and a printed handbook published in 1660 titled *Conduites pour les exercices principaux qui se font dans les séminaires ecclesiastiques* (General conduct for the principal exercises practiced in ecclesiastical seminaries), written by a former seminarian of Saint-Nicolas-du-Chardonnet and resident of its priestly community named Matthieu Beuvelet. Although normative in nature, these sources nonetheless bear the trace of private prayer's progressive publicness in early modern seminary education.

Assembly

The publicness that infused devotional exercises derived first from the fact of assembly. Publicness consisted both in the quality of being common or accessible to all, like public land, and in the quality of being exposed, made known, or put on display. By frequently gathering seminarians together into one place, the techniques used at the Seminaries of Saint-Sulpice and Saint-Nicolas-du-Chardonnet to teach silent prayer made devotional acts public in both these ways, establishing a particular prayer method as common to all and requiring seminarians to practice that method in front of others. The entry for the term 'public' published in Antoine Furetière's *Dictionnaire universel* captured the interrelationship between assembly as a circumstance that endowed its participants with the kind of publicness attributed to goods that anyone could use and assembly as the occasion for exposure. Furetière used 'public' in the first sense when he wrote, 'Public is said of an assembly open to everyone, or to a select few', and then used it in the second sense when he gave the following examples: 'It takes boldness to appear in public. Lawyers speak in public. Preachers preach in public.... One also says that an Author has given his works to the public when he has them printed....'[27] Although seminary directors made private devotion into a public event in order to ensure conformity – their aim was for all the churchmen living at the seminary to acquire the same ethos or 'spirit' and thus form an identifiable community – the publicness fostered through assembly nonetheless provided the fodder for public-making. The types of assemblies in which seminarians learned and practiced prayer created conditions suitable for constituting a public by fostering a type of relationality crucial to public formation, described by Warner as 'stranger sociability.'[28] Stranger sociability occurs when 'we've become capable of recognizing ourselves as strangers even when we know each other', and it creates a public insofar as the people it joins are 'unite[d] ... through participation alone' rather than through some other kind of membership.[29] Stranger relationality in turn facilitates the free circulation of ideas. Seminary directors had to put tight controls on the circulation of people and texts in order to restrain stranger sociability's public-making potential.

The seminary itself amounted to a sort of extended assembly – France's earliest seminaries grew out of ten-day retreats for clergymen who wanted to be ordained – and fostered stranger sociability by bringing young men from diverse backgrounds into contact with each other. Most seminarians received their first lessons in prayer before entering the seminary, either through instructional sessions offered by seminary directors for men interested in joining the priesthood, or during ten-day spiritual retreats in which the archbishop of Paris required clergymen to participate before receiving ordination.[30] After entering a seminary, instructional sessions occurred regularly. Seminarians learned the basics of silent prayer in a weekly, hour-long lesson, or *conférence*, on Sunday mornings at Saint-Nicolas and on Saturday evenings at Saint-Sulpice.[31] These gatherings established relations among strangers, assembling men who ranged from laymen with no ecclesiastical experience to priests who wanted to improve their skills, from country folk to city dwellers, and from poor boys to rich sons.[32]

In addition to classes, which gathered small groups of seminarians throughout the day, three larger types of assemblies punctuated daily life: meals, Masses, and morning prayers. These assemblies physically gathered all members of the seminary together, creating a 'public' in Furetière's sense of a gathering open to all but not necessarily in Warner's sense of a relation among strangers united through participation. Whereas meals separated seminarians into two 'tables' or lunch hours, thereby dividing the community, and Masses joined seminarians into a single ritual body around the altar through ceremonial action, thereby obscuring each person's particularity, the assembly for morning prayers provided a foundation for stranger sociability by gathering all the seminarians together in a way that displayed their common participation while underscoring each person's irreducibility and essential equality before God. The way seminarians entered the *salle des exercices* for morning prayers conveyed the assembly's underlying egalitarianism and its emphasis on each individual. Meals and Masses, which organized participants hierarchically according to ecclesiastical rank, required them to arrange themselves by rank upon entering the dining hall or to walk to church in procession.[33] For morning prayers, by contrast, seminarians arrived one at a time by themselves. The rules alerted them that 'You must deliver yourself to the classroom a little while before the hour when the prayer commences' and advised them to leave their rooms 'by a quarter before five-thirty so as to be able to find yourself [there] for the beginning of the prayer or meditation which starts precisely at five-thirty'.[34] However, the rules specified nothing further about exactly how they were to arrive, which meant that the general rule of indifference applied. As a version of the rules from circa 1710 stated, 'One must (as we in fact do, thank God) place ourselves indifferently, sometimes after, sometimes before...'.[35] During morning prayers the hierarchical relationships that structured all the other seminary activities gave way to a universal self-abnegation before God.

Gathered in prayer, seminarians could see themselves as an association among strangers. Technically, a churchman could experience his wretchedness while conducting his silent prayers alone in his room. The simple act of making all the seminarians engage in silent prayer in the same room gave visible expression to the potential public forged through their participation. The gestural sequence seminarians observed during the prayer assembly displayed both their unity and their individuality, passing from kneeling to standing and from synchronized action to independent movement. Prayers began with 15 minutes of genuflection, after which seminarians could kneel or stand as they saw fit.[36] Used by priests and laypeople alike, genuflection expressed the personal nature of devotional prayer. According to Jean-Claude Schmitt, this gesture, in which Catholics knelt on both knees with their bodies erect, became 'the normal attitude of prayer' in the Middle Ages, signaling a shift toward 'a more individual kind of prayer that is addressed to God in front of an object, like the crucifix, materializing the divine presence'.[37] Genuflection aided and expressed prayer's inward movement through, in Schmitt's words, 'a sort of 'folding' of the body upon itself'.[38] By kneeling, the person praying signalled the desire to encounter God individually. Standing, in contrast, signaled collectivity, respect, and readiness for action. For example, during Mass all the faithful stood to hear the Gospels read so as to show, in Olier's words, that 'they are ready to march'.[39] By starting with 15 minutes of synchronized genuflection, a gesture emblematic of devotional privacy but here done in unison, the morning assembly made manifest the bond created through prayer. By then permitting seminarians to choose their posture the assembly conveyed their individuality, while the practice of standing provided a physical reminder that things learned in prayer were to be put into circulation, made to march.

An emphasis on individuality, however, does not by itself establish stranger sociability. Seminarians could very quickly become friends or enemies when living and praying together every day in close quarters. A public, though, relates strangers, not friends. Seminary rules imposed stranger sociability upon seminarians by requiring them to address each other as *Monsieur* and to use the plural form of 'you' – *vous* – that signalled distance and courtesy.[40] Rules also prohibited modes of address that fostered familiarity, like nicknames and all forms of touching, whether for greetings or games.[41] Meanwhile, the prefect 'watch[ed] carefully over discontentment, familiarities that are too great, and vicious discourses during recreations, leagues, cabals or bad unions that could occur among seminarians' so as to prevent them from growing.[42] By guarding against alliances and cliques, the seminary rules ensured that an element of strangeness characterized seminary friendship.

The mode of speech used by seminary instructors teaching students how to pray enhanced stranger sociability by being at once personal and impersonal, another quality attributed to publics by Warner. He writes, 'Public speech can have a great urgency and intimate import. Yet we know that it was addressed not exactly to us but to the stranger we were until the moment we happened to be addressed by it.'[43] Seminary instructors sought to communicate with their students using a simultaneously personal and impersonal mode described in the rules as 'zeal'. Zeal touched each person in an urgent and immediate way, while at the same time ignoring the differences among people and thus addressing them all in the same way. For example, the guidelines for the instructor who presided over the weekly lesson on prayer specified: '[T]his conference must be done with very great zeal and a desire to powerfully excite and to carry all the churchmen to a daily practice of ... silent prayer.'[44] An instructor's zeal addressed students personally in that, if successful, it 'abundantly filled' them with the attitude of prayer.[45] And yet zeal aimed at forming all seminarians with a common ethos, the 'ecclesiastical spirit' which, from Olier's perspective, transcended differences in 'age and condition' through austerity and self-mortification.[46] Professorial zeal divested seminarians of the social distinctions with which they entered the seminary – family, rank, financial prosperity or poverty, level of education – and regarded each of them in light of a standardized vision of the perfect churchman, creating the opportunity for new kinds of association by removing seminarians from their traditional ties.

Although the publicness that infused prayer assemblies had public-making potential as a result of the ways in which conferences on prayer and prayer sessions favoured stranger sociability and distanced seminarians from traditional ties, prohibitions within seminaries on the circulation of people and information prevented the potential public constituted through prayer assemblies from self-organizing, and therefore from flourishing as a public in the sense envisioned by Bronwen and Yachnin. Rules short-circuited the self-organizing dynamic crucial to the making of a public by preventing seminarians from meeting together in private or talking with each other repeatedly during recreational hours. Seminarians could not enter each other's rooms or even approach one another's doors without permission from the prefect.[47] Nor could they spend their free time in groups of less than three, talk with the same people during recreation every day, or consistently socialize with seminarians from the same 'country,' meaning home town or region.[48] These rules impeded seminarians from forming groups that might critique seminary practices or deviate from seminary doctrine.[49]

Prohibitions on the circulation of ideas further limited the self-organizing capacity of any seminarians who did manage to meet together or who flouted the rules in order to speak their minds. They could not study any books other than those assigned for a class or recommended by an instructor, lend or borrow any books without permission from the seminary Superior, or lend or keep 'bad books, romances, plays, defamatory libels, or [books] counter to morals, Religion, or the state'.[50] Seminary rules circumscribed their conversations too. They could not teach or ascribe to ideas classified as 'bad doctrine' by the church or the seminary directors, nor could they 'converse with each other about the news of the world, gazettes, or affairs, either public or private, that could offend in any way one's neighbor'.[51] Without the liberty to assemble at will or read, share, and discuss ideas, the stranger sociality that the publicness of devotional practices imparted to seminary life could not easily give rise to unexpected associations, or publics, and instead remained within the control of seminary directors. Focused ultimately on standardizing pastoral practices like ceremonies rather than on providing a liberal arts education, seminary directors curtailed the self-organizing aspects generated by publicness so as to create a community, a 'house', instead of its less predictable cousin, a public.

Exposure

Publicness derived not only from the fact of assembly, but also from the experience of exposure. At the seminaries of Saint-Sulpice and Saint-Nicolas, both the instructional sessions during which seminarians learned about prayer and the morning assembly in which they practiced prayer used oral presentation and spectatorship to expose a seminarian's otherwise invisible, inner work to the evaluative gaze of his peers and superiors. This performance of a difference between interior and exterior is part of what gave devotional exercises in France's early seminaries their public character. The pedagogical techniques that seminary instructors used to bring the inward work of prayer to light had the potential to foster a public in the substantive sense because the spiritual interior exposed through discussion and spectatorship was neither empty nor solitary. To the contrary, seminary instruction revealed that the *oraison* established a non-kinship association with a virtual community – God, the saints, angels – that existed only by virtue of attention, a feature of publics. Warner asserts that publics are 'constituted through mere attention'.[52] Unlike membership in a social class or nation, which persists even if a person falls asleep or stops thinking about it, 'a public exists only by virtue of address'; only by virtue of the 'active uptake' of a text or communication.[53] As opposed to institutions, publics 'commence with the moment of attention, must continually predicate renewed attention, and cease to exist when attention is no longer predicated'.[54] When not established in the context of assembly and exposure, however, the virtual community accessed through the *oraison* remained self-contained and could not circulate, limiting its public-making potential. Seminary exercises exposed this invisible community so as to teach seminarians how to participate in it, and in doing so created texts and signs that circulated within and beyond the seminary in ways prone to foster a self-organizing devotional public.

Before considering how seminary pedagogy exposed the inner work of prayer, the public-making potential of this inner work merits a brief examination. The inner work that was taught and then exposed through *oraison* exercises consisted in a relentless effort to renew and maintain attention on a text by means of which seminarians focused their prayers. This inner work by its nature thus entailed a public-making capacity. Although everyone gathered to kneel at five-thirty in the morning, prayer actually began the previous night when each seminarian read a short meditation to 'prepare their spirits in advance' for the morning exercise.[55] Beuvelet presents this as the commencement of the next day's active attention to the text:

> You must read attentively the subject of the Meditation, with the intention of doing it well the next day, and plan for how you will do it, like determining which affections and resolutions you will produce.[56]

In the morning, seminarians reflected on the text again immediately after waking. The seminary rules instructed them: 'You must as you get dressed go over in your mind the subject upon which one must meditate...'.[57] Upon arriving at prayers, the same text served as the nucleus around which they built their hour-long *oraison*. 'As soon as the *Oraison* has started,' the rules urged them, 'one must apply himself to the proposed subject of meditation, without detracting from any of the time destined for this exercise'.[58] Two more exercises throughout the day – both of which were also conducted in an assembly – returned the seminarians' attention to the text from the previous night. These exercises trained seminarians to gauge what Warner might call the success of the 'active uptake' of the meditational text. The *examen particulier* in the afternoon before lunch provided the occasion for seminarians to evaluate their behavior in light of the resolutions made during prayer, while the *examen général* undertaken in the evening before reading a new meditation required them to consider the entire day's activities through the lens of the previous night's meditation topic.[59] Prayer, like a public, ceased to exist if attention failed. The *oraison mentale* trained seminarians to continually renew their attention.

The meditation text provided a point of entry, an attention gateway, for the active uptake that constructed a virtual community through the act of prayer. Depending on the prayer, this community might consist of the various parts of the praying person's self (mind, will, heart, and soul), the three divine persons who compose the Christian trinity (God the Father, Jesus Christ his son, and the Holy Spirit), the Blessed Virgin, saints, and guardian angels, as well as other praying souls. For example, the prayer began by putting oneself in the presence of God, invoking His assistance or the assistance of an intermediary like a saint, and then presenting to oneself the prayer topic under God's watchful eye.[60] Once presented, the topic provided the focus of everyone's attention for the duration of the prayer. A discourse ensued, still oriented by the meditational text but aimed at helping the praying person's will to form resolutions that could be carried out during the rest of the day. To explore the types of interactions possible during the *oraison* would require a much longer essay, but one called a 'colloquium' aptly represents the conversational, reflexive, multidimensional character of the *oraison* interaction. Beuvelet defines the colloquium as 'a certain discussion [*entretien*] of the soul with God, with the angels, the saints, or even with ourselves'.[61] A colloquium, according to Beuvelet, could serve as the prayer's conclusion, or the praying person could summon a colloquium during the body of the prayer. The *oraison* exercise, although interior and therefore not prone to circulate or to recruit the attention of strangers, nonetheless had the character of a discussion carried out in private among a select number of participants about a text that had a wider readership. Silent prayer in seminaries not only assumed that seminarians participated in a specific reading public, it also figured the prayer experience as a contained example of that public's interactions.

Oral presentation and spectatorship exposed the inner work of silent prayer, bridging the relatively contained and non-circulating virtual community assembled through the *oraison* with the material, circulation-prone assembly of priests gathered in seminaries. This bridging effect introduced strangers into the intimate community forged by a seminarian during his *oraison*, making the virtual community accessed through silent prayer more like a public. At the same time, this bridging placed prayer's hidden colloquium into circulation, making it the fodder for a human public of the kind imagined by Warner. Oral presentation exposed the inner work of the *oraison* most fully when seminarians first learned to pray. This was also the period during which seminary pedagogy introduced what could be considered strangers into the prayer interaction most aggressively. A letter written in 1695 to Louis Tronson, Saint-Sulpice's superior general in Paris, by a Sulpician seminary instructor in the town of Limoges named Thomas Bourget, gives an idea of this exposure. Bourget tells Tronson that seminarians at Saint-Sulpice's seminary in Limoges learned to pray during a series of *entretiens*, or conferences, before even joining the seminary, and then adds, 'We also make them do the *oraison* out loud for several days'.[62] Bourget does not describe precisely how this exercise unfolded – did everyone say a prescribed prayer or did each participant construct their own prayers in front of everyone else? – but whatever the specifics, the practice of conducting the *oraison mentale* out loud in an assembly of people who were not yet even seminarians made strangers privy to the virtual communities established by each praying person, while also making strangers an integral part of the discussions conducted with invisible participants like God and the saints during the prayer. Oral presentation added stranger sociability to the practice of silent prayer.

Once participants were enrolled in a seminary, *oraison* pedagogy continued to introduce an element of stranger sociability into the practice of silent prayer, although in a less intrusive way. At Saint-Sulpice, and upon occasion at Saint-Nicolas, the seminary director presented the *oraison* meditation orally rather than distributing it in text form, incorporating in this way the director's voice into the *oraison* conversation. An outside voice joined the *oraison* conversation again every afternoon during the *examen particulier*, when seminarians 'listen[ed] on their knees and attentively' as a seminary instructor read aloud a text about 'a subject of self-examination on some virtue, some vice, or some imperfection.'[63] In response to the oral presentation of the examination topic, seminarians evaluated their spiritual progress since the morning, placing the *examen* in dialogue with the morning's prayer resolutions. The *oraison* conversation widened still further in that each seminarian's spiritual director assigned him a specific vice or virtue on which to reflect for a longer period of time – a month or two[64] – thereby adding his voice both to the silent prayer colloquium that guided seminarians as they formed resolutions in the *oraison*, and to the multiple voices and texts at play in the interior dialogue undertaken during the *examen particulier*. The successive oral presentations of texts and meditations throughout the day expanded silent prayer's invisible community so that it encompassed other seminary residents.

The weekly lessons on the *oraison mentale* placed prayer's hidden colloquium on display, and into circulation, by positioning some students as spectators called upon to observe and judge the prayers of their fellow churchmen. This exercise, which at Saint-Sulpice was called the *répétition de l'Oraison* (meaning both prayer repetition and prayer rehearsal) required seminarians to recount their *oraison* experience in front of their instructor and peers.[65] According to the guidelines for the prefect at Saint-Nicolas, the instructor asked two or three seminarians to describe 'to all the company the good feelings he had during the meditation, the order he kept [in his meditation], the affections and resolutions he formed, etc.'.[66] Once several people had shared, the prefect called on other students to 'point out the faults that they observed in the practice of their fellow seminarians,' and then 'advis[ed] them gently and charitably of the failings against which they must be on guard so as to profit from the prayer'.[67] The rules regarding the *répétition* at Saint-Sulpice brim with anxiety that this exercise might turn into a performance, please an audience, and circulate in non-sanctioned conversations, an anxiety that suggests the *répétition*'s public-making potential. After insisting on mandatory attendance, the rules say:

> [T]hose who are interrogated to repeat their oraison must report simply the manner in which they performed their meditation, the sentiments with which they were touched, the reflections they made, and the resolutions they took, without trying to give an eloquent or well-studied discourse.[68]

The rules also warned the assembly to 'listen attentively to those who are interrogated, to avoid laughing at their way of speaking even if it is defective in some way, and to never talk with each other afterward about the faults that you thought you noticed in the discourse you heard, nor make fun of it'.[69] The *répétition* thus intentionally made the inner work of prayer a topic of discussion, launching it into the authorized channels of circulation within the seminary community. The *répétition* also, inadvertently, incited non-authorized channels of circulation through which talk about prayer performances travelled, perhaps along with jokes and opinions about not only the way fellow seminarians described their prayers but also the content of their prayers. The display and spectatorship of the *oraison*'s inner dialogue connected the spiritual community accessed through prayer to the embodied one present in the seminary, making private prayers a matter of general concern.

Unhampered, the publicness with which seminary instructors infused the oraison by teaching it through oral presentations and making use of spectatorship had the potential to develop into a self-organizing public. Not only did the *oraison* itself have a conversational structure, but it assumed that the people who prayed were already participants in a reading public, the public that consumed devotional texts. In the seminary, the prefect crafted the daily meditation from his own readings, and after a seminarian left the seminary to work as a priest, he selected a daily meditation for himself based on the devotional books in his own collection. The oral representations that seminarians produced of their *oraison* created a public in the even more immediate sense of an audience complicit in and eager to talk about a performance. These characteristics created pathways for the flow of ideas. To hamper this flow and craft a reproducible identity for the seminary as an institution, seminary instructors worked tirelessly to prune, shape, and eliminate circulation pathways that, if allowed to develop organically, could alter the prevailing norms, attitudes, and perspectives in the seminary.

In addition to the limits on the circulation of people and information already discussed, one other method for gaining control over the public-making potential of the *oraison* responded to the unpredictability of oral presentation and spectatorship. Seminary rules discouraged extemporaneous performances, whether from presenters or the people who watched and listened to them. This policy extended beyond the prayer lessons and exercises to encompass all seminary activities. On Saturday evenings and feast days at Saint-Sulpice, for example, during the hour when the superior gave a lesson on prayer methods, seminarians who had already completed their university studies gave a presentation on 'some matter of piety related to the holiday.'[70] Although the rules demanded that seminarians at this stage keep themselves in a constant state of readiness to speak during the lesson, implying preparedness for making an improvisational contribution, the rules also demanded that they 'never expose themselves to speak without having prepared and learned by memory beforehand what they must say'.[71] Likewise, auditors were instructed to 'observe a great silence and great modesty at lessons (during which one must never speak if one is not questioned), in the dining hall, in the dormitory, in the cloak room, and generally everywhere ...'.[72] Even during recreation, seminarians were encouraged to prepare in advance, if not the content of their conversation, the intentions with which they would converse.[73] While other types of monasteries, convents, and schools imposed similar restrictions on spontaneous behaviour – the seminaries were not unique in this way – such restrictions nonetheless enabled seminary instructors to direct and curtail avenues of circulation created through performances rather than texts. Control over performances in turn made it easier to channel the public-making potential generated through display and spectatorship into the creation of a community-specific style of expression: a style aimed at differentiating churchmen from the larger public beyond seminary walls rather than at incorporating more strangers into their ranks.

Conclusion

Silent prayer as practiced in France's early seminaries infused private devotion with publicness by requiring seminarians to conduct their *oraison* in an assembly, and by using oral presentation and spectatorship to expose the inner work carried out during prayer. Prayer in this context facilitated types of interactions that could forge associations among clergymen, and potentially even among their lay associates, based on shared interests, desires, or opinions rather than on rank, class, family, or even the priestly vocation seminarians were in the process of acquiring. The publicness of private devotion at Saint-Sulpice and Saint-Nicolas-du-Chardonnet fostered stranger sociability, promoted forms of address characterized by impersonal intimacy, and created pathways for the circulation of ideas through the mixing of people from diverse backgrounds, through texts, and through performances. In France's seventeenth-century seminaries, devotion did not jeopardize public-making. Rather, seminary directors exerted tremendous energy to create something they valued more, an ecclesiastical community with recognizable boundaries and institutional longevity. Only through vigilant efforts to impose order on the circulation of people, texts, and ideas that resulted from prayer's publicness did seminary directors manage to rein in the potentially self-organizing dynamic set in motion through the *oraison*. Making a community was harder than making a public.

Notes

1. 'Reglement général du Séminaire de S. Sulpice', 1682, Paris, Bibliothèque nationale de France (BN), Ms. Fr. 11760, f. 105r–v; M. Baudrand, 'Mémoire sur la vie de M. Olier et sur le séminaire de Saint-Sulpice', in L. Bertrand (ed.), *Bibliothèque sulpicienne ou histoire littéraire de la Compagnie de Saint-Sulpice* (Paris: Alphonse Picard et Fils, Éditeurs, 1900), 437; 'Livre dans lequel sont escrits tous les Reglemens de chaque office, et Exercice du Seminaire desquels le Prefet doit avoir une parfaite connoissance', late seventeenth century, Paris, Archives nationale de France (AN), MM 475, f. 250r–251v.
2. 'Reglement général du Séminaire de S. Sulpice,' BN, Ms. Fr. 11760, f. 106v: ('la priere et oraison mentale en commun, partie à genoux et partie debout'). All translations are the author's unless otherwise noted. Non-standard spellings from early modern sources have been preserved.
3. Baudrand, 'Mémoire sur la vie de M. Olier et sur le séminaire de Saint-Sulpice', 437–8: ('chacun lit tout bas, à genoux et tête nue, un chapitre du Nouveau Testament'); 'Reglement général du Séminaire de S. Sulpice', BN, Ms. Fr. 11760, f. 109r–110v.
4. 'Reglement général du Séminaire de S. Sulpice', BN, Ms. Fr. 11760, f. 114v: ('on fera en commun la priere du soir et l'examen de conscience'); For a description of the afternoon activities, see Baudrand, 'Mémoire sur la vie de M. Olier et sur le séminaire de Saint-Sulpice', 438–40.
5. Émile Goichot, *Les Examens particuliers de M. Tronson: Essai sur la formation du prêtre 'classique,'* edited by René Heyer (Strasbourg: Presses Universitaires de Strasbourg, 2005), 30: ('L'apport essentiel de Saint-Sulpice a été en effet d'institutionnaliser en exercice public l'acte de dévotion privée').
6. See 'Directoire des prieres que l'on recite au matin, a midy, et au soir, avant et aprés [sic] chaque exercice public du seminaire' in 'Reglement du seminaire paroissial de Sainct Nicolas du Chardonnet, pour l'usage du prefect', seventeenth century, Paris, AN, MM 474, f. 57.
7. See César-Pierre Richelet, 'Public', *Dictionnaire françois, contenant les mots et les choses, plusieurs nouvelles remarques sur la langue françoise: ses expressions propres, figurées & burlesques, la prononciation des mots les plus difficiles, le genre des noms, le régime des verbes, avec les termes les plus connus des arts & des sciences, le tout tiré de l'usage et des bons auteurs de la langue françoise* (Genève: Chez Jean Herman Widerhold, 1680), http://gallica.bnf.fr/ark:/12148/bpt6k509323/f814; See also Antoine Furetière, 'Public', *Dictionnaire universel, contenant generalement tous les mots françois, tant vieux que modernes, & les termes de toûtes les sciences et des arts...* (La Haye: Chez Arnout & Renier Leers, 1690), http://gallica2.bnf.fr/ark:/12148/bpt6k50614b.
8. Dictionary author César-Pierre Richelet defined the substantive form of public as 'the bulk of the multitude'. See Richelet, 'Public': ('Le gros de la multitude').
9. Bronwen Wilson and Paul Yachnin (eds), *Making Publics in Early Modern Europe: People, Things, Forms of Knowledge* (New York and London: Routledge, 2010), 1.
10. Michael Warner, *Publics and Counterpublics* (New York: Zone Books, 2005), 74, 76, 67.

11. See, for example, Steven Mullaney, Angela Vanhaelen, and Joseph Ward, 'Religion Inside Out: Dutch House Churches and the Making of Publics in the Dutch Republic', in Bronwen Wilson and Paul Yachnin (eds), *Making Publics in Early Modern Europe: People, Things, Forms of Knowledge* (New York and London: Routledge, 2010), 25–36; See also Warner's discussion of sermons in *Publics and Counterpublics*, 82–5. He argues that the sermon is a form that best achieves its religious aims precisely when the hearer does not experience it as public speech.

12. Dom Gregory Dix, *The Shape of the Liturgy* (New York: The Seabury Press, 1983), 1.

13. See Bernard Chédozeau, *Chœur clos, chœur ouvert: De l'église médiévale à l'église tridentine (France, XVIIe-XVIIIe siècle)* (Paris: Les Éditions du Cerf, 1998), 15–16, 24–30; Some churches with closed chancels would throw open the chancel door during the elevation, when the celebrant raised the consecrated Eucharist above his head, but more than one ecclesiastical synod prohibited this practice. See Édouard Dumoutet, *Le Désire de voir l'hostie et les origines de la dévotion au saint-sacrement* (Paris: Gabriel Beauchesne, 1926), 58.

14. Jean-Jacques Olier, *Explication des cérémonies de la grande messe de paroisse, selon l'usage romain. Par un Prestre du Clergé* (Paris: Jacques Langlois, 1656), 7: ('des predications par les yeux').

15. See, for example, Matthieu Beuvelet, *Conduites pour les exercices principaux qui se font dans les séminaires ecclesiastiques, dressées en faveur des clercs demeurans dans le Seminaire de S. Nicolas du Chardonnet* (Lyon: Chez Hierosne de la Garde, en ruë Merciere à l'Esperance, 1660), 126–7; See also Jean-Jacques Olier, 'Projet de l'establissement d'un séminaire dans un diocèse, où il est traité premierement de l'estat & de la disposition des sujets, secondement de l'esprit de tous leurs exercices, par un prestre du clergé', printed document with handwritten notes and rough draft manuscript by Olier (Paris: Chez Jacques Langlois, Imprimeur & Libraire ordinaire du Roy, vis à vis la Fontaine Ste Geneviesve, 1651), Archives de la Compagnie des Prêtres de Saint-Sulpice (SS), Ms. 20, f. 17, 19.

16. Jean-Jacques Olier, 'Autographes de M. Olier, fondateur du Séminaire de St. Sulpice: Divers écrits, tome I', before 1657, SS, Ms. 14, f. 188: ('lhabit interieur ... qui doibt rejaillir sur lexterieur').

17. 'Entretiens des ordinands sur les matieres de devotion', SS, Ms. 157, f. 2r: ('qui s'addone a l'Oraison me[n]tale en fait beaucoup mieux les fonctions de l'Estat Ecclesiastique Car comme en l'oraison on en conçoit Evidemment l'importance et dignité, et qu'on y recoit les sentiments d'affections et de respect on s'y applique avec bien plus d'esprit attention, et modestie: Ainsy on presche beaucoup mieux, on celebre mieux la messe...'); This manuscript contains ten 'entretiens' or lessons on the devotional practices required by priests and was probably composed between 1634 and 1657. For more information, see Gérard Carroll, *Un Portrait du prêtre: les retraites de 10 jours pour les ordinands*, vol. 1 (Paris: Pierre Téqui, 2004), 167–9.

18. See Olier's discussion of interior and exterior exercises in Gilles Chaillot, Paul Cochois, and Irénée Noye (eds), *Traité des Saints Ordres (1676), compare aux écrits authentiques de Jean-Jacques Olier (†1657)* (Paris: Procure de la Compagnie de Saint-Sulpice, 1984), 45.

19. Beuvelet, *Conduites*, 19: ('la Preparation, le corps de l'Oraison, & l'action de graces').

20. Beuvelet, *Conduites*, 20: ('Se mettre en la presence de Dieu', 'Invoquer son assistance,' 'Se presenter le sujet de l'Oraison').

21. Beuvelet, *Conduites*, 21: ('En quoy consiste la seconde partie de l'Oraison? Elle consiste en trois choses principalles: aux Considerations de l'entendement & aux Affections & aux Resolutions').

22. Beuvelet, *Conduites*, 21–6.

23. Beuvelet, *Conduites*, 26–7.

24. Beuvelet, *Conduites*, 28: ('Resolution est un propos determiné, & un dessein que l'on forme dans l'Oraison pour policer ses mœurs, pour corriger quelque défaut, ou pour pratiquer quelque vertu').

25. Beuvelet, *Conduites*, 29: ('trois petits actes').

26. The practice of keeping track of mistakes occurred in the context of the spiritual self-examination, during which seminarians evaluated whether or not they had kept the resolutions made during morning prayers. See Beuvelet, *Conduites*, 37; See also Claude de la Croix, *Le Parfaict ecclesiastique ou diverses instructions sur toutes les fonctions clericales. Cy-devant disposées en tables par M. Claude de la Croix, prestre du Seminaire de S. Nicolas du Chardonnet. Et depuis redigées en livre, corigées & augmentées par des ecclesiastiques du mesme seminaire. Divisées en quatre parties, & enrichies de figures en taille-douce. Ouvrage autant utile que necessaire aux seminaires & communautez, tant seculieres que regulieres; à tous curez, & autres ecclesiastiques, pour exercer dignement leurs charges, & se bien acquiter de leurs devoirs. Où les laïques mesmes pourront connoistre la sainteté du service divin, & l'excellence du sacerdoce. Dedié à Messeigneurs les Archevesques & Evesques deputez du clergé de France* (Paris: Chez Pierre de Bresche, Libraire & Imprimeur ordinaire de la Reyne, ruë S. Jacques, vis à vis les Charniers S. Benoist, à l'Image saint Joseph & saint Ignace, 1666), 89–90.

27. Furetière, 'Public': ('Public se dit aussi d'une assemblée ouverte à tout le monde, ou à quelques personnes choisies. Il faut avoir de la hardiesse pour paroistre en public. Les Advocats parlent en public. Les Predicateurs preschent en public... On dit aussi, qu'un Auteur donne ses ouvrages au public, quand il les fait imprimer...').

28. Warner, *Publics and Counterpublics*, 75.

29. Warner, *Publics and Counterpublics*, 74–5.

30. On the pre-ordination retreats, see Carroll, *Un Portrait du prêtre*, 1:62–73.

31. Pasté, *Abrégé du reglement du Seminaire Paroissial de S. Nicolas du Chardonnet, pour l'usage des Seminaristes* (Paris: Chez Pierre Trichard, ruë Saint Victor, proche S. Nicolas du Chardonnet, au Chef Saint Jean, 1672), 4; Pasté, *Abrégé du reglement du Seminaire Paroissial de S. Nicolas du Chardonnet, pour l'usage des Seminaristes* (Paris: Chez Pierre Trichard, ruë Saint Victor, proche S. Nicolas du Chardonnet, au Chef Saint Jean, 1677), 9; At Saint-Sulpice these conferences took place on Saturdays and feast days. See Baudrand, 'Mémoire sur la vie de M. Olier et sur le séminaire de Saint-Sulpice', 439; The length of the conference is given in 'Livre dans lequel ...', AN, MM 475, f. 60r.

32. On the types of students who entered Saint-Sulpice, see Gwénola Hervouët, 'Le Séminaire de Saint-Sulpice, 1642–1700: étude sociologique et religieuse' (Mémoire de maîtrise sous la direction de M. le Professeur Bely, Université de Paris IV-Sorbonne, 1999), 12–13, 17–18, 28.

33. For dining hall rules, see 'Livre dans lequel ...', AN, MM 475, f. 186r–193r; For the procession to Mass, see 'Reglement général du Séminaire de S. Sulpice', BN, Ms. Fr. 11760, f. 118r–v.

34. 'Reglement général du Séminaire de S. Sulpice', BN, Ms. Fr. 11760, f. 106v, 106r: ('Il faut être rendu à la Salle des éxercices [sic] quelque peu de temps avant

l'heure ou l'oraison commence;' 'Il faut partir de sa Chambre au plus tard à l'avant quart de cinq heures et demie afin de pouvoir se trouver au commencement de l'oraison où méditation qu'on commence à cinq heures et demie précises').

35. 'Règlement général du Séminaire de Saint-Sulpice', 1710, Paris, SS, Ms. 1342, f. 73: ('On doit (comme on le fait aussi Dieu merci) se placer indifferemment, tantost apres, tantost devant').

36. 'Reglement général du Séminaire de S. Sulpice', BN, Ms. Fr. 11760, f. 107r.

37. Jean-Claude Schmitt, *La Raison des gestes dans l'occident médiéval*, Bibliothèque des histoires (Paris: Éditions Gallimard, 1990), 299: ('Durant le Moyen Âge central, l'agenouillement devient l'attitude normale de la prière: une prière plus individuelle qui est adressée à Dieu le plus souvent devant un objet, tel le crucifix, matérialisant la présence divine').

38. Schmitt, *La Raison des gestes*, 300: ('une sorte de 'repli' du corps sur lui-même').

39. Olier, *Explication des cérémonies de la grande messe de paroisse*, 298: ('pour faire voir qu'on est prest à marcher').

40. 'Règlement général', SS, Ms. 1342, f. 70–1.

41. 'Règlement général', SS, Ms. 1342, f 71.

42. 'Livre dans lequel ...', AN, MM 475, f. 15r: ('Il veille soigneusement sur les mescontentements et sur les familiaritez trop grandes & les discours vicieux dans les recreations, ligues, cabales ou mauvaises unions qui pouroient arriver parmy les seminaristes – pour ne les point causer croistre...').

43. Warner, *Publics and Counterpublics*, 76.

44. 'Livre dans lequel ...', AN, MM 475, f. 60r: ('[C]ette conference se doit faire avec tres grand zele et desir dexciter puissamment et de porter tous les Ecclesiastiques a la pratique journaliere ... de l'oraison mentale').

45. 'Livre dans lequel ...', AN, MM 475, f. 60r: ('d'en remplir avec abondance tous les Seminaristes').

46. Olier, 'Projet de l'establissement d'un séminaire', SS, Ms. 20, f. 35, 37–41: ('le Seminaire ... comprend tous les sujets qui se viennent former à l'Esprit Ecclesiastique, & de ceux-là il y en a de toute sorte d'aage & de condition').

47. Seminary rules expound at length about the importance of not entering each other's rooms. See, for example, 'Reglement général du Séminaire de S. Sulpice', BN, Ms. Fr. 11760, f. 124r–v; Pasté, *Abrégé du reglement ... de S. Nicolas du Chardonnet (1672)*, 14; 'Règlement général', SS, Ms. 1342, f. 60–5.

48. 'One must spend recreation several together, being never less than three and not trying to spend it frequently with the same people or with those from your country.' See 'Reglement général du Séminaire de S. Sulpice', BN, Ms. Fr. 11760, f. 112v: ('Il faut faire la recréation plusieurs ensemble, n'être jamais moins de trois et ne pas affecter de se trouver fréquemment avec les mêmes personnes, ou avec ceux de son païs').

49. At Saint-Nicolas, the rules explicitly prohibited the circulation of negative opinions about the seminary: 'Take care when with each other to never speak badly, disapprove, blame, or condemn the House rules or the conduct of the Superiors; and even more so to undertake any affair or form any plan that could wrong the House directly or indirectly...'. See Pasté, *Abrégé du reglement ... de S. Nicolas du Chardonnet (1672)*, 13–14: ('Prendre garde êtans les uns avec les autres, de ne jamais mal parler, desaprouver, blâmer, ny condamner les regles de la Maison, ou la conduite des Superieurs; ny encore moins entreprendre aucune affaire ou

former aucun dessein qui puissent prejudicier à la Maison directement ou indirectement').

50. See the list titled 'Faults for which one will be excluded from the Seminary' in 'Reglement général du Séminaire de S. Sulpice', BN, Ms. Fr. 11760, f. 120v, 128v: ('lire, prêter ou vouloir garder des mauvais livres, romans, Comédies, libelles diffamatoires, ou contre les moeurs, la Réligion et l'état').

51. 'Reglement général du Séminaire de S. Sulpice', BN, Ms. Fr. 11760, f. 128v: ('Enseigner ou soutenir une mauvaise doctrine'); Pasté, *Abrégé du reglement ... de S. Nicolas du Chardonnet (1672)*, 13: ('Ne s'entretenir de nouvelles du Monde, de gazettes ny d'affaires publiques ou particulieres, qui puissent prejudicier en quelque façon que ce soit au prochain').

52. Warner, *Publics and Counterpublics*, 87.

53. Warner, *Publics and Counterpublics*, 87.

54. Warner, *Publics and Counterpublics*, 88.

55. 'Conférences épiscopales', late seventeenth century, BN, Ms. Fr. 14428, f. 122r: ('preparer les esprits par advance').

56. Beuvelet, *Conduites*, 20: ('Il faut lire attentivement le sujet de la Meditation, avec dessein de la bien faire le lendemain, & prevoir quelque façon, & comme determiner quelles affections & resolutions on y produira').

57. 'Reglement général du Séminaire de S. Sulpice', BN, Ms. Fr. 11760, f. 106r: ('Il faut aussi pendant qu'on s'habille repasser dans son esprit le sujet sur lequel on doit méditer').

58. 'Reglement général du Séminaire de S. Sulpice', BN, Ms. Fr. 11760, f. 107r: ('Dés que l'Oraison est commencée, on doit s'apliquer au sujet de méditation proposé, sans rien retrancher du temps destiné à cet Exercice').

59. Beuvelet defines the *examen particulier* as 'a little review that is done one or several times per day on some vice or imperfection that one wants to correct in oneself, or on some virtue that one wants to acquire.' He defines the *examen de conscience* as the review 'that is done of the entire day in the evening before going to bed.' See Beuvelet, *Conduites*, 36, 33 ('C'est une petite reveuë qui se fait une ou plusieurs fois le jour, sur quelque vice ou imperfection, dont on se veut corriger, ou sur quelque vertu que l'on veut acquerir'; 'C'est celuy qui se fait de toute la journée le soir avant que de se coucher').

60. Beuvelet, *Conduites*, 20–1.

61. Beuvelet, *Conduites*, 30: ('Le Colloque est un certain entretien de l'ame avec Dieu, avec les Anges, les Saints, ou bien avec nous mémes').

62. Letter XXXVI, from M. Bourget to Tronson, 8 April 1695 in Louis Tronson, *Correspondance de M. Louis Tronson, troisième supérieur de la Compagnie de Saint-Sulpice: Lettres Chosies, annotées et publiées par L. Bertrand*, edited by Louis Bertrand, vol. 1 (Paris: Librairie Victor Lecoffre, 1904), 415: ('On leur fait aussi pendant quelques jours l'oraison tout haut...').

63. 'Reglement général du Séminaire de S. Sulpice', BN, Ms. Fr. 11760, f. 110r: ('écouter à genoux et attentivement ... un sujet d'examen particulier sur quelque vertu, quelque vice ou quelque imperfection').

64. 'Reglement général du Séminaire de S. Sulpice', BN, Ms. Fr. 11760, f. 110r.

65. 'Reglement général du Séminaire de S. Sulpice', BN, Ms. Fr. 11760, f. 107r.

66. 'Livre dans lequel ...', AN, MM 475, f. 61r: ('a toute la compagnie des bons sentimens qu'il a eu dans la meditation et de l'ordre qu'il y a gardé, des affections et resolutions qu'il y a formé, &c.').

67. 'Livre dans lequel ...', AN, MM 475, f. 61r: ('interroger quelque autre pour remarquer les defauts qu'ils ont observé dans le procedé de leurs confreres;' 'on les avertit doucement et charitablement des manquemens ausquels ils doivent prendre garde pour profiter de l'oraison').

68. 'Reglement général du Séminaire de S. Sulpice', BN, Ms. Fr. 11760, f. 107r–v: ('[C]eux qui sont interrogés pour répéter l'Oraison doivent rapporter simplement la maniere dont ils ont fait leur méditation, les sentimens dont ils y ont été touchés, les réflexions qu'ils ont faites, et les résolutions qu'ils ont prises, sans s'attacher à faire des discours éloquens ou étudiés').

69. 'Reglement général du Séminaire de S. Sulpice', BN, Ms. Fr. 11760, f. 116v: ('écouter attentivement ceux qui sont interrogés, éviter de rire de leur maniere de parler quand même elle seroit defectueuse en quelque chose, et ne jamais s'entretenir ensuite avec d'autres des fautes qu'on croiroit avoir remarqué dans les discours qu'on y a entendus, ni en faire des railleries').

70. 'Reglement général du Séminaire de S. Sulpice', BN, Ms. Fr. 11760, f. 116r: ('sur quelque matiere de pieté relative à la fête').

71. 'Reglement général du Séminaire de S. Sulpice', BN, Ms. Fr. 11760, f. 116r: ('ne s'exposeront jamais à parler sans avoir auparavant préparé et appris de mémoire ce qu'ils doivent dire').

72. Pasté, *Abrégé du reglement ... de S. Nicolas du Chardonnet (1672)*, 14: ('Observer un grand silence & une grande modestie aux Conferences (durant lesquelles on ne doit jamais parler si l'on n'est interrogé) au Refectoir, au dortoir, au chausoir, & generalement par tout...').

73. Tronson advised the seminarians at Saint-Sulpice to adopt an intention for that afternoon's recreational conversations while walking from the dining hall to the garden, where seminarians took their recess. See Louis Tronson, 'Entretiens', late seventeenth century, SS, Ms. 50, f. 178v.

Works cited

Baudrand, M. 'Mémoire sur la vie de M. Olier et sur le séminaire de Saint-Sulpice', in L. Bertrand (ed.), *Bibliothèque sulpicienne ou histoire littéraire de la Compagnie de Saint-Sulpice*. Paris: Alphonse Picard et Fils, Éditeurs, 1900, 369–466.

Beuvelet, Matthieu. *Conduites pour les exercices principaux qui se font dans les séminaires ecclesiastiques, dressées en faveur des clercs demeurans dans le Seminaire de S. Nicolas du Chardonnet.* Lyon: Chez Hierosne de la Garde, en ruë Merciere à l'Esperance, 1660.

Carroll, Gérard. *Un Portrait du prêtre: les retraites de 10 jours pour les ordinands.* Vol. 1. 3 vols. Paris: Pierre Téqui, 2004.

Chaillot, Gilles, Paul Cochois, and Irénée Noye (eds). *Traité des Saints Ordres (1676), compare aux écrits authentiques de Jean-Jacques Olier (†1657)*. Paris: Procure de la Compagnie de Saint-Sulpice, 1984.

Chédozeau, Bernard. *Chœur clos, chœur ouvert: De l'église médiévale à l'église tridentine (France, XVIIe-XVIIIe siècle)*. Paris: Les Éditions du Cerf, 1998.

'Conférences épiscopales', late seventeenth century. Ms. Fr. 14428. Bibliothèque nationale de France (BN).

Croix, Claude de la. *Le Parfaict ecclesiastique ou diverses instructions sur toutes les fonctions clericales. Cy-devant disposées en tables par M. Claude de la Croix, prestre du Seminaire de S. Nicolas du Chardonnet. Et depuis redigées en livre, corigées & augmentées par des ecclesiastiques du mesme seminaire. Divisées en quatre parties, & enrichies de figures en taille-douce. Ouvrage autant utile que necessaire aux seminaires & communautez, tant seculieres que regulieres; à tous curez, & autres ecclesiastiques, pour exercer dignement leurs charges, & se bien acquiter de leurs devoirs. Où les laïques mesmes pourront connoistre la sainteté du service divin, & l'excellence du sacerdoce. Dedié à Messeigneurs les Archevesques & Evesques deputez du clergé de France.* Paris: Chez Pierre de Bresche, Libraire & Imprimeur ordinaire de la Reyne, ruë S. Jacques, vis à vis les Charniers S. Benoist, à l'Image saint Joseph & saint Ignace, 1666.

Dix, Dom Gregory. *The Shape of the Liturgy.* New York: The Seabury Press, 1983.

Dumoutet, Édouard. *Le Désire de voir l'hostie et les origines de la dévotion au saint-sacrement.* Paris: Gabriel Beauchesne, 1926.

'Entretiens des ordinands sur les matieres de devotion', Paris, between 1634 and 1657. Ms. 157. Archives de la Compagnie des Prêtres de Saint-Sulpice (SS).

Furetière, Antoine. 'Public', *Dictionnaire universel, contenant generalement tous les mots françois, tant vieux que modernes, & les termes de toûtes les sciences et des arts...* La Haye: Chez Arnout & Renier Leers, 1690. http://gallica2.bnf.fr/ark:/12148/bpt6k50614b.

Goichot, Émile. *Les Examens particuliers de M. Tronson: Essai sur la formation du prêtre 'classique'*, edited by René Heyer. Strasbourg: Presses Universitaires de Strasbourg, 2005.

Hervouët, Gwénola. 'Le Séminaire de Saint-Sulpice, 1642–1700: étude sociologique et religieuse', Mémoire de maîtrise sous la direction de M. le Professeur Bely, Université de Paris IV-Sorbonne, 1999.

'Livre dans lequel sont escrits tous les Reglemens de chaque office, et Exercice du Seminaire desquels le Prefet doit avoir une parfaite connoissance', late seventeenth century. MM 475. AN.

Mullaney, Steven, Angela Vanhaelen, and Joseph Ward. 'Religion Inside Out: Dutch House Churches and the Making of Publics in the Dutch Republic', in Bronwen Wilson and Paul Yachnin (eds), *Making Publics in Early Modern Europe: People, Things, Forms of Knowledge.* New York and London: Routledge, 2010, 25–36.

Olier, Jean-Jacques. 'Autographes de M. Olier, fondateur du Séminaire de St. Sulpice: Divers écrits, tome I', before 1657. Ms. 14. SS.

———. *Explication des cérémonies de la grande messe de paroisse, selon l'usage romain. Par un Prestre du Clergé.* Paris: Jacques Langlois, 1656.

———. 'Projet de l'establissement d'un séminaire dans un diocèse, où il est traité premierement de l'estat & de la disposition des sujets, secondement de l'esprit de tous leurs exercices, par un prestre du clergé', printed document with handwritten notes and rough draft manuscript by Olier. Paris: Chez Jacques Langlois, Imprimeur & Libraire ordinaire du Roy, vis à vis la Fontaine Ste Geneviesve, 1651. Ms. 20. SS.

Pasté. *Abrégé du reglement du Seminaire Paroissial de S. Nicolas du Chardonnet, pour l'usage des Seminaristes.* Paris: Chez Pierre Trichard, ruë Saint Victor, proche S. Nicolas du Chardonnet, au Chef Saint Jean, 1672.

———. *Abrégé du reglement du Seminaire Paroissial de S. Nicolas du Chardonnet, pour l'usage des Seminaristes.* Paris: Chez Pierre Trichard, ruë Saint Victor, proche S. Nicolas du Chardonnet, au Chef Saint Jean, 1677.

'Reglement du seminaire paroissial de Sainct Nicolas du Chardonnet, pour l'usage du prefect'. Paris, Seminary of Saint-Nicolas-du-Chardonnet, seventeenth century. MM 474. AN.

'Reglement général du Séminaire de S. Sulpice'. Paris, 1682. Ms. Fr. 11760. BN.

'Règlement général du Séminaire de Saint-Sulpice'. Paris, 1710. Ms. 1342. SS.

Richelet, César-Pierre. 'Public'. *Dictionnaire françois, contenant les mots et les choses, plusieurs nouvelles remarques sur la langue françoise: ses expressions propres, figurées & burlesques, la prononciation des mots les plus difficiles, le genre des noms, le régime des verbes, avec les termes les plus connus des arts & des sciences, le tout tiré de l'usage et des bons auteurs de la langue françoise*. Genève: Chez Jean Herman Widerhold, 1680. http://gallica.bnf.fr/ark:/12148/bpt6k509323/f814. Last accessed 15 June 2013.

Schmitt, Jean-Claude. *La Raison des gestes dans l'occident médiéval*. Bibliothèque des histoires. Paris: Éditions Gallimard, 1990.

Tronson, Louis. *Correspondance de M. Louis Tronson, troisième supérieur de la Compagnie de Saint-Sulpice: Lettres Chosies, annotées et publiées par L. Bertrand*, edited by Louis Bertrand. Vol. 1. 3 vols. Paris: Librairie Victor Lecoffre, 1904.

———. 'Entretiens'. Paris, late 17th century. Ms. 50. SS.

Warner, Michael. *Publics and Counterpublics*. New York: Zone Books, 2005.

Wilson, Bronwen, and Paul Yachnin (eds). *Making Publics in Early Modern Europe: People, Things, Forms of Knowledge*. New York and London: Routledge, 2010.

3

The Durban Passion Play: Religious Performance, Power and Difference

Michael Lambert and Tamantha Hammerschlag

The 'wave of secularization' which, Habermas notes,[1] characterized almost all European countries after the Second World War and was predicated on the separation of church and state, was simply not the case in apartheid South Africa in 1952, when the Durban Passion Play was first performed. In fact the National Party, which came into power after the post-war elections in 1948, sought to blur the boundaries between church and state, deliberately using a version of Calvinist Christianity to underpin the racist ideology that shaped its politics. This symbiosis of ideology and theology spawned a religion that *included* the white, Afrikaans-speaking oligarchy and its supporters and *excluded* the largely black majority of the population. Roman Catholicism was at that time a minority religion allied to the ruling elite because of the colour of almost all its clergy. All of the performers of the Durban Passion were white. The Church was opposed to the ideology of the ruling oligarchs, yet fearful of alienating them. This situation seems to us to illustrate the complexities and ambiguities of negotiation in a public space, which was anything but a space of rational argument.

It is thus not without significance, we shall argue, that the play chosen for this very public statement of 'Catholicness' at the provocatively-titled Marian Congress in 1952 was a Passion Play, not from the theatrical tradition which characterized the Enlightenment, but a play from the rural, pre-Enlightenment tradition of mediaeval mystery plays with a para-liturgical, didactic function. To 'interpret' the 'truth' of the Gospels was regarded as beyond the capacity of human actors. The Durban Passion Play nevertheless offered a particularly racist interpretation that made a claim to Gospel 'truth'. In the following account of the origins of the Durban Passion Play, and the subsequent relationship between the Durban Catholic Players' Guild (DCPG) and the polity, we shall attempt to tease out the complexities and ambiguities referred to above, and examine what possible 'messages' about race and identity this particular performance of religion in public embodied.

History of the Passion Play

In 1952, in order to celebrate the centenary of the establishment of the Natal Vicariate and the arrival in Natal[2] of the Oblates of Mary Immaculate, the organizing committee of the National Marian Centenary Congress in the Archdiocese of Durban staged a Passion Play as one of the events leading up to the Congress.[3]

Denis Hurley, Archbishop of Durban from 1951 until 1992, notes in his memoirs that 'as the preparations went forward we fired the imagination of an Irish Oblate with a natural instinct for theatre, Father Noël Coughlan OMI'.[4] Coughlan obtained permission from the mayor and community of Oberammergau, a village in Bavaria in southern Germany, to stage an abridged version of their famous Passion Play. According to legend, the Oberammergau Passion Play was first performed in 1633, 'when the village was afflicted by the plague which carried off many inhabitants in a short period of time'.[5] In the midst of their despair the village vowed to perform a Passion Play every ten years, a tradition which continues to this day and involves almost every member of the community; some of the roles have been handed down from generation to generation within specific families.

The Durban Passion Play was first performed in 1952 in the Durban City Hall. The City Hall was an ornate Edwardian building in the very heart of the city, built in a grand neoclassical style and housing all the important offices of municipal government. After five performances there, the Durban Passion Play was staged once again outdoors at the Greyville Race Course on the first evening of the Marian Congress.[6] In his memoirs, Archbishop Hurley comments that 'the interest, spirit and enthusiasm generated by the Durban Passion Play (named the Oberammergau of South Africa) was such that those who participated made a vow to stage the play every five years'.[7] In 2011 the play was staged for the 13th time by the Durban Catholic Players' Guild (DCPG), a group of amateurs from various religious denominations, 'drawn to this form of Christian witness', who, like the villagers in Oberammergau who inspired them, receive 'no material or monetary gain'.[8]

Historical, political and religious context of the first performance

When the Durban Passion Play was first staged in 1952, South Africa had been under National Party rule for four years, ever since the post-war elections of 1948 that brought the neo-fascist, Afrikaner nationalist party to power.[9] By 1952 most of the legislation which underpinned the ideology of apartheid or 'separate development' had been enacted: the *Prohibition of Mixed Marriages Act of 1949* and the *Immorality Amendment Act of 1950* made sexual intercourse between white and black persons illegal, the *Population Registration Act of 1950* classified every person according to race, and decreed that each 'population group' had to live in its own area and use its own facilities (schools, hospitals, cinemas, toilets, etc.), the *Group Areas Act of 1950* legislated, on the basis of racial classification, where people could live or own land or property, the *Suppression of Communism Act of 1951* gave the Minister of Justice extraordinary powers to ban any person or organization deemed 'subversive', and the *Bantu Education Act*, promulgated a year after the first performance of the play, seized control of black education from the churches and mission schools and placed it in the hands of the government, which deliberately embarked on a policy of education for submission.

To understand further the context in which the Passion Play was first performed it must be noted that at this stage South Africa was nominally a Christian country, dominated by a white elite and a zealous form of Calvinist Protestantism. The first printed record of the word apartheid occurs in a speech given by a minister in the Dutch Reformed Church (DRC), which manipulated biblical texts to justify the racist policies of the National Party.[10] Furthermore, even if South Africa regarded itself as a parliamentary democracy in which, technically, church and state were separated, there is no doubt that the ruling party exploited its links with the DRC in order to imbue its policies with a divine authority. Although the Catholic Church had been active in South Africa for more than a century, especially in its network of mission schools and hospitals, Catholics constituted a minority religious community, 'almost totally dependent on bishops, priests and religious from overseas' and 'therefore loath to jeopardize the religious freedom it enjoyed'.[11] This anxiety was largely responsible for the fact that, despite the segregationist legislation that was patently immoral and impinged on the church's beliefs and activities, no response to the government's policies and its violent suppression of dissent had, before 1952, been forthcoming from the Catholic bishops.[12] Significantly, a few months *after* the Marian Congress in Durban, the Catholic bishops of South Africa issued their 'first-ever joint statement on race relations', which asserted, in a carefully argued (and typically Catholic) distinction between 'fundamental' and 'contingent' rights, that the right to human dignity was 'fundamental' and that racial discrimination was an offence against human dignity.[13] In reaction to this statement, the official mouthpiece of the DRC (*Die Kerkbode*) attacked the Catholic Church by publicizing a document provocatively entitled *Die Roomse Gevaar* ('The Roman Danger'), which set out a programme for dismantling Catholic influence in South Africa. One of its proposals was that the government should seize control of all Catholic schools, hospitals, and orphanages, which should be subject to Protestant beliefs in accordance with the government's policy of 'Christian National Education'.[14]

In a national context 1952 was indeed a momentous year in which to hold a *Marian* Congress and stage the first Passion Play. Nothing could be more inimical to the South African version of Calvinist Protestantism than the Catholic's Church's devotion to the Virgin Mary. 1952 was also the year in which the ruling National Party was celebrating the tercentenary of the arrival from the Netherlands of the first white settlers at the Cape of Good Hope in 1652. Black political groups such as the African National Congress (ANC) and the South African Indian Council (SAIC) vigorously opposed this celebration of white colonialism, which came in the wake of oppressive legislation that further entrenched white domination. The Catholic Church carefully chose Durban for the Marian Congress in 1952, not simply because the Oblates had arrived there a century before, but also because of the city's complex political history.

Although it was not the provincial capital, Durban was the most important city in the province of Natal. Natal had been a British colony from 1856 until the Union of South Africa in 1910.[15] Amongst the white settlers, largely of English, Irish and Scottish descent, English was the predominant language. Voters in the province generally resisted Afrikaner nationalism and, significantly, voted against South Africa becoming a republic in 1961.[16] The predominant religious affiliation amongst the white settlers was a Protestant Christianity, especially Anglicanism and Methodism, that was noticeably more tolerant of Catholicism than the form of Calvinism espoused by the ruling party. In Durban there was also a small but active Jewish community. The city also hosts one of the world's largest diasporic Indian communities, largely descendants of the indentured labourers who had been imported by the British in 1860. Among them, Hinduism and Islam prevailed. The religion of the black *isiZulu*-speaking majority was Christianity in its various forms, largely because of the aggressive work of Catholic and Protestant missionaries who competed for African souls; there were also various forms of African traditional religion.

After the performances of the Passion Play at the end of the Marian Congress in 1952 a parade of floats organized by its producers moved through central Durban from the City Hall to Albert Park. In his memoirs, Archbishop Hurley comments on this pageant: 'fifteen magnificent floats suitably spaced within the procession depicted the mysteries of the rosary. ... [T]hey added dramatic and artistic significance to the procession, which culminated at a special altar erected in Albert Park with an act of consecration to Mary Assumed into Heaven and benediction of the Blessed Sacrament. A recorded message from Pope Pius XII was broadcast by radio.'[17] Kearney rightly notes that this was the 'most open display of Catholicism that Durban had ever seen': it is estimated that 30,000 people participated in the procession, 'including 210 priests and 480 nuns of fifteen congregations, with more than 50,000 spectators'.[18] The procession was prominently reported in Durban's major English-speaking newspaper, the *Natal Mercury*,[19] which had the largest circulation of any Natal newspaper at the period; and in the national Catholic weekly, the *Southern Cross*.[20] Although the *Natal Mercury* could hardly be described as left-wing, it positioned itself in its editorials as critical of the government's policies, as did most of the English-speaking press at the time. The *Mercury*'s contribution to the circulation 'amongst strangers' of discourses about the extravagant public performance of the tenets of a faith, distrusted by the ruling oligarchy, may well have contributed to the creation of what Warner terms a 'counterpublic', significantly generated by this performance of the procession. It has been impossible to assess how the procession was received by adherents of the Islamic, Hindu, and Jewish faiths. The procession passed by stores owned and staffed by members of these religious groups. It is reasonable to surmise that this 'counterpublic' generated others, both compliant and resistant. Even the *Mercury*'s role in the creation of this 'counterpublic' is beset with irony: the Catholic performance of the private in public seemed to challenge the very Englishness of the newspaper which endorsed the separation between the public and private, and contributed to the blurring of the two spheres so evident in the ruling party's dangerous liaison with the Dutch Reformed Church.

In the context of the religious beliefs of the white settler community on a national and local level, this procession (and the 100-foot column topped by a statue of the Virgin Mary erected on the Greyville Race Course) can be read as an oppositional protest, publicly challenging the non-Catholic viewer to confront those elements of Catholic belief which mainline Protestantism considered objectionable: the rosary, belief in the Assumption of the Blessed Virgin, and the very theatricality of the rituals themselves. The Benediction of the Blessed Sacrament, which climaxed in the elevation of the consecrated host enshrined in a gold monstrance, was particularly spectacular, let alone the performance of the Passion Play itself. The very fact that the Marian Congress and this final procession focused on a revered *female* figure within Catholic Christianity may well have resonated with the Hindu community, but not with the Muslim or Jewish or Reformed Christian communities within the city, whose organizational structures by and large remain patriarchal.

On a political and social level, the Congress, the Passion Play, and the procession were fraught with the kinds of ambiguities displayed by the attitudes of the Catholic Church towards Jews in Nazi Germany. There was evident opposition to the government's racism, yet Catholics were hesitant to express this openly for fear that confrontation might unleash an attack on the Church – which, in South Africa, it eventually did. There is nothing to suggest that the Congress or the public performance of some of the basic tenets of Catholic belief challenged or undermined in any way the government's segregationist policies, which were being endorsed on a national level by the tercentenary celebration of white colonization. On the contrary, the Congress, the Passion Play, and the procession seem publicly to have endorsed colonialism, separatism, and white domination. The inspiration for the Marian nature of the Congress was Canadian; the Oblates were, in origin, a French order. The two organizers of the Congress were 'dynamic'

American Oblates. Of the 21 priests and 24 lay people who attended the first meeting of the Marian Congress in 1951, there was not a single black African amongst them, although there was a special 'African' committee appointed to organize African events such as a separate 'African mass'.[21] Many years later Archbishop Hurley was 'embarrassed at how whites had dominated the whole event',[22] which 'betrayed how "European" the Church of Durban still was at that time'.[23] Photographs of Congress events in the Oblate Archives reveal that this was indeed the case: the cast of the Passion Play was entirely white and the stands at prestigious Greyville Turf Club and Racecourse were obviously segregated into white and black sections, in accordance with the recently-passed legislation.[24] How the Catholic Church managed to get the Turf Club to agree to host a multiracial event of this magnitude in 1952 is a story of expedient alliances. Leo Boyd, a former mayor of the city and a member of both the executive committee of the Natal provincial government and the Turf Club, happened to be a Catholic, as did the racecourse manager.[25] What the large segregated audience of black viewers made of this performance of the pivotal events in a 'white' Christ's life, produced in a venue which smacked of white elitist wealth (the racecourse) and capitalist decadence (gambling), can only be guessed at. With the advantage of hindsight, it seems to us to endorse a very European and trans-Atlantic version of Christianity, subtly linked to those old bedfellows of colonial religion – capitalism and power – even if, by their very presence, the black members of the audience challenged the separatist policies of the ruling Nationalists.

The Durban Passion Play was thus mired from its very inception in the kinds of political and identity problems which have bedeviled the Catholic Church in Africa: how does an international church with its hierarchical apex in Rome become truly African, or South African? How does the Church speak to power, if that power, as was the case in South Africa, could retard and forbid its fundamental evangelical and missionary work?

The Passion Play after 1952

In the years after 1952, before the freeing of Mandela in 1990 and the first democratic elections, the DCPG developed a mutually beneficial relationship with the Durban establishment by forming links with various departments of municipal government – for example, the Durban Symphony Orchestra and Choir. The Passion Play found a permanent home in the City Hall. Some programmes name the Town Clerk's department as co-producer. The regular mayoral messages (in both English and Afrikaans) clearly indicate that holding the Passion Play every five years was good for Durban's economy, as audiences were drawn from all over the country. The use of the two official languages in the programmes (and not only for the mayoral messages) suggests that there existed the need to foster cordial relationships with the Afrikaans-speaking Protestant community, perhaps a hangover from the 'white' politics of the 1950s when South Africa's most pressing political problem seemed to be the relationship between Afrikaans and English-speaking South Africans.[26] The choice of language shows that the Catholic Church was still painfully aware of its position as a minority church, now openly hostile to the government's segregationist policies. A bilingual programme was the least the DCPG could do to ensure the polity's support every five years.

Significantly, the first use of *isiZulu* in the Passion Play programme occurs in 1987, as civil unrest breaks out all over the country and South Africa edges towards majority rule. This programme also names a Catholic brother as 'Zulu interpreter', and for the first time, the Archbishop's message (in English and *isiZulu*, but not Afrikaans), explicitly links the understanding of Christ's passion, death and resurrection with the 'pain of a difficult social and political transformation' in South Africa. Archbishop Hurley, whose home had been bombed by right-wing supporters of the government and who had taken part in a very public trial as a witness against state brutality, clearly felt that it was time to position the Play in a more overtly political struggle against the government.[27] In contrast to the Archbishop's message, the mayor's message was in English and Afrikaans but not *isiZulu*, and comments on the beauty of the 'spectacle' and congratulates the local producers on their 'outstanding success', thus distancing himself, the city, and the performance from the Archbishop's politics.

In 1997 the link between the church and the public was ruptured when the Passion Play moved into the Playhouse Theatre across the road from the Durban City Hall. In this new venue the play was produced in association with the state-funded Playhouse Company. A new script with a new sub-title, 'There lived a man...', was devised, which moved away from the previous 'didactic pageant style' and invited the audience 'to share the last days of Christ on earth in a more intimate manner'. The break with the public polity and the association with a professional theatre company heralded a new emphasis on theatricality and interpretation, rather than fidelity to the Gospels and the Oberammergau tradition. However, for the 'jubilee' production in 2000, the DCPG announced in the programme that it was returning 'to the pageant style of the original script' which, together with the revolving set, made the visual effect of the production 'both meaningful and dramatically moving'. The new script, directed by an outsider from Pretoria, did not meet with the approval of the Players' Guild. It is precisely this return to the pageant style and original script which met with negative criticism in a review of the 2005 production, published in *the Mercury*: the reviewer, influenced by Mel Gibson's 'gritty' film version of the *Passion*, lamented the absence of interpretation of any of Christ's significant relationships in the play.[28]

The profound changes in political circumstances in South Africa and the move to the right in the Catholic Church can certainly be detected in the messages in Passion Play programmes from the current Archbishop of Durban, Cardinal Napier, the first black man to hold this office. Napier's ostensibly non-political messages suggest that he conceives of the Passion Play's primary purpose as dramatic reinforcement of 'what we normally read about or listen to during the Holy Week and liturgical celebrations',[29] which could deepen personal spirituality. This is precisely how the DCPG and its members appear to conceive of the play's purpose through programmes,[30] newspaper interviews with performers, and notes to the director.[31] It is 'didactic' theatre, a form of Christian testimony which provides a unique spiritual journey for both cast and audience. What if there were Jews, Muslims, or Hindus in the audience? What possible 'messages' might the text of the play itself contain for them? Can the performance of a Passion Play by a minority faith within Christianity in South Africa, in a multicultural and multifaith city, ever distance itself from the politics of the past and present, considering South Africa's divisive history and the fact that the play is predominantly performed by members of the white minority?

The text, anti-Semitism, and the position of Jews in South Africa

The Oberammergau text consists of three major elements: verse, prose dialogue based on selected texts from the New Testament dealing with Christ's passion, crucifixion and resurrection, and solo and choral songs based on 'prophetic' texts from the Old Testament. It was revised between 1811 and 1815 by a Catholic priest, Father Othmar Weis, and once again between 1860 and 1870 by an 'ecclesiastical counsellor', Joseph Daisenberger.[32] It was this last version of the text that Coughlan used for his abridged Durban version in 1952, a version that had yet to be purged of its infamously anti-Semitic 'bloodguilt' passages.

The accusation that Jews committed deicide is an age-old justification for anti-Semitism and Christian antagonism towards Judaism. It was not until 1965, 13 years after the first performance of the Durban Passion Play, that the Second Vatican Council formally repudiated this accusation with the *Nostra Aetate*.[33] As the Passion Play directly affects Jews living in a predominantly Christian society, an analysis of its public performance needs to take into account the position of Jews in South Africa.

A survey conducted by Simon Herman during the Second World War revealed that English-speaking white South Africans felt no compunction at expressing overtly anti-Semitic prejudices.[34] Afrikaner Nationalists shared these prejudices, supported Nazi Germany, and espoused anti-Semitic rhetoric. Questioning the right of Jews to be regarded as 'white',[35] they 'focused increasingly on the Jew as an explanation for Afrikaners' political misfortunes'.[36] Jews were associated with British imperialism and capitalism and, in line with Nazi propaganda, were accused of promoting communism and seen as plotting to 'give South Africa to the Natives'.[37] After the Afrikaner National Party's victory in the 1948 elections, Jewish fears were somewhat allayed by the assurance 'that the "Jewish Question" would be laid to rest.'[38]

However, Jews still felt vulnerable as a marginal group, and the South African Jewish Board of Deputies chose not to challenge the apartheid state, proclaiming that 'Jews participate in South African public life as citizens of South Africa ... and have no collective attitude to the political issues which citizens are called on to decide.'[39] Thus, having been granted the status of 'white' with all its attendant privileges, the Jewish authorities maintained silence about racial prejudice. Jewish resistance to apartheid was evident in the outspoken actions of individuals, and was forced outside the ambit of communal religious life.[40]

When the Passion Play was first performed in 1952, given the prevalent anti-Semitic climate, one can assume that the casting of the Jews in the role of villain was received without question by the majority of the Durban audiences. The play claimed to conform to the Gospels and served a well-established ethnic assumption. Neither the text nor the performance interrogated the revolutionary possibilities inherent in the story, choosing to stick rigidly to convention and bypassing anything that could destabilize either preconceived assumptions or the white hegemonic status quo.

How were the archetypal villains, the Sanhedrin, read in 1952, so soon after the end of the Second World War? Did some Afrikaners' classification of themselves as the 'chosen race' allow the Sanhedrin to take on the guise of the Afrikaner? Natal was predominantly English-speaking, and still longing for independence from the rest of South Africa. In claiming a right to the land, some early Afrikaner Nationalists, seemingly unaware of the irony, drew a parallel between themselves and the diasporic tribe of Israel, presenting themselves as akin to the Jews in that they mythologized themselves as God's 'chosen people', previously stateless and now the beneficiaries of divine generosity in being bequeathed South Africa.[41]

The extent of the villainy of the Sanhedrin can only be appreciated in relation to the other character often discussed in analyzing the bloodguilt: Pontius Pilate. In the Durban Passion Play he is still portrayed as rational and conservative. In costume and performance he is lent a degree of *gravitas* and respectability, a portrayal that serves to heighten the guilt of the Sanhedrin. In his preface to an English version of the Oberammergau play of 1890, William T. Stead writes that he sees Pilate as akin to an English magistrate or colonial ruler. Stead exonerates Pilate's behaviour as he sees it as part of a 'typical colonial dilemma'.[42] He finally concludes that 'it was only when the Sanhedrin threatened to denounce him to Caesar as an enemy of the Emperor that he unwillingly gave way. Here and there, no doubt, there are among our English magistrates and judges fanatical believers in abstract right, who would have risked the Empire rather than let a hair of Christ's head be touched; but the average English magistrate – especially if the accused was "only a nigger" – would shrug his shoulders at such Quixotism as folly and worse. It is better, they would say, that one man should die even unjustly than everything should be upset.'[43] Although Durban in 1952 was vastly different from Stead's world, Pilate, as a rational yet compromised victim, may have had considerable appeal for a predominantly white, English-speaking company, identifying in 1952 with England and the crumbling Empire, and later keen to wash their hands of complicity in the apartheid system.

Anti-Semitism may not be as prevalent today as it was in South Africa in the 1950s, but it has not disappeared. Moreover, South Africa's racial problems have not miraculously evaporated after the demise of apartheid. The 2011 text used by the DCPG still attempts to present a depoliticized version of the Gospels, and does not confront or grapple with either the issue of anti-Semitism or South Africa's racial problems. The present Durban text shows little evidence of the post-Holocaust sensibilities that demanded the revision of the Oberammergau text. Helig points out that in 1969, after *Nostra Aetate*, the Oberammergau text was modified, removing 'some of the more offensive anti-Jewish passages'.[44] The 2011 Durban text differs from that of Oberammergau in that it is significantly shorter, having omitted the prologues as well as the choral singing. The Biblical prophecies linking the Gospels to the Old Testament and encouraging an intellectual justification for belief in Jesus as Messiah are also omitted. The omission of the commentary serves to place the Durban text more sharply within the genre of realism, a style that is more familiar to the majority of the current South African audience, which has little theatrical exposure. Presenting religious mythology in a predominantly 'realist' way has political repercussions. As Brecht pointed out, sustained narrative promotes heightened feeling, not thinking.[45] Thus the shorter, sharpened dramatic experience of events central to Christian belief may aid a cathartic outpouring, but does not encourage reflexivity or social analysis of any sort and, in fact, may well contribute to the reinforcement of racial stereotyping.

In contrast, the commentary in Greek choral style of the Oberammergau version serves an inclusive humanism, and may function to mitigate the potentially anti-Semitic content. The prologue challenges the audience to:

Let our eyes and hearts
Be turned to Him united in gratitude.
Greetings also to you, brothers and sisters of the people
Who brought forth the Redeemer.
Let no-one try to find the blame in others;
Let each of us recognize
His own guilt in these events.[46]

This overt self-reflexivity is lacking in the Durban text. Dawn Haynes, the most recent director of the Durban Passion play, stated in a conversation with the authors that she has left the text largely untouched. She felt the text was devoid of any anti-Semitism, especially as she has implemented a significant change to the text: the removal of the word 'Jew' when referring to bloodguilt.[47]

The Durban programmes, in contrast to those of Oberammergau, do not attempt to divorce the play's enactment of Jewish bloodguilt from possible anti-Semitic consequences. Writing on the 1990 Oberammergau text, theologian Rudolf Pesch goes to great lengths to combat the charge of anti-Semitism by emphasizing Jesus' Jewishness. He points out that Jesus is addressed as 'Rabbi' in the play, which also occurs in the Durban version, and speaks a few words of Hebrew. He includes present-day Christians as inheritors of the bloodguilt, and refers to all religious strife between Christians, Muslims and Jews as '[tearing] our world apart'. He writes that 'the blood from the body of the Messiah which we spilt when we fought each other, burned heretics, and gassed Jews not only cries to heaven, it has also "fallen on us and our children."'[48]

Like post-war Germany, South Africa is a country dealing with the aftermath of a heinous political system. Although it is understandable that anti-Semitism is a lesser concern in South Africa than it is in Germany, it is ironic that the DCPG continues to perform the Passion in an apparent political vacuum. The actors are predominantly white, with a smattering of Indian, African, and 'Coloured' performers.[49] The Players do not draw on the rich musical traditions with which they are surrounded. There is no Zulu *isicathamiya* singing, nor is any attempt made to draw on Durban's Indian heritage. On a political level, the story of the Passion finds countless resonances in the South Africa of both the past and that of the present. During the period that the Passion has been performed in Durban, South Africa has seen the arrest of Nelson Mandela (to whom messianic qualities are often ascribed) as well as his later ascent to political power. The country has teetered on the cusp of a revolution and a bloody civil war, a struggle that was fought in close proximity to Durban. Moreover, KwaZulu-Natal has one of the highest HIV infection rates in the world.[50] As the arrival of the plague in Oberammergau was the original inspiration for the text, alluding to our own plague and exploring this theatrically could potentially radicalize the experience. If the play were allowed to resonate more with its social context, and move beyond a western interpretation – a stained-glass window come to life – it might make use of its potential to be a volcanic theatrical, political, and religious experience. As it stands, the play remains aesthetically western, with little sense of collective guilt (be it for apartheid or for general inhumanity) reflected in performance or in the discourse that surrounds it.

The Sanhedrin of the Durban Passion Play remain the demonic Jews of the mystery plays. They are tied into the literary stereotype of the Jew as bloodsucker and uncouth monster. In performance, the actors playing the Sanhedrin engage in much stereotypical hand-wringing and head nodding.

Their costumes are generically eastern, dressed as they are in bloodthirsty red and sinister black, and are instantly distinguishable from the pious followers of Christ. Theatrically this is effective, as they are, after all, the villains of the piece. In the version we saw, the actors playing the Sanhedrin gave fiery and believable performances, lifting the emotional register of the play beyond the monotony of amateur dramatics. At a stretch one could suggest that the Sanhedrin's black cloaks and hats echo the clothing of Orthodox religious Jewry, and thus are visually aligned with modern Jewry rather than with the Pharisees of the New Testament. The disciples, too, make use of Jewish prayer shawls, emphasizing Jesus's Jewish roots.

The Christus in the Durban Passion Play is submissive and serene, his struggle not especially evident. Angela Tilby correctly states that 'in Gethsemane Jesus was overcome with panic and more or less broke down. The Gospels are quite upfront about this. They do not portray Jesus as heroi- cally calm or confident; he is a wreck. Some ancient Gospel manuscripts go as far as to say that in his anguish his sweat fell to the ground like great drops of blood (Luke 22:44).'[51] In this respect the Durban text is not as faith- ful to the Gospels as it claims. Also omitted is the encouraging voice of the Angel in the Oberammergau text, which urges the desolate Jesus to:

Bear the sickness of mankind!
Take the sufferings on yourself!
Heal them through your wounds!
The Lord delights in His broken servant,
He saves him who gives his life in atonement![52]

In the Durban text 'a light appears growing in intensity and slowly fades',[53] diminishing Jesus's distress. In the performance that we saw, Jesus's apparent lack of agony detracted from his human suffering and made his 'passion' less tragic.

The Durban Passion receives wide support. It plays to full houses, a rarity in South Africa where theatres regularly struggle for audiences. It is lauded in the press and the audiences appear to be fully engaged. Catholic parishes throughout KwaZulu-Natal and beyond regularly arrange transportation for audience members, some from remote rural areas. Whereas the cast remains predominantly white and does not reflect the South African demographic, the audiences do, and are thus predominantly black and Zulu-speaking. This racial inversion smacks of white didacticism, harking back to the missionary enterprise, the centenary of which was celebrated in 1952.

Conclusion

In contemporary South Africa the boundaries between church and state have been firmly drawn. South Africa's progressive constitution forbids any discrimination on the basis of race, religion, or sexual orientation, which would have been unthinkable in 1952. In such a context the performance of a religious play in a multifaith city by a minority religion, one that has lost its link with the polity yet perpetuates the public 'othering' of different races and religions, is deeply problematic. Even the mayor's message in the latest programme of the Durban Passion Play (2011) is no longer couched in pietistic tones, but is embedded in the discourse of theatre rather than religion. The secularization of South Africa's public sphere has been late in coming, but it has arrived. Performing the Durban Passion Play in public, in the 'pageant style' of the original script, represents a dogged adherence to apartheid-era religious traditions, embedded as they were in constructs of difference and colonial Christianity. It could be argued that performing the play in public at a state-funded theatre affords the Catholic or Christian performer the space to 'practice' subjective identity and thus empowers the religious person in a very secular context (the commercial theatre). Yet this kind of personal empowerment, which disempowers others by perpetuating western iconography in an African context, privileges the individual at the expense of the collective – and nothing could be more un-African than that.

Notes

1. Jürgen Habermas, 'Religion in the Public Sphere', *European Journal of Philosophy*, 14(1) (2005): 1.
2. Natal is a province on the eastern seaboard of what was then the Union of South Africa.
3. See *Memories: The Memoirs of Archbishop Denis Hurley OMI*, Paddy Kearney, ed., (Pietermaritzburg: Cluster Publications, 2006), 80–3, and Paddy Kearney, *Guardian of the Light* (Pietermaritzburg: University of KwaZulu-Natal Press, 2009), 61–9. At this stage nearly all the clergy in the Archdiocese were Oblates. Since the patron of this order was the Virgin Mary, 'it was decided that... the celebration should take the form of a Marian Congress along the lines of one that had been held a few years before in Canada to mark an Oblate occasion in that country' (Archbishop Denis E. Hurley, in Kearney, *Memories,* 80). The National Marian Centenary Congress established the organizing committee, along with twelve subsidiary committees, in 1951.
4. Kearney, *Memories,* 82–3.
5. Franz Dietl, 'Preface,' in *The Oberammergau Play of the Suffering, Death and Resurrection of Our Lord Jesus Christ*, revised by Othmar Weis and Joseph Alois Daisenberger (Oberammergau: The Village of Oberammergau, 1990), 7.
6. Kearney, *Memories,* 83.
7. Kearney, *Memories,* 83.
8. 'Message', in 'The Durban Passion Play Programme' (Durban: Durban Catholic Players' Guild in association with The Playhouse Company, 2011).
9. For a recent account of South Africa's political history between 1948 and 1953, see Hermann Giliomee and Bernard Mbenga, *New History of South Africa* (Cape Town: Tafelberg, 2008), 308–23.

10. Giliomee and Mbenga, *New History*, 259, 391. In 1982 the World Alliance of Reformed Churches expelled the Dutch Reformed Church of South Africa.
11. Kearney, *Guardian*, 63.
12. Further inhibiting factors were the absence of a formal structure for the bishops, such as a synod which met regularly, and the views of the apostolic delegate, opposed to any kind of open confrontation with the government, which would threaten the position of the Church (Kearney, *Guardian*, 63–4). For a full discussion of these factors, see Kearney, *Memories*, 86–95. The apostolic delegate was, interestingly, a Hollander (Kearney, *Memories*, 93).
13. Kearney, *Guardian*, 65–7. The statement drafted by Archbishop Hurley, who was to play so courageous a role in the struggle against apartheid, was later regarded by him as 'primitive' and 'horribly patronizing', especially as the right to vote was regarded as 'contingent' upon the gradual evolution of black South Africans into political maturity (Kearney, *Guardian*, 66–7).
14. Kearney, *Guardian*, 67–8.
15. Giliomee and Mbenga, *New History*, 192.
16. T.R.H. Davenport, *South Africa: A Modern History*, 2nd edn (Bergvlei: Southern Book Publishers, 1989), 399.
17. Kearney, *Memories*, 83.
18. Kearney, *Guardian*, 62.
19. *Natal Mercury*, 1 May 1952.
20. *The Southern Cross*, 7 May 1952.
21. Kearney, *Memories*, 80–3; Kearney, *Guardian*, 61–2.
22. Kearney, *Guardian*, 62.
23. Kearney, *Memories*, 83. See also J.B. Brain, *The Catholic Church in Natal over 150 Years* (Durban: Oblates of Mary Immaculate, 2002), 108.
24. See Kearney, *Memories*, 82–3. Brain, *Catholic Church*, 108 has an impressive and intimidating photograph of the nuns in procession, wearing habits that are definitely pre-Vatican II. All are white persons.
25. Kearney, *Memories*, 82. See also the photograph of the mayoral couple with Archbishop Hurley in Kearney, *Memories*, 52.
26. Davenport, *South Africa*, 361–81. Alan Paton's biography *Hofmeyr* (Oxford: Oxford University Press, 1994) provides an excellent background to this relationship.
27. See Kearney, *Guardian*, 221–7 (the trial).
28. A. Bolowana, 'Sticking Close to Scripture', *The Mercury* (Durban) 8 March 2005, 9.
29. 'Message,' in 'The Durban Passion Play Programme,' 3.
30. For instance, see the messages in the 1973, 1978, 1982, 2000 and 2011 programmes.
31. See the interviews with Co van Doorn (a hairdresser who played Christ) in the *Daily News*, 31 March 1987, p. 11, and *Sunday Tribune*, 5 April 1987, p. 3; with Joseph Couve de Murville (a student who played John the Beloved and the understudy Christ) in *The Berea Mail*, 18 March 2005, p. 9; with Denise Rankin (a teacher who played Mary) in *The Highway Mail*, 18 March 2005, p. 5; and with Robin Paul (a financial planner who played Christ) in *The Sunday Tribune* 20 March 2005, p. 4. *The Sunday Tribune* and *The Daily News* have a wide circulation within the Durban area and the province of KZN as a whole. Personal notes from members of the cast and the audience were generously loaned to the authors by the current director of the Passion Play, Dawn Haynes. Only published articles are listed in the bibliography.
32. 'Introduction' in Othmar Weis, *The Oberammergau Passion Play*, revised by Joseph Alois Daisenberger (Village of Oberammergau, 1990), unnumbered.

33. Jocelyn Helig, *The Holocaust and Antisemitism: A Short History* (Oxford: Oneworld, 2003), 301.
34. Richard Mendelsohn and Milton Shain, *The Jews in South Africa* (Johannesburg and Cape Town: Jonathan Ball, 2008), 121.
35. Mendelsohn and Shain, *The Jews*, 135.
36. Mendelsohn and Shain, *The Jews*, 109.
37. Mendelsohn and Shain, *The Jews*, 109.
38. Mendelsohn and Shain, *The Jews*, 134.
39. Mendelsohn and Shain, *The Jews*, 135.
40. Mendelsohn and Shain, *The Jews*, 135.
41. Hermann Giliomee, *The Afrikaners: Biography of a People* (Cape Town: Tafelberg, 2003), 178–9.
42. William Stead, *The Story That Transformed the World: or, the Passion Play at Oberammergau* (London: Office of the Review of Reviews, 1890), 156.
43. Stead, *The Story*, 157.
44. Helig, *The Holocaust*, 211. The 1984 and 1990 texts contained further revisions.
45. Bertolt Brecht, *Brecht on Theatre: The Development of an Aesthetic*, trans. John Willett (London: Methuen, 1964), 201.
46. Weis and Daisenberger, *Passion Play*, 11.
47. Interview with Dawn Haynes, Michael Lambert and Tamantha Hammerschlag. Pietermaritzburg, 2011.
48. Weis and Daisenberger, *Passion Play*, 112.
49. These racial categories are still commonly used in South Africa and are not thought to be pejorative. 'Coloured' refers to people of mixed race.
50. *The 2010 National Antenatal Sentinel HIV and Syphilis Prevalence Survey in South Africa* (Pretoria: Department of Health, Republic of South Africa, 2010).
51. Angela Tilby, *Son of God* (London: Hodder & Stoughton, 2001), 138.
52. Weis and Daisenberger, *Passion Play*, 49.
53. Dawn Haynes, ed., *Passion Play 2011 Script* (Durban: The Durban Catholic Players Guild, 2011), 28.

Works cited

Bolowana, A. 'Sticking Close to Scripture', *The Mercury* (Durban), 8 March 2005, 9.
Brain, J.B. *The Catholic Church in Natal Over 150 Years*. Durban: Oblates of Mary Immaculate, 2002.
Brecht, Bertolt. *Brecht on Theatre: The Development of an Aesthetic*, trans. John Willett. London: Methuen, 1964.
Davenport, T.R.H. *South Africa A Modern History*, 2nd edn. Bergvlei: Southern Book Publishers, 1989.
Dietl, Franz. Preface to *The Oberammergau Play of the Suffering, Death and Resurrection of Our Lord Jesus Christ*, revised by Othmar Weis and Joseph Alois Daisenberger. Oberammergau: The Village of Oberammergau, 1990, 7–9.
Giliomee, Hermann. *The Afrikaners: Biography of a People*. Cape Town: Tafelberg, 2003.
────── and Bernard Mbenga. *New History of South Africa*. Cape Town: Tafelberg, 2008.
Habermas, Jürgen. *The Structural Transformation of the Public Sphere*, trans. T, Burger. Cambridge, MA: MIT Press, 1989.
──────. 'Religion in the Public Sphere', *European Journal of Philosophy*, 14(1) (2006): 1.

86 *Performing Religion in Public*

Haynes, Dawn (ed.). *Passion Play 2011 Script*. Durban: The Durban Catholic Players Guild, 2011.

Helig, Jocelyn. *The Holocaust and Antisemitism: A Short History*. Oxford: Oneworld, 2003.

Hlongwane, A. 'A Passion to Portray Christ', *Sunday Tribune* (Durban), 20 March 2005, 4.

Kearney, Paddy (ed.). *Memories: The memoirs of Archbishop Denis Hurley OMI*. Pietermaritzburg: Cluster Publications, 2006.

Kearney, Paddy. *Guardian of the Light*. Pietermaritzburg: University of KwaZulu-Natal Press, 2009.

Lynch, E. 'Durban gears up for Passion Play', *The Southern Cross* (Southern African Catholic Bishops' Conference newspaper), 1–7 December 2004, 1.

Mendelsohn, Richard and Milton Shain. *The Jews in South Africa*. Johannesburg and Cape Town: Jonathan Ball, 2008.

Paton, Alan. *Hofmeyr*. Oxford: Oxford University Press, 1994.

Pesch, R. 1990. 'His Blood Be On Us and On Our Children', in O. Weis and J.A. Daisenberger (rev.), *The Oberammergau Play of the Suffering, Death and Resurrection of Our Lord Jesus Christ*. Oberammergau: The Village of Oberammergau, 1990, 109–13.

Stead, William. *The Story That Transformed the World: or, the Passion Play at Oberammergau*. London: Office of the Review of Reviews, 1890.

Tilby, Angela. *Son of God*. London: Hodder & Stoughton, 2001.

Warner, Michael. *Publics and Counterpublics*. New York: Zone Books, 2002.

Part I Discussion

Simon W. du Toit, Tamantha Hammerschlag, Michael Lambert, and Joy Palacios

Joy Palacios: Consistent themes emerge among our three chapters. One is of the form and political impact of religious performance in relation to governmental authority. The second is similar, considering the form and political function of religious performance in relation to the sense of place, or security, that a religious group has.

Michael Lambert: I'd like to add the notion that the puritans in their theatrical sermon performances were, in a sense, responding to the very theatricality of Catholic and Anglican ritual.

Simon W. du Toit: A fourth theme has to do with the question of consumption and circulation.

Palacios: We're also asking, 'What is a public, what is a counterpublic, and how does religious performance shape these phenomena?'

du Toit: The publics we're looking at are limited in particular kinds of ways, and challenged by the powers of the government. Perhaps we should return to the first question, about the relationships between publics and the governments under which they exist.

Palacios: In early modern England and in modern South Africa there is a contentious relationship between the government and a minority religious group that performed a public. The public I'm looking at is really limited by decision. The directors of this potential public limit it in order to create something else.

Lambert: A public that resists the government is different from one that confirms or supports the government. The seminarians would support and reinforce some of the state's notions, rather than contest them. Joy, you offer a useful distinction, between performance *in* public, and the creation of publics *by* performance.

du Toit: For Habermas the church provides a legitimating authority that supports the authority of the monarchy and of sovereign public statements. When religious bodies are divided and a minority group forms, that legitimating authority perhaps becomes questionable. Do these religious performances we analyze contribute to or challenge the legitimating authority of religion under a non-democratic government?

Palacios: In the context of the Durban Passion Play the answer is multiple. In 1952 the decision to stage the Passion Play might have emboldened the Catholic authorities to make a statement against apartheid. Certainly they decided to have both African and European audience members in the same stadium. Michael and Tamantha, as your chapter follows the Passion Play's history towards the present, you highlight moments when the Catholic authorities become more cautious.

Lambert: In some cases the Catholic Church seemed afraid of finding itself the persecuted minority. It didn't want to openly contest government policies. The Church had an ambiguous relationship with the state, forming a public that contested and yet supported the state simultaneously. The moment that the Church takes what was really private, the Mass, and opens it up and performs it in public, religious ideas start circulating. This was the first time that the streets of Durban had seen any Christian event performed in public.

Tamantha Hammerschlag: I would say that as the play distances itself from any kind of political activity, and thinks of itself as just a religious event, it becomes appropriated by the government.

du Toit: I'm wondering if you came across any evidence of government action in South Africa in response to any aspect of the Durban Passion Play. For example, English monarchs and church authorities passed laws and issued orders controlling public speaking and preaching, beginning long before Elizabeth's reign, in order to protect and maintain their power and to protect and control orthodoxy.

Lambert: Not that I'm aware of. The Passion Play must have annoyed the government, because during that period there was a restriction on the importation of Irish and German missionary priests. The Catholic Church was told to find its clergy locally rather than import them. The use of Afrikaans in the programmes, which starts in the 1960s, was definitely a way in which the Church was flirting with the government, because there were Afrikaans-speaking people in the audience. The only kind of reaction we can talk about is that the Reformed churches considered the Passion Play to be the sort of theatre which they could go to without feeling guilty.

du Toit: Perhaps the religious nature of the performance allowed the political aspect of it to remain subliminal and submerged.

Hammerschlag: The producers shied away from provoking the government by not opening up the revolutionary potential that is within the Passion Play. It presents itself as the work of an amateur theatrical group that performs the play to a wide audience, but for a religious or evangelical purpose rather than in any way as a political statement.

Palacios: What do you think it is about the performance that prevents its potential political implications from being perceived as such?

Lambert: I think that comes from the claim to be as faithful to the Gospels as possible, not realizing that in making that claim that it involves interpretation. The Church offers a faithful representation of the events in Christ's life, but in doing so, they are arranging those events so as to create an emotional catharsis. It can't possibly be neutral.

du Toit: Your chapter marks precisely that development in history, in the ways in which the play has been interpreted variously, according to the historical conditions.

Lambert: As with the emancipation of the Catholics in the early nineteenth century, bringing the enemy out of the closet – in this case the "Roman danger" – and naming the enemy makes them easier to control, and the same might be said of the apartheid government in relation to the Catholic Church.

Hammerschlag: The issues of white guilt and how the play would reflect on the Jewish community are not usually interrogated. Overtly political interpretations are also discouraged. Jesus's political radicalism is limited, and there was no association drawn with political figures such as Nelson Mandela. Even now, such an interpretation would have political ramifications. They shy away from that.

Lambert: Shying away from it is in itself a political choice.

Hammerschlag: That reluctance seems to connect with the theme of place, and the way people begin to associate freedom of expression with certain places, whilst in other areas they feel constrained. Even when there is an overt adoption of civil rights people may still feel silenced because of an undercurrent of prejudice, so they form counterpublics.

Palacios: So geographic place combines the explicit and visible contours of the place and the undercurrents of cultural history. At the end of your chapter, Simon, you mention that the puritan church was a placeless church, and that made me think about the priests I'm looking at; they had a clear place. I inferred from Tami and Michael's paper that the Catholic Church in South Africa was a minority church, but it did have a place. Their places of worship were not circumscribed. I wonder if the need to engage in active public-making has some link to this possession or non-possession of a place. It seems like for the puritans, who didn't have a place, the use of prophetic speech as a way of forming a public was more urgent than it was for the priests I'm looking at in France, and maybe for the Catholic Church in South Africa.

du Toit: One of the goals of Stockwood's sermon performance was to re-inscribe Scriptural authority on the civic order, the sense of place in the City of London. He believed that in a Biblical civic order, theatres ought to be banned from the city.

Lambert: In South Africa, I don't think that the place of the Catholic Church was secure. They had the sense that their place was actually insecure, and that explains their slightly collaborative tendencies with the apartheid

authorities. It's the insecurity of the sense of place that set up the ambiguities we've been talking about.

Palacios: So they had a place, but they needed to hang onto it. Simon, were
the puritans allowed to gather to worship?

du Toit: The puritans were dissenters within the dominant church. They
essentially took over certain Anglican parishes. As Stockwood came into
London he had to cross the Thames at London Bridge, and immediately
to his left as he approached the bridge was St Saviour's Church, which was
a puritan stronghold. Why was it located outside the city, in one of the
liberties? Attached to the notion of place is the idea of what is proper – de
Certeau's notion that the sense of place is based in a set of practices that
establish the order of the proper. Warner draws on that sense of propriety
and place when he refers to the struggle of the gay community to find
a geographic place that can serve as the scene for the performance of
identity.

Lambert: The Catholic Church was almost embarrassed by the evangelical
aspect of the Durban Passion Play, there was something improper about
it, because that's considered rather Protestant. When the Catholic Church
performs an aspect of its interiority in public, there is a slightly hesitant
approach to theatricality, to performing religion in public.

du Toit: That antitheatricality becomes an occasion for religious bodies to
mark their boundaries.

Lambert: When a religious practice is centred in something as theatrical
as the Mass, the reactant group attacks religious theatricality, but it also
adopts theatricality, in puritan sermon performance, for example.

Palacios: When one group charges another group with theatricality in worship, it's a delegitimizing strategy. Any yet, the theatrical nature of the
Durban Passion Play, particularly when it was in its pageant-like form,
allowed its potentially political meanings to remain submerged. When
religious performance in public takes on a theatrical aspect does that
enhance or diminish its political impact?

du Toit: So much depends upon how the audience receives that theatricality. If
it's received as a legitimate correspondence to interiority and the construction of 'truth', then performance magnifies the political force of religious
speech. Among puritans that kind of vociferous and heated style of preaching was a marker of interiority and truthfulness that circulated within the
puritan public, and therefore it had force and reliability. This question is
searching for the roots of legitimacy and authority. When is performance
marked as hypocritical or illegitimate, and when is it accepted as legitimate
and authoritative? The locus of authority seems to shift, and it seems to
shift in concert with other cultural conditions such as the available technologies of communication, or patterns of consumption.

This brings us back to our fourth theme. Joy, you mark boundaries of
consumption within meals, and the parallel between the daily ritual of

the meal and the celebration of the Mass. I'm interested in the ways in which consumption and circulation construct authority, and the boundaries around those practices. The fact that seminarians were not allowed warm conversation. Interiority was not allowed to circulate. There seems to be a broader connection between kinds of consumption and kinds of production and circulation. Did circulation and consumption within the seminary extend beyond its walls to the laity?

Palacios: Many of the manuscripts I study probably did not circulate widely, but there were also published texts aimed at teaching priests how to behave properly, and the prefaces often make it clear that the priests publishing these documents thought that they would help lay people to organize their religious practice, while at the same time enabling laypeople to appreciate what priests were doing. It would take more work to figure out whether those documents would create a public in Warner's sense, or in Habermas's sense. There are certainly texts that circulate, and there's a reading public so there's a market, but it would be a matter of figuring out what kind of social interaction those documents actually facilitated. I don't yet have other sources to help me know how lay people actually used these documents.

du Toit: Performance circulates within a religious community, and may circulate outside a religious community, and yet because the church authorities and the government authorities seem to have been collaborating in such an intense way in that period of French history, this performance doesn't seem to have occasioned any kind of concern from the authorities on the one hand, or resistance at the lay level on the other. With respect to this question of legitimation and authority, the authorities seem to have remained very much in control. There doesn't seem to have been much anxiety about authority as a question.

Palacios: There is one caveat that I don't discuss in the chapter, which is that the bodily appearance of the seminarians did get marked by their prayer practices and by the kinds of devotional and liturgical practices they promoted among the laity. As a result, they were labeled as *les dévots*, the devout, or as zealous. There was critique among laypeople that these seemingly devout people were hypocrites.

You could argue that the public manifestation of religious practice promoted a public among the laity who found the trope of the devout clergyman or the devout lay person useful in creating plays and pamphlets as a form of critique. For example, there's pretty strong evidence that the costume worn by the character Tartuffe in the début of Moliere's play would have resembled a seminarian's garb. The play might be a poke at the kind of religiosity these counter-reformers in France's seminaries were trying to create. Just a couple of decades earlier, the costume of the lower clergy would not have been as recognizable because the seminaries hadn't yet started to standardize it.

du Toit: So the figure of the *dévot* was already circulating as a public figure of religiosity, and then it becomes a target for Moliere. This particular model of what it is to be religious is starting to circulate outside the church and be subject at least to lay uptake if not lay resistance and criticism.

Palacios: Which parts of the Passion Play would be best described as public-making or as a public? How does the category of the public fit into the history of the Durban Passion Play?

Lambert: The very pageant itself, performing in the streets, must have provoked a number of responses amongst different communities, although we don't have direct evidence of it. We could only tap into Catholic material that was almost hagiographical. We tried to find evidence that would show it was received differently by Islamic, Jewish, or Hindu scholars, but there wasn't any available evidence apart from vague reports in the newspapers, which, at that stage, were dominated by Anglican, High Church, English editors who were embarrassed by popery in the streets.

Hammerschlag: Dawn Haynes, the director of the Passion Play, said in conversation that there were people who would faint in the auditorium, and people who were incredibly moved by it, and so presumably it did have a strong effect on certain audience members.

Lambert: The Passion Play attracts people from all walks of South African life. Particularly now, it attracts rural black people, and many of them are not English speaking. They sit through this performance of the Passion done largely by white people, in English, which in itself of course raises all sorts of problems.

du Toit: And was there a marked emotional reaction amongst the black members of the audience?

Lambert: Yes, absolutely.

Hammerschlag: They're a very responsive audience, very engaged.

du Toit: The affective reaction is crossing racial lines, bringing ethnicities together at a time when they're politically deeply divided. That seems like an almost subversive act, and yet its politics seem to have remained on a subliminal level. We spoke earlier about the possible connections between the people organizing and administering the Passion Play and the people in the nascent resistance movements, the African National Congress and so forth. It seems clear that there really is no evidence of any such connection.

Lambert: No, there isn't.

Hammerschlag: The only person we've noted in the programmes who might possibly have made that connection is David Horner, who was involved in the trade union movements in the theatre, and founded the Drama Department at the University of Witwatersrand. He doesn't feature hugely as a political activist, to the best of my knowledge. None of the other people named in the programme seem to be politically involved.

Palacios: Simon, in your chapter, you talk quite a bit about prophetic speech and performative speech, and both of those seem to have a relationship to a religious counterpublic. Are those kinds of speech the same? Did sermonic performance have a particular kind of publicness?

du Toit: I view puritan prophetic speech as performing a view of history that transcends the immediate present. In the prophetic moment the speaker feels himself or herself to be moved by the Holy Spirit and called into the presence of a Biblical experience of time. In that sense prophetic speech has a salvific function and intention, calling people to repentance, but it is performative in the sense that those who practiced it were self-conscious about their performance. The practitioners of this affective style were critical of the many ministers in the nascent Anglican Church who weren't capable of preaching. The Anglican authorities published *The Book of Homilies*, and those who weren't capable of preaching were invited to read sermons from this book. Their reading ministry was not accounted to have any efficacy as far as the radical Protestants were concerned, and so the performative nature of puritan preaching in the Austinian sense of the word, which calls upon the emotional state of the preacher, also marks its efficacy in the Holy Spirit.

Palacios: Can you talk a bit more about how you envision the puritan counterpublic? Your chapter traces a market for this kind of speech, especially in the sermon-gadding where people cross parish boundaries to hear different preachers. What kind of counterpublic do you think this prophetic speech fostered?

du Toit: Warner suggests that counterpublics are not only resistant to a dominant public, but that they are self-conscious about it; they are reflexive about their minority status. Stockwood complains that he and others have been termed with this odious word 'puritan'. Those who identified with the radical reform wing of the church despised the term, in part because of its lack of precision. There were many different kinds of resistant Protestant groups in England in that period. There were sects springing up all around the country: Brownists, the Family of Love, Sabbatarians, and later the Muggletonians – groups with bizarre names. These different schismatic splinter groups were often all thrown in a bucket together and called 'puritans', and that was upsetting for strict Calvinists like Stockwood.

Palacios: What kind of public do you think Stockwood wanted to create? Which of these smaller groups was he really trying to address?

du Toit: Stockwood was addressing two audiences. He was performing a hail to those who shared his religious position, and saying to them, 'My fellow reformer, it's time for us to stand up and call for our acceptance and recognition.' At the same time he was self-consciously critical of the government, and resistant toward the oppression that the bishops had visited upon the radical wing of the church. The puritans were analogous to the counterpublics that Michael Warner describes. They clearly performed their sense of difference, not only in what they said but also in how they performed their religious lives. Sermon-gadding and the many other puritan religious practices formed a cultural life that included others who were strangers, who would not have been known to each other. That demonstrates the stranger sociability to which Warner alludes. A person who lived as a puritan adopted prophetic speech practices that would have flaunted their puritan status.

Palacios: So would it be fair to say that one way in which Stockwood contributes to forming a counterpublic is in appropriating this term 'puritan', and then turning it into a hail?

du Toit: I think that the speech itself became a style of performance; I wouldn't want to call it a dialect, but an idiom, a pattern of speech that became so recognizable that it was caricatured on the stage. Puritans constantly peppered their speech with Scriptural references and phrases. They also were fond of marking their sense of difference by stigmatizing cultural practices such as the theatre. By so doing they performed themselves in such a way that they were recognizable as puritan among those who didn't know them.

Palacios: I'm wondering what this style can tell us about the contours of the counterpublic. I can see that there is a style that is recognizable among people who are not part of that public, and I can see that the people who are part of that counterpublic share these performance practices, although they don't always agree with each other on doctrinal subtleties, so maybe these religious practices help link them together despite their differences.

Hammerschlag: I suppose also that what constitutes a counterpublic shifts.

du Toit: Habermas suggests that publics are grounded in discursive circulation, and develop a legitimating authority so that the locus of authority in a democracy is not held in the hands of the government, but in the hands of the public. That process of challenging the locus of legitimate authority is historically critical to the idea of a public. For puritans, the Reformation in England was never fully completed. For them, the locus of legitimate authority did not lie in the person of the monarch, but, rather, it lay at the local level. Rather than resisting the discourses of a dominant public, the puritan counterpublic was defined by its resistance of centralized, sovereign religious authority. Sixteenth-century puritans were politically loyal, but dissented on a religious level.

Palacios: We've seen how religious performance in public can both challenge and reinforce government authority, and, conversely, how government can limit the sense of place a public can perform.

Lambert: Yes, and the theatricality of performance is linked to the sense of place. It can easily become antitheatricality.

Hammerschlag: The state can also appropriate religious performance to serve its own ends.

du Toit: In all our chapters, the conditions of consumption and circulation helped us mark a view of a public's proper place. Each of these threads has an impact on how publics and counterpublics form and dissipate.

Thanks very much for your contributions to this project.

Part II
Visceral Publics

4
Church on/as Stage: Stewart Headlam's Rhetorical Theology

Tom Grimwood and Peter Yeandle

> We who live in large towns know only too well that the
> people are perishing for the lack of beauty quite as much
> as for the lack of knowledge. ... Having for three centuries
> worshipped a God of gloom, having had Manichaeism and
> Puritanism established over us by the state, we have learned
> to think that there is some contradiction between the love
> of beauty and the love of God. Counteracting all this the
> Theatre has been at work with its heavenly mission; there
> the contemplation of beauty has been made possible for
> the people; there, in spectacular drama, pantomime, bal-
> let, comic opera, burlesque; there, with the art of the scene
> painter and the musician and the dancers with their poetry
> of vital motion, their artistic and unconventional dress,
> and the harmonious blending of beautiful colours; there
> the people have been educated, i.e., taken a little out of
> themselves, received hints of how beautiful this world will
> be when at last order has overcome chaos and when God
> is seen in perfect beauty. (Stewart Headlam)[1]

The history of Christianity shows an interconnected yet complex relationship with the practice and techniques of rhetoric. From St Paul to
St Augustine, Richard Whately and John Henry Newman to C.S. Lewis, theologians have used performative aspects of rhetoric to demarcate the reach
and limits of the Church's identity within society. Often overlooked in this
history of 'rhetorical theology' is the Reverend Stewart Duckworth Headlam
(1847–1924) and his controversial Church and Stage Guild (founded in
1879). Headlam was one of the most public Christian figures in late-Victorian London: he stood bail for Oscar Wilde, served as character witness for
Charles Bradlaugh and other high-profile secularists, shared a platform with
Irish Nationalists and sponsored, as well as led, socialist marches. Headlam's
licence to preach was revoked in 1882 not only because of his association

with radicals, but also for the reason that he defended the moral integrity of ballet dancers and argued that theatrical space was sacred. His brand of sacramental socialism meant, for him, the ballet dancer performed divine grace, and the stage was endowed with a spiritual potential equivalent to that of the Church. Headlam was thus a preacher without a pulpit, who, through print media and spoken word performance, created his own distinctive theological space by conceptualizing his audience – of otherwise 'secular' agents – in congregational terms. That is, Headlam understood his audience to be formed by a series of layers: the workers, the destitute and the oppressed to whom he spoke directly; their employers, exploiters and oppressors he addressed through the very publicness of his performance. He used his Church and Stage Guild to coerce established Anglicanism into reconsidering its view of the stage (including notorious arguments with two Bishops of London).

This chapter argues for Headlam's inclusion in the history, not only of Christian Socialism, but also of religious performance and the public sphere. It will suggest that Headlam's controversial interlinking of Church and theatre used multiple audiences in order to not only push the moral boundaries of late-Victorian society, but also reconfigure the boundaries of the Church itself as a distinctly figurative institution. It is our argument, consequently, that by defining his own 'public' and his own 'space', Headlam challenged both the accepted spatial and institutional dimensions of religious and political performance. In doing so, his combination of radical politics and theological critique not only influenced the development of Victorian public opinion, but conceptually redrew the boundaries of how such opinion could be formed.

But what history is it that Headlam should be included within? Writing on the role of rhetoric within the Christian faith, David Jasper notes:

> Theology has always been obsessed with power and authority – the authority, perhaps, of God, or the Church, or individuals within the Church. Through rhetoric and rhetorical criticism we come to see how the Western tradition has defined itself in text, has been defined by text, and reconstitutes itself through repeated experiences of discontinuity, through an entextualising process which both forms community and perhaps suggests the nature and purpose of the religious community.[2]

Jaspers' emphasis on the 'textual' here may initially suggest a blasé distinction between 'text' and 'world' (or the 'theory' and 'practice' distinction that have haunted postmodern debates over public space in the past[3]). But for Jaspers, the role of rhetoric within faith is rather to identify and engage with the significant words and actions as the binding foundation of a community otherwise discontinuous and fractured. Rhetoric is thus a process of 'entextualizing' – recognizing oneself not so much within a discourse, but related to a discourse that is constantly being rewritten. The distinction, then, is not between text and world, or theory and practice, but between the idea of Christian community as a kind of moral ontology,[4] and as a performance *of* community bounded by its rhetorical structure. What rhetoric offers us, contra the moral approach to community, is a way into the notion and identity of Christian community that emphasizes *performance*. In doing so, it arguably takes less risk with its own piety: it is, to be blunt, far easier to *describe* ideal moral communities than to negotiate the practical 'entextualizing' of their performance. As Karl Barth suggested,[5] as much as theologians (particularly at the tail end of the nineteenth century) may have lauded the Church *as* a community, there are, in reality, many 'dead' churches: not dead in the sense of unattended or forgotten, but rather in the sense of failing to constitute a public performance of Christian community. As such, it would not be entirely wayward to suggest that rhetoric and Christianity interlink specifically when the practice of defining Christian community is at work; perhaps more so, as Jaspers rightly suggests, defining community when it is *fractured*. In this sense, the rhetorical performances of Christian mission are key sites of the tensions between the ideal community and the practically realized one, particularly regarding the limits of such a community. To this extent, the 'public' is a constant site of negotiation between the speaker who rhetorically identifies and constructs his audience, and the audience who necessarily supersedes that construction.

Headlam's use of such entextualizing rhetoric must be placed in the context of late nineteenth-century England. By the 1880s and 1890s, a greater majority than before were heeding demands for greater religious intervention in confronting the social injustices wrought by poverty. Mid-century economic confidence, sustained by evangelicalism, rejected such demands: poverty was perceived the fault of the individual, not the system. However, economic crises in the 1870s exposed fragilities within *laissez-faire* ideology. According to K.S. Inglis, this transition to economic uncertainty marked a new 'spirit of the age' or paradigmatic shift.[6] A number of factors made churchmen rethink their position. Fewer people attended church, and, despite an unprecedented programme of church building in the East End,[7] fear spread that too many of London's poor were beyond the reach of the church. The increasing popular appeal of secularist activists, evidenced by booming participation of workers at their lectures, caused intense anxiety amongst a number of clergymen about the moral degradation of the British working classes. In turn, this prompted a large number of left-leaning clergy to demand active, practical engagement with those most in need of spiritual succour.

It is no surprise, then, that the 1880s and 1890s witnessed an emergence of a cultural vacuum in which moral critiques of capitalism, such as those of Ruskin, could now become popular.[8] Indeed, there is a distinct Ruskinian influence on Headlam's lauding of the theatrical as means to social betterment.[9] At the same time, this fracturing was not simply about loss of lay attendance, but concerned theological and political disputes as well. Anglican groups concerned with social reform – the Christian Social Union, the Christian Socialist Society, or the Socialist Quaker society – were often at theological loggerheads with one another.[10] Headlam's rhetoric of 'sacramental socialism', which argued for a distinct relationship between the ritual of Christian worship, theatrical performance, and social reform, was thus both a challenge to the 'established' Church and also an attempt to create a unity of purpose around issues of social responsibility. To attempt such a unity, Headlam purposefully spoke to, and, indeed, interpellated a public sphere otherwise demarcated (and, indeed, delimited) from theological discourse. By addressing not a pre-established audience but rather the very media through which address itself is instigated – that is to say, addressing social reform in terms of the methods of theatrical performance – Headlam's crusade was not simply moral, but also topological. In other words, Headlam's significance lies in his rhetorical reconfiguring of the space of debate, both conceptually and materially.

Rhetoric, theology, and the grammar of assent

The question, however, is not so much whether Headlam 'entextualized' community within his rhetorical performances, but rather what made his particular performance of entextualizing distinctive and significant. The contexts of Headlam's activities were both practical and theoretical. Practically, his involvement with the fraught relationship between the Church of England and the theatre, and in particular the music-hall ballet of the East End, led him to actively challenge the distinction between theatre and religious ritual. In *The Function of the Stage* (1889), Headlam not only argued that pleasure should be the primary yardstick by which to measure the success of popular amusements, but that pleasure itself was godly:

> ... [I]nstruction, education and edification may all accrue from plays, but pleasure *must*: a work of art has failed its object if it does not give pleasure. ... The moral ministry of the stage depends upon the fact, that we can be made better people by being made brighter and happier people. ... Overworked and worried, living too often in gloomy streets, surrounded with mud, dirt, grime, meagreness, can you overestimate the ennobling, healing, exhilarating influence of merely a bright, spectacular ballet, quite apart from any plot or story ... ? Suppose, if you like, that the story goes for nothing, there is still the poetry of vital motion, there is still the beauty of form, music, and colour. And this is why the ballet becomes such a useful touchstone for the clergy, to see whether they are Mahommedans or Christians, Manichaeans or orthodox Churchmen. They have to face the fact, whether they think the human body an evil

thing or the temple of the Holy Ghost. Tragedies and comedies may be supposed to appeal mainly to the Intellect – the ballet does not do so any more than a sunset does.[11]

For Headlam, beautiful dancing, if contemplated with moral eyes, served a sacramental function by revealing divine grace. As an Anglo-Catholic, Headlam subscribed to Catholic sacramental liturgy, and claimed a sacramental function for the ballet as the outward visible sign of an inward spiritual grace. He was clear: 'We have constantly affirmed that stage dancing should be treated as a genuine art; from a theological standpoint we have declared that the Corps de Ballet is part of the Body of Christ'.[12] Ruskin, in *The Poetry of Architecture*, urged the use of the word 'poetry' to denote the intellectual and emotional essences of art.[13] It is no surprise, therefore, that Headlam invoked the ballet as sacramental by labelling it 'the poetry of motion' and 'outward spiritual sign of an inward spiritual grace' (as sacrament is defined in the *Book of Common Prayer*).[14]

Theoretically, his performative[15] interventions within this relationship itself took place within an intellectual context of the ecclesiastical rhetoric which Headlam both invoked and subverted. For nineteenth-century ecclesiastical rhetoric, at least up until the end of the century, was no less concerned with the issue of the fracturing of community, and the need to look to its boundaries. The 'somewhat embarrassing' position that English Christianity found itself in regarding declining Church attendance from the industrial working class, as well as the pressing claims of new factions within Christianity itself, was certainly noted by academic theologians and Churchmen alike.[16] However, the key for the main writings on the subject of rhetoric was how to defend the fundamental truths of Christianity against the criticisms of the Atheist, the Agnostic, the Socialist, and the Nonconformist. Richard Whately's 1846 textbook *Elements of Rhetoric*, for example, shows rhetoric to be a primarily forensic activity, concerned with the justification of a priori truths. It served the pulpit orator in 'his task of conveying to an unlettered congregation the indisputable doctrines of the Christian faith', as well as defending said faith against rationalistic critiques.[17] It is not surprising that such a foundation of ecclesiastical rhetoric informed the converted Roman Catholic John Henry Cardinal Newman when he discussed issues of disagreement and community in his seminal essay on the *Grammar of Assent*.[18]

Newman disagrees with Whately's claims that there are accessible a priori truths useful to public debate, as these are, for Newman, frequently found to be wanting in real life argument. Nevertheless, Newman maintained that stable consensus is the necessary foundation of public discourse. While essentially a defence of Christianity in changing times, the purpose of Newman's essay was not simply to critique an over-reliance on rational logic as an arbiter of all things, but also to justify a particular sense of public agreement whereby the uncertainties of real life situations could neverthe-less be used to provide a firm foundation for truth. In this sense, its appeal to the rhetorical nature of argument was an appeal to a particular model of the 'public', and in particular that public's 'illative sense', which was, in brief, the idea that conviction and belief was formed by multiple and varied smaller reasons and probabilities that were impossible to reconstruct for-mally. Evidence for conviction was thus variable, not scientific; but this does not stop the basic tenets of Christian community from being the best beliefs to have. In essence, Newman presents a rhetorical theory here which reflects what we might now term Western political pluralism: a discourse of com-munity that allowed for variation and difference in belief, which, through such variation, ultimately led to assent on fundamental belief.

Such an appeal to assent obviously carries its own assumptions over the nature of the community, whether ideal or real. As Jasper notes, the theological interest in a rhetoric of assent often draws upon what Matthew Arnold termed the 'Hellenism' of Christian thought.[19] That is to say, despite its attention to the variability of public discussion, secular or otherwise, it is ultimately governed by the final unity that they will assent to. The purpose of religious performance is not to strike out into ambiguous territory (what Arnold terms 'Hebraism'), but rather to return the territories of ambiguity back home to the newly found security of assented truth. To this extent, the purpose of rhetoric, for both Newman and Whately, was – whether ultimately leading us to rational certainty or consensual probability – to forego its Classical requirements. Whereas Classical Rhetoric insisted on five parts of a discourse – invention, arrangement, style, performance and memory[20] – the ecclesiastical rhetoric of the nineteenth century saw its pur-pose instead to primarily clarify and type the invention and arrangement of arguments. Performance, in the theatrical sense in which Classical orators were well versed, was excised from the rhetorical foundations of Newman's 'public'. Assent, in Newman's formulation, was above all a principle of invention, given that all arguments require the stasis of agreement between interlocutors on what is being spoken *about*. Here, according to Newman, assent 'becomes a sort of necessary shadow' to the probabilities of concrete reasoning.[21] In other words, assent is both a work of faith (which any kind of public discourse necessitates; that is, that people must agree on certain truths in order to understand one another) and the basis of community (in discerning the nature of assent, more fundamental truths of human inter-action can be affirmed); but this remains distinctly forensic in nature and overtly optimistic in application.

In contrast to the implicit idealization of consensus in Newman's rheto-ric, Headlam's rhetorical practice was situated amid recognition of the shifts and changes in the ascription of concepts and identities, at both the social and intellectual level.[22] Following F.D. Maurice, Headlam thus recognized the need to challenge the 'otherworldliness' of the stagnant theological orthodoxies. As such, the reaches of a purely forensic rhetoric are not enough for Headlam's 'entextualizing' practices. Furthermore, it is Headlam's reintroduction of performance as a central part of his rhetorical theology that specifically challenges the notion of assent that Newman sees as necessary to public discourse.

This performance, we would argue, manifested itself in two ways. First, his physical performances upset the boundaries between secular and religious: in particular his merging of the theatre and ballet with the rituals of Christian worship. Second, his oral and written performances – his sermons, writings in the newspaper he edited, the *Church Reformer*, and other widely-read essays – meant debates about theatre, as well as his theological justifications for the sacred calling of stage artists, gained widespread attention and prompted considerable debate about aesthetics, ritualism, and working-class poverty relief. In doing so, Headlam's use of rhetorical techniques allowed him to speak to multiple publics within single performances; not only pushing the moral boundaries of late-Victorian society, but also reconfiguring the boundaries of the Church itself as a distinctly *figurative* institution that was capable of engaging with and acting in the growing secular sphere. In other words, Headlam's performative rhetoric exposed 'the power games of the Christian tradition' at work in the concept of assent as an ideal public, and, in doing so, entextualized a fractured community through the motif of the stage.[23]

Stewart Headlam, the 'most bohemian Priest' in all London

It was not only the nineteenth-century rhetoric textbooks that shunned the role of performance. The Church had maintained its animosity towards the theatre throughout the nineteenth century. It was not uncommon for clergy to denounce performers and theatrical space. The Oxford Churchmen's Union forbade its members to attend the theatre: 'the influence of the theatre tended to sin'.[24] Mimicry was seen as the devil's work, and the presumed desire of actors to be the centre of attention was condemned as vanity incarnate.[25] The following view expressed in an editorial in the *Christian Commonwealth* was not uncommon:

> at the theatre, all the evils that waste property, corrupt morals, blast reputations, impair health, embitter life, and destroy souls are to be found. There vice in every form lives, moves, and has its being ... The only way to justify the Stage is, as it ever has been, and as it is ever likely to be, is to condemn the Bible. The same individual cannot defend both.[26]

Attitudes were at their most hostile when considering stage dancers: to some 'evangelical sensibilities', the relationship 'between the female body and public display' exposed the precarious sexual mores of Victorian theatregoers;[27] the dance was perceived as an enticement to male lust, ballerinas themselves synonymous with prostitutes.[28]

Despite its association with the sinful side of life, ballet was central to nineteenth-century pantomime performance and was a requisite component of music-hall shows throughout the year. It was hard and poorly paid work, requiring serious physical and mental training.[29] The activities of the few, it seems, were inaccurately given as exemplification of the morals of many. The conflict between the beautiful presence on stage and the off-stage girl from the slums was not lost on Headlam either. For Headlam, the incongruity between dancing as pure and *beautiful* labour, and impure illicit eroticism, owed not to the moral failings of the girls, but to the unchristian attitude of the Church. 'For too long', according to Headlam, Christians had 'contented themselves with simply denouncing the evil of the stage'; instead, the Church should have worked hard to lessen the evils felt by those hardworking, and, crucially, Christian, performers.[30] Headlam's first curacies had been in some of the most deprived areas of London, perhaps most notably at St John's Church, Drury Lane, where he had come into frequent contact with those employed in the theatre industry. Headlam had seen first-hand how poverty had driven dancers and actresses away from honest employment; he baulked at young girls being 'sold' to nefarious continental dancing companies.[31] But, for Headlam, the worst abuse he observed was the exercise of Christian prejudice which would abuse performers their right to communion, irrespective of their good hearts.

Headlam made his thoughts on this clear in a lecture, 'Theatre and Music Hall' (10 October 1877) at a secularist Hall of Science, in Bethnal Green, a venue at which he had become close friends with Charles Bradlaugh (about whom more in a moment). His lecture was well received by many: he had praised theatrical entertainment as 'pure and beautiful' and encouraged young folk to attend to learn moral lessons. Not unsurprisingly, the lecture itself and its subsequent publication in the *Era* were both abhorred by his ecclesiastical superiors. Indeed, it was his refusal to rescind his support for the stage and to show contrition for his criticisms of the Church that led to his first Episcopal censure. Given the enmity felt towards the stage, it is little surprise that the Church authorities should take serious offence. It was that censure that so outraged Headlam and led him to establish the Church and Stage Guild in 1879, 'a society of members of the dramatic profession, clergymen and others, who feel it their duty ... to get rid of the prejudices widely felt by religious people against the stage, and by theatrical people against the Church'.[32] The objectives of the Guild were 'to try and get the Clergy to take a Christian view of the Stage'.[33] So, Headlam's defence of ballet dancers sprang from his experience of the economic factors and effects of stereotyping which had driven some young girls into vice. Moreover, the support he was given by wider elements in society encouraged him to challenge doctrine.

Headlam's support for the performing arts, however, was deeply embedded within his own theological system. His support for the arts was no mere attention-seeking act of defiance; Headlam's whole eschatology was grounded in Christianity as secular, performative, and sacramental.[34] The theatre, as he makes clear in the extract at the head of this chapter, brought pleasure. In an open letter to entertainers of 1881, Headlam wrote: 'To artists we say: "your calling is a sacred one ... your art tends to give cheer and pleasure to vexed and worried lives."' He assured those who felt derided by Churchmen their work was 'not in vain in the Lord',[35] and argued that 'we should honour those who work [on the stage], we should protect their fair fame and reputation from insolent patronage and ... religious fanatics'.[36]

For Headlam, actors were to be praised, indeed celebrated, since they did not work for themselves, but for their audience. His theological cue for this was undoubtedly the work of F.D. Maurice, and in particular his theology of 'vocation': individuals were divinely endowed with talents with which to live their lives and contribute to their community.[37] In a diatribe against celebrity actors who might seek the limelight for personal gain, he argued that, in contrast, true divinely appointed actors

> ... must please the immediate public or they cannot fulfil their sacred calling at all. This fact, it seems to me, is not sufficiently considered by those who criticise Stage work in all its departments. It is a fact which adds immense importance to the work of the actor, the singer and the dancer, for it prevents them from shirking present day difficulties and indulging in the luxury of despising the present and working for the future. Their art cannot appeal to the select few of all generations, they must get at the heart of the people of their own day, catch their conscience, interpret their life, find out what it is that will give them pleasure.[38]

If actors were to be revered, then ballet dancers – in Headlam's worldview – were sacrosanct. His own straightforward ambition was made clear in his preface to a dancing manual he published in 1888: 'my chief object in producing this book is to enable the public to understand better than they do at present how difficult the art of dancing is, and so to induce them to appreciate more fully the Dancers and their work'.[39] More than this, though, the ballet to him was as central to his worldview as the drive towards the reform of land tax and the promotion of incarnation theology. When asked what his life had stood for, Headlam replied: 'The Mass and all that it means of organised Church life, with the living present Christ at its centre and object of worship; [and] the Ballet and all that it means of anti-Puritanism and the love of beauty in a Kingdom of Heaven to be established on earth'.[40]

Dancing revealed divine beauty. It was sacramental. Headlam questioned the morals of those who condemned dancing: 'Your Manichean Protestant, and your Superfine Rationalist, reject the Dance as worldly, frivolous, sensual and so forth; and your dull stupid sensualist sees legs, and grunts with some satisfaction'. In contrast, the sacramentalist knows that 'we live now by faith and not by sight, and that the poetry of vital motion is the expression of unseen spiritual grace'.[41] Headlam consecrated theatrical space: 'He is with us now in the Theatre as well as in the Church. ... [T]hose who minister to the lighter needs of life are God's servants equally with others'.[42] 'We have constantly affirmed that stage dancing should be treated as a genuine art; from a theological standpoint we have declared that the *Corps de Ballet* is part of the Body of Christ'.[43]

This relating of ballet performance and ritual is, of course, dressed in a distinct rhetoric of community. The specific naming of Manichean Protestants or Superfine Rationalists is not by chance: both are 'positions' that emphasize the atomistic individual who rejected the world and its heterologies; both, moreover, are positions that blur nominal boundaries between heretic and Christian. This in turn creates an audience identity bound both by community and by 'truth': not the truth of Newman's 'assent', whereby rhetoric creates a space of agreement between disparate parties that presumes a universal agreement, but rather, an entextualizing truth that demands the audience reassess the boundaries of those who are true to the values of Christianity and those who are not – whether they declared themselves Christian or not. According to Orens, Headlam believed that 'Catholic Christianity ... lifted the veil from the eyes of the faithful, allowing them to perceive God's sacramental presence in society, in nature, and in their own bodies. The ballet, Headlam believed, was the paradigm of this worldly holiness'.[44] In this sense, not only did the aesthetics of theatrical performance lead Headlam to a sacramental theology, but the rituals of Christian worship were themselves also reflections of the beauty of the ballet. But Headlam was not simply opening up the boundaries of theology towards a broader, 'secular' public, in the way that Newman suggested in his model of assent. For Headlam, the key to sacramental nature of his faith led him to address, and call forth, an agonistic audience; and it is here that the significance of his rhetorical theology to the idea of the 'public sphere' can become visible.

Textual performance and the entextualizing of community

While historians have been quick to forget Headlam, he was notorious in his day. Indeed, Headlam's understanding of performance was not limited to observing the ballet, but based on his own participation in public speaking. His articles were published in periodicals and newspapers as diverse as the *National Reformer*, the *Pall Mall Gazette* and the *Era*; his activities were written about in the most widely read daily papers (*The Times*, *Daily News* and *Telegraph* differed in opinion but shared their fascination); and the satirical press, *Punch*, *Judy* and *Fun* made many a comment about the Dancing Priest. Headlam's influence on other radicals and literati was acknowledged: the notorious Rhymer's Club (whose members included Arthur Symons and Edgar Jepsom), the Arts and Crafts Movement (Selwyn Image, William Morris). George Bernard Shaw learnt his skills as a public speaker under Headlam's tutelage at the Guild.[45] While we lack a sense of Headlam's voice as a speaker, analysis of his words as delivered through the medium of print reveal a sense of Headlam's construction of audience, and his rhetorical interventions in such audiences, principally through the paper he edited from 1884, the *Church Reformer*. Its title a deliberate mimicking of the contemporary secularist Charles Bradlaugh's *National Reformer*, Headlam's monthly publication provided a documentary record for the papers and correspondence of his socialist Guilds, theatrical, literary, art and music reviews, as well as expositions of the hypocrisies of the Anglican Church and promotions of socialist causes (such as education, poverty, unions and leisure). Each month, Headlam provided a front-page editorial in which he would preach on politics, theology, or theatre, often combining all three. Within the provision of the paper, we can already see Headlam's combination of politics, theology, and the performing arts. We can also see that, while Headlam may well have been (post-1882) a preacher without a Church, he was far from a preacher without a pulpit or congregation.

Within this congregation were the workers of Stepney, Shoreditch, and Bethnal Green, where Headlam held curacies between 1873 and 1882, as well as actresses, actors, and dancers who he had met in his first curacy at St Thomas's on Drury Lane. His message was often directed at these two groups in direct terms: 'you who with tired bodies work your hardest to line the pockets of the rich yet receive no earthly gain', 'you who would give your time to the hallowed function of the stage', and so on. The aim of such an address was not simply to acknowledge or to inspire, but also to empower.

The nature of this empowered audience is complicated, though, by the wider public audience of Headlam's work. In this sense, and noticeably different to the contemporary communitarian ecclesiology that has followed in his wake (John Milbank, Stanley Hauerwas, Oliver O'Donovan, and so on), Headlam was also concerned with an agonistic audience: he spoke to those who rejected his theology, his socialism, or his God. This audience was far less explicit in Headlam's speaking: partly, perhaps, because it is obvious that a socially active and visible preacher working in London would have the capacity to reach audiences beyond his immediate congregation without too much effort; but perhaps also in part because of Headlam's distinctive sense of how the boundaries of community are formed. While often addressing the thorny issue of where 'Church' stops and 'secular' begins, there is no sustained opposition in Headlam's rhetoric between Church and non-Church. This is because what Headlam calls 'Church' is often presented as being in need of reform; but furthermore, a reform more commonly called for from outside of the Church. As such, the work of the Church – and here Headlam typically invokes the motif of the Kingdom of Heaven as a transformative moment of the present, reminiscent of Rauschenbusch – is done by those who may not realize they are working for the Church at all. For example, in his obituary to renowned atheist Charles Bradlaugh, Headlam commends the 'grand secular work and the example of his thoroughness' on social issues. While Bradlaugh claimed that he himself did not know God, Headlam argues that nevertheless 'God knows him'. Furthermore, this is 'a root, foundation truth without which the world would be unbearable: a truth which is annoying to argumentative "atheists" and narrow religionists, but which the great mass of the people receive with joy when it is put before them'.[46]

The 'foundation truth' is not only that Bradlaugh's good works within society were commendable, but it is this – and not his criticisms of the Bible – that leads God to know him. Undoubtedly, Headlam recognizes the irony of an Anglican priest commending the work of an atheist over and against his fellow Christians, and, indeed, the tone of the essay remains ironic throughout: claiming that Bradlaugh's 'aggressive Atheism has done us [Churchmen] much good'. 'The Church can never thank him too much for having exposed, and brought back into a high light, so that all their ugliness might be made manifest, many monstrous travesties of the Catholic Faith'.[47] In this reappraisal of his work, Bradlaugh becomes one of Headlam's 'us': 'he was fighting ... as a freelance on our side', and in bringing to light the bad practices of the Church was in fact 'clearing the ground for us'. Conversely, if Bradlaugh is a valued member of Headlam's community, then, his criticisms turn to Bradlaugh's detractors as obstacles to him realising the foundational Christian truth of his work. Bradlaugh's critical 'nonsense' of the Bible was no different to that of Christian commentators, Headlam suggests, and it is 'we who are to blame' for allowing the Church to become absorbed in Biblical dogmatics at the expense of social reform.[48] As Atherton comments, 'the secular was used to interpret Christianity',[49] and for Headlam, his reworking of Christ as secular was central to his gospel of social reform: 'As far as I understand the life and character of Jesus Christ, he was far more of a secularist than many religious people seem to think'.[50]

There are two points to make on this. The first point is that this employment of irony emphasizes Headlam's willingness to interrupt the typical narratives of assent advocated by Newman, Whately, et al. As de Man argues, the ironic is the necessary undoing of any systematic narrative through digression, reversal, or nonsense.[51] Such undoing is, of course, best emphasized in overtly theatrical characters – the character of the fool, for example, who breaks the 'fourth wall' of the theatre and speaks to the audience, thus collapsing the integrity of the play by bringing to the fore an unavoidable awareness of staged performance. But Headlam's theatrics are not aimed at collapsing the cohesion of the performance. Thus, the second point is that the ethical core of Headlam's rhetoric is less concerned with undermining the Church, and more concerned with demonstrating the flexibility of the Church community's boundaries. For Headlam, the need was to remind believers that faith was to be *performed* by their actions; by prioritizing not simply the revolutionary ideals of ecclesiological ethics, but also by showing, displaying and performing in public the needs of the meek over the mighty. By embracing the ballet and the theatrical, Headlam's activities not only undermined the moral boundaries of the existing Church tradition, but also reaffirmed the saving grace of Christian community *as a form of performance.*

Arguably, the commitment to the openness of these boundaries drives Headlam's assertion of action over words. 'I need not say one single word to you', he argues in one sermon, 'in proof of our assertion that social and secular matters need attending to by Churchmen, as to the evil physical and moral conditions under which great masses of people live; you know them only too well'.[52] There is no need for words, it seems, when the physical reality of the world is so apparent; and likewise, for Headlam, the Kingdom of Heaven is on earth,[53] not in the textbooks of the 'Christian commentators' he deeply mistrusts. This mobility allows Headlam to present his case for the Guild of St Matthew both as a theologico-political movement that he invites others to respond to, and as a fundamentally binding aspect of the Christian community. In other words, it allows him to switch between identifying his audience as Englishmen, Christians, the morally concerned, and, in some cases, *both* opponents *and* friends of the Guild. For example, in his sermon on 'The Guild of St. Matthew: An Appeal to Churchmen' of 1890, he begins by defending his Guild against the audience, and in particular the charge that the Church itself needs no 'guilds' or other 'societies' to belong to in order to do its work.[54] He then justifies the work of the guild as bearing witness to truths which 'in the stress of ordinary parochial and diocesan affairs, might be forgotten or neglected'. The Guild is therefore not a breakaway rival to the traditional base of the Christian community: in fact, quite the opposite. Headlam argues that it is one of 'the best preventatives against that most fatal sin, the sin of Schism'.[55]

His effort, then, is to introduce alterity into the familiarity of communal practices (for example, by drawing out the theatrical element of worship), not to destabilize that practice, but to widen its implications to the secular as well as the religious audience. In contrast to an agreeable community of shared values, such as Newman's rhetoric of assent, Headlam specifically engaged in a distinctive entextualizing process: not simply representing the underrepresented, and speaking for the excluded, but in doing so attempting to perform a reconceptualization of these representations themselves. The ballet dancer is not simply the working girl, but an instrument of God's righteousness; the secularist is not simply someone who has turned away from the Church, but a representative figure of a Church which has turned from its central values.

It is perhaps too tempting to view Headlam as some kind of forward-thinking revolutionary whose championing of the excluded and the dispossessed speaks to our 'modern' sensibilities. This is certainly a difficult interpretation to resist, but it risks obscuring some of the more key aspects of Headlam's public performances: in particular, his 'entextualizing' of the complex communal relations between public and private, tradition and novelty, and ritual and rupture. It would be wrong to suggest that Headlam provides any kind of theory of Christian rhetorical performance, of course, but his performances remain distinctive, in an applied sense.

Of course, it is not enough to claim that Headlam's cause was persuasive simply because he literally stood on a stage and consecrated theatres. This may work for late modern audiences, of course – Headlam becomes an instantly palatable figure as soon as we see he embraces egalitarianism, opposes dull delivery of religious ritual and stands up for social injustice – but this goes only as far as appeasing a rather straw-man contemporary sense of what it is to be a 'good speaker'. As de Man pointed out, one can never 'step outside' of rhetoric in this sense, and if Headlam appears to speak to our contemporary sensibilities, then this is something to handle with a certain suspicion, rather than embracing him as 'one of us' too quickly. Rather, Headlam's writing encapsulates a performative politics. By harnessing the power of ritual and repetition central to the Anglican Eucharist, and demonstrating its affiliation with the theatre, Headlam was able to emphasize the mobility of what he saw as the central truths of Christian community. It is this mobility of performance that is the key to Headlam's entextualizing practices, and gives him a deserved place in the history of Christianity and rhetoric.

Notes

1. Stewart Duckworth Headlam, 'The Stage', Sermon preached at St Michael's, North Kensington, 7 August 1881, printed in Headlam, *Service of Humanity, and Other Sermons* (London: J. Hodges, 1882), 22–3.
2. David Jasper, *Rhetoric, Power and Community* (Basingstoke: Palgrave, 2003), x.
3. Such debates are understandably wide-reaching, but for examples of a range of discussions on the relationship between the 'theory' of textuality and narrative and the 'practice' of public space, see Henri Lefebvre, *The Production of Space* (Oxford: Blackwell, 1991), 17; Frederick Jameson, 'Marx's Purloined Letter', in Michael Sprinker, ed., *Ghostly Demarcations* (London: Verso, 1999), 28–30; Richard Rorty, *Contingency, Irony and Solidarity* (Cambridge: Cambridge University Press, 1989), 82; Wendy Brown, *Edgework: Critical Essays on Knowledge and Politics* (Oxford: Princeton University Press, 2005).
4. See, for example, Frank G. Kirkpatrick, *The Ethics of Community* (Oxford: Blackwell, 2001).
5. Karl Barth, 'Christian Community and Civil Community', in *Community, State and Church: Three Essays* (Garden City: Doubleday & Co., 1960).
6. K.S. Inglis, *Churches and the Working Classes in Victorian England* (London: Routledge and Kegan Paul, 1963), 250–71.

7. F. Knight, *The Nineteenth-Century Church and English Society* (Cambridge: Cambridge University Press, 1998), 61–8.
8. See, for example, G. Cockram, *Ruskin and Social Reform: Ethics and Economics in the Victorian Age* (London: Tauris Academic, 2007), 40–66; Jose Harris, 'Ruskin and Social Reform', in Dinah Birch (ed.), *Ruskin and the Dawn of the Modern* (Oxford: Clarendon, 1999), 7–33.
9. One of us has discussed Ruskin's influence on Headlam and late-century Christian Socialism in more depth: P. Yeandle, 'Art, Ethics, Pleasure: The Influence of John Ruskin on the Reverend Stewart Duckworth Headlam', *Nineteenth-Century Prose*, 38(2) (Fall 2011): 109–32; 'John Ruskin and the Christian Socialist Conscience', *Ruskin Review and Bulletin*, 8(2) (2012): 14–21.
10. As Peter d'A. Jones makes clear, so disparate were the individuals and denominations that constituted the Revival that 'their activities, even as socialists, were far from ecumenical in spirit'. *The Christian Socialist Revival, 1877–1914: Religion, Class and Social Conscience in late-Victorian England* (London: Oxford University Press, 1968), 5.
11. Headlam, *The Function of the Stage: A Lecture* (London: Frederick Verinder, 1889), 9–11, 21–2.
12. *Church Reformer*, 5/6 (1886), 133–4.
13. Michael Bright, 'The Poetry of Art', *Journal of the History of Ideas* 46(2) (1985): 259–77.
14. Headlam's notion that the dancer could reveal divine grace drew from Ruskinian teaching on beauty. For Ruskin, the dancer, like a tree, can be instinctively felt to be perfect. For Headlam, the dancer performed grace and inspired spiritual emotions. As Sara Atwood argues, Ruskin's dissatisfaction with Darwinian science was that it rendered vision technical, rather than moral (Sara Atwood, 'The Soul of the Eye: Ruskin, Darwin, and the Nature of Vision', *Nineteenth-Century Prose*, 38(1) (Spring 2011): 127–46). Hence, Headlam not only identified with Ruskin's argument in *Modern Painters* 3 that 'to see clearly is poetry, prophecy and religion – all in one' (Cook and Wedderburn, *Collected Works of Ruskin*, 5.333), but with Ruskin's insistence in *The Queen of the Air* (1869) that 'the body is only the soul made visible ... [and] ... the presence of life is asserted by characters in which the human sight takes pleasure' (19.358).
15. The word performative, of course, has many different uses regarding public performance and oration. We use it here in the same sense that Tracy Davis describes whereby performativity links the 'performance' on the stage to its multiple and conflicting effects outside of the theatre, in terms of public response, effects on moral taste, social acceptance and so on. Reflecting on the historiography of theatre scholarship, Davis notes that 'one of the most significant developments has been the broadening of focus from repertoire, production values and architecture to an inclusive view of performance beyond theatre buildings. ... [Performance scholars] now have the confidence to take on the debates arising from various disciplines and fields and contribute simultaneously to multiple ongoing controversies in theatre studies and elsewhere'. Davis and Holland, 'Introduction: The Performing Society', in *The Performing Century: Nineteenth-Century Theatre's History,* eds. Davis and Holland (Basingstoke: Palgrave, 2007), 3. This is made possible by the nature of performance as a repeated iteration of language (be it literary, visual or physical), which allowed for multiple meanings to be contained within one site of production.
16. C. Walsh, 'The Incarnation and the Christian Socialist Conscience in the Victorian Church of England', *The Journal of British Studies* 34(3) (1995): 351.

17. Douglas Ehninger, 'Introduction', in Richard Whately, *Elements of Rhetoric* (Carbondale, IL: Southern Illinois University Press, 1963 [1846]), xi.
18. John Henry Cardinal Newman, *An Essay in Aid of a Grammar of Assent* (Westminster: Christian Classics Inc., 1973 [1870]).
19. Jasper, *Rhetoric, Power and Community*, 115.
20. See Quintilian, *The Institutes of Oratory*, trans. H.E. Butler (Cambridge, MA: Harvard University Press, 1980).
21. Newman, *Grammar of Assent*, 159.
22. Many of these shifts and changes could also be said to be characterized by a reflexive concern for the limits of identity, whether as a group or a concept. For example, M.B. Reckitt argues that it was the economic recessions of the 1870s that first saw the concept of 'unemployment' being used extensively. Unemployment, as opposed to simple vagrancy, infers a performative aspect of the concept of employment that both identifies its boundaries (that is, the physical actions of those who are working and those who are not) and reaffirms its normalcy (that is, that one who is not working should be working; that to be unemployed is to be dispossessed of employment, rather than a separate act altogether). M.B. Reckitt, *Maurice to Temple: A Century of the Social Movement in the Church of England* (London: Faber, 1947).
23. Jasper, *Rhetoric, Power and Community*, 117.
24. Quoted in Donald Hole, *The Church and the Stage: the Early History of the Actor's Church Union* (London: Faith Press, 1934), 12.
25. Jonas Barish, *The Anti-Theatrical Prejudice* (London: University of California Press, 1981), 295–49.
26. Headlam, 'Some Darkened Christian Truths III', *Church Reformer*, 2(9) (1883): 1.
27. Anne Witchard, 'Bedraggled Ballerinas on a Bus Back to Bow: The "Fairy Business"', *19: Interdisciplinary Studies in the Long Nineteenth Century*, 13 (2011): February 5, 2013, http://19.bbk.ac.uk.
28. See Alexandra Carter, *Dance and Dancers in Victorian and Edwardian Music Hall Ballet* (London: Ashgate, 2005), 24–5. Such a view was not without foundation, of course: many young girls had grown up to become sex workers because it was the only work available to them once they were too old to dance. Many others, as a series of reports by Social Purity Alliance authors confirmed, had become tempted by older men making offers of money, gifts and status which should have been ignored. As Mrs Laura Ormiston Chant complained, when employed in the theatre or music hall, 'every attraction a woman possesses is pressed into the side that tends to evil and sorrow'. Quoted in Joseph Donohue, *Fantasies of Empire: The Empire Theatre of Varieties and the Licencing Controversy of 1894* (Iowa City: University of Iowa Press, 2005), 30.
29. Jane Pritchard, 'Collaborative Creations for the Alhambra and the Empire', *Dance Chronicle*, 24(1) (2001): 55–82. This was not lost on commentators: as Anne Witchard notes, 'the tension between the aestheticized identity of the ballet girl as she appeared on stage across the glare of the footlights and her accessible self shivering in the street outside was a crucial component of her undeniable erotic appeal' (Witchard, 'Bedraggled Ballerinas', 8). See also Deborah Jowett, *Time and the Dancing Image* (Berkeley: University of California Press, 1988), 44.
30. Quoted in D. Hole, *The Church and the Stage: the Early History of the Actor's Church Union* (London: Faith Press, 1934), 12.
31. For example, he frequently returned home from missions to Brussels and Paris having rescued Londoners from the white sex trade.

32. For further discussion, see Richard Foulkes, *Church and Stage in Victorian England* (Cambridge: Cambridge University Press, 1997), 169–77.

33. Headlam, 'The Stage', *Service of Humanity*, 31.

34. As he explained, 'my own enthusiasm for the stage is the result of my strong religious conviction'. Headlam, 'The Stage', 15.

35. Headlam, 'Some Darkened Christian Truths, III', 2.

36. Headlam, 'The Stage', 23.

37. For further analysis, see Torben Christensen, *The Divine Order: A Study in F.D. Maurice's Theology* (Leiden: E.J. Brill, 1973), 91–7.

38. Headlam, 'Applause', paper read to the Church and Stage Guild and reprinted in *Church Reformer*, 5(5) (May 1886): 111–13. See George Bernard Shaw's comment in his paper on 'Art as Fool's Paradise' that Headlam cared about acting life behind the stage – true Christian.

39. *Theory of Theatrical Dancing: Edited from Carlo Blasis's Code of Terpsichore, with the Original Plates* (London: Frederick Verinder, 1888), preface.

40. F.G. Bettany, *Stewart Headlam: a biography* (London: J. Murray, 1926), 207. Themes such as these had earlier been elaborated upon by the Revd E. Husband, who labelled himself a disciple of Headlam, in a paper presented to the Church and Stage Guild: 'True art is a heavenly thing', Husband argued, continuing: 'It is the gift of God. ... What has God made some men Actors for? ...He has made some men Actors, so that they may act. It is a gift, and a gift to be used for the instruction and amusement of mankind, not to be placed under a Calvinistic bushel or be buried in a puritan napkin. I have heard many sermons in my life, but some of the noblest lessons I have ever been taught have been from the stage ...'. Revd E. Husband, 'A Sermon', paper presented to the Church and Stage Guild and reprinted in *Church Reformer*, 4(6) (1885): 137.

41. Headlam, *The Laws of Eternal Life* (London: Frederick Verinder, 1888), 51.

42. Headlam, 'The Stage', 27.

43. Headlam, 'Review of the Cenci', *Church Reformer*, 5(6) (1886): 133–4. This was a review of a private performance (set to stage by the Shelley Society) since it was refused licence by the Lord Chamberlain.

44. J. Orens, *Stewart Headlam's Radical Anglicanism: The Mass, the Masses and the Music Hall* (Chicago: University of Illinois Press, 2003), 63.

45. The Church and Stage Guild facilitated the teaching of elocution to Churchmen by actors; more than this, Headlam was insistent on the importance of public processions, usually swathed with colour and grandeur. Headlam spoke at Hyde Park Corner, in Secularist Lecture Halls, in pubs, in the foyer of Drury Lane theatre and to workers in their workplaces. So well regarded was his commitment to radicalism that he was invited to preside over the funeral and lead the 200,000-strong procession for the socialist martyr, Arthur Linnel, who died as a result of injuries inflicted by police during the Bloody Sunday protests of 1887.

46. Headlam, 'Charles Bradlaugh', *The Church Reformer* (March 1891), 51–2.

47. Headlam, 'Charles Bradlaugh', 51.

48. Headlam, 'Charles Bradlaugh', 52.

49. Atherton, J. 'Social Christianity in Context', *Social Christianity: A Reader*, ed. J. Atherton (London: SPCK, 1994), 17.

50. *National Reformer*, 24 December 1882, 453–4. It is worth noting that, typically, 'secularists' were less rampant atheists, and generally agnostic. Hence Headlam could comment that the 'Secularists have, in fact, absorbed some of the best Christian Truths which the Churches have been ignoring'. Headlam, *The Sure*

Foundation: An Address Given before the Guild of St Matthew at the Annual Meeting, 1883 (London: Frederick Verinder, 1883), 10. One can understand, however, the misgivings his superiors may have had when he asked 'how much nearer to the Kingdom of Heaven are these men in the Hall of Science than the followers of Moody and Sankey', cited in Bettany, *Stewart Headlam*, 50.

51. Paul de Man, *Aesthetic Ideology* (Minneapolis: University of Minnesota Press, 1996).
52. Headlam, 'The Guild of St. Matthew: An Appeal to Churchmen', *The Church Reformer* (November 1890), 244.
53. Headlam, 'Charles Bradlaugh', 52.
54. '[S]ome of you may be inclined to say that the Church itself is the one and great Society to which you belong, and that you are not disposed to concern yourselves with other societies which, whatever may be their object, if they are composed of true and loyal Churchmen, can only be doing work which the Church itself is bound to do; and this is indeed quite true' (Headlam, 'The Guild of St. Matthew', 243).
55. Headlam, 'The Guild of St. Matthew', 243.

Works cited

Atherton, J. 'Social Christianity in Context', in J. Atherton (ed.), *Social Christianity: A Reader*. London: SPCK, 1994, 10–49.

Atwood, Sara. 'The Soul of the Eye: Ruskin, Darwin, and the Nature of Vision', *Nineteenth-Century Prose*, 38(1) (Spring 2011): 127–46.

Barish, Jonas. *The Anti-Theatrical Prejudice*. London: University of California Press, 1981.

Barth, Karl. *Community, State and Church: Three Essays*. Garden City: Doubleday & Co., 1960.

Bettany, F.G. *Stewart Headlam: a Biography*. London: J. Murray, 1926.

Bright, Michael. 'The Poetry of Art', *Journal of the History of Ideas*, 46(2) (1985): 259–77.

Brown, Wendy. *Edgework: Critical Essays on Knowledge and Politics*. Oxford: Princeton University Press, 2005.

Carter, Alexandra. *Dance and Dancers in Victorian and Edwardian Music Hall Ballet*. London: Ashgate, 2005.

Church Reformer, 5(6) (1886): 133–4.

Cockram, Gillian. *Ruskin and Social Reform: Ethics and Economics in the Victorian Age*. London: Tauris Academic, 2007.

Cook, E.T. and Alexander Wedderburn (eds). *The Works of Ruskin: Library Edition*. London: George Allen, 1903–12.

d'A Jones, Peter. *The Christian Socialist Revival, 1877–1914: Religion, Class and Social Conscience in late-Victorian England*. London: Oxford University Press, 1968.

Davis, Tracy and Peter Holland (eds). *The Performing Century: Nineteenth-Century Theatre's History*. Basingstoke: Palgrave, 2007.

de Man, Paul. *Aesthetic Ideology*. Minneapolis: University of Minnesota Press, 1996.

Donohue, Joseph. *Fantasies of Empire: The Empire Theatre of Varieties and the Licencing Controversy of 1894*. Iowa City: University of Iowa Press, 2005.

Ehninger, Douglas. 'Introduction', in Richard Whately. *Elements of Rhetoric*. Carbondale: Southern Illinois University Press, 1963 [1846].

Foulkes, Richard. *Church and Stage in Victorian England*. Cambridge: Cambridge University Press, 1997.

Harris, Jose. 'Ruskin and Social Reform', in Dinah Birch (ed.), *Ruskin and the Dawn of the Modern*. Oxford: Clarendon, 1999, 7–33.

Headlam, Stewart Duckworth. 'Review of the Cenci', *Church Reformer*, 5(6) (1886): 133–4.

———. 'Applause', reprinted in *Church Reformer*, 5(5) (1886): 111–13.

———. 'Charles Bradlaugh', *The Church Reformer*, 10(3) (1891): 51–2.

———. 'Some Darkened Christian Truths III', *Church Reformer*, 2(9) (1883): 1–2.

———. 'The Guild of St. Matthew: An Appeal to Churchmen', *The Church Reformer*, 9(11) (1890): 243–8.

———. 'The Stage', sermon preached at St Michael's, North Kensington, 7 August 1881, printed in Headlam (ed.), *Service of Humanity, and Other Sermons*. London: J. Hodges, 22–3.

———. *The Function of the Stage: A Lecture*. London: Frederick Verinder, 1889.

———. *The Laws of Eternal Life*. London: Frederick Verinder, 1888.

———. *The Sure Foundation: An Address Given before the Guild of St Matthew at the Annual Meeting, 1883*. London: Frederick Verinder, 1883.

———. *Theory of Theatrical Dancing: Edited from Carlo Blasis's Code of Terpsichore, with the Original Plates*. London: Frederick Verinder, 1888.

Hole, Donald. *The Church and the Stage: the Early History of the Actor's Church Union*. London: Faith Press, 1934.

Husband, Revd E. 'A Sermon', paper presented to the Church and Stage Guild and reprinted in *Church Reformer*, 4(6) (1885): 137.

Inglis, K.S. *Churches and the Working Classes in Victorian England*. London: Routledge & Kegan Paul, 1963.

Jameson, Frederick. 'Marx's Purloined Letter', in Michael Sprinkler (ed.), *Ghostly Demarcations: A Symposium on Jacques Derrida's Spectres of Marx*. London: Verso, 1999, 26–67.

Jasper, David. *Rhetoric, Power and Community*. Basingstoke: Palgrave, 2003.

Jowett, Deborah. *Time and the Dancing Image*. Berkeley: University of California Press, 1988.

Kirkpatrick, Frank G. *The Ethics of Community*. Oxford: Blackwell, 2001.

Knight, F. *The Nineteenth-Century Church and English Society*. Cambridge: Cambridge University Press, 1998.

Lefebvre, Henri. *The Production of Space*. Oxford: Blackwell, 1991.

National Reformer (December 1882): 453–4.

Newman, John Henry Cardinal. *An Essay in Aid of a Grammar of Assent*. Westminster: Christian Classics Inc., 1973 [1870].

Orens, J. *Stewart Headlam's Radical Anglicanism: The Mass, the Masses and the Music Hall*. Chicago: University of Illinois Press, 2003.

Pritchard, Jane. 'Collaborative Creations for the Alhambra and the Empire', *Dance Chronicle*, 24(1) (2001): 55–82.

Quintilian, *The Institutes of Oratory*, trans. H.E. Butler. Cambridge, MA: Harvard University Press, 1980.

Reckitt, M.B. *Maurice to Temple: A Century of the Social Movement in the Church of England*. London: Faber, 1947.

Rorty, Richard. *Contingency, Irony and Solidarity*. Cambridge: Cambridge University Press, 1989.

Torben, Christensen. *The Divine Order: A Study in F.D. Maurice's Theology*. Leiden: E.J. Brill, 1973.

Walsh, C. 'The Incarnation and the Christian Socialist Conscience in the Victorian Church of England', *The Journal of British Studies*, 34(3) (1995): 351–74.

Witchard, Anne. 'Bedraggled Ballerinas on a Bus Back to Bow: The "Fairy Business"', *19: Interdisciplinary Studies in the Long Nineteenth Century*, 13 (2011). Last accessed February 5, 2013. http://19.bbk.ac.uk.

Yeandle, Peter. 'Art, Ethics, Pleasure: The Influence of John Ruskin on the Reverend Stewart Duckworth Headlam', *Nineteenth-Century Prose*, 38(2) (2011): 109–32.

———. 'John Ruskin and the Christian Socialist Conscience', *Ruskin Review and Bulletin*, 8(2) (2012).

———. 'Christian Socialism on the Stage? Henry Arthur Jones's *Wealth* and the Dramatisation of Ruskinian Political Economy', in Keith Hanley and Brian Maidment (eds), *Persistent Ruskin: Studies in Influence, Assimilation and Affect*. Aldershot: Ashgate, 2013. 93–104.

5
The Intolerable, Intimate Public of Contemporary American Street Preaching

Joshua Edelman

It is hard to imagine an act more offensive to the Habermasian conception of the public sphere as a place of open, egalitarian, and democratic dialogue than street preaching. The act of shouting out a religiously divisive message without invitation, nor differentiation, nor concern for its effect, nor effort to mould the means of speech to the context of speaking represents no sort of public hail that Jürgen Habermas would recognize. Street preaching is not part of a dialogue between (potential) equals who choose to participate in debate; instead, one speaker rudely takes up a privileged position in a monologic effort to convince a (generally unwilling) audience of the truth and power of his religious message by means of performance.[1] If we were, charitably, to call this the putting forward of an argument, that argument would have to be seen as a directly sectarian, anti-rationalist, and exclusionary one. There is no public dialogue here.[2]

Nor can the social grouping created by street preaching fit into Michael Warner's notion of a public (or counterpublic).[3] It is not a grouping based on the notions of shared identity and the potential inclusion of strangers. There is at least a minimal similarity between the street preacher's audience and Warner's definition of a public, no matter how temporary: both are relationships amongst strangers created by an address that is both targeted at those persons assembled and yet impersonally addressed, and both organize themselves (to the extent that they are organized) around the simple fact of attention.[4] The problem comes from the last of Warner's criteria: that a public must act through its circulation of discourse, and that such action is a form of poetic world-making. If this were to hold for the public of street preaching, what would it imply about the nature the world? A public is characterized by the address that gives rise to it;[5] in street preaching's case, that characterization is not just of sinfulness, but of ignorance of that sinful nature. This is an important distinction. Much Christian preaching hails its public as sinful; the fallenness of humanity and its need for redemption is a central point of Christian doctrine. But street preaching does more than this. It does not draw its audience's *attention* to its need for redemption.

Rather, it casts them as lacking a basic understanding of their own human nature. Of course, no reasonable person would think of themselves as ignorant in this way, or could easily be persuaded to do so. Street preachers thus put their audience in a far more difficult position than church preachers do. It is not that this position is intoler*ant*; that is, is does not (necessarily) reject the egalitarian norms of democratic discourse. Rather, it is intoler*able*, hailing its public as ignorant and its speaker as wise in a way that is both infuriating and unsustainable. The public that street preaching builds is thus an 'intolerable public' – one of which no reasonable person could accept being a part. It is not possible to willingly and consciously accept one's self as ignorant in this manner.

This is what keeps the street preacher's audience from becoming a proper counterpublic. Warner argues, 'Addressees are socially marked by their participation in this kind of discourse [i.e., the constituting address of a counterpublic]. Ordinary people are presumed to not want to be mistaken for the kind of person who would participate in this kind of talk or be present in this kind of scene'.[6] The public of street preaching, however, never chose to receive this address, and cannot easily or speedily evade it.

This underlines the assumption of voluntarism inherent in the Habermasian public sphere that Warner continues through his notion of a public. Neither can fairly account for the ways that we can be seized by social groupings without our will or consent. The street preaching example is useful in that it provides a clear case of such an unwilling public. It makes manifest the ways in which we can be co-opted into publics we did not choose and which characterize us against our will. This does not make them any less acts of poetic world-making. In the more traditional language of performance studies, I know of no other form where the audience so often and so vociferously *rejects* the performer's hail of them. This rejection is, I would argue, structurally necessary to the performance of street preaching, at least in the American evangelical Christian mode that is the focus of my examples here. If the public were not to be depicted as ignorant sinners, there would be no need to preach to them. And, of course, no one will assent to such a depiction. In fact, an audience which actively rejects that depiction is seen as a mark of a successful preacher. Street preaching, then, must *not* establish a Habermasian public sphere or a Warnerian welcoming public if it is to do its job. For the same reason, it cannot adopt the playful, jesterly posture associated with carnival and aesthetic performance. It requires public rejection to function. Neither the discursive public sphere nor the carnival can be so clearly and definitively rejected.

It is not the mere existence of American street preaching that offers a challenge to Warner's idea of the construction of a public, as well as to Habermas's notion of the public sphere. Failed publics and illegitimate public speech say little about their successful cousins. Rather, it is the *success* of street preaching in creating a potent and affective public, which, even if temporary and occasional, can speak with a significant voice to the role of religion in American society. In particular, the community created by street preaching can be surprisingly intimate, building microsocial bonds between strangers, even if those bonds are not on a basis of essential camaraderie and shared commitment to a discourse. This shows us one example of the role religion can play in building up forms of public affect and discourse in opposition to the ways that Habermas and Warner suggest. However, the example also offers an opportunity to look critically at the ways in which both free association and coercion can have their roles in creating a sense of publicness. It is tempting, at times, to see all publics and public spheres as unalloyed *goods,* spaces for healthy communality and democratic negotiation. But publics can be coercive as well as constructive. Much of Habermas's exclusion of religion from the public sphere was an attempt to avoid divisions that cannot be reasonably overcome. When we remove that exclusion, perhaps we should not be too sanguine about the results. But nor should we blind ourselves unnecessarily to the potency of the communal affect that can be created by this anti-discursive form of social poesis.

The practice of street preaching that I am considering here is a minor but significant contemporary religious practice, one that derives largely from the history of American evangelical Christianity and is now organized through informal and online channels which themselves have built up a form of community. As a first example, let us first take the preacher Jesse Morrell. While I cannot claim Morrell as representative of all street preachers, he does have a following through his own Open Air Outreach website, his membership in the Southeast Open Air Preachers Association (SOAPA), and the numerous videos of his work posted on YouTube. While these clips are not hugely popular (they have a few thousand views each), they serve as a model for others who wish to follow in his footsteps.

One relatively prominent video shows him preaching to students on a college campus.[7] He wears a grey three-piece suit and tie and carries both a small bible and a five-foot-tall black-and-yellow sign that reads, 'Forsake all your sin and follow the Lord Jesus Christ'. The spectacle draws a small crowd, and he stands above them behind stone pillars and a metal fence. The sign and bible are used as barriers. Even when he takes their questions, he does little to engage with them directly or address their concerns. His sign, his costume, and his vocal delivery separate him out hugely from his audience, and his language (a combination of implorings and awkward confessions about his past sinful life delivered in a slow, lilting cadence) do nothing to lessen this distance. In none of his videos does he seem to convince – or even engage directly with – a single listener.

In truth, what does he think he's accomplishing? Let me stipulate that Morrell is not insane. His website and videos required work: supplies, setup, a cameraman, editing, and so on. The music and transitions he adds to his videos are not sophisticated, but they are not childish. This is a serious documentation of a thought-out piece of work. Why does he do this, and why is he so proud of it that he chooses to present himself online (to a much larger public) in this way?

Like other public discourses, street preaching functions as a form of world-making (or poesis, in Warner's terms). The performance asserts certain truths about the world: that sinners are condemned to an eternity in hell unless they repent, turn from their evil ways and towards Christ. Further, it casts Morrell as the knowledgeable saved and the audience as the ignorant damned. This is a simple and important message that must be shared, and Morrell therefore takes up the obligation to spread it, creating a world in which the reality of sin and repentance is inescapable.

Perhaps the relevant question, then, is why more of Morrell's fellow Evangelical Christians do not join him. There are tens of millions of Evangelicals in America, many of whom passionately share the core of Morrell's beliefs on the need to reach out to the unsaved, even if they differ in theological details. Street preaching, however, remains a very rare method to accomplish this. Far more common is evangelism based in service – shelters, clinics, soup kitchens, and the like. Gina Welch's *In the Land of Believers* chronicles her time doing missionary work in Alaska with Jerry Falwell's Thomas Road Baptist Church; while they proudly claimed over a hundred conversions from the trip, never once did they preach on the streets to an uninvited public.[8] Even those who do engage in street preaching often see it as a means to prompt more private conversations in which the real work of evangelism can be done. The closest thing to street preaching recommended by the North American Mission Board of the Southern Baptist Convention is called 'Prayer Walking'. It involves teams from churches walking through neighbourhoods to pray, silently, for all those who live in them. The evangelical imperative is fulfilled through the occasional one-to-one conversations initiated by members of the public, in which they will be handed a prayer card inviting them to visit the church.[9]

Many Christians object to street preaching on soteriological grounds; theologically, they do not believe that salvation is akin to a piece of knowledge that can be passed from a person who has it to one who does not. Others disagree, seeing no contradiction between the imperative to preach the Gospel in public and the Holy Spirit's control of the impulse to conversion. These debates are beyond this book's remit, of course. But there are two non-theological objections that many Christians have to street preaching which deserve attention. Both are artefacts of the modernity that Habermas associates with the development of print culture and the notion of the public sphere. They are not, thus, either novel or specific to a certain conception of Christian theology and are ones that could be leveled against other examples of religious performance in a modern public sphere.

The first objection is that street preaching is *awkward*. Publicly drawing attention to another person's failings is a violation of courtesy, especially when that person is a stranger. When it is done outside of a practice in which a certain level of criticism is formalized and expected (such as a political debate or a rap battle), those who point out others' failings in public appear to be unable to negotiate the sort of generally accepted social practices (*artes de faire,* per de Certeau) that make mundane sociality possible.[10] Street preachers such as Morrell seem to fall into this category, even if their social skills are much greater in other contexts.[11]

It is not just criticism that is awkward in public, but the public discussion of matters considered too personal for public discussion. Sexuality is the most obvious case, but what makes it difficult to discuss is not a taboo but its relationship to passionate emotion. It is not just that these emotions are not necessarily shared; rather, Habermasian public discourse lacks the language to speak about affect as a topic of communal concern, a fact that motivates much of Ann Cvetkovich's work.[12] Public discussions of all private passions share this difficulty, including religious passions.[13] In his chapter in this volume, Simon du Toit discusses the puritan effort to combat just this awkwardness through the politicizing of religious interiority—that is, in making religious commitment and faith an issue of public concern and not merely private interest.

In the context of contemporary, post-puritan, diverse America, this effort has been both effective and fraught. It has led to a public détente in which there is both a high importance placed on religiosity and signs of inner religious conviction (in candidates running for political office, for instance) and a disinclination towards the public discussion of theological differences between specific religions. While religiosity is valued, it is seen as private. The American notion of religious freedom as a phenomenon of the private sphere is therefore more than just a separation between church and state. It has become what de Tocqueville viewed as a religious marketplace geared to the consumer. Different denominations can make their case, but, ultimately, the individual's right to decide their religious allegiance is sacrosanct. Street preaching pushes too hard against this right by publicly accusing people of making an incorrect religious choice. Such correction is possible in the safety of the counterpublic community of a formal church environment, but not in the public sphere itself.[14] Street preaching is therefore rude, even offensive. It becomes what Slavoj Žižek, in *The Puppet and the Dwarf,* calls 'a threat to culture'.[15] And uncultured, rude troublemakers rarely make welcome neighbors.

This leads to the second objection: street preaching is *ineffective.* In the marketplace of belief, as in the marketplace of commodities, the undesired product has no value. Any form of evangelism that does not lead to more converts, then, is a waste of time. By this logic, contemporary street preaching is quite pointless. Clearly, an argument for spiritual conversion made by a loud stranger on a street corner which establishes little or no connection to its audience is in fact no argument at all, all the more so when that stranger's words are either incomprehensible or banal and he seems incapable of normal sociality.

The revivalist giants of previous centuries of public preaching spoke outside partially because they could find no large enough space to hold everyone who wanted to hear them, often on short notice. The attraction was the magnetism of the performance, the thrill of the event, and the solidarity of the large crowd. But the magnetism, thrill, and crowd have all gone, and without them, it is hard to see why a hearer would be led to conversion through street preaching.

Preachers such as Morrell have long had answers to both these objections. The rudeness objection is answered by an appeal to the Biblical example and Christian history. Moses, Joshua, Ezra, Nehemiah, Jesus himself, and, of course, Paul are all cited as models and justifications for the contemporary street preacher.[16] They, too, were seen as rudely upsetting the social conventions of their times. When that list is extended to the heroes of Protestantism such as Knox, Wycliffe, Wesley, and Whitefield, an annoyed or even hostile response to preaching is almost as deeply encoded as the message and the method of delivering it. In this tradition, preachers *ought* to be rude troublemakers; if preaching does not make trouble, it is not being done properly. In the words of Charles Spurgeon, one of the leading nineteenth-century English preachers:

> I am somewhat pleased when I occasionally hear of a brother being locked up by the police, for it does him good, and it does the people good, also. It is a fine sight to see the minister of the Gospel marched off by the servant of the law![17]

Morrell, too, proudly features online videos of occasions when he has been confronted by the police.[18] He chooses to present himself online through videos that show his audience ignoring him, jeering at him, interrupting him, and even spitting on him. It is in his interest to portray himself as the target of mockery and scorn; after all, look at what happened to Paul.

That expectation of hostility leads to the second objection – that street preaching is ineffective. And this is where questions of the nature of the public created by street preaching come into focus. Not only do street preachers expect hostility from their audiences; they actively require it as justification for their work. The nineteenth-century revivalist preachers, who found large, engaged, and respectful crowds in the streets and in tents, nonetheless portrayed themselves as soldiers doing battle with a social enemy. Their performances defined themselves as more socially offensive than they actually were. But why would a social practice choose an offended audience for itself?

I would argue that it is because of the particular way in which the act of street preaching hails its public. To the street preacher, his public is *deficient* in a fundamental way – they are unable to see their own, sinful nature. This sinfulness does not simply infect a separable private sphere of human life that could be called religious or spiritual. Rather, it is virulent, consuming the whole person, including their sense of judgment. The term for this in the Protestant theological tradition is 'total depravity', deriving from the Augustinian concept of original sin; it claims that there is no aspect of a person or society which is untouched by humanity's essentially sinful nature. Any preacher's audience is necessarily made up of such people.

The public's apparent hostility to the Christian message is thus explicable and dismissible. Therefore, guides for street preachers often counsel *against* measuring success by overt conversions. One of the most prominent street preaching websites for the American audience is called Living Waters; it publishes advice and tools for street preachers (a website, books, tracts, videos, and so on), and runs an online training programme called the School for Biblical Evangelism.[19] One of the group's most popular products is an 'Evidence Bible' – an edited version of the KJV with commentary and guidance for missionaries by Ray Comfort, which is excerpted on its website.[20] One page advises preachers to 'Aim for Repentance Rather than a Decision':

> The Bible tells us that as we sow the good seed of the gospel, one sows and another reaps. If you faithfully sow the seed, someone will reap. If you reap, it is because someone has sown in the past, but it is God who causes the seed to grow.[21]

So conversion takes the fullness of time and the grace of God, and a street preacher should not expect immediate results. But the site goes farther, citing 2 Timothy 2:25–6, which defines the goal of Christian 'gentle instruction' to sinners as the 'hope that God will grant them repentance leading them to a *knowledge* of the truth, and that they will *come to their senses* and escape from the trap of the devil' (NIV, my italics). The website's reading of this passage takes the language of entrapment and ignorance very seriously:

> Scripture tells us that sinners are blind. They cannot see. What would you think if I were to stomp up to a blind man who had just stumbled, and say, 'Watch where you're going, blind man!'? Such an attitude is completely unreasonable.[22]

Taken together, these passages clearly show that it is Comfort's view that the purpose of street preaching is *not* to offer the gift of sight. That is beyond human power. Rather, it is to hold up a picture of salvation in front of the blind. Of course, this picture cannot be accepted, because it cannot be seen. But the picture will be so self-evident once it *is* seen, and so crucially important, that the preacher is compelled to hold it up anyway. This is only possible if the preacher himself is free of this curse of blindness.[23] To justify his work, a street preacher *must* preach to a blind and unaccepting public. Otherwise they would already be saved and he would have no reason to preach to them.

No sane audience member would choose to place themselves in this blind, stumbling role. It is not how we rightly expect to be treated by those who wish to speak to us in public. Habermasian coffeehouses were places of *willing* debate; those who entered them did so because they wished to be part of a public discussion on the terms on offer, which were based on a predictable equality of all participants. Warner's publics may not be as symmetrical, but they still require active assent from those involved in them.[24] So the responsibility falls to the preacher to *cast* his public in that way against their own will. And here is where the idea that the public is deficient morphs into the more potent idea that the preacher's public is deviant.

It thus becomes important for the preacher to maximize the distance between himself and his audience. Recall how Morrell chose to set himself up in a space physically distant and separated from his audience by a fence, colonnade, and enormous sign. This is a pattern one can observe in many photographs of contemporary street preachers; they often cloak themselves in signs and platforms that come physically between them and their audience. Compared to the unobtrusive way most pop singers use microphones, for example, street preachers tend to hide behind bulky amplification systems.

But the distance is not just physical; in his preaching, Morrell uses as a case study of sin his own former unsaved life as 'a drug dealer street fighter gangster rapper in the rough streets of Connecticut'. He is casting his audience, sinners as he was, as not only spiritually deviant, but culturally deviant, too. This is a very old pattern: missionaries have long drawn a connection between the natives' need for salvation and their need for European culture and civilization.[25] Of course, the language of this message has to be couched differently today, but it is still present in the idea of a deviant public on which this kind of street preaching relies.

The next pair of examples brings this tension to the surface in a particularly lucid and uncomfortable way. They come from what appears to be the most prominent media outlet for today's evangelical street preachers, The Way of the Master.[26] The ministry is run by anti-evolution campaigner Ray Comfort and former teen heartthrob Kirk Cameron, who is probably best known to American audiences for his role in the 1980s sitcom *Growing Pains*. The Way of the Master produces a weekly television show for broadcast on Christian networks, a radio programme, and sells DVDs and associated tools for the aspiring street preacher. Its website is slick, if over-produced: it features selections from the ministry's catalogue, helpful tips and techniques, and video clips from the television programme. These clips show Cameron and Comfort on the street preaching to the unsaved, generally through tightly controlled discussions with individuals or small groups that John

Fletcher calls 'quasi-Socratic'.[27] As befits the medium, they are more highly produced than Morrell's YouTube efforts. Though the camera cannot always resist Cameron's face, it generally focuses more on the preachee than the preacher, unlike the camera following Morrell.

The targets the site chooses to highlight are telling. One clip, titled 'Kirk witnesses to hardened gang members at Santa Monica', characterizes Cameron's audience as deviant – spiritually, of course, but also socially, intellectually, racially, and even sartorially. Shot on the Santa Monica beach, it shows Cameron speaking with three shirtless men, two in sunglasses and one heavily tattooed. 'We're from the ghetto', they announce at the top, and Cameron attempts (badly) to translate the phrase 'the Ten Commandments' into Spanish. The clip is edited with a backing track of bouncy, synthesized, vaguely Latin music evoking early 1980s pop. The site also includes interviews with a pink-haired girl and a Christian transvestite. Cameron, of course, never shares their deviant clothing or regionally-marked accents.

The social gap is never as clearly marked as in a clip described on the website as 'one of our favorites'. Cameron's target is a black New York man who goes by the name of P-Nasty. He is introduced in a montage of a New York street scene smoking a cigar, grinning, flashing a hand sign, and wearing a puffy leather jacket, baseball cap, and gold chain. He is being interviewed (apparently in front of a Broadway theatre) by Ray Comfort. He is a deeply charming and human character, and plays with meaning and ambiguity in answering Comfort's rigidly scripted questions through what Henry Louis Gates might call 'signifyin(g)'.[28] Comfort asks him, for instance, if he had ever lied. When P-Nasty admits he has, Comfort asks, 'What does that make you?' 'A human being', he replies, repeatedly resisting Comfort's effort to get him to label himself a liar. Comfort does have obvious affection for P-Nasty and is preaching with his benefit in mind, but he cannot engage with his interviewee's playfulness.

And because of that refusal to play, this interaction is not that of a dialogue between equals but rather the imposition of a hegemonic script on a subaltern subject who struggles to resist it.[29] For all his queer playfulness, the best P-Nasty can do is to neutralize it, making for a friendly but basically ineffective encounter on both sides. No one really comes away changed, and there is no ludic space for interaction between them. Each sees the other as irreparably blind. Comfort cannot tolerate P-Nasty's deviance, and P-Nasty cannot tolerate being the kind of public that Comfort insists on making him into.

This quality of playless ignorance, I argue, is the characterization that contemporary American street preaching imposes on the public it addresses.[30] And like P-Nasty, I find it both intolerable and remarkably difficult to escape from. When confronted with a street preacher, I *am* placed into his ignorant public by his performative action and affectively resent the fact as intuitively unjust.

But this is not, of course, the only way that street preaching can work. The practice also contains within it the seeds of a different sort of public discourse, one that is no less religious or imposed but far more intimate.

To explain how this is possible, we need to begin by noting that it is essential to both Warner's and Habermas's publics that its members are, to a certain degree, depersonalized; they are being addressed not as a particular individual, but as the occupier of a position already created by the public-making discourse. The public sphere is defined as a relationship between strangers rather than between friends or enemies. In addressing a public, one necessarily addresses (potentially) everyone and no one in particular. This is what allows Jon Foley Sherman, in his discussion of intimate yet public performance art, to refer to its audience as a 'micropublic', rather than a personal encounter with the Levinasian Face.[31] Even if audience members are being spoken to (or physically touched) one at a time, they are being attended to as replaceable members of a public, not as individuals.[32]

David Wittenberg tests the limits of this necessary generality by pushing smartly on the spatial metaphor inherent in terms like 'public sphere', 'public square', and so on. While they often are taken to denote a network of ideas and argument, their language is one of the sharing of a common physical space, and much of their power comes from this invocation of various spaces of public gathering (*agora*, forum, marketplace, town square, et cetera.) If these terms are taken to denote a space, he argues, a speaker may need to enter into that space in order to address a public or participate in one. We enter a space not as interchangeable beings but as embodied, particular individuals. We need to 'go out' into public in order to participate in it, in Wittenberg's terms, and in so doing we put ourselves forward as individuals and must throw off the safety of a wholly depersonalized public discourse. This is the trap, Wittenberg argues, that Kierkegaard fell into when he appeared in public as an individual and not a mere voice.[33] His arguments had been powerful and provocative when disembodied, but his personal appearance established a new form of discourse that did not match them and thus ruptured the public discourse he had established.[34]

What Kierkegaard could not endure was the exposure of himself as an embodied individual to the scrutiny of the public gaze. The danger and power of this intimate exposure, though, is the driving force behind much of contemporary performance's interest in identity and the performing body. And so, I would suggest, a performance studies approach can help us explain how a street preacher can make *use of* his own bodily occupation of space in the public sphere to evoke a powerful intimacy, one that is every bit as imposed and rude as the examples we have seen but far more effective.

As I have argued, the public is cast so negatively that the *only way* it could become tolerable is if the preacher takes that public role on himself. Morrell's preaching, like Cameron and Comfort's, is based on the assumption of a fundamental difference in knowledge between them and those they preach to. But this assumption is not necessary, practically or theologically. Per Rancière, the teacher need not know more than the student to be an effective instructor.[35] The Christian doctrine of original sin insists that *all* human beings are sinners, including those who have been saved. And so, when the preacher goes out in public to exhort the blind public, he may also accept that that he is exhorting himself. The embodied nature of performance facilitates this; by physically taking up a vulnerable position within the public square and subjecting himself to the scrutiny of the public, he can achieve an intimacy that more formal, discursive forms of public discourse cannot. Doing this requires him not to *place* controversial arguments and ideas forward that a necessarily impersonal public can take up, but to *confront us himself* as a brother human being, not as the bearer of an argument.[36] That taking-up is an act of generosity and love that those who see it have little choice but to accept. This forced intimacy is rude and undemocratic; it is not based on the co-participation of potential equals. But this is a trait it shares with much contemporary performance art and one that is in no way a disqualification for the building of a public.

An example of the intimacy of this sort of vulnerable preaching may help illustrate this point. This case is, in my view, the single most effective piece of street preaching that I have uncovered. The preacher is named Patrick Ersig. He is a large man with a bushy red beard and a ponytail, and he wears a T-shirt, cargo shorts and glasses. In his online videos, he walks around Cass Park in central Detroit with no amplification save for his own cupped hand. He has no props or objects separating himself from his audience: none of Morrell's signs, books, or barricades. He paces about the park, screaming and waving his hand in the air, his voice cracking and straining. It seems that he is trying to convince himself as much as anyone else, and that makes for a compelling performance. Slowly, and with the occasional 'amen', he preaches:

> There's hope! There is hope! The devil's been lying to somebody here today! He's been telling them there's no hope. That there's no hope for you. That you're done with. But I'm here to tell you that there is hope. There is hope in the resurrection power of Jesus Christ. That devil is a liar! That devil is a liar! And I'm sick of him lying to people![37]

He is not successful in changing the theological views of any of his spectators in this clip and I cannot imagine that he ever would be. He gives no one else a chance to speak and ignores codes of quotidian social practice. He falls into the same trap of social awkwardness that Morrell did. He has no invitation from his audience to preach. He is not establishing a public that I would ever choose to be a part of, and yet in that he has already placed me there, it does not strike me as a place from which I must quickly flee.

This is only possible because Ersig places no boundaries between his audience and himself, whether physical or doctrinal. He dresses like his audience and moves among them, and seems to need the hope every bit as much as we do. His opponent is not sinners he seeks to convince but an (external) lying devil. Unlike Morrell, he does not preach against cultural practices (such as rap or homosexuality). Unlike Comfort, he is not presenting a logical argument as part of a theological debate. Instead, he offers a message of comfort, without offering a space to refuse it. Implicit in his call is that this hope is *necessary*, and this is an idea that is as socially awkward for him to express as it is for his audience to recognize (as we must) as true.

This joint awkwardness creates a curious sort of public intimacy. It is not based on an argument he makes or a relationship that I as audience member have with him; neither of these exists. Rather, his action presents me with a powerfully felt, abstract connection between all people as such (in this case, our need for hope). This resembles what anthropologist Victor Turner called *communitas,* an antihierarchical feeling of group solidarity, which he argued could arise from group status-transforming events such as pilgrimages and rites of passage and serve as the emotional undergirding of more stratified social orders.[38] Here, however, the feeling is imposed by a single (unauthorized) performer, rather than welling up from the actions of the group, and comes as an unexpected and unwelcome irruption into accepted public discourse, rather than an expected and valorized punctuation to it. Ersig's poetic construction of a public, then, represents a form of *communitas* stripped of all social acceptance or standing.

In watching the video of Ersig's work, I see myself as the counterpoint to Warner's example of the balletgoer who falls asleep during the performance but nevertheless counts as part of its public because he chose to come there, even if he does not attend to the dance.[39] I attend to Ersig's performance even if I did not choose to hear it because, compellingly, it *casts me,* it forces me to be a character in its dramatic narrative. Now, I can reject that characterization; indeed, I *must* reject it if I wish to stay a stranger to him and his church. But my rejection of it does not erase the intimacy he has achieved, or the way that it has placed me as part of the public of people in need of hope. This 'imposed intimacy' is a particular contribution that the public performance of religious action can make to our understanding of the public sphere; without either its religious or perfomative aspects, this intimacy would not be possible.

Allowing myself to go out in public means making myself vulnerable to being placed into publics that I do not like, accept, understand, or tolerate, or one that is antithetical to my social expectations of rational public discourse. Most often, street preachers make use of this vulnerability to characterize me as part of a public of which I cannot tolerate being a member. Yet Ersig, by embracing Kierkegaard's fate and taking on the burden of the public display of his own deviancy, forces me – and all those around me – into a public we can neither accept nor ignore. The intimacy he imposes on me and my neighbours cannot but shape my position in the public sphere, even against my will. Its effectiveness is not conditioned on my acceptance or agreement. This suggests that the public sphere that shapes our politics is one that can be performed as well as debated. We will need to develop a way of talking about the justice of such performances that does not either misconstrue them as arguments or deny their potency in imposing a powerful idea and affect of public life.

Notes

1. I use the masculine pronoun here and throughout in that I have found essentially no examples of contemporary female street preachers in my research. I will use the term 'audience' for those who listen to the preacher (or do not) to highlight the perfomative nature of the activity.
2. For Habermas's most current thinking about religion in the public sphere, see Jürgen Habermas, 'Religion in the Public Sphere', *European Journal of Philosophy*, 14(1) (2006). and Jürgen Habermas, 'Why we need a radical redefinition of secularism', in Eduardo Mendieta and Jonathan VanAntwerpen (eds), *The Power of Religion in the Public Sphere* (New York: Columbia University Press, 2011).
3. See, primarily, Michael Warner, *Publics and Counterpublics* (New York: Zone Books, 2005).
4. Warner takes pains to note that the 'cognitive quality' of this attention is far less important than the simple fact of it. Those who hear an address are part of its public even if they 'have wandered into hearing range of the speaker's podium in a convention hall only because it was on [the] way to the bathroom'. Michael Warner, 'Publics and Counterpublics', *Public Culture*, 14(1) (2002): 61.
5. Warner, 'Publics and Counterpublics', 82.
6. Warner, 'Publics and Counterpublics', 86. Warner is not exactly clear on exactly *who* presumes that 'ordinary people' would not want to be that 'kind' of person. I believe Warner implies this presumption is shared both by members of the counterpublic and by members of society in general.
7. He was at the University of North Alabama in October of 2008. Jesse Morrell, Open Air Outreach, 'Sinner SPITS on Preacher Jesse Morrell', YouTube video, uploaded 2 January 2009, last accessed 26 January 2013, http://youtu.be/uuuEoRvl2U. Photos and additional videos can also be found on his website, last accessed 26 January 2013, http://www.openairoutreach.com.
8. Gina Welch, *In the Land of Believers: A Journey into the Heart of Evangelical Amerca* (New York: Metropolitan Books, 2010).
9. The NAMB's guide is Thomas Wright, *Taking Prayer to the Streets: Prayerwalking Guide* (Alpharetta, GA: North American Mission Board [Southern Baptist Convention], 2009), available online at the NAMB website at http://www.namb.net/taking-prayer-to-the-streets/, last accessed 4 February 2013. The cards are reproduced as appendices in Wright's guide.
10. See Michel de Certeau, *The Practice of Everyday Life*, trans. Steven Rendall (Berkeley: University of California Press, 1984).
11. When Morrell speaks in a different context – preaching inside a church or welcoming visitors to his website, for example – the difference is quite striking. His rhetorical skills are sharper and his tone is far more approachable. Even his gestural language in using a microphone and Bible change; there is no sense of

a barrier between speaker and audience. See, for instance, his online sermon at http://youtu.be/7feYLaJBz1g, last accessed 4 February 2013.

12. See Ann Cvetkovich, 'Public Feelings', *South Atlantic Quarterly*, 106(3) (2007). Also, Ann Cvetkovich, *An Archive of Feelings: Trauma, Sexuality and Lesbian Public Cultures* (Durham, NC: Duke University Press, 2003).

13. Paula Neuss, for instance, sees an awkwardness in talking about or portraying God as the common thread in her survey of British productions of mystery plays in the 1970s. See Paula Neuss, 'God and Embarrassment', in James Redmond (ed.), *Drama and Religion* (Cambridge: Cambridge University Press, 1983).

14. Of course, a church environment can be extended out of church buildings and onto a city's streets, but those who do this work do not generally call it street preaching. For an example see Claire Maria Chambers, 'Street Church and Service as Salutation: The Public Ecclesiology of the South of Market Episcopal Churches', *Performance Research*, 12(2) (2011).

15. Slavoj Žižek, *The Puppet and the Drawf: The Perverse Core of Christianity* (Cambridge, MA: MIT Press, 2003). 7.

16. There is nothing new about this response. Rev. T.S. Bacon, in a published and circulated sermon from 1855 Louisiana, tells fellow street preachers to expect ridicule and hold to the Biblical example. 'Do you ever read the Acts of the Apostles? If so, are you not at times struck with the heroic devotion of those first Christians, and persuaded that they were right, and that we ought to be like them?' T.S. Bacon, *A defense of street preaching: A sermon preached in Trinity Church, Natchitoches, La., on Advent Sunday, 1855* (New Orleans: Sherman, Wharton & Co., 1856), 11.

17. Charles H. Spurgeon, *Letters to my Students* (London: Passmore and Alabaster, 1877), 88.

18. See, for instance, Jesse Morrell, 'Police Hassle Street Corner Preacher Jesse Morrell', YouTube video, uploaded 21 November 2009, last accessed 26 January 2013, http://youtu.be/s87Y--hUq7M. Also, Jesse Morrell, 'Preacher Jesse Morrell Falsely Arrested at Alabama A&M University', YouTube video, uploaded 5 November 2009, last accessed 26 January 2013, http://youtu.be/doBKjgLBey8.

19. See http://www.livingwaters.com/. Living Waters is the publishing arm of the Way of the Master ministry, discussed below. Last accessed 26 January 2013.

20. Ray Comfort (ed.), *The Evidence Bible* (Bellflower, CA: Bridge-Logos Publications, 2003).

21. Living Waters, 'Aim for Repentance Rather than a Decision', last accessed 4 February 2013, http://evidencebible.com/witnessingtool/aimforrepentance.shtml.

22. Living Waters, 'Watch it Blind Man!', last accessed 4 February 2013, http://www.livingwaters.com/witnessingtool/watchitblindman.shtml.

23. How preachers can be assured that they do, in fact, have clear and correct access to salvific truth in a form their preaching can communicate is a theological problem which different preachers address differently, and is more than can be addressed here.

24. Recall, for instance, Warner's welcoming of the reader as his public at the beginning of his essay, Warner, 'Publics and Counterpublics', 49.

25. See, for example, Laura M. Stevens, *The Poor Indians: British Missionaries, Native Americans, and Colonial Sensibility* (Philadelphia, PA: University of Pennsylvania Press, 2004).

26. 'The Way of the Master' homepage, http://www.wayofthemaster.com/ , last visited 4 February 2013. The ministry uses Living Waters, discussed above, as its publishing arm.

27. Fletcher sees more of a difference than I do between the 'extreme forms of confrontation' practiced by Morrell and the 'more common' confrontational techniques of Way of the Master, but helpfully contrasts them with the 'conversational' methods that have gained more. John Fletcher, 'Getting to Know You (and by the Way, Are You Going to Hell When You Die?): Evangelical Outreach to Post-Christian Publics', in Robert B. Shimko and Sara Freeman (eds), *Public Theatres and Theatre Publics* (Newcastle: Cambridge Scholars Publishing, 2012), 83–5. These clips can be found both at http://www.wayofthemaster.com/watchwitnessing.shtml and on the site's associated YouTube channel. Last accessed 26 January 2013.

28. See Henry Louis Gates, *The Signifying Monkey: A Theory of African-American Literary Criticism* (Oxford: Oxford University Press, 1988).

29. Artaud (or at least Derrida speaking in his name) would substitute the word 'theological' for 'hegemonic' in this sentence, which might give Christians pause about the nature of the doctrine being preached here. See, principally, Jacques Derrida, 'La parole soufflée', in *Writing and Difference* (Chicago: University of Chicago Press, 1978).

30. For more on this, see the connections drawn between Habermas and Bakhtin in John Michael Roberts and Nick Crossley (eds), *After Habermas: New Perspectives on the Public Sphere*, The Sociological Review Monographs (Oxford: Blackwell, 2004).

31. Jon Foley Sherman, 'Plural Intimacy in Micropublic Performances', *Performance Research*, 16(4) (2011). The performances discussed here the work of Felix Ruckert, particularly the piece *Consulto* for which Sherman was a performer (Museum of Contemporary Art, Chicago, 2003). Briefly, Sherman's argument is that his relationship with his spectators (who he calls 'attendants') is a form of 'ambiguous opening to others' based on the perceptual encounter on the phenomenological model. Because of its awareness of its own incompleteness, this form of opening does not exclude social structures such as the nature of publicness. Sherman places this ambiguity in contrast to the definite but pre-rational imperative of the Levinasian face-to-face encounter.

32. David Wittenberg goes farther, arguing that in Michael Warner's theories, the crowd gathered in a theatre understands itself not as the theatrical public being addressed by a play but rather as 'a coincidental cross section of the larger mass of people who "could have been there" instead'. David Wittenberg, 'Going out in Public: Visibility and Anonymity in Michael Warner's "Publics and Counterpublics"', *Quarterly Journal of Speech*, 88(4) (2002): 428.

33. After calling on the Copenhagen satiric newspaper *The Corsair* to satirize and mock him for reasons of an aesthetic debate, Kierkegaard found himself attacked and harassed on the streets of Copenhagen. This was a traumatic event for Kierkegaard, who came to a different understanding of public speech as a consequence of it. For more, see Roger Poole, *Kierkegaard: The Indirect Communication* (Charlotte, VA: University of Virginia Press, 1993), especially p. 188f.

34. Wittenberg, 'Going out in Public', 432.

35. See Jacques Rancière, *The Emancipated Spectator* (London: Verso, 2009).

36. Levinas, of course, remains the most important ethical philosopher of our responsibilities to our neighbour. But for an interesting contemporary set of explications of the ethics and politics of neighbourliness from a psychoanalytic perspective, see Slavoj Žižek, Eric L. Santner, and Kenneth Reinhard, *The Neighbor: Three Inquiries in Political Theology* (Chicago: University of Chicago Press, 2005).

37. See Patrick Ersig, 'Patrick – There is Hope in Jesus', YouTube video, uploaded 19 June 2006, last accessed 26 January 2013, http://youtu.be/AWj-9Ph5yKw.

38. The notion of *communitas* was developed in much of Turner's work, but for its original introduction (and, I would argue, its most useful presentation), see Victor Turner, 'Pilgrimages as Social Processes', in *Drama, Fields, and Metaphors: Symbolic Action in Human Society* (Ithaca, NY: Cornell University Press, 1974).
39. Warner, 'Publics and Counterpublics', 61.

Works cited

Bacon, T.S. *A Defense of Street Preaching: A Sermon Preached in Trinity Church, Natchitoches, La., on Advent Sunday, 1855*. New Orleans: Sherman, Wharton & Co., 1856.

Chambers, Claire Maria. 'Street Church and Service as Salutation: The Public Ecclesiology of the South of Market Episcopal Churches'. *Performance Research*, 12(2) (2011): 65–73.

Comfort, Ray (ed.). *The Evidence Bible*. Bellflower, CA: Bridge-Logos Publications, 2003.

Cvetkovich, Ann. *An Archive of Feelings: Trauma, Sexuality and Lesbian Public Cultures*. Durham, NC: Duke University Press, 2003.

———. 'Public Feelings'. *South Atlantic Quarterly*, 106(3) (2007): 459–68.

de Certeau, Michel. *The Practice of Everyday Life*, trans. Steven Rendall. Berkeley: University of California Press, 1984.

Derrida, Jacques. 'La Parole Soufflée', in *Writing and Difference*. Chicago: University of Chicago Press, 1978.

Ersig, Patrick. 'Patrick – There is Hope in Jesus'. YouTube video, uploaded 19 June 2006, last accessed 26 January 2013. http://youtu.be/AWj-9Ph5yKw.

Gates, Henry Louis. *The Signifying Monkey: A Theory of African-American Literary Criticism*. Oxford: Oxford University Press, 1988.

Habermas, Jürgen. 'Religion in the Public Sphere', *European Journal of Philosophy*, 14(1) (2006): 1–25.

———. 'Why We Need a Radical Redefinition of Secularism', in Eduardo Mendieta and Jonathan VanAntwerpen (eds), *The Power of Religion in the Public Sphere*. New York: Columbia University Press, 2011.

Morrell, Jesse. 'Sinner SPITS on Preacher Jesse Morrell'. YouTube video, uploaded 2 January 2009, last accessed 26 January 2013. http://youtu.be/uuuEoR-vI2U.

———. 'Police Hassle Street Corner Preacher Jesse Morrell'. YouTube video, uploaded 21 November 2009, last accessed 26 January 2013. http://youtu.be/s87Y--hUq7M.

———. 'Preacher Jesse Morrell Falsely Arrested at Alabama A&M University'. YouTube video, uploaded 5 November 2009, last accessed 26 January 2013. http://youtu.be/doBKjgLBey8.

Neuss, Paula. 'God and Embarrassment', in James Redmond (ed.), *Drama and Religion*. Cambridge: Cambridge University Press, 1983.

Rancière, Jacques. *The Emancipated Spectator*. London: Verso, 2009.

Roberts, John Michael, and Nick Crossley (eds). *After Habermas: New Perspectives on the Public Sphere*, The Sociological Review Monographs. Oxford: Blackwell, 2004.

Sherman, Jon Foley. 'Plural Intimacy in Micropublic Performances', *Performance Research* 16(4) (2011): 52–61.

Spurgeon, Charles H. *Letters to My Students*. London: Passmore and Alabaster, 1877.

Stevens, Laura M. *The Poor Indians: British Missionaries, Native Americans, and Colonial Sensibility*. Philadelphia: University of Pennsylvania Press, 2004.

Turner, Victor. 'Pilgrimages as Social Processes', in *Drama, Fields, and Metaphors: Symbolic Action in Human Society*. Ithaca, NY: Cornell University Press, 1974.

Warner, Michael. 'Publics and Counterpublics', *Public Culture*, 14(1) (2002): 49–90.

———. *Publics and Counterpublics*. New York: Zone Books, 2005.

Welch, Gina. *In the Land of Believers: A Journey into the Heart of Evangelical Amerca*. New York: Metropolitan Books, 2010.

Wittenberg, David. 'Going out in Public: Visibility and Anonymity in Michael Warner's "Publics and Counterpublics"', *Quarterly Journal of Speech*, 88(4) (2002): 426–33.

Wright, Thomas. *Taking Prayer to the Streets: Prayerwalking Guide*. Alpharetta, GA: North American Mission Board (Southern Baptist Convention), 2009.

Žižek, Slavoj. *The Puppet and the Dwarf: The Perverse Core of Christianity*. Cambridge, MA: MIT Press, 2003.

Žižek, Slavoj, Eric L. Santner, and Kenneth Reinhard. *The Neighbor: Three Inquiries in Political Theology*. Chicago: University of Chicago Press, 2005.

6
Faith, Fright, and Excessive Feeling

Kris Messer

In a church-based performance in central Florida, *Remember the Magic*, 'a tornado abruptly ends the championship basketball game and ends the lives of Coach Wyatt, Robb, and Dina and brings to light the importance of choosing a saving and personal relationship with Jesus Christ'.[1] This staged tragedy gains weight through its performance in a geographical area in which natural disasters are common occurrences. Shared experiences of the past underscore the commonalities connecting those inside and outside of publicly articulated communal boundaries. These interstices create multiple opportunities for the definition and display of Christian identity in public performance.

The performances discussed in the following pages – Judgement House, *Tribulation Trail*, and *Nightmare* – share their ability to work on audiences and participants through this intermingling of the secular and the spiritual, as well as through their unremitting physicality, which mirrors the suffering of both Christ and Christians. In these works the performative display of religious belief traces the borders of faith and troubles the ability to differentiate between public and private spheres of action. As Ann Pellegrini noted in 2007, Hell Houses make use of affect in order to function as vital and effective political performance. Performers and audience members are worked over and, themselves, work through the force of affect; they are 'invested (or reinvested) in a deeper structure of religious feeling that can tie together disparate, even contradictory, experiences, bodily sensations, feelings, and thoughts'.[2]

These performances, as well as many others like them, are crafted from headlines, hot-button issues, Halloween thrills, and horror flicks, and are performed in the spaces of participants' day-to-day lives and on the bodies of family and friends. They are struck through with corporeal suffering, emotional outpouring, scenes of tangible damnation, hopeful eternity, and even apocalypse, all of which contribute to the creation of spiritual identity. This spiritual identity rendered by performing beliefs on live bodies circulates in the public realm – beyond church borders – as counter, other, outside. The relationship between the embodied nature of performance and the socially constructed portrayal of Christian and secular character types in the *mise en scène* enables the communities performing these works to enact the spiritual and social implications of their beliefs on bodies whose concrete existence circumvents the reasoned discourse of the Habermasian public by travelling in the channels of literal liveness. It is in this battle with the performing body that the notion of a public is laid bare. Performances that work on the body and the spirit by twining those realms with the day-to-day and the commercial enterprise of Halloween create performative gaps, as Pellegrini terms them; these gaps are the very moments in which public discourse falls in on itself unable to reason the irreconcilable made present by simultaneous deployment of the physical poetics of love and hate, joy and sorrow, reason and rage.[3]

The discourse of the public sphere seeks to foster civilly articulated and egalitarian communication in service of a healthy democratic polity, while articulating the ways in which relational differences structure (or should structure) political and social life. However, the relationship between a particular community and the larger public within and to which that community expresses itself is fraught with the 'personal relations of domination', as Habermas argues in *The Structural Transformation of the Public Sphere*.[4] Community is dependent on relations of similarity and difference, which are inherently based in dominance – us and *not* them. The articulation of communal identity rests on divergences, inequalities, authenticities, and embodied practice, all of which are deployed to consume (subsume) those outside communal bounds.

One's individual subjectivity is cobbled out of motivations that intersect and compete on the fields of economic, spiritual, and biological experience; these motivations, though sometimes coherently externalized as a unified performance, often exist discreetly parcelled and disconnected from the performance one believes they are displaying and the actuality of how one may be read in their social environment. This multivalent toolbox of selfhood – sometimes rationally presented and framed, other times emotionally excessive and spilling out of the frame, and more often than not deploying tactics that simultaneously utilize both the rational boundary markers and the overflowing expressive content – troubles easy generalizations about one's place in public exchange. The performance of spiritual beliefs teeters in the space of distinction between rational discourse and embodied experience; it is in this ever-contested space that the public sphere can be viewed as an aspirational ideal that influences the form that highly personal religious expression takes within the realm of social engagement. Identities, the very currency of public participation, are imaginary structures; to perform, form, and *re*form them one must deploy sloppy and contradictory tactics. As such, there is no public – only a Platonic ideal of public fraternity, a dialogue, which, like a religious paradise or a post-apocalyptic Kingdom, hovers above messy social interactions and casts its shadow upon the world below. This public of pure form structures behaviours through its imagining, but it is never able to be rendered through our contradictory, sloppy, embodied actions. The notion of 'the Public' then becomes a discursive strategy to be deployed to shape the tools and terms of practice, but one that can only be recognized as theory, instigating, inspiring, and initiating our day-to-day experiments in communal identity and interaction. The following pages examine distinct intersections between religious individuals and the techniques by which religious performance shapes the exchange between private and public personhood.

The politics of the Christian right and the 'family values' agenda play a significant role in both individual and communal visions of what 'America' should – or should not – be. This agenda is deeply connected to supporting governmental actions and social structures that encourage familial formation along patriarchal lines. Among outreach programmes sponsored by self-identifying evangelical Christian congregations in recent years, there has been a proliferation of religious performances, which in their methods work to *re*-present traditional social behaviours and familial order by portraying what happens when the patterns of godly living (often conflated with patriarchal and conservative understandings of an essential set of values that structure social action) are not respected. Judgement House is one of the most widespread and influential forms in this genre. In its own words, the Judgement House organization aims to present 'a dramatic walk-through presentation about the truth of people's choices and their consequences both in this life and the next ... a Judgement House presentation becomes an "agent of change"...'.[5]

Tom Hudgins, founder and president of New Creation Evangelism, Inc., created the first Judgement House in 1983; it was remarkably successful for the participants, and the experiences of the youth in that first congregation were quite significant. Several of them went on to become youth pastors or ministers; some even present Judgement House in their communities today. In the first years after Judgement House began, and before Hudgins founded New Creation Evangelism, Inc., he would often receive requests for scripts or for advice about staging a Judgement House from other youth ministers around the nation and he did his best to keep up with them. However, he was often dismayed by the ways that this diluted the quality, content, and message of his work, and so he decided to create a more fully organized structure for the distribution of the scripts. The organization Hudgins created to distribute scripts has grown in scope; he now works full time for New Creation Evangelism, Inc. Though he is affiliated with Calvary Baptist Church in Clearwater, Florida, he no longer serves as youth pastor there in order to dedicate his resources to his own project. Judgement House is actively seeking to make inroads into other nations, as well as reflecting on the inclusivity and efficiency of its structure. The organization's strategic plan focuses on enhancing and expanding their web presence, extending into other forms of drama outreach, increasing collaborations across faith, cultural, and linguistic boundaries, and strengthening the regional network structure by creating offices throughout the United States, as well as in countries such as Mexico, Costa Rica, El Salvador, and Brazil.[6]

Operating within this franchise structure, so-called Covenant Partner Churches are furnished (for a fee) with scripts that allow congregations to tailor scenarios to the needs of their specific communities. The fee that congregations pay goes to support the development of future scripts, sponsor travelling support vans to help with performances, fund training conferences, pay Hudgins' and staff salaries, and develop Judgement House's operations.

At a Judgement House event, audience members proceed through a series of rooms set up all over the church grounds, in and out of Sunday school classrooms, gymnasiums, cafeterias, libraries and sanctuaries, parking lots, and roads. The trail they follow is draped and labyrinthine, transforming straightforward hallways into a network of break rooms, prayer rooms, and performance spaces. After proceeding through the earthly storyline, which ends in some form of calamity, the groups faces Judgement where each audience member's name is called, along with the characters. The audience then travels to Hell or Heaven (most often performed in the church sanctuary) and finally to a room of prayer where the significance of the event is explained one last time.

The tangled web: web of lies

> Erica finds herself in a familiar pizza restaurant, and in the company of an oddly dressed Reynaldo who is more than happy to offer her the drink into which he has quietly added a common date rape drug. Moments after Erica is finished with the drink, Reynaldo is leading her out of the restaurant, and into the final stages of his dark fantasy, when Bill literally runs into his daughter and her abductor. In the ensuing struggle Erica loses her life, Bill loses his daughter, and Trish loses her double-life leading father to the justice system.[7]

The Judgement House script *Web of Lies* begins with an execution by lethal injection and the story traces the path of how the executed arrived at each moment of personal and public justice. Before each scene the guide soberly lays out what one is about to witness, framing the event for audience members and connecting the spectacle to specific passages in scripture. As the guide states before the first scene in the *Web of Lies* script:

> Tonight's journey begins in a prison cell where Alexander Johnson has been served his final meal on this earth. He has been involved in

a horrific act of violence and sentenced to death by lethal injection. How on earth can someone end up in this type of situation? I wonder how his mother must be feeling. Where is his father and what happened to cause Alexander to become another death row statistic?[8]

This quote sets up the concerns of the text, both direct and indirect. What caused Alexander (AJ) to go wrong? We will find out, but already we know that negligent fathering might be to blame. While Alexander's father hurt him and he hurts his daughter, they are both free to choose their own spiritual destiny. While good family structure can protect a person, it cannot decide for them, as the guide tells us at the scene's conclusion: 'Sin whispers to the wicked...'.[9] Alexander's father may have contributed to his downfall, but it was his inability to take personal responsibility that sealed his fate. In a world in which having a strong nuclear family structure appears to participants to be less and less supported, these performances present an alternate path to salvation for those whose experiences lie outside the bounds of Norman Rockwell, *Leave it to Beaver,* and *Father Knows Best*. While it is important to note that a good family can guide, it cannot *save*; a bad family can harm, but it cannot *prevent* salvation.

The content of the script consistently alludes to the social structure of contemporary America: slumber parties, pizza parlours, internet chatrooms, *American Idol*, Facebook. When police respond during the tragedies that mark every Judgement House, they wear the actual uniforms and drive the cruisers that local law enforcement officers use every day. This presentation of contemporary life violently fractured by physical tragedy thrusts participants into a spiritual dilemma that comes to a climax in the space of a heavenly courtroom in front of a robed judge with a gavel who calls forth the characters and audience members by name. It also frames a contest between one's actions in the public sphere and the notion of individual choice. In the end, no matter your contributions to the social world, you are left alone with your choices. The audience's experience is structured as spatially and contextually parallel to the experience of the characters as they plead the case for their salvation; when one's name is called and one physically steps forth one must process one's place in the schema.

In *Web of Lies*, Erica, the young woman who meets her violent demise, her young male acquaintance who is trying to help her off her troubled path, and their murderer all confront the same question: did they accept Christ? The answer to that question dictates their salvation; it is not their deeds as social actors, but their personal responses to the choice of faith that structures their narrative closure. The script sounds a Calvinist echo in its tight parallel between salvific personal choices and proper behaviour of its characters. Erica, the victim who advertised herself in a sexually open manner on a social networking site, and her murderer, the father of a friend who posed as a young man on the same site, both go to Hell, while the young man who intervenes between the two is Heaven-bound. This split of characters and their fates functions as social poesis. Those who deviate from proper behaviour are corrupted by their deeds; sin is not merely shunning salvation as the script would have you believe, but punishment is also meted out to those who step outside sanctioned social roles. If you sneak into the basement during a horror movie to behave illicitly you get killed; if you sneak out of the youth group slumber party at Judgement House to meet a man at a pizza parlour you get shot and go to Hell.

In contrast to other performances in this genre, a Judgement House does not overtly attempt to represent reality as a twisted and morally remiss playground, but as a legitimate social system through which the Christian navigates, utilizing their faith and its rewards as a guide. The reality it seeks to create is the social structure, as participants believe it operates. The narrative metes out a judgement that is systematic and bears relation to everyday life. In the judgement room, the audience stands before a heavenly judge who wears robes that one would see in any American courtroom. He is seated at a bench, and is old, male, usually white, pounds a gavel, and calls everyone in the audience to judgement by name. In this way, Judgement House references a normative social structure.

As indicated by Judgement House's simultaneous treatment of civic ceremony and personal spiritual choice, these performances provide participants with the vocabulary to articulate their place in the idealized public sphere, while providing (through that articulation) a tool for intra-communal bonding. Didactic performances have the capacity to distil complex situations into recognizable categories. They do this through the oversimplification of narrative structure, genre, and character type, the interpretational openness of the performance's aesthetics, their recourse to both prophetic (and varyingly interpreted) religious symbolism, as well as to the artefacts of popular consumer culture. All of these techniques make these performances, in Warner's words, 'ongoing space(s) of encounter', which are heavily involved in 'world-making'.[10] Yet, while these performances may delimit by hailing their creators and audience members, they cannot control how individuals structure their responses in the live instances of the performative exchange. A public performance of communal identity categories implicitly questions its own boundaries. For instance, the antagonistic tone of public discourse directed at those engaged in performances such as those discussed in the following pages solidifies for participants their positions as truth-bearers, salvation-bringers, and outsiders to a world that needs saving.

Performance is transactional, as Kershaw points out in *The Politics of Performance*: '[P]erformance is "about" the transaction of meaning, a continuous negotiation ... to establish the significance of the signs and conventions.'[11] Participants in these events consistently define themselves in opposition to the 'other', the non-believer. In turn, what they perceive as a challenge to the legitimacy of their faith-marked identity provides the

outline for a public portrayal of both the outsider and the Christian identity
categories that participants construct for performance. These outlines for
identity are brought into flesh and performed on participants' own bodies
and on the bodies of their fellows in faith: their neighbours, friends, and
family members. In an interview, Medrith Woody, director of the North
Roanoke (Virginia) Baptist Church's Judgement House, demonstrates the
power of eliding personal identity with socially structured character types.
In reference to her church's Judgement House performance of the script
Collision, Woody states:

> The message in *Reality on the Highway [Collision]* is, there is [this] char-
> acter in it Natalie, and you'll, you'll get to know Natalie she is just a
> wonderful person I mean she is just a good kid and she's a cheerleader in
> this play and she just kind of reaches out and helps people and, and in
> the Judgment scene, which is in this room, you see Natalie realize that
> it's not about being a good person, that gets you to Heaven and she goes
> to Hell in the Judgment scene and it is very, very powerful. Our daughter
> plays that role, and I mean she literally screams at the top of her lungs,
> I mean, to where it just sends chills down your spine as she's screaming
> and they're throwing her in.[12]

Natalie's tragic flaws – her pride, youth, and brash insistence that she
thought she would have 'more time' – blare out from behind the harsh
strobe lighting, heat, and heavy smoke as she wails and pleads while being
handled by two large, masked, robed and backlit demons three feet from the
crowd. The strength of this spectacle is aided by the fact that many of the
people watching this event *know* the actress playing Natalie from school,
church, and work, and know her to be a 'good' person. Witnessing Natalie
suffer viscerally and palpably before being tossed into eternal damnation
after a tragic death that is not at all her own fault is to understand one's own
relation to sin and salvation more fully.

Judgement House works in broad strokes, operating largely on 'American'
cultural types: the cheerleader, the good kid, the soldier, the rebel, the jock,
and the out-of-luck working man. In Judgement House, 'ritual forms of solidarity are usefully promoted because ... they focus on common symbols...
ritual does not appear to communicate common understandings of its
central symbols'.[13] It is the scope of these symbols that allows participants
to intersect with them on their terms, supporting the notion that cultural
and social positioning vis-à-vis the performance (spectacle and text) rests
on openness. The relationship between the character of Natalie, as a 'good
kid' (middle class, Christian, white, well liked), and the actress playing
Natalie as a 'good kid' draws on standard categories of 'Christian' and 'all-
American' identity. The performer literally embodies the standard of the
category she presents. The conflation of character and performer reinforces

in its circulation an almost mythic and nostalgic identity that in actuality is far more complicated than the corollary relationship drawn here would suggest. Natalie is: (1) an attractive young white woman, (2) a cheerleader, and (3) a 'good kid' who reaches out to help others; yet, her one flaw – lack of *explicit* faith – nullifies all her 'good' earthly qualities. As Mary Douglas explains, 'The physical experience of the body, always modified by the social categories through which it is known, sustains a particular view of society ... there is a continual exchange of meanings so that each reinforces the categories of the other.'[14]

Natalie's violent journey to Hell is replete with recognition and reversal, in the genuinely tragic sense. One is left watching Natalie come into her own wisdom, but too little and too late. Community-based performances such as this ask the spectator and the participant to critically redraw their boundaries; to understand that what connects them to Natalie is both the mythologized 'Americanization' of her character and the damnation of her soul. It is clear that while these arguments reference identity categories stabilized through a secular public discourse, their tools lie in the personal relevance of religious experience. One must assess Natalie and apply one's faith position in relation to her. The drama itself relies on (and in fact forces) not only reflection but also self-definition. While investment in the story being told during a performance is significant, being free to articulate shared beliefs across geographical, class, age, and cultural bounds also creates community. That community is understood through the image of an ideal and fraternal public, but one can only work towards this ideal through personal, individual, internal, and bodily choice. An audience member's individual choice in public space finds its most forceful articulation in the moment of a character's damnation, because whether one eschews the message, accepts it, or takes exception to it, one must find some way of making meaning in negotiation with it.

On the trail

Tribulation Trail, produced by Mount Vernon Baptist Church (formerly Metro Heights Church) in Stockbridge, Georgia, takes personal identification within the context of spiritual world-building to the next level in its depictions of the Rapture and Tribulation in a wooded outdoor setting. Performances of *The Trail* began in the early 1990s and they garner about 30,000 paid visitors per run, which lasts three to four weekends in October. The co-dependent relations amongst violence, fear, and space in the performance of *Tribulation Trail* underscore the preponderance of fear and violence as mediums for communication in the contemporary world, secular and religious. If a visitor rejects Christ during the performance, she will experience the terrors one has witnessed; if she welcomes him, she will be active in creating terror. Here, secular suffering of the unredeemed, whether staged or projected upon attendees, is necessary for the meaningful Rapture of those who believe. One must tell, name, and chew up destruction in order to choke it down; the enactment of the post-apocalyptic world familiarizes Christian participants with readings of horror. Performance makes violence more palatable and allows for the consumption of pop-cultural apocalypse imagery in Christianized format.

When we reach the demarcation line where the grassy field beneath our feet slowly curves upward it is our turn to move forward. An ancient woman sits engulfed in a folding chair wearing a sweatshirt airbrushed with a wolf howling at the moon, and even though it is past dusk, a huge sun hat; she drinks out of a Big Gulp cup. She stands with great effort to relay to us 'The rules of *The Trail*'. Her voice strains against the excited whispers of our group, composed of part of a student group from Brazil, a father and three tween-age boys, and my husband and me. The elderly woman tells us no cameras, no flash photography, and to follow our guide for our own safety. A young man dressed in militaristic black garb emerges from the woods; the Brazilian girls giggle. He motions for us to 'come along' and we pick our way up the hill into the darkening woods, stepping over tree roots up an incline until confronted by a beach within a forest; a fire glows and a man in ragged robes sits with his head in his knees. As we assemble in a semi-circle, he lifts his head and speaks quietly from the Book of Revelation. As his frightening speech meanders on, our guide motions us forward saying, 'What was John talking about? Let's go see.'

We emerge from the thickly wooded area into a vast open field with a living room and kitchen ahead of us; it is a box set abandoned, as if some- one ripped the roof and fourth wall off of a small suburban rancher. On the right of the room are two white-robed figures; in relation to the black-robed figures circling the edge of the playing space, they recall an angelic presence. In the living room a teenage boy plays with a gaming system. In the kitchen his mother slams the refrigerator door, cursing. The demons draw closer, as her anger mounts. The man of the house enters and asks about dinner; a heated verbal fight ensues, with one black robed figure standing behind and controlling the movements of the man, the other controlling the woman: mirrored puppeteers. As the argument climaxes, he extends to strike her. As he does so all of the performers begin to move in slow motion, with the exception of the white-clad figures who place themselves between the cou- ple. At this moment the man comes to and shakes the demon's grip from his upswung arm; the demons retreat to the edge of the audience, lurking. The family embraces. The young man suggests a prayer and then ordering pizza. As they pray, the white-robed figures flanking them raise their arms and point towards the distance; the black-robed demons scuttle into the darkness, forward into the space where we are headed. The scene, the only one that happens in our place and time, pre-apocalypse, exists to connect us to the event and makes us think about the choices we make every day.

As we move deeper into the open field, armed guards halt our progress. Four large jets of flame shoot up stories-high into the air. We hear the sound of shots, and when the flames shoot up again, we see, standing on an uplit podium, what appears to be a demonic presence in black robes, macabre mask, with all his visible flesh painted red. A pre-recorded and distorted voice blasts through the night air. The performer's body twists and contorts as he calls forth each of the Four Horsemen of the Apocalypse, and each time he does so an appropriately-clad figure on horseback rides in and positions himself in front of one of the flame jets. When they are in place the flames sear the night again, the light goes out, and the horsemen thunder off across the field into the distance, the darkness preceding us.

The walk between each area takes at least three minutes, which creates a reflective period for processing events with those sharing the experience. How other group members respond to the event can shape one's experience drastically; a church group and a group of tipsy thrill seekers have very different reactions. Additionally, the terrain is not easy to navigate; this difficulty is natural, not man-made, lending credence to the spectacle. The simultaneous sensations of vastness and enclosure afforded by the space make for a disorienting journey. It mirrors the participants' relationship to the message. As participants, we are within the community of our small group traipsing through the Georgia night, as well as in the spiritual community that surrounds us, but we remain alone in our relations with God. What we choose is ours to know. We are cut off from the world outside the performance space, just as the proposed Rapture would make strange the world as we know it. Alienated from our surroundings, turned around through forest and field, we search for connections with other audience members and look for relations within the temporal cues of the spectacle. We listen for the sounds, trying to place ourselves: that is where we were, that is where we are going.

We are led into a round wooden enclosure with a large screen on the back wall. In an interview Carla Reeves, who co-directed *The Trail* (until church leadership changed in 2006) and who selected many of the video clips shown in this portion of *The Trail*, explains the significance of the footage she selected:

> All day these pictures impact on us, but not in one instant. I tried to bring up all the things that impact on us from the world, different types of stories – entertainment and tragedies, to show pollution, to make it clear that the problems aren't in one place – entertainment, morality, news events. ... I was proud; it's impactful when you watch it on the screen all coming together.[15]

She is right about the impact. Under bright stars in the crisp night air, in an open expanse of field stretched out between stands of trees, images of death, destruction, opulence, greed, and chaos flash before one's eyes. The sense of extremity is heightened by the bucolic nature of the field and the sparkling night sky.

The narrative's pace picks up, mirroring the chaos of life in the seven-year Tribulation period after the Rapture. We plunge through an atmosphere of crime, prostitution, drug use, starvation, empty unearthed graves left hollow from the Raptured bodies, and a camp in which Christians are executed for not taking The Mark. We are offered an opportunity to take The Mark, and we watch others do so; however, we are rushed forward before we can either accept or reject it. We see people ransacking the trunks of cars for food. In the trunks are dead bodies. Armed guards then shoot the looters as they crouch on the ground, eating like animals.

Finally, an iconic long-haired Christ in white robes stands far above us, bathed by white warm light and in a gold and white environment. The soundtrack identifies him as 'Our Saviour, King' while the Anti-Christ, dressed in a power suit and sporting horns, is on our level. Christ casts the Anti-Christ back into Hell and once more we are treated to a huge wall of flame. We move on to see Christ seated before a throne, judging those who have taken The Mark and those who remained steadfast. We walk about another three minutes in the woods and then are confronted with a pala-tial, bedazzling vista, complete with two streams running along its sides. We cross over small golden bridges in order to bask calmly in the craft store glory of the Kingdom.

Most people go to performances that depict such dire circumstances in order to affirm an already existing faith and to participate in a practiced communal expression of that faith, as well as to literalize their interpre-tation of the text of Revelation. Practitioners are aware that the event's strength lies within the community, and while they aim to put on a good show for all who come, they understand *The Trail* as a way for believers to witness the end of times – the Rapture and Tribulation – that they will never get to see except from box seats in Heaven. The performance affirms and rewards the path that most of its attendees have laid out for their lives, as well as giving them a titillating peek at the horror of the end. As Noel Carroll writes in *The Philosophy of Horror*, 'monsters are not wholly other but derive their repulsive aspects from being contortions performed upon the known'.[16] Like the monster pieced together from exaggerated combinations of human characteristics which we recognize, revel in, and revile, *The Trail* contorts a proposed known – the Rapture and Tribulation – to form a mon-strous realm attached to the real in which participants recognize their place, revel in the adventure, and revile their hand in creating it.

While performances such as *Tribulation Trail* afford audiences and partici-pants a way to imagine an improved and/or altered social order, they also can point up the sharp discontinuities between social utopias and the actual social world of the participants. Large sectors of the American public believe that their world should change, or change 'back', and they work actively to make those changes. As Carla Reeves, *The Trail's* former director, notes in a taped telephone interview:

> When I grew up you knew people on your street, what was happening in their lives, in their families. ... You could knock on their doors...get help if you needed or help other people. People had problems with each other, but we knew each other. Now you could live somewhere your whole life and not know your neighbour really at all. ... People move in and out all the time.

The performance creates nostalgic meaning and projects the fulfilment of prophecy on the existent world, creating a space for participants to voice concerns about the path of American politics in a performance that asserts the primacy of religious feeling in public affairs. Performance is, first and foremost, a site in which the contemporary world is examined through negotiation, personal experience, and emotional and aesthetic response.

In contrast to *The Trail's* post-apocalyptic world, *Nightmare* operates in the realm of statistically tangible events. It is a gore-oriented project that takes on the task of showcasing the leading killers of teens in the United States: drunken driving, gang violence, suicide, and drug use. Housed in a warehouse space built by the Believer's Church in Marshfield, Wisconsin, *Nightmare* uses a rotating cast of volunteers from several local churches.[17] Marshfield's *Nightmare* performances open a doorway into a public debate that would otherwise exclude religious emotionality by proving the strength of that emotionality through the force of live performance. When entering *Nightmare,* one is physically searched, even signing a waiver agreeing to be touched, but not to touch in return. Audience members are herded into a disorienting, tight circular space after being patted down, because, as the militaristically dressed armed guard who shuffles groups into the enclosure illuminated only by ricocheting strobe lights says, 'You never know, you might not be crazy, but someone you are in here with might be. Even a pen could kill you in tight quarters like this.' This distrust of one's fellows serves to divide audience members, pushing them into their own fear and away from a sense of group unity. Throughout *Nightmare* isolation pervades the experience, forcing one inward. The audience group is divided physically by the spectacle itself. In the car accident scene the individual audience members are scattered around the wreckage of automobiles and bodies; in the drug den bodies again divide participants; and in the second of three crucifixion-centred scenes the cross lies in the middle of the floor and the audience surrounds Jesus and his torturers on all sides, his broken body and the blood at one's feet serving as the focal point.

Physical sensation is paramount in *Nightmare* and all the situations within the display are representative of extreme bodily and emotional suffering. The audience is uncomfortable, not only because of fright; they are uncomfortable because of the unpleasant physical world of which they are a part: the stale smell of alcohol in the air; the tight quarters; the prosthetic-limbed heavy breathing demons wending throughout each small pack of audience members; the heat in Hell; the cold in the outdoor scenes; the cage in which each audience group is transported across a dank marsh, full of hands reaching up from the floor and out from the walls, as the tormented shrieking emanating from other cages hangs throughout the space.

In its representations of the 'real' world the performance showcases a car accident with real wrecked cars, a gang shooting, a drug den, domestic violence, and a suicide. Though campy at times, the scenes of the 'real' are bloody and uncomfortable; human bodies are contorted and writhing. A narrated voiceover, struck through with a scary demonic voice, urges characters towards their ultimate destructive choices and provides the skeleton of a plotline. This disembodied narration also serves to focus attention on the performer's expressive bodies and the sounds of their torment. Here, the day-to-day goings-on of life are directly linked to the spiritual and physical torments of Hell. In the absence of God, the production implies, life is harsh, brutal, worth next to nothing at all; it is Hell. *Nightmare* makes an effort to mediate the divide between emotion and reason by emphasizing Christ's tangible suffering and graphically portraying his death. Hell's terror, in both the Hell scenes and the 'real' scenes, is presented with excessive intensity, thus making Christ's sacrifice more pressing and ever more graphic and physically tangible.

The display of *Nightmare* argues for Hell as a literal physical reality, and bodily suffering as a part of that reality, linking the imperfect suffering body of the average participant with the perfect suffering embodied in the tortured body of Christ. The scenes exceed their bounds, spraying audience members with warm salty water as they stand witness to a suicide, for example. After being surrounded by gushing blood, and standing right next to the cross while Jesus is nailed to it then hoisted up as blood pours forth from his wounds, directly after a whole scene in which shirtless men whip him, the final empty white room of *Nightmare* forges a space in which one is left reimagining the horror one has witnessed. The importance of one's personal reaction to the preceding spectacle is evident in director Stacy Remus's description of the last performance space in *Nightmare*:

> We want to lead people to a vision of their lives, of life, and let them decide what impact *Nightmare* has on them. What is their world like? How far are they from what they saw? The last room is there for you, the audience, to reflect on what you saw before, to think about it before you go back into the world ... a world that is not in a lot of ways that different. These are the top killers of teens in the United States. ... That is real.[18]

The very structure of the event reflects the ideal public. It is a concert of multiple voices from throughout Marshfield engaged in public discourse about the top killers of teens in the United States, and the audience is asked to consider, reflect, and respond. However, there is a tension between social values and the loss of a cohesive fraternal public in what many *Nightmare* participants view as a corrupt social world that skews the actual existence of a public. In this situation, public dialogue becomes rhetorical gesture: a vessel to contain intense physical, personal, and emotive responses.

The tension between values and the way they appear to be applied in the social world is made manifest in the ways that bodies are broken, feminized, and subjugated to the forces of the material world within *Nightmare*'s spectacle. Sin and suffering are equated with a feminized and/or youthful posture; aside from Christ, all the victims of violence are women and the young. The 'good' Christian participant is responsible for linking their victory over sin and the sinful world to Christ's victory over human sin and suffering. The world that the broken body of Christ represents – one rife with sin, on the wrong track, devoid of moral values, and engaged in an attack against the good Christian – gives the religious participant the strength to go on. In the final tally, *Nightmare* guides participants to see the brutality performed on the bodies in the spectacle as tantamount to the social, spiritual, physical, and emotional brutalities of a social world gone awry. The layering of the social world, public discourse about social issues, and emotive experience turns the impact of performance inward in highly personal, idiosyncratic ways. This intense internalization is mediated by recourse to an imagined public, which gives form, but not content, to the exchange. As Remus asserts in an interview:

> We are becoming more liberal in Marshfield and we want to remind people of the dangers we see – the city doesn't let us hang our signs in town or send pamphlets into school. ... People are looking away and that is when things go wrong, and most kids don't even realize what is making this peer pressure or fighting, bullying.[19]

When asked about *Nightmare*'s relationship with the Marshfield community, Remus brings up a protracted court battle over a statue of Jesus in a Marshfield public park as a marker for when the balance of power shifted away from what she perceives as Marshfield's traditional or conservative worldview towards a more secular one. In 1998, the year of the first *Nightmare* performance in Marshfield, the Freedom from Religion Foundation, a non-profit organization that 'works as an umbrella for those who are free from religion and are committed to the cherished principle of separation of state and church',[20] filed a suit against the City of Marshfield on behalf of Clarence Reinders, a Marshfield resident, for an alleged violation of the separation clause. The original judge dismissed the case after a group of citizens formed the Henry Praschak Memorial Fund and purchased the statue and the land on which it stood from the city, creating the Henry

Praschak Wayside Memorial Park. However, the Freedom from Religion Foundation appealed the ruling on the grounds that a reasonable person would have no knowledge that the land was not maintained by the city, and thus they would not know that the city did not endorse the public display of religion. Tensions in the town mounted; there were acts of vandalism against the statue, churches, the judge, and Reinders. The case was heard on appeal in Chicago's 7th Circuit Court of Appeals and then sent back to the US District Court Judge, who ruled for the construction a four-foot-tall iron fence around the statue, to be flanked by two signs with the declaration that the statue is in a 'PRIVATE PARK: The enclosed property is not owned or maintained by the City of Marshfield, nor does the city endorse the religious expression thereon.' The Freedom from Religion Foundation was upset with the final outcome due to the height of the wall; they had requested a cement wall ten feet high, and four signs.

While the Marshfield case may have been anticlimactic, with neither side feeling particularly vindicated, it surely feeds into Remus's perception about the changing place of religion in the public discourse of Marshfield. No matter what one may feel about traditional family structures, the position of marriage in society and the inclusion or exclusion of religion from public spaces, assumptions that have existed for some time are being questioned. As this excerpt from *The Opinion* section of the *Marshfield News Herald* points out:

> Anti-God groups are hard at work to remove the presence [of] God from our society. Alabama: removal of a Ten Commandments monument from a judicial building. ... Ohio: removal of Ten Commandments monuments from four high schools, privately held student prayer meetings being forced from school grounds, the removal of Benediction from graduation ceremonies, the change of the word 'Christmas' to 'holiday' and a myriad of other examples ... They are attempting to push us – to push God – into backrooms and basements.[21]

These feelings find outlet in national events such as the 'Justice Sunday' gatherings in which thousands of Christians are encouraged to pray for the judiciary appointment process and to support conservative social issues. Judicial decisions that intersect on the battlefield between progress and nostalgia, such as those made regarding the statue in Marshfield, are often hard to apprehend fully from either side. What does seem clear, however, is that for a variety of reasons, personal, political, and spiritual, every decision is felt strongly and often taken personally by those on both sides of the issue. It is because community members perceive their strongly held beliefs to be curtailed, dismissed from reasoned public discourse, misapplied, or misunderstood that opposing parties, religious and secular, have such a difficult time respecting, discussing, and engaging the multiple sides of such issues. As Reinders's statement below suggests, the blade cuts both ways, and the secular side of the debate is not free from recourse to emotionality and reactionary discourse:

> [O]ur successful defence of the first amendment will be long immortalized. We have encaged behind an iron fence for all to see the central figure of a major religion. ...Whenever anyone looks at the idol in its newly-imprisoned setting he/she will see the fruits of our labors. ... The idol cannot now be viewed except through our American secular lens...[22]

This shift in attitude towards the statue, in Remus's view, marks an assault on Christianity's presence in and connection to civic life, a presence she sees as having been accepted as a neutral base of operation in Marshfield for as long as she can remember. It denotes a change, not necessarily in the composition of the community itself, but in the beliefs about family structure, marriage, work, moral (that is, religious) education, and the sanctity of human life that the churched community espouses. *Nightmare*'s very existence postulates that the slippage of these beliefs leads to the problems that the performance seeks to confront: drugs, gangs, domestic violence, drunken driving, and suicide. Remus does not blame this slippage on demographics, but rather on the transformation of the core beliefs of the community as a whole and on the perceived change in the freedom by which community members are able to operate from an *assumed* common belief system:

> It is not so much people moving in to Marshfield, there have always been changes. It is just what people think is important. I'll give you an example: we used to hang a sign on a railway bridge, don't know if you saw it? That goes over the main street in town. It cost fifteen dollars to hang the sign for *Nightmare* and we do it every year, last year someone saw it there and complained that the sign was for a religious event and shouldn't be allowed to hang there, because the bridge is the city's. People can't leave it alone. I mean don't come. Now, all sorts of signs hang there, and we paid, but the City of Marshfield made us take it down. It's just an event; it doesn't say come to Jesus. Just the date and location and some graphics.[23]

Many Christian participants have channelled their apprehension about assaults on their way of life into these performances. The fears actuated in these performances reflect uncertainty about who might be allies and who might be enemies in an age of multinational co-operation and corporations, instability in gender roles and practices, alternative lifestyles, anxiety about national borders and national identity, and so on. In a public conversation in which church members often feel their voices are discounted as backward, or in which they feel unable to be heard because they consider the recipients of their message to be fogged over by sin, churched participants view the live medium as a compelling way to deliver their speech and be heard.

Performance is not logically or reasonably, but *viscerally* public. Its tools are connected to representations of the social world, but the ways in which one relates to the ideas that inhabit a performance are primarily embodied, partially beyond rational discourse, and outside the bounds of logical exploration, much like religious experience. Countervailing forces such as the state, the market, and social movements may tighten or free expression with varying degrees of strength and efficacy; therefore, performance and identity are vital sites of social, political, and cultural battles over the local connotations and significances of who may speak in public and how they may be heard.

It is my contention that the performative combination of embodied religious belief and the secular circumstances of an imagined public heightens, and thus renders transparent, the constructed nature of the public. This constructed entity structures the terms of our social exchanges, and, in so doing, excludes forms of embodied understanding that can only be expressed and apprehended in the physical realm. Performances act on the sensory level to compel participants to formulate revised versions of self in relation to this formal and idealized public that, in turn, structures the poetic and aesthetic terms of the performance.

Notes

1. Judgement House/New Creation Evangelism, Inc., 'Our Scripts, *Remember the Magic* Summary', http://www.judgementhouse.org/Our-Scripts_7_pg.html, last accessed 9 November 2007. Indexed on CD.
2. Ann Pellegrini, '"Signalling Through the Flames": Hell House Performance and Structures of Religious Feeling', *American Quarterly* 59(3) (2007): 915.
3. Pellegrini, 'Hell House', 916.
4. Jürgen Habermas, *The Structural Transformation of the Public Sphere: an Inquiry into a Category of Bourgeois Society,* (Cambridge, MA: MIT Press; 1991), 17.
5. Judgement House/New Creation Evangelism, Inc., 'What is Judgement House?', http://www.judgementhouse.org/whatisJH.html, last accessed 22 January 2013.
6. For discussion of the goals of Judgement House outreach see Judgement House/ New Creation Evangelism, Inc., 'About Us', http://www.judgementhouse.org/ mission.html#, last accessed 23 January 2013. Also, specific information about the goals of Judgement House was discussed with Tom Hudgins in an interview with the author, Clearwater, Florida, 15 July 2007, tape recording. Since 2007, Judgement House has come under new leadership and they have pulled back on some of their overseas missions, though Hudgins remains involved.
7. Judgement House/New Creation Evangelism, Inc., 'Our Scripts, *Web of Lies* Summary', http://www.judgementhouse.org/Our-Scripts_7_pg.html, last accessed 2009. Indexed on CD.
8. Judgement House Writing Team as inspired by Karen Rines, *Web of Lies* (Clearwater, FL: New Creation Evangelism Inc., 2007), 7.
9. Judgement House Team, *Web of Lies,* 9.
10. Michael Warner, *Publics and Counterpublics* (New York: Zone Books, 2005), 90.

11. Baz Kershaw, *The Politics of Performance* (New York: Routledge, 2001), 16–17.
12. Medrith Woody, interview by author, North Roanoke, Virginia, 22 April 2006, tape recording.
13. Catherine Bell, *Ritual Theory/Ritual Practice* (New York: Oxford University Press, 1992), 183.
14. Mary Douglas, *Natural Symbols: Explorations in Cosmology*, 2nd edn (New York and London: Routledge, 1996), 69.
15. Carla Reeves, telephone interview with the author, 12 July 2007, tape recording.
16. Noel Carroll, *The Philosophy of Horror or Paradoxes of the Heart* (New York and London: Routledge, 1990), 167.
17. In this discussion I have chosen to focus on the *Nightmare* in Marshfield; however, there is a much larger *Nightmare* in Tulsa, Oklahoma whose project shares similar aims and narrative structures.
18. Stacy Remus, telephone interview with author, 10 November 2007, tape recording.
19. Remus.
20. Freedom from Religion Foundation Website, 'About FFRF', http://ffrf.org/about, last accessed 24 January 2013.
21. Terry Wiersma, 'Minority of Citizens Dictating to Majority', Opinion Section, *Marshfield News Herald*, 6 September 2003.
22. Clarence Reinders, 'We Done Good', *Freethought Today*, http://ffrf.org/outreach/awards/freethinker-of-the-year-award/item/11910-clarence-reinders, last accessed on 24 January 2013. Reinders was the plaintiff in the suit against the City of Marshfield, begun in 1998 and won on appeal in May of 2000. He was subsequently named the FFRF's 'Freethinker of the Year' for 2000.
23. Remus.

Works cited

Bell, Catherine. *Ritual Theory/Ritual Practice*. New York: Oxford University Press, 1992.
Carroll, Noel. *The Philosophy of Horror or Paradoxes of the Heart*. New York: Routledge, 1990.
Douglas, Mary. *Natural Symbols: Explorations in Cosmology*, 2nd edn. New York: Routledge, 1996.
Freedom from Religion Foundation. 'About FFRR'. http://ffrf.org/about. Last accessed 24 January 2013.
Habermas, Jürgen. *The Structural Transformation of the Public Sphere*. Cambridge, MA: MIT Press, 1991.
Hudgins Tom. Interview with the author. Clearwater, Florida, 15 July 2007. Tape recording.
Judgement House/ New Creation Evangelism, Inc. http://www.judgementhouse.org/. Last accessed 23 January 2013.
———.'Our Scripts, *Web of Lies* Summary' and '*Remember the Magic* Summary'. http://www.judgementhouse.org/Our-Scripts_7_pg.html. Last accessed 12 January 2009. Indexed on CD.
Judgement House Writing Team, as inspired by Karen Rines. *Web of Lies*. Clearwater, Florida: New Creation Evangelism Inc., 2007.
Kershaw, Baz. *The Politics of Performance*. New York: Routledge, 2001.
Pellegrini, Ann. '"Signalling Through the Flames": Hell House Performance and Structures of Religious Feeling', *American Quarterly*, 59(3) (2007).
Reeves, Carla. Telephone interview with the author, 12 July 2007. Tape recording.

Reinders. Clarence, 'We Done Good'. *Freethought Today*. http://ffrf.org/outreach/awards/freethinker-of-the-year-award/item/11910-clarence-reinders. Last accessed 24 January 2013.

Remus, Stacy. Telephone interview with the author, 10 November 2007. Tape recording.

Warner, Michael. *Publics and Counterpublics*. New York: Zone Books, 2005.

Wiersma, Terry. 'Minority of Citizens Dictating to Majority', Opinion Section, *Marshfield News Herald*, 6 September 2003.

Woody, Medrith. Interview with the author, North Roanoke, Virginia, 22 April 2006. Tape recording.

Part II Discussion

Joshua Edelman, Tom Grimwood, Kris Messer, and Peter Yeandle

Joshua Edelman: Kris talks at one point about public dialogue becoming rhetorical gesture. I'm interested in the relationship between the *hail* – the rhetorical gesture that names the public – and the nature of the public that act of naming conjures up. And the way that can flip back on itself. The public that exists can constrain the sort of rhetoric that is available – clearly enough – but that rhetorical gesture can also call a public into being, which can then condition the next piece of rhetoric. That relationship is something that all three of our examples wrestle with.

Tom Grimwood: I think we should distinguish between the two notions of hailing the audience that we're dealing with here. First is the post-nineteenth century, 'modern audience' of the public sphere. But second is a tension around audience and representation embedded deeply within the history of Christianity itself, both within modernity and before. The whole idea of Christian ritual is based on a reproduction of a central event that is (for all intents and purposes) *not* reproducible. This is something that struck me about Kris's chapter, actually – how much there's this strange mimetic quality in the performances. They're playing on genre-based typical mimetic qualities, such as those from horror films – but at the same time, there's this mimetic excess that has such a long history in Christianity.

Kris Messer: Excess in the sense of an overwhelming physical, phenomenal experience. There's a community that's created by those who have experienced it, and that community in turn offers access to speaking about that excess, and how that physical experience relates to a spiritual realm. Because a lot of the moments in the performance that allow for spiritual reflection are very personalized, there tends to be disjuncture between how they're experienced by different people. I see the function of this hailed community as allowing people to work out this disjuncture, while keeping those experiences – I hesitate to say authentic, but keeping them similar enough that they feel that they are still correctly spiritual.

Grimwood: Pete and I would argue Headlam is doing is almost the opposite of a performance like Judgement House. In Kris's chapter there is constant

153

tension between transgression and appropriation. Generally speaking, American evangelicalism has this strange seeding-together of the Christian narrative with all the hallmarks of consumer culture and postmodern cynicism, as if the Judgement House is trying to take authority over those secular symbols and performances, and say 'this is the correct spirituality'. We can have *A Nightmare on Elm Street,* but we can reconstruct the horror genre and appropriate the power of its performance, so that it ends the right way. For Headlam, it is the other way around: he is saying that a ballet performance far exceeds anything the Church is doing in terms of its Christian values. Ballet has something to teach the Church.

Edelman: I think there's a basic tension between, on the one hand, Headlam's effort to take that metonym of the church as a building and push the walls out as much as he possibly can and blur any definite boundaries, and on the other, the effort I see in Hell House to draw that line as clearly and narrowly as possible. Secular public opposition to Hell Houses is necessary for the performance to function. You can see the drawing of that line – or its blurring – in the relationship between performer and audience. That's the tension I saw between Morrell and Ersig. Pete, your use of 'figurative church' seems to mean not just that the building represents the congregation or the body of Christ, but that we can't know the limits of the building, that the walls are invisible, that they're always moving out, and that's the opposite of what your example is saying, Kris.

Messer: I do see the expansiveness of Headlam's vision, and I see how he turns something that was seen as sinful into something of great beauty. But I'm not sure that this narrowing was the goal of Judgement House. The point was that it allowed for a more personal interaction with the material. But that personal exchange serves to call up a demon that's not there. As opposed to calling up beauty. It teaches people that there needs be something to be afraid of, and thus you've got to look around and find that somewhere. In Marshfield, there's a sense that daily, ordinary things ought to be turned into something of significant concern. Because that keeps people thinking about their relationship to sin and salvation.

Grimwood: The link I see between the chapters comes from the visceral, embodied nature of our examples, but I was also thinking about it in terms of public speaking, where the confrontation itself can be a visceral force. Embodiment is complicated, it's not rational, and it tends to lack ready-made boundaries. I felt Kris's chapter was less about the boundaries themselves between good guys and bad guys, and more about trying to take control of the transgression of that boundary. In relationship to Josh, I was thinking about public preaching in two historical senses. On the one hand, there's street preaching in the modern public sphere – it's distasteful, it's offensive – but on the other, there's a self-sacrificial element. Remember the seventeenth-century Catholic martyrs who preached and were put to death. In the chapel of the Venerable English College in

Rome where they train Catholic priests, there are paintings of horrific death scenes, basically saying this is what you'll face back in England. I don't know if these acts of public speaking are not so much about 'here's us that's good and there's them that's bad,' but more about the visceral sacrificial element that runs all the way through the heart of Christianity.

Edelman: I think you're right to link viscerality to Christian notions of sacrifice. I feel that viscerality in the conformational examples of the street preaching has this kind of emotionally generative function, and I feel like controlling the fear, deploying it, managing it appropriately, had a similar function in Kris's example, and I wonder if the experience of pleasure had a similar function in Headlam's. Pete, is that the case?

Peter Yeandle: Very much so. One of the critiques Headlam makes against orthodox Anglicanism is that it seeks to control through fear. In his sermon 'The Gospel of Joy', he writes that God designed people to experience pleasure. If they work hard, they deserve to experience beauty through leisure; rest is its own divine reward. Headlam had an argument with the archbishop who said, I can't really encourage a church and stage guild, because it's not really that different from endorsing a church and publicans guild. Headlam had no problem saying, why can't there be a church and pub guild, because we need to bring joy to the world? He's very much seeking to critique the established church's attempts to control through fear by arguing instead that the enjoyment of pleasure is itself holy.

Yeandle: Headlam's concern with pleasure was about three things, really. First, pleasure is the yardstick by which you judge the social utility of art, including ballet and theatre. Second, God didn't just intend people to be cogs in the industrial wheel, but to celebrate their hard work through their leisure. And third, the notion of pleasure helps him discursively construct his audience. He's using Ruskin quite explicitly to argue about a kind of collective response. When critically reviewing a play, for instance, he's saying, if only all eyes saw with the same moral conscience, then you'd have the revelation of the sacraments. He's constructing an ideal audience, and pleasure is part of that.

Edelman: As Tom has indicated, maybe this isn't just a modern problem. There is something about performing church as a gesture *out*, towards the transcendent, which cannot be represented, as a problem that predates the modern and is foundational to what the church is.

Grimwood: It's less about a public sphere of rational dialogue, and more about an internal dynamic within a performance based around this idea of propriety and mimesis. Part of my concern is that I think all this talk of boundaries can overemphasize the distinction between the performance and the audience in ways that aren't helpful. The two are bound together, both part of that mimetic dynamic. In fact, we, as cultural theorists, as historians, as performance theorists, represent and create a performance of our own in that way; it's difficult to separate out our work from 'the event'.

Edelman: Kris's example calls for 'audience participation', to put it crudely. It doesn't give them a safe space from which to observe; they're forced to make choices for which they're responsible.

Messer: In your chapter, Josh, discussing the position of having to choose where to ally in the moment of being preached to, it seemed similar to the sort of moment I've often felt in a Judgement House judgement scene, in which I don't particularly wish to be judged, but they have your name on a piece of paper, and the heavenly judge calls everyone up by name up to a podium. There's this moment where you have to assess where you are and move forward. Coming from the perspective of knowing I'm going to write about it, it created in me a very similar response: that lack of choice. I felt like the performance space structured both an internal reflexive choice and an external choice I had to make right away – it seemed very similar to the choice that the participants in the street preaching moment have to make.

Grimwood: A footnote about viscerality: if you think about the concept of the demonic in Christianity, you realize it works in the context of a higher, 'good' authority. Why are demons scary? Tertullian writes that demons are hideous because they parody resurrection. Which is doubly bad, because they reproduce a momentous, singular event, in a way that mocks the whole idea of the Christian miracle. So they're only allowed to exist as demons and have that power if, at the end, they are vanquished by the singular event of resurrection. The choice has to have already been made. So if we look at Judgement House in the context of public sphere theory, we say, well, that's unacceptable because you haven't been given a free choice. But if we think about its internal dynamics, when then of course the choice was never there, because we wouldn't recognize the demonic aspects *as* demonic unless the choice had effectively already been made. I don't want it to sound like I'm defending Judgement House!

Edelman: No, it doesn't sound like that. You're pointing out that like the street preaching, Judgement House is making use of a certain trope, a trope of parody, that it needs in order to make itself clear.

Grimwood: Yes. And it's a performative trope, based on repetition and mimesis.

Edelman: Yes, exactly. Kris, one of my questions to you was how the audience *recognized* these figures as demonic. And you said that these are either traditional conventional images – horns and red tail – or those taken from film genres of greedy suit-wearing baddies, and perhaps even with specific visual reference to the *Left Behind*[1] films. One of the things that are interesting to me is how these secular tropes from horror movies or daytime television operate alongside the traditional Christian ones of salvation and judgement. There's this very postmodern quality to it.

Messer: To me, that equalizing of those tropes speaks to the idea of street preaching, of reaching people where they are.

Edelman: So it's a generous act, on some level?

Messer: Yes, it is. It's saying that these things, like horror movies or social networking or whatever, exist in the world, and there has to be a structure to utilize and deal with them. They're given a similar weight because they're similar to people's daily experiences. It mingles our tangible day-to-day lives and our spiritual world. And to me, it seems really interestingly connected to the experience of street preaching, of bringing one's body and belief to where people are. Particularly in your last example of Patrick Ersig, that bringing of the message into someone's space is a very powerful way to build connection.

Grimwood: Is there an element of appropriating the 'external' tropes from horror movies into a 'correct' Christian narrative? It made me think of Josh's discussion of P-Nasty. It becomes a struggle for the right to define a certain sort of deviance and appropriate it into a narrative. Who's right in this discussion that's not actually a discussion? Here's the guy who has all the symbols and the figuration of a particular character set, but who has the right to say if he's a liar or not?

Yeandle: Headlam is doing something slightly different with respect to ballet. He does tell the stories of the ballet dancers who have suffered, but he isn't trying to impose an external narrative on them. He frequently gives the example of when he had his first curacy: two women came to him for ministry because they were turned away from the main church service because of their career in the arts. And he does liken their story to what would happen if Jesus were reborn now. But the point is that the arts and artists are to be embraced on their own terms as a site of divine beauty and grace that, in a sense, is *superior* to what the church is offering. Not that either ballet or ballet dancers need to be reappropriated into a Christian narrative for church use. The opposite, in fact.

Edelman: This brings up questions of gender. I think there is something disturbing about the way that Headlam idealizes the female dancing body as the symbol of grace, compared, for example, to the way the cheerleader is used in some of the performances Kris describes.

Yeandle: This is a question that always comes up. I'd argue that he made a decision early on that he is going to stand up for the most oppressed and maligned, not necessarily those who were oppressed through capitalist exploitation, but through Christian stereotyping. Attitudes towards ballet dancers illustrate this polarized opinion within the church. Some would look at the female body and see sin, but Headlam would want to say that it's not the female body that is in sin, but the soul behind the eyes that look. Theologically, that allows him to create the argument that true beauty and divine grace can be revealed through the female body, but the onus is on the eyes of whose who are looking to be able to see without prejudice. This is part of his strong theological argument about sacramental revelation and the ways in which Christianity has become blinded to the visceral Christ.

Grimwood: There's also a rather ironic link to the history of the Western Church, in which the malleable female body has been a form for expressing political dissent: the mystics, the holy anorexics, Catherine of Siena. In these cases, the female body becomes a site of political dispute. Headlam wouldn't talk about this; it's almost the flip side of what he's trying to express.

Messer: In Judgement House performances, women are the ones who die, often quite brutally. Very much like in a horror movie. Often, there's a link from that brutality not just to sin but also to an uncomfortable political world. There's a sense that something is slipping beyond control in the political realm that enables women's bodies to act outside traditional ways. This gets linked to certain nostalgic ideals, of course.

Edelman: Women's bodies are a kind of index of a political slippage?

Messer: Right. And yet, the way that women are represented as the victim, generally the very bloody victim, is closely linked to Christ's body, which is also brutalized, feminized. To me that represents a taking-on of that sin. Within the spectacle, the body of Christ is shown to take the role of bridging and consuming that sin. In terms of the narrative progression through the nightmare, the brutalized spectacle of women's bodies leads us and prepares us to see the very bloody preparation for the crucifixion.

Grimwood: The risk of this kind of religious practice of taking on so many contemporary cultural tropes is that you wind up with this sort of bloody mess. Sacrifice, which is absolutely essential to the Christian narrative, becomes so entangled with punishment of the sinful, that it becomes unclear. If you think about the horror genre, the death of the girl is almost always some kind of punishment, because she's attractive or she's just being a girl. In effect, what gives the piece moral coherence is what you call the narrative progression, Kris. It's not the images themselves but rather the physical act of walking through the building and seeing all these chaotic mixtures of different tropes.

Messer: Also, the narrative keeps referring back to chance – this could happen to anyone at any time. And so I find irony in the fact that it's not anyone at any time, but a very specific set of characters: women and young people, those traditionally seen as weaker and needing strong guidance and boundaries. They are more susceptible to whatever it is that will create this mass chaos. I look at the irony as operating with the idea of chance from within those sorts of very strict narrative structures.

Edelman: Pete, I just want to go back and pick up your reference to the visceral Christ – it's a very helpful concept. Perhaps there's something in the Christian story that draws on the visceral more than it does the polemical. That the primary Christian act is a visceral reconstruction or a visceral memory before it puts forward an argument. That has an effect on the nature of what the Christian community is, and on what Christian life and worship are. Is that fair?

Yeandle: I think so. One of the things Headlam shares with others in the Christian Socialist revival is a Christ of action and physical substance. They use socialist language. Christ is the holy carpenter, the mass is the great communist occasion, and baptism is the great sacrament of equality – things like this. Christ as secular, as a social worker, as a role model for emulation as well as a religious icon for worship. Our chapter attempts to capture the idea of an active Christ who forces the acknowledgement that the established church had lost its moral authority to represent Jesus because it was representing a static Christ and not Christ as action.

Grimwood: Yes. It's reappropriation of a certain mimesis, a certain performativity. We don't want this mimetic quality expressed by a cross on an altar or on a painting – we want it in a performance, because performance is contemporary, it attaches itself to the tropes of socialism and activity.

Edelman: And the crucial link between the visceral and the socialist and the Christ of action is the idea of pleasure as a basic human right.

Yeandle: Yes. Agreed.

Grimwood: I'm speaking very generally here, but Headlam's invocation of Christ is obviously taking place at that point in the broader history of theology where there's an interest in Christ as a person rather than as a divine entity. And this gets combined with a specifically nineteenth-century sense of immanence – a sense that it's all happening now, this is the end of history, as Hegel said, so this is when we have to do it. And one of the points we tried to make about the rhetorical aspect of Headlam's work is that you don't base this sort of ministry on the idea that at some point in the future we'll all agree on things and in the meantime we can look for ways that we can all get on. No. Instead, you provoke because the point is to do it now.

Edelman: There was a tactical decision in terms of rhetoric not to wait for agreement – to get on with it. In both Kris's and my examples, people are not asking for agreement. They're finding another way to get on with it and do their work. This is part of the larger book's challenge to Habermas. Agreement might be far less necessary than he seems to think it is, even dialogue moving towards agreement might be far less necessary. There might be other things that can do that job in its place.

Thank you all for your contributions to this discussion. It's been a pleasure.

Note

1. The *Left Behind* series is a set of best-selling action novels by Tim LaHaye and Jerry Jenkins that narrate a premillenial dispensationalist version of the end of the world, based on an evangelical reading of the book of Revelation. The sixteen-book series has sold over 65 million copies. For an academic engagement with the series, see Glenn Shuck, *Marks of the Beast: The Left Behind Novels and the Struggle for Evangelical Identity* (New York: NYU Press, 2005).

Part III
Publics and Commodification

7

Congregations, Audiences, Actors: Religious Performance and the Individual in Mid-Nineteenth-century Nottingham

Jo Robinson and Lucie Sutherland

On 30 November 1860, the *Nottingham Journal* reported to its readers that the 'anomalous practice of conducting public worship in a theatre, commenced in London last winter, has extended to Nottingham':

> On Saturday night placards were posted on the walls in the poor, thickly populated areas of the town, announcing that a religious service would be held in the Theatre, St. Mary's Gate, and inviting the attendance of persons who were not in the habit of going to places of worship.[1]

The 'novelty of such a service at such a place', reported the paper, caused an 'immense and noisy crowd' to attend: 'all parts of the building were crowded, and when the doors were closed numbers were left outside'. The police officers who were present to assist the doorkeepers 'were altogether unable to preserve anything like order', although the sermon itself, it was noted, secured 'marked attention, unbroken by any interruption'.

There is an inherent anxiety evident in the way the *Journal* reports this anomalous event, portraying unease at the juxtaposition of secular and religious leisure pursuits.[2] Indeed, the reporting of this service, and of the ones that followed it in the theatre and in other secular venues in the town, mixed religious and theatrical discourses to convey the complex reactions provoked by these public performances of religion, which took place in unexpected public spaces and in which differing expectations of behaviour and performance came into conflict. Writing of the second such service a week later, for example, the *Journal* reported that:

> The behaviour of the 'congregation' was certainly more orderly when they had taken their places, but at times the old spirit of the gallery would make itself apparent by the emission of those sounds with which it is so intimately connected.[3]

Here practices from one public – that of the theatre audience – seemed to bleed through into those of another – the religious congregation. Once more, the *Journal* demonstrates anxiety at the move from church to theatre, and this is soon focused on the nature of the individuals making up those publics, and their appropriate place within the society of the town, seeming to argue for a kind of physical and behavioural restraint that should be practised by bourgeois citizens. By the time of the third service, held on 9 December 1860, the *Journal* reported that the preacher, Captain Orr, had issued a warning to particular members of the assembled congregation:

> The services at that place were not, he said, intended for them, but for the masses who would not attend religious services elsewhere. He was afraid that to gratify a feeling of curiosity some persons had left their own places of worship to occupy seats there, which, judging by the crowd he saw in the street, would have been filled by others who would not go to the churches and chapels they had left.[4]

Repositioning the form and content of religious practice within the established cultural context of a theatre building was a process of commodification that positioned worship within the sphere of leisure, and this surely accounts for the anxiety espoused by the *Journal*. The newspaper focuses upon a vicarious curiosity that motivated a section of society to attend, whose position in that society was distinguished, to some extent, by allegiance to legitimate sites of worship.[5] For a paper in sympathy with the Anglican tradition, consistency in worship practice embodied ideals of control, legitimacy and restraint in ways that service 'for the masses' in a site of commercial entertainment could not.

Taking our cue from such reports of congregations occupying different kinds of public spaces, and the articulation of anxiety both over which 'public' was the invited audience for these services and the appropriateness of their performed behaviours in what was intended to be an ordered, attentive religious context, this chapter addresses the place, practice and performance of audiences for formal religious events in Nottingham in the mid-nineteenth century. Analyzing the range of faith-related activities and competing secular events available to residents of the town, we demonstrate how, by mapping choice, attendance and practice, the role of the individual subject within the public spheres of religion and wider society may be more fully understood.

The concept of mapping is integral to this work. Charting the geography of religion within modern societies, Lily Kong recognizes that

> socially constructed religious places overlap, complement or conflict with secular places and other socially constructed religious places in the allocation of use and meaning. [...] Even while the sacred is often constructed,

and gathers meaning in opposition to the secular, place is often multivalent, and requires an acknowledgement of simultaneous, fluctuating and conflicting investment of sacred and secular meanings in any one site.[6]

While Kong herself addresses modern geographies of religion, her notion of the overlap, complement or conflict between sacred and secular spaces is key both to the approach of this chapter and to the wider research project which underpins it: the 'Mapping Performance Culture: Nottingham 1857–1867' project, funded by the UK Arts and Humanities Research Council and led by Jo Robinson and Gary Priestnall at the University of Nottingham. This interdisciplinary collaboration between theatre history and geography has sought to investigate the performance culture of one provincial town via the creation of a web-based, interactive map that draws on an extensive database of performance events within the 11 years covered by the project.[7] The map, which operates primarily in terms of space but also in terms of time, has the ability to 'play' events across the years 1857–67. It can thus prompt exploration of Kong's 'multivalent', 'simultaneous, fluctuating and conflicting' usage and meanings of sites, as it situates the various sites of performance – whether key venues such as established churches and concert halls, or more ephemeral performance spaces such as circuses and portable theatres – within the town in relation to one another and to their patterns of public usage for different kinds of performance events.[8]

This stressing of connections and relationships between different performance events and between the members of the audiences or congregations who may have attended them is key to our argument here for, as Michael Booth reminds us, the Victorian audience 'lived in its own culture and its own network of economic and social relationships; it did not exist only in auditoriums for the benefit of the scholar'.[9] This is just as true of congregations: congregation members were, and remain, employers, workers, and potential members of the audience for other events. Thus the individual member of any congregation – whether in established church, dissenting chapel or a member of the public attending a religious service in a secular venue – must be situated within a complex of interrelationships between congregations and other audience communities, and between religious and other cultures within the wider society in which he or she lives.[10] Within such complex interrelationships, this chapter argues that religious performance, within and beyond places of worship, provided an opportunity for individuals in the provincial town of Nottingham to exercise choice and foreground subjective identity in a rapidly expanding and changing urban environment.

The religious landscape of Nottingham

It is essential to acknowledge that such playing out of subjectivity was made possible, but also circumscribed, by the increasing fragmentation of social interaction and the development of separate leisure time, as identified by Peter Bailey in his *Popular Culture and Performance in the Victorian City*. As 'the coherent and readily comprehensible pattern of social life [...] was increasingly exchanged for a pattern of life notable for its discontinuities of experience in terms of time, space and personnel', Bailey argues that

> segregation and the introduction of new work routine compartmental-
> ized social classes and the basic activities of work, leisure, and home life
> to such a degree that man the social actor was obliged to play out his
> encounters in an even greater number of discrete situational settings.[11]

Amongst other concerns, such fragmented societies gave rise to anxieties that the practices and sites of established religion were failing to meet the needs of every individual with newfound time for leisure; indeed, such anxieties seem to have prompted the 'anomalous practice of conducting public worship in a theatre' with which this essay began. For while Nottingham was not yet a city in the period we are examining, Bailey's words on societal changes during the nineteenth century may be usefully applied to the town, which witnessed rapid expansion during Victoria's reign, with a population increase from 53,091 in 1841 to 239,745 in 1901.[12] The lack of land for building within the town boundaries prior to the enclosure of common land on the town's periphery in the 1840s, together with the reliance of Nottingham's key industries – lace and hosiery – on small units of production, meant that the 'discrete situational settings' identified by Bailey were clearly marked, making church and chapel a potentially important site for instilling a sense of society and community; the challenge was to attract individuals to join and remain with any given community.

In such circumstances, competition between different denominations for congregations was perhaps inevitable on both a national and local scale: David Cornick highlights the advantages of the 'dissenting "denominations" [that] were able to respond to the changes wrought by industrialization more rapidly and flexibly than the Church of England'.[13] Such nonconformist groups – that is, those established in opposition to or as distinct from the Anglican Church – had, Cornick notes,

> two inherent advantages – they were financially and legally free, and they
> possessed a theology of lay ministry (expressed in many forms, from the
> strictly organized to the chaotically *laissez-faire*) which enabled them to
> liberate plant and personnel with ease.[14]

Such advantages were apparent at the local level, as our analysis of the Nottingham returns in the 1851 Religious Census demonstrates. On 30 March 1851, for the first and only time, the government carried out a survey of the whole of England and Wales in order to establish how many places of worship were open, how many sittings were provided by each place, and how many of those sittings were occupied at morning, afternoon, and evening services: the results reveal complex variations of religious practice across nation and regions. In Nottingham, the census recorded 38 places of worship, nine of which were controlled by the Church of England including some new satellite churches set up in the outskirts of existing parishes. The rest, with the exception of one Jewish synagogue and the Catholic Church of St Barnabas, were associated with nonconformist and dissenting religious groups, and on the Sunday of the census, total attendance at those venues was significantly higher than for the established Churches: 10,394 for evening service, compared with 4,524 for the nine Church of England sites (comparative figures for morning service, including children or 'Sunday Scholars' attending Sunday school activities at the premises, were 9,839 and 6,237 respectively).

Although these details provide some idea of religious provision within the town, the data were not without controversy: the established Anglican Church 'argued that instead of estimating attendances [... the] enumerators should have asked people to give their religious affiliation',[15] suggesting that the Church of England acknowledged that attendance – or non-attendance – at the many available 'discrete situational settings' might be prompted by factors other than faith. Thus, while the census data record the physical manifestation of religion in Nottingham at the middle of the nineteenth century, the motivation of attendees is much less certain. The equivocation and defensiveness in such comments, recorded in the census alongside the raw data, provides evidence of the precise form of competition between the Anglican Church and nonconformist denominations that resulted in a wide range of activities offered to the individual by representatives of established religious groups within the town.

One response of denominations to such a competitive field was the construction of more places of worship throughout Nottingham. Nonconformist groups certainly monopolised parts of the expanding town after enclosure was undertaken in the 1840s, and, in the thirty years after the 1851 Census, the Methodists alone built more than twenty new chapels and missions. The Church of England also erected new buildings, with the large central town parishes recorded in the 1851 Census – St Mary's, St Peter's and St Nicholas' – subdividing, throughout the latter part of the nineteenth century, into smaller parishes, each with a church building. For example, by 1871, St Mary's had been subdivided seven times. George Harwood, a preacher and writer closely connected to the Methodist movement in Nottingham, noted the steadily increasing number of religious venues in his diary of 1863:

> Nottingham has, during the last few years, increased very fast both in houses and inhabitants, and the religious bodies seem to be trying to outstrip each other in providing for the additional population. The

Church of England has added several new churches, and is adding more. The Unitarians are building a Chapel in Pease Hill Road, Mr. Little has recently opened the Methodist Independent Church in Great Freeman Street. The New Methodists have purchased a piece of ground on Woodborough Road for the purpose of building a chapel thereon. A piece of ground has been secured for the same object in Great Alfred Street by the United Free Church. The Wesleyans of the North Circuit have built a small chapel in Hartwell Street, and we of the South Circuit are about to erect a good chapel in the Meadows.[16]

The wide choice of locations that resulted from all of these developments were aimed at a variety of social and economic groups, an attempt to provide new sites of worship for congregations, many at a remove from secular events in the town centre. These new sites did parallel secular places of entertainment, however, in staking the claim of precise religious denominations to a place within the distinct civic identity of one regional town. Yet the result of this increase in religious venues was, of course, increased competition for potential attendees; a returning congregation was required to pay for the construction and consequent upkeep of these buildings, so denominations needed to find ways to attract new members, and consolidate their audiences.

There were also other, competing claims on leisure time, some of which claimed their own moral qualities: at the opening of the New Theatre Royal in Nottingham in September 1865 the theatre's manager, Mr Walter Montgomery, argued:

> With a well-conducted theatre, and with a company of ladies and gentlemen, what is to prevent the drama from fulfilling its great mission, viz., a teacher of the highest morality, nay, even the gentle hand-maiden of religion. [...] there is nothing inconsistent in the following of our profession and the 'wearing the light yoke of that Lord of Love who stilled the rolling wave of Galilee'.[17]

Here the *Express*, inclined to sympathize with nonconformist – and more specifically Methodist – ideals, advertises the moral integrity of the venue. However, in summarizing the speech, the paper also reveals that Montgomery may be just as concerned to attract a literary elite within the town, as he chooses to quote lines from the New Testament that had been incorporated by Tennyson (then Poet Laureate) in to *Enoch Arden*, published in 1864. The reporting of this speech enhances the sense of vigorous competition between different sites associated with culture, leisure and faith within the town that would potentially appeal to the same individuals within Nottingham. Secular and religious venues existed within close geographical proximity and in strong tension with each other, inevitably resulting in a competitive form of the 'overlap, complement or conflict' identified by Kong. Our analysis in this chapter of the approaches taken by these venues to the attraction, creation and sustaining of different audiences and congregations within Nottingham, which identifies shared strategies and methods, thus helps to illuminate our understanding of both congregations and audiences and of the wider social networks within the town by highlighting issues of choice and agency which may sit at odds with more conventionally understood habits of faith. In this light, religious performance can be seen not just as a demonstration of such faith, but rather as another site within public discourse in which the urban individual could develop and practice his or her subjective identity.

Practising religion, exercising choice

Although any such identity would be delineated to a significant extent by socioeconomic parameters including gender and profession (or the absence of the latter), practices such as religious worship in theatres, and the colonization of disparate urban environments by different religious groups, portrays a concern with expansion over consolidation in a manner that provided a greater degree of choice for the individual. These groups responded to the rapid development of Nottingham as an industrial centre – one manifestation of the economic liberalism that had become dominant in line with industrial development since the latter half of the eighteenth century – through the expansion of facilities for potential worshippers. The result was a broader range of choice, albeit choice demarcated by the particular strategies and aims of each distinct faith group. With this analysis of the religious landscape of Nottingham in mind, it is perhaps unsurprising that developers and administrators of these new religious venues and of nonconformist sites of worship in particular were keen to capitalize on the increased mobility and leisure time of subjects in this changing urban environment. In such an environment, relationships between individuals and particular churches can be seen as marked by choice rather than habit: religious historian Horton Davies argues that 'sermon-tasting' – the practice of visiting many different churches to hear notable orators preach – 'was a favourite diversion that also counted as a duty and was thus doubly attractive to the Victorians', and notes the sustained popularity of the practice within nonconformist denominations particularly throughout the nineteenth century.[18] 'People from a broad range of social and educational backgrounds attended the services of various notable preachers', suggests Joseph Meisel:

> Certainly, some did so out of curiosity or because it was the thing to do; but the fact that these preachers were famous enough to make attendance broadly fashionable indicates the extent to which hearing leading religious orators provided entertainment value.[19]

The diary of George Harwood, whose comments on the growth of religious venues in the town we have already seen, provides a specific example of this mobility between religious venues as both preacher and worshipper in Nottingham:

> *Sunday 30 April, 1865:*
> Walked to Carlton, and at 10½ preached in our Chapel there on Judas, with remarkable freedom. Rode down with Mrs. Taylor to Carlton field and had dinner. Spent the afternoon with Mr. Taylor in conversation about Methodist affairs. [...] After tea, walked through Colwick to Nottingham, and went to Halifax Place Chapel where I heard the Rev. James Daniel, of Wrexham, preach on Martha and Mary.[20]

Harwood's exercise of choice was not exceptional; regular advertisements in Nottingham newspapers, which listed times for special services and sermons alongside the competing demands of theatres and other entertainments in and around the town, suggests an awareness of such practices by different denominations, with each venue working to publicize what was distinctive about the particular form of worship or entertainment they were providing. Such advertisements also reveal the commercial imperatives underpinning a broad programme of services: effective marketing worked to attract individuals who could be encouraged to donate money to ensure the maintenance of church buildings and associated educational institutions.

One example of such advertising can be found in the *Nottingham Journal* of 17 June 1865, where an announcement provided information on the annual fundraising drive, in Anglican venues, for the Nottingham branch of the Church Missionary Society (see Figure 7.1). Potential members of the congregations for these sermons are presented with listings for individual venues that seem to encourage choice between churches in the town centre and surrounding villages according to the speakers who would be present (the relative success of these listings is indicated by a report in the *Journal* of 19 June 1865 of the funds raised at the sermons).[21] The listing of 12 simultaneous morning sermons and 13 evening sermons, happening at the same time as services in nonconformist and dissenting chapels, remind us that individuals could select an event according to shifting preferences and demands. Within the public sphere of performed religion, then, changing conditions within the urban environment opened up the possibility of individual agency in the exercise of choice between available faith-based activities.

Such agency was not limitless, and, indeed, the advertising used to evidence its existence here also directs and limits its exercise, as Michael Warner's work on publics and counterpublics makes clear:

> The self-organized nature of the public does not mean that it is always spontaneous or organically expressive of individuals' wishes. Although

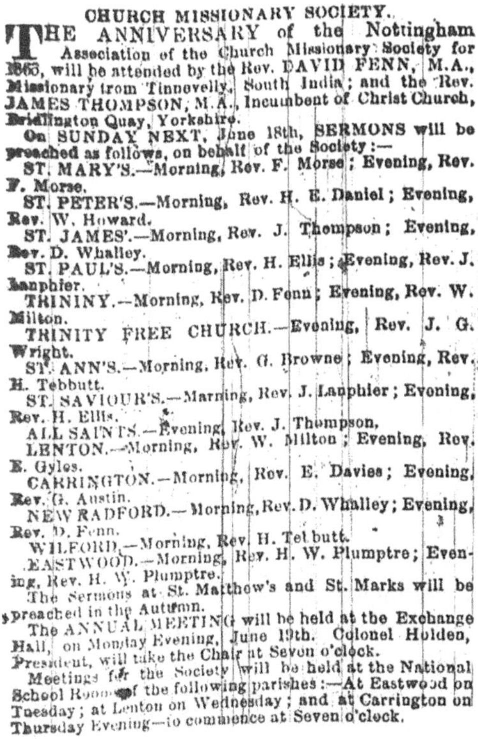

CHURCH MISSIONARY SOCIETY.

THE ANNIVERSARY of the Nottingham Association of the Church Missionary Society for 1865, will be attended by the Rev. DAVID FENN, M.A., Missionary from Tinnevelly, South India; and the Rev. JAMES THOMPSON, M.A., Incumbent of Christ Church, Bridlington Quay, Yorkshire.

On SUNDAY NEXT, June 18th, SERMONS will be preached as follows, on behalf of the Society:—

ST. MARY'S.—Morning, Rev. F. Morse; Evening, Rev. F. Morse.

ST. PETER'S.—Morning, Rev. H. E. Daniel; Evening, Rev. W. Howard.

ST. JAMES'.—Morning, Rev. J. Thompson; Evening, Rev. D. Whalley.

ST. PAUL'S.—Morning, Rev. H. Ellis; Evening, Rev. J. Lanphier.

TRININY.—Morning, Rev. D. Fenn; Evening, Rev. W. Milton.

TRINITY FREE CHURCH.—Evening, Rev. J. G. Wright.

ST. ANN'S.—Morning, Rev. G. Browne; Evening, Rev. H. Tebbutt.

ST. SAVIOUR'S.—Marning, Rev. J. Lanphier; Evening, Rev. H. Ellis.

ALL SAINTS.—Evening, Rev. J. Thompson.

LENTON.—Morning, Rev. W. Milton; Evening, Rev. E. Gyles.

CARRINGTON.—Morning, Rev. E. Davies; Evening, Rev. G. Austin.

NEW RADFORD.—Morning, Rev. D. Whalley; Evening, Rev. D. Fenn.

WILFORD.—Morning, Rev. H. Tebbutt.

EASTWOOD.—Morning, Rev. H. W. Plumptre; Evening, Rev. H. W. Plumptre.

The Sermons at St. Matthew's and St. Marks will be preached in the Autumn.

The ANNUAL MEETING will be held at the Exchange Hall, on Monday Evening, June 19th. Colonel Holden, President, will take the Chair at Seven o'clock.

Meetings for the Society will be held at the National School Room of the following parishes:—At Eastwood on Tuesday; at Lenton on Wednesday; and at Carrington on Thursday Evening—to commence at Seven o'clock.

Figure 7.1 *Nottingham Journal*, 17 July 1865, p. 8
Image courtesy of Nottingham Local Studies Library, Nottingham City Council

> the premise of self-organizing discourse is necessary to the peculiar cultural artifact that we call a public, it is contradicted both by material limits – means of production and distributions, the physical textual objects, social conditions of access – and by internal ones, including the need to presuppose forms of intelligibility already in place, as well as the social closure entailed by any selection of genre, idiolect, style, address, and so on.[22]

But while marketing shapes the nature of the choices that can be made, it is still important to note that the very process of selecting a given event, on the part of the social actor – an aspect of the 'self-organizing discourse' – remains a demonstration of individual agency within the public sphere. In place of regular and consistent religious observance at one location as a mark of respectability (most particularly among the middle-class residents who would be in a position to purchase newspapers and respond to the advertisements) the publicity afforded to exceptional Sunday services implies instead the possible operation of a more flexible economy of religious performance practice, based on taste, choice, and social contexts as well as purely religious affiliation. Such flexibility was, as has been noted, delineated and defined by the range of facilities and activities established and administered by religious groups within the town. The variety and simultaneity of events does, however, establish the presence of multiple and competing religious and secular events that were available within the still fairly restricted confines of the mid-nineteenth-century town.

Competition and responsiveness: new sites and new performances

In the light of this more flexible economy of religious practice, different denominations sought to provide a number and variety of activities at different locations that competed with alternative religious and secular events in Nottingham. As with the reports of religious services in the theatre with which this chapter began, religious leaders recognized that established venues might not best serve the needs of potential congregations. Indeed, the Religious Census returns of 1851 make it clear that the recent consecrations of new venues in Nottingham were prompted by the needs of new areas of population developing in the growing town, with the opening of the Lancasterian School Room as a place of worship on 26 December 1846 said to be 'owing to the remoteness of the population of that Neighbourhood from the parish Church'.[23] Thus, secular sites throughout the town were pressed into use for faith-based activities, most particularly for nonconformist acts of worship, demonstrating the versatile responses to industrial development outlined by Cornick.

An example from the *Nottingham Journal* of 28 August 1857 illustrates such an approach:

> On Tuesday last, about 300 Sunday scholars were provided with a first-rate tea, on the new Cricket Ground, Bath Street, at the nominal charge of 2d. a head, the expense being defrayed by voluntary subscriptions, promoted by some members of the Primitive Methodist Connexion. The treat originated in a singular movement, which has already excited great interest among the religious community. Seven boys assembled on the Cricket Ground, one Sunday evening in May, with the view of establishing a juvenile prayer meeting. The novelty of the thing soon attracted attention, and the meetings have been continued every Sunday evening since; not only children, but their parents and other grown up friends have been induced to attend.[24]

Of interest here is both the site where this event took place – a secular sporting arena – and the role of young residents in the town in initiating attendance.

However, of particular significance to an analysis of how denominations attracted their congregations is the manner in which, by developing an initial, spontaneous gathering into a formal event, the Primitive Methodist Connexion enhanced their status and profile within the town. As Harvey, Brace and Bailey observe in writing about Methodist parades and tea treats elsewhere:

> Moving out of the chapel, parades acted to extend the reach of the institution amongst people who were not normally part of its constituency. It is necessary to understand parades as part of putting religion on display, of articulating belief and of performing faith as a group. Parades and tea treats reaffirmed faith, rewarded attendance and acted as a vehicle for recruitment and retention of members.[25]

The young Methodists inscribed the presence of one denomination within the town through public display, mobility standing for prominence in Nottingham, and advertising religious faith through practice, to a broad public.[26] This example also reminds us of the role played by another prominent aspect of religious practice during this period: the Sunday School. This developed into a mid-week activity during the summer months, and therefore frequently took place on the same day as secular events, raising questions about simultaneity and choice-making among the individuals who were potentially both congregation and secular audience. On the same Tuesday as the 'first-rate tea' at the Bath Street Cricket Ground, a festival procession through the town followed by a tea party at Trent Bridge Cricket Ground was arranged for scholars attending the Anglican Trinity Sunday and weekday schools – one example, perhaps, of a very open competition between opposing religious denominations, with a recognized nonconformist group using a permanent sporting venue. This permanence argues for the prestige and legitimacy of its 'putting religion on display', to use the term introduced by Harvey, Brace and Bailey. A number of alternative leisure activities were also taking place in the town, further emphasizing the need for awareness that concurrent events were always competing for attendees. While certain events would appeal to very different audiences, some classes of residents might experience both religious and secular events. For example, the 28 August 1857 edition of the *Journal* (which reported on the religious activities at the two cricket grounds) also noted that, during that same week, H. Corri's opera company was appearing at the old Theatre Royal in St Mary's Gate, and that a picnic party on the banks of the Trent was organized by the landlord of the Carrington Arms. We can add to these entertainments some of the regular attractions in the town, such as an exhibition of history and natural history at the Mechanics' Institute, which had attracted 'a large number of persons, young and old, to examine the collection'[27] and, every day of the week including Sundays, when entrance was free, the pleasures of the Nottingham Arboretum, established in 1852.

Here is a varied potential programme of activities within a limited area. Access to some events might be limited by cost or, in some cases, by temperance or antitheatrical concerns, but otherwise all were available to the population of Nottingham – a population who could even, as in the case of the Primitive Methodist Connexion 'treat', initiate these events by their presence in secular spaces in the town, providing further evidence of the 'self-organizing discourse' present within Nottingham, albeit modified by precise social and economic contexts.

Returning to the winter of 1860, and the services in secular venues with which this chapter began, the final service of that year took place in what might at first seem to be an even stranger venue, as the *Nottingham Journal* of 28 December 1860 reported:

> On Sunday evening the Polytechnic Hall, Broad-Street, was the scene of ceremonies very different to those practised generally in that temple of wonders. The gentlemen who have for some time past been engaged in holding religious services at the Theatre it seems have disagreed with the Manager or lessee, and wishing most probably to increase the anomalous nature of the ceremony obtained the use of the Colosseum.[28]

The choice of the Colosseum Music Hall – once a Sunday School, but now 'converted, or rather perverted, into a place of low amusement' according to the anonymous critic Asmodeus, whose *Revelations of Life in Nottingham*, a series of articles reprinted from the *Nottingham Telegraph*, reveal him as a consistently conservative, critically moral voice – was indeed an interesting and anomalous choice for the preachers, one which illustrates the layering of 'simultaneous, fluctuating and conflicting sacred and secular meanings' onto individual locations.[29] Affording a single venue many functions not only echoes Kong's discussion of religious sites, but also places the onus on individual attendees to select from an increasingly sophisticated range of both venues and events.

Such examples establish religious worship in the mid-nineteenth-century industrial town as dynamic and evolving, dependent to some extent upon the choices made by individual residents. Of course, it is important to recognize that not every worshipper moved around the town, choosing different events in which they might participate. Most notably, by the middle of the nineteenth century, a steadily increasing number of children were attending Sunday or weekday schools run by Anglican and nonconformist churches and chapels, forging a consistent relationship between these children, their families, and the relevant site of worship, which, as we have seen above, often required new buildings to accommodate them, and the raising of funds to support them.

Whether a visiting preacher or a regular speaker, the performance given by an individual religious practitioner – the sermon – remained the single, consistent fundraising device employed across denominations. In addition to financial implications, the role of the individual orator, renowned on a national or a local level, in attracting an audience and consequently authorizing a space was paramount, and of particular interest to our analysis of competing religious and secular attractions. Yet, as we have already seen, the role of the preacher in the mid-nineteenth century was under pressure; the anxiety expressed by Anglican ministers in the 1851 Census alludes to factors within and beyond religious practice, as developments in education, literacy, print culture and the entertainment industry competed with religious worship. Davies notes that 'the Victorian preacher was far from being immune from competition'.[30] Those delivering sermons had to find methods to make individual venues attractive, and to encourage a returning audience to attend faith-based events. In addition to bringing the congregation in through advertising, it is apparent that preachers, as much as their audience, could move around the town of Nottingham, co-opting secular spaces to attract spectator-worshippers.

One final example demonstrates how this practice appealed to the individual as they selected religious activities. In February 1865, religious and secular entertainments became intimately and obviously related, as the old theatre at St Mary's Gate was again utilized for a religious service. As the *Journal* reported:

> Yesterday, two religious services were held in the theatre, St. Mary's-gate. The preacher was the Rev. James Caughey, the American revivalist, who had been specially engaged for the purpose, bills distributed during the previous week, inviting the public to 'come and hear the wonder of the world preach Jesus only.' The services, which were held in the afternoon and evening, attracted very large congregations, the stage being thronged by auditors and the other parts of the house crowded. After the evening sermon there was a prayer meeting, which was conducted in a most excited manner, a hymn being sung in the gallery and prayer offered on the stage at the same time. Penitent sinners were also handed over the orchestra and footlights from the pit, and conducted to a private service at the back of the stage, the drop scene being lowered to hide the persons engaged in this latter service from the gaze of the rest of the congregation. The promoters of the services were, we believe, the friends worshipping at Park-row chapel, where Mr. Caughey is engaged to preach every evening this week.[31]

Caughey's presence in the theatre, as with the service in 1860 described at the beginning of this chapter, was an unusual event within the town, prompting significant press coverage. However, where the reports of services in the theatre in 1860 exhibit concern over the melding of theatrical and religious discourses within a single space, here the distinction between stage and auditorium and between religious and secular space seems to have been

deliberately diminished during the service, as both the dedicated performance space and order of service were undermined in a frenetic, revivalist
entertainment where Caughey's audience could experience a degree of
physical and emotional intimacy. The complex use of the space created an
effect that could not be achieved in a site of worship, the theatre providing
a range of hidden and public spaces and the useful 'drop scene' that allowed
Caughey to stage conversion and revelation.

This special service was organized by administrators of a Methodist
chapel, who, demonstrating the flexibility of response noted by Cornick,
chose to hire a secular place of entertainment for the appearance of an
internationally renowned preacher.[32] The interactive service simultaneously
authorized a particular type of worship that could be associated with one
chapel in Nottingham and provided an arena in which residents in a rapidly
expanding urban environment, confronted with multiple, competing activities that occurred during their leisure time, were encouraged to become part
of a practicing and involved congregation.

By charting such events as examples of the choices that were available to
a growing population, it is possible to scrutinize the prominence of competing repertoires and the potential for congregational mobility in Nottingham.
Mapping the alternative performances and entertainments – religious and
secular – that were available at particular moments has established that,
while it may not be possible to chart exact attendance and participation, the
analysis of choice within an altering urban landscape can demonstrate how
the social actor achieved a measure of agency within institutional frame-
works, including that of organized religion.

Notes

1. 'Religious Service at the Theatre', *Nottingham Journal*, 30 November 1860, 5.
2. This anxiety was in line with the position of the *Nottingham Journal* as a paper with
   moderate Tory sympathies and a primary allegiance to the established Anglican
   Church.
3. 'Religious Service at the Theatre', *Nottingham Journal,* 7 December 1860, 5.
4. 'The Theatre', *Nottingham Journal,* 14 December 1860, 5.
5. This process is in line with Jürgen Habermas's understanding of the operation
   of and developments within the English public sphere by the mid-nineteenth
   century. See particularly 'From a Culture-Debating (kulturräsonierend) Public to
   a Culture-Consuming Public' in *The Structural Transformation of the Public Sphere*,
   trans. Thomas Burger (Cambridge: Polity Press, 1992), 159–74.
6. Lily Kong, 'Mapping "New" Geographies of Religion: Politics and Poetics in
   Modernity', *Progress in Human Geography*, 25(2) (2001): 212.
7. 'Mapping the Moment: Performance and Culture in Nottingham, 1857–1867',
   University of Nottingham, last accessed 5 February 2013, www.nottingham.ac.uk/
   mapmoment.

8. For further information on the AHRC, please see www.ahrc.ac.uk. We also acknowledge the help of our project partners: Nottingham City Libraries; Nottinghamshire County Archives; and the Manuscripts and Special Collections team at Nottingham University. For a fuller description of the project, see Jo Robinson et al., 'Mapping the Moment: A Spatio-temporal Interface for Studying Performance Culture, Nottingham, 1857–1867', *International Journal of Humanities and Arts Computing*, 5(2) (2011): 103–26.

9. Michael Booth, *Theatre in the Victorian Age* (Cambridge: Cambridge University Press, 1991) 10.

10. Kong (in 'Mapping "New" Geographies') usefully highlights the importance of understanding religion as 'a matter for historical and place-specific analysis' – our approach here – 'rather than taken as *a priori* theory' (p. 226). As a result, her understanding of the secular also shifts and fluctuates as her discussion moves across different contexts.

11. Peter Bailey, *Popular Culture and Performance in the Victorian City* (Cambridge: Cambridge University Press, 1998), 35.

12. Roy A. Church, *Economic and Social Change in a Midland Town: Victorian Nottingham 1815–1900* (London: Cass, 1966), 232 and 236.

13. Quoted in John Beckett, in *A Centenary History of Nottingham* (Manchester: Manchester University Press, 2007), 351–84, which examines the breadth of religious practice within Nottingham during the nineteenth century. Although Church of England, Methodist, Baptist and Independent congregations were predominant, and most relevant to our work in this chapter, further faith groups were also represented through single places of worship. Beckett and Brian H. Tolley calculate that 27.6 per cent of all congregations recorded in the 1851 Religious Census were present at nonconformist and Roman Catholic services (364).

14. Quoted in Beckett, *A Centenary*, 363.

15. Michael Watts (ed.), *Religion in Victorian Nottinghamshire: the Religious Census of 1851*, 2 vols, Centre for Local History Record Series 7 (Nottingham: University of Nottingham Adult Education Department, 1998), vii.

16. George Hodgkinson Harwood, *The Journal of George Hodgkinson Harwood, 1860–7*, Nottinghamshire Archives, M23,788, 5 December 1863.

17. *Nottingham and Midland Counties Daily Express*, 26 September 1865, 3.

18. Horton Davies, *Worship and Theology in England*, 4 vols (Princeton: Princeton University Press, 1962), vol. 4, 284.

19. Joseph S. Meisel, *Public Speech and the Culture of Public Life in the Age of Gladstone* (New York: Columbia University Press, 2001), 163.

20. George Harwood, *The Journal of George Hodgkinson Harwood*, Sunday 30 April 1865.

21. Figures for funds raised across the individual churches are reported as follows: St Mary's £20 11s. 0½d.; St Peter's £14 5s.; St James's £27 9s.; Trinity £27 12s. 10½d.; Lenton £21 1s. 10d.; New Radford £14 8s.; Carrington £10 1s.; New Radford £15 2s.; Wilford £4 6s. 8d.; annual meeting £40 4s. 10d.

22. Michael Warner, *Publics and Counterpublics* (New York: Zone Books, 2005), 416.

23. Alan Rogers, 'The 1851 Religious Census Returns for the Borough of Nottingham'. *Transactions of the Thoroton Society* 76 (1972): 84.

24. 'Sunday School Treat', *Nottingham Journal*, 28 August 1857, 8.

25. David C. Harvey, Catherine Brace and Adrian R. Bailey. 'Parading the Cornish Subject: Methodist Sunday Schools in West Cornwall, c. 1830–1930', *Journal of Historical Geography* 33 (2007): 44.

26. Considering the ways in which the field of performance – both religious and secular – in Nottingham was affected and inscribed by practices of movement and walking has been a key part of the work of the *Mapping the Moment* project. See Joanne Robinson, 'Mapping the Field: Moving Through Landscape', *Performance Research*, 15(4) (2010): 86–96.
27. *Nottingham Journal*, 28 August 1857, 5.
28. 'Natural History at the Mechanics' Institution', *Nottingham Journal*, 28 August 1857, 5.
29. 'The Colosseum', *Nottingham Journal*, 28 December 1860, 5.
30. Kong, 'Mapping "New" Geographies', 212.
31. 'Preaching in the Theatre', *Nottingham Journal*, 27 February 1865, 2.
32. Park Row Chapel was built in 1855 to house an offshoot of the Methodist movement, the Wesleyan Congregational Free Church. Its history echoes the story of multivalent usage outlined here: the building was subsequently used by various Methodist groups before being purchased by the Church of England in 1872 and renamed St. Thomas' Church. Caughey was an American evangelist who made several trips to Nottingham, perhaps most notably in 1844, when among his converts was William Booth, founder of the Salvation Army.

Works cited

Bailey, Peter. *Popular Culture and Performance in the Victorian City*. Cambridge: Cambridge University Press, 1998.

Beckett, John. *A Centenary History of Nottingham*. Manchester: Manchester University Press, 2007.

Booth, Michael. *Theatre in the Victorian Age*. Cambridge: Cambridge University Press, 1991.

Cornick, David. 'Post-Enlightenment Pastoral Care', in G.R. Evans (ed.), *A History of Pastoral Care*. London: Cassell, 2000, 362–82.

Habermas, Jürgen. 'From a Culture-Debating (kulturräsonierend) Public to a Culture-Consuming Public', in *The Structural Transformation of the Public Sphere*, trans. Thomas Burger with Frederick Lawrence. Cambridge: Polity Press, 1992.

Harvey, David C., Catherine Brace and Adrian R. Bailey. 'Parading the Cornish subject: Methodist Sunday Schools in west Cornwall, c. 1830–1930'. *Journal of Historical Geography*, 33 (2007): 24–44.

Harwood, George Hodgkinson. *The Journal of George Hodgkinson Harwood, 1860–7*. Nottinghamshire Archives. M23, 788.

Kong, Lily. 'Mapping "New" Geographies of Religion: Politics and Poetics in Modernity', *Progress in Human Geography*, 25(2) (2001): 211–33.

Nottingham Journal (Nottingham, George Burbage, from 1787). In the University of Nottingham Library, special collections.

Robinson, Joanne. 'Mapping the Field: Moving Through Landscape', *Performance Research*, 15(4) (2010): 86–96.

Robinson, Jo, Gary Priestnall, Richard Tyler-Jones, and Robin Burgess. 'Mapping the Moment: A Spatio-temporal Interface for Studying Performance Culture, Nottingham, 1857–1867', *International Journal of Humanities and Arts Computing* 5(2) (2011): 103–26.

Rogers, Alan. 'The 1851 Religious Census Returns for the Borough of Nottingham', *Transactions of the Thoroton Society*, 76 (1972): 74–87.

Warner, Michael. *Publics and Counterpublics*. New York: Zone Books, 2005.

8
Sufi Ceremonies in Private and Public

Esra Çizmeci

The *Sema*[1] (commonly known as whirling) ceremony is practiced as the spiritual journey of dervishes (student and devotees of Sufism). Listening to religious hymns and whirling, the dervish transcends the ego and matures through love. The repetitive whirling carries the dervish to an extraordinary mental state. The dervishes claim that they return from this spiritual journey able to love the whole of nature and all living beings without discriminating with regard to belief, class or race. *Sema* is performed as a tourist attraction, dance and/or worship in various public and private settings such as cultural centres, train stations, Sufi lodges and private homes in today's Turkey. Analyzing Sufi rituals such as *Sema* ceremonies, I argue that Sufi ritual performances inspire means of compassion and harmony for both secular and non-secular Turks.

According to Jürgen Habermas, religious arguments, having the potential to weaken democratic values such as social egalitarianism, are not valid in the public sphere. However, religious practices and ideas are primary sources of certain values that support the principles of multicultural citizenship, imposing both respect and unity. This chapter aims to discuss two related issues: first, the Turkish government's attempt to publicize the Sufi *Sema* ceremony as a secular performance without emphasizing the ceremony's religiousness; and, second, the functions of *Sema* performances in today's Turkey which hover between the secular and religious and between the public and the private.

Origins and history of Sufism and Sufi ritual performance

Scholars have often described the complicated history between Sufism and Islam. The links between the two have often been downplayed, due both to an Orientalist understanding amongst some scholars in service of the colonialist ideals of Europe and the United States and to the particular scholarship produced by orthodox *ulema* (Muslim scholars). However, contrary to this Orientalist scholarship and conservative *ulema*, the partnership between modern Sufism and Islam that is visible in Sufi rituals is far stronger than has been claimed. In order to understand the key connections and differences, it is necessary to trace the transforming relationship between early Sufism and Islam in Anatolia. Ahmet Yaşar Ocak, historian of Turkish religion and culture, writes:

> [I]f we look at the phenomenon of Sufism – as it was until the end of the 11th century – from the perspective of social history, we can state the following fact ... Sufism was actually formulated by the members of a settled, 'superior' culture, who found the monotheism of Islam, imposed on their cultures by foreign war-like Arab conquerors, who in addition to all else, were from an 'inferior civilization', too simple and plain. Their efforts were directed towards ensuring the revival, survival and preservation of this culture, within the religion of the conquerors, by using the templates and general principles of that religion. That's why Sufism can be seen as a 'parallel religion' within Islam.[2]

While analyzing Sufism as a parallel religion within Islam, what needs to be made clear is that Sufism is distinguished from mainstream Islam by its concept of God. While in conventional Islamic theology, God created the world as other than Himself, in Sufi belief all creation was originally one with God. Conservative Islam believes in the principle of *tawhid*, meaning disconnection of Allah from all the rest of the creation and His Unity. However, Sufism disagrees with the division of Allah from the rest of the creation. In Sufism, creation is seen as the manifestation of the Creator. Sufis believe in the transformation of the human expressed in the notion of *al-insan al-kamil*, which means the search of an ideal person 'who is equipped with superior divine qualities and is placed within the *al-wallaya* (sainthood) theory, through which theory an alternative to the Islamic institution of prophets is implied'.[3] The Sufi concept of human as semi-divine contradicts Islamic law due to the principle of *tawhid*. Therefore, in the eleventh century, in order to encourage the development of Sufi *tariqats* (orders or brotherhoods), Sufi dervishes started to improve their relations with orthodox Islam, adapting their beliefs into others more attuned to orthodox Islamic ones.

Members of *tariqats* aimed to systematize their practices, believing that organization was necessary for the expansion of Sufism. To do so, *tariqats* developed their theory of knowledge, embracing the doctrines of orthodox Islam. In this developed theory, a dervish must follow obedience to the *Shari'ah*, Islamic law, which made Sufism far more acceptable to Islamic orthodoxy. Beginning to follow Islamic law, Sufis, instead of declaring that they *were* Allah, were to seek abolition of the self *in* Allah. As Ocak points out,

> Sufism acquired characteristics that made it more acceptable in the eyes of society, of political authorities and of at least some of the scholars. As

the *tariqat* began to appear from the 11th century onwards, the epics narrating the miracles of the sheiks created a halo of charisma around them, with the result that during the following centuries the great majority of Muslim public opinion began to consider Sufism as something inseparable from Islam and even to identify it with Islam.[4]

Starting in the eleventh century, different *tariqats* formed around the memories of various Sufi *Pirs*, spiritual leaders. In the fourteenth century, by the time the Ottoman Empire was formed, Sufism was already recognized as a cultural Islamic movement comprised of different *tariqats* and Sufi ritual practices played a central role in the spiritual life of the Ottoman Sufi *tariqats*. However, Islamic orthodoxy was disapproving of the rituals and ceremonies such as *Sema* and certain forms of *zikr* (remembrance of God) that were also reflective of an idea that a dervish seeks to become one with Allah.

Although the Quran does not offer prohibitions against music and dancing, during the Ottoman Empire, the orthodox *ulema* persistently rejected the practice of *Sema* rituals of Sufi orders. However, considering the importance of Quranic names (used to define God) and the auditory aspect of the Quran, the recitation of these names was of critical importance for Sufi practitioners and thus Sufis practiced *Sema* and/or *zikr* in order to experience religious feeling. For dervishes, the practice of *zikr* is crucial for Sufi spiritual growth because repeating God's names allows them to fully release worldly desires and become one with their beloved. *Zikr* rituals of Sufism involve repetition of God's Quranic names, whirling, chanting, and vigorous physical activities. They are rapturous experiences in which the seekers can revise his or her[5] everyday worship; recognize the infinite; feel a sense of harmony, love and energy; realize the meaning of divine reason through continued reflection upon readings of sacred texts; refine the subtle faculties of the mind; and release worldly desires.

However, it is important to note that beginner Sufi students were not allowed to practice *Sema*. All Sufi leaders believed that to practice *Sema*, a *mureed* (student of Sufism) had first to complete the study of Quranic texts, and could only start practicing whirling and music after they had internalized Islamic doctrines. It was believed that an untimely experience of *Sema* would only inspire sensual rather than spiritual feelings. Abu Hafs Suhrawardi, founder of the Suhrawardi Sufi order, stated:

> Music does not give rise, in the heart, to anything which is not already there: so he whose inner self is attached to anything else than God is stirred by music to sensual desire, but the one who is inwardly attached to the love of God is moved, by hearing music, to do His will. What is false is veiled by the veil of self and what is true by the veil of the heart, and the veil of the self is a dark earthy veil, and the veil of the heart is a radiant heavenly veil. The common folk listen to music according to

nature, and the novices listen with desire and awe, while the listening of the saints brings them a vision of the Divine gifts and graces, and these are the gnostics to whom listening means contemplation. But finally, there is listening of the spiritually perfect, to whom, through music, God reveals Himself unveiled.[6]

Whirling, practiced by Sufi orders such as Mevlevi, Kadiri and Rifai, requires a high level of self-discipline in order for a dervish to go beyond his or her visible self. Training different features of the inner self is the central point of this self-discipline toward the divine unity.[7]

In the thirteenth century, during the time of Mevlana Celaleddin-i Rumi, the *Sema* ceremony was not yet organized in its complete form; however, the whirling was practiced as a spiritual discipline. According to Turkish historian Metin And, during Rumi's time, the whirling was performed 'anytime and any place'[8] to connect the dervish's mind to the infinite, initiating an emotional relationship between human being and God. Mevlevi *Sema* was systematized by Rumi's son Sultan Veled, and then the ceremony took its final form with the organization of Sultan Veled's grandson, Pir Adel Çelebi. *Sema* performed as a Mevlevi *zikr* involved vocal and instrumental compositions, readings from the Quran, recitation of verses from *Mesnevi* (spiritual teachings of Rumi), singing of the *'Naat-i Serif'* (poem of Mevlana praising Muhammed), meditative walking and saluting positions, and whirling. It was an inspirational spiritual force during the Ottoman Empire. Kudsi Erguner, who was a member of the Mevlevi brotherhood, writes that during the Ottoman Empire, *Sema* was performed in public spaces and 'was conceived of both as a ritual which would benefit the participants and as a spiritual concert which would spread spiritual benefit among the audience as well'.[9] Scholars describe the whirling ceremony as 'an aesthetic sight and experience' and as holding 'an aura of spirituality'.[10] Due to the religious and societal importance of *zikr* and *Sema* for Sufi *tariqats*, Sufi *mureeds* continued to perform their ritual performances in public settings such as streets until the prohibition of the rituals by the Turkish government in 1925.

Secularization of Sufi ritual performances: the Turkish state and Sufism

Mustafa Kemal Ataturk, the founder of the Turkish Republic in 1923, was an innovative military man with strong attachments to science, evolution and modernity. According to Ataturk's modernization plans for Turkish society, dervish lodges were to be closed immediately in order to transform the long-existing religious Ottoman culture into a rapidly evolving intellectual culture built on western scientific knowledge instead of Islamic religious education. His idea of modernization was committed to the notion that Turkey had to free itself of the Ottoman Islamic cultural beliefs and values that, he believed, bound the country to a remote and unsophisticated way of life. Ataturk wanted Turkey to move away from Ottoman customs and embody a more European lifestyle. He intended to realize this plan over an extremely short period, between 1923 and 1932, convincing the nation to strictly dedicate itself to carrying out his design for the Turkish Republic.

On 13 December 1925, the new secular regime of Turkey officially banned all Sufi *tariqats*, under Article 1 of Law 677. To reinforce secularization, Sufi *tariqats* that had been recognized as religious institutions in the Ottoman Empire were converted to secular foundations, societies and clubs. The performance of Sufi rituals was banned after the Sufi lodges were closed. Ritual accoutrements, including costumes and musical instruments, were confiscated and put on display in museums as vestiges of Turkish heritage.[11]

Due to the well-known hospitality of Sufi dervish brotherhoods (that is, their openness and generosity to visiting guests),[12] Ataturk was aware of their influence on society. As Anne Marie Schimmel suggests, Sufi *tariqats'* 'adaptability made the orders ideal vehicles for the spread of Islamic teachings'.[13] Sufi saints played guiding roles in people's lives because of the emphasis of divine love, trust, and togetherness in their teachings rather than a focus on the rules of orthodox Islam. In a public speech in 1925, Ataturk said:

> the aim of the revolution which we have been and are now accomplishing is to bring the people of the Turkish Republic into a state of society entirely modern and completely civilized in spirit and form. This is the central pillar of our Revolution, and it is necessary utterly to defeat those mentalities incapable of accepting this truth ... I flatly refuse to believe that today, in the luminous presence of science, knowledge, and civilization in all its aspects, there exist, in the civilized community of Turkey, men so primitive as to seek their physical and mental well-being from the guidance of one or another *şeyh* [spiritual leader]. Gentlemen, you and the whole nation must know, and know well, that the Republic of Turkey cannot be the land of *şeyhs*, dervishes, disciples, and lay brothers. The straightest, truest Way [*tariqat*] is the way of civilization.[14]

Ataturk's ideology was applied to the education system of the newly formed republic and influenced the minds of young Turkish citizens, convincing them they should not be affiliated with any Islamic organization, including the Sufi *tariqats*.

Şeb-i Aruz ceremonies: *Sema* performed in public

The secularization of the *Sema* ceremony started 25 years after the closure of Sufi lodges. In 1953, when ambassadors from the United States visited Konya (the Turkish city that is known as the birthplace of the Mevlevi Sufi order) as part of the European Recovery Program, the town's mayor contacted Sufi musicians and asked them to organize a performance of the ceremony. Following the first performance in 1953, the mayor initiated a festival, known today as *Şeb-i Aruz* (the Wedding Night – the day Rumi unites with God), to commemorate Rumi's passing. The mayor invited the members of the former Mevlevi Sufi order, including *şeyhs* and dervishes who were known to have continued to practice their traditions in their private homes, to perform their *Sema* ceremony in a sports hall. Kudsi Erguner, a musician from a Sufi family, reports that, 'The governor of the province told them that the festival was not meant to be anything more than a folklore performance. The governor warned them that they could get into serious trouble. This was a paradox bordering on absurdity.'[15] According to Erguner, even though the ritual was presented in a sports hall, the very presence of the *şeyh* made the space sacred for the Mevlevi dervishes.

However, in the 1960s, following the coup in which the Turkish military overthrew the elected government to impose the pro-western, secular form of government established by Ataturk, army officials and television cameramen started to attend ceremonies.[16] This disturbed *şeyhs*, who during one of the performances chased the cameramen out of the space, causing the government to ban the members of the Sufi community of Istanbul from the *Şeb-i Aruz* celebrations in Konya. As an alternative, the following year non-dervish performers were trained to enact the ceremony.

Authorization for trained dancers to perform at the celebrations and the exclusion of the *şeyhs* and dervishes should not be seen as a weakening of Sufi culture and *Sema* ceremony. It is true that the government tried and failed to undermine the religiousness of *Sema*. The government, by utilizing *Sema* ceremony as a secular tourist attraction, expected to stimulate the Turkish economy rather than promoting Sufi religious values. This action taken by the government should be seen as an unplanned strengthening of the religious *Sema* and its role in reviving Sufism in Turkey, because the growing number of enactments of *Sema* in the twentieth century enabled the Turkish audience to remain familiar with the spiritual teachings of Sufi mystics.

It is true that the Turkish government's decision to advertise the ceremony as folklore and the use of the ceremony for political speeches discomforted the Sufi *şeyhs*, who had controlled and practiced *Sema* as a religious ritual for centuries. However, witnessing a growing number of enactments of *Sema*, especially in Turkish cities such as Istanbul and Konya, *şeyhs* and dervishes familiarized themselves with the regulations of the secular world and started to take every opportunity to practice their whirling ritual for tourists, continuing to inspire secular Turkish artists and scholars to create work inspired by *Sema*.

UNESCO-driven Sufi ritual performances

In 1973, the Turkish government's intentions became more apparent when, in collaboration with UNESCO, the government observed the 700th anniversary of Rumi's passing, formally recognized as the Year of Rumi. With this designation, the Turkish government permitted Sufi practitioners to travel to London, Paris and across the United States to perform their (ostensibly) secular ceremonies. For the government, the designation by UNESCO and visibility of *Sema* outside of Turkey was the perfect opportunity to announce the strength of secularization and the serene position of Islam in Turkey. In honour of Rumi's 800th birthday, UNESCO also announced that 2007 would be the 'Year of Mevlana Celaleddin-i Rumi and Tolerance'. The designation of *Sema* and Rumi as part of UNESCO's World Intangible Cultural Heritage increased the visibility of Sufism and Sufi rituals as secular commodities of Turkish culture once again.

As David Smith argues, UNESCO's effort to promote the survival of 'traditional folklore, knowledge, and artistic expressions throughout the world, including oral traditions and expressions, performing arts, social practices, rituals and festive events' misrepresents performance's religious significance. Smith writes of the problematic way in which the organization has tried to organize knowledge, which reflects back to the historical western prejudice against non-empirical epistemology: 'The Western philosophical tradition has largely marginalized and discounted knowledge which cannot be represented in propositional form (and, preferably, written down).'[17] The information provided for the public on the UNESCO website, while informing the reader that 'today the performances have been mostly deprived of their religious significance',[18] was overgeneralized. It is true that Sufi *dedes* (senior dervishes) in today's Turkey organize the performance of the ceremony for tourists; however, most of the ceremonies organized by Sufi practitioners themselves encourage the public to focus on *Sema*'s religious significance for dervishes. On the other hand, producers and directors who were interested in documenting Sufi music, art and rituals in Turkey used these public enactments to create film and performance projects that brought forth the religious significance of the ritual. Taking inspiration from a variety of Sufi rituals performed by *dedes* and dervishes, more and more artists and scholars became familiar with Sufi arts, music and ceremonies. Through the visibility of the *Sema* ceremony's aesthetic qualities, religious Sufism has become more visible both in and out of Turkey.

In the last ten years, artists both within and outside the country, including the famous Turkish composer Orhan Şallıel, the Turkish performer Yılmaz Erdoğan and the American theatre director Robert Wilson, as well as journalists and fiction writers, have been inspired by Sufi culture and have created public performances of the whirling ceremony. In addition, articles, books, and art projects inspired by *Sema*, and the enactments created to represent *Sema* as a religious ceremony, demonstrated an increasing interest in Sufi dervishes and Sufi culture. Orhan Şallıel, together with a performance artist and producer, Yılmaz Erdoğan, created a representation of Rumi's life, poetry, and the *Sema* as part of UNESCO's celebration of the 800th birthday of Rumi. Due to the popularity of Erdogan in Turkey, the visibility of Sufism reached new audience members, who had neither seen nor heard anything about Sufism. Salliel's performance event was a valuable example of the ceremony taken out of its original context and commodified for the purpose of creating a multidisciplinary performance piece that nevertheless stimulated mystical feelings. According to the critic Elif Tunca, 'this new project [was] not like any other – particularly with its spiritual aspect, which Şallıel believe[d] [was] the most important.'[19] Pointing out the role of *Sema* as a religious ritual performed for the purification of a dervish's soul, Şallıel collaborated with the popular Turkish choreographer and dancer Ziya Azazi, who created an adaptation of the Mevlevi whirling, exploring the trance-like qualities of the ritual.

Azazi's performance used the high-speed ecstatic repetition of whirling and affectionate arm and hand movements, suggesting devotion, reflecting the experience of an intense emotional state and Mevlevi dervishes' search for love and joy. In his interview with *Le Monde*'s Rosita Boisseau, Azazi said: 'I try to go deeper into the movement to achieve extreme power and awareness ... the repetition of whirling carries you away like the current of a river or the flow of time until you reach an extraordinary mental state.'[20] His fast moves were highlighted by his use of *tennures* (long dervish skirts) in different colours (black, white, yellow and red), which he removed one by one at the end of his performance, hiding himself under the red skirt, taking the shape of the red sheepskin mat of the Mevlevi *şeyh*, and physically depicting the spiritual journey that the dervish desires to take to become a spiritual leader.

Through the exploration of symbolic images and movements expressed as the search for mystical love, Azazi's performance portrayed the dervishes' desire to go beyond the rules of society and religion. In Sufism, the most eloquent expressions of the soul are recognized as 'poetry, music, and the *Sema,* which embodies the unquenchable quest for beauty and perfection'.[21] Azazi's hand movements, reaching out and then touching and embracing himself as he whirled, expressed the dervish's body whirling with passion, searching the memory of his beloved, and seeking to disengage any thoughts apart from God. Azazi moved around the space so fast as he whirled with his black skirt in front of the black theatre curtains that he seemed as if he was flying above the musicians on stage. At times, it was hard to track his movements. The shape of his body looked like a shadow, suggestive of the dervish's journey beyond the material body.

The modern adaptations of the whirling ritual such as Azazi's dance performance are encouraging a youthful and energetic image of Sufism in Turkey. Nicholas Birch states, 'Many secular Turks used to respond to the word *tarikat* with a grimace of distaste ... however, since the 1990s, secular fears have increasingly centered on political Islam' while Sufism is seen as a 'moderate alternative'.[22] With the increase of the popular enactments created about Sufi rituals, Sufism is seen as a more appropriate option for secular-minded Turks. As Turkish scholar Metin And states, 'Alongside the cultural impact of Mevlana's verses, paeans to love, and humanistic Sufism, the ritual whirling ... continues to exert wide influence outside the realm of Islam'.[23] Azazi's performance generated an unrealistic picture of the Sufi dervish, neglecting the difficulty of a dervish's self-discipline and *nafs* (ego) training; however, in terms of accessibility to the secular audience, his whirling performance was able to present the joy of experiencing Sufi spiritual life. Watching him whirl was reminiscent of the human being's need to experience rapture and freedom.

Performing *Sema* in the Yenikapi Mevlevi Lodge

Many artists in Turkey seek to recreate Sufi rituals such as the *Sema* ceremony as spectacle, modifying the religious aspects of the whirling ritual and altering it into a modern dance performance; however, it is still possible to see enactments of Sufi rituals that have not been secularized in this way. Mainly in Istanbul, due to the high population of Sufi dervishes, it is possible to see Sufi rituals performed in the private homes of Sufi *şeyhs* that are old houses, apartment buildings, and flats used as *dergahs* (Sufi lodges).[24] These performances are reflective of religious feelings such as compassion, love and unity and are seen by small numbers of non-dervish secular and orthodox Muslims. In the *dergahs,* the presence of the *şeyh* radiates a gentle but unquestioned authority. He is exceedingly kind and attentive to his dervishes and their visiting friends who arrive at his *dergah. Tariqats* in Turkey, due to the legal restrictions imposed on Sufi orders, choose not to expose these spaces to the public unless a member of the Sufi order invites an entrusted friend. An invitation to a gathering at a private (mostly secret) *dergah*, says a secular Turkish friend, 'is an extremely rare occasion that brings to the surface once elapsed spiritual feelings'.[25] What is inspiring in these private *dergahs* 'is the dervishes's performance of certain tasks such as cooking, cleaning, serving the dinner, and *zikr* ceremonies, and *şeyh's* performance of *sohbets* (talks)'.[26] In most of the private *dergahs,* dervishes exclude the performance of whirling as a *zikr* ceremony, thinking that *Sema* has become more of a secular public show that is about the worldly experience of Sufism rather than dervishes's spiritual journey. Most of the private *tariqats* prefer to perform *zikr* ceremonies that are more about the vocalization of God's names in sitting and standing positions, moving to left and right, as they repeat Allah's names.

In such a performance of *zikr,* as the tempo increases, the dervishes start using shorter versions of God's 99 names listed in the Quran such as 'Allah hay; hay, hay; etc.'. The cycle of names changes with the singer's loud notification or through the change of music. The performance of *zikr* depends very much on the abilities of the singer, who is usually the *şeyh* or one of his *mureeds* (dervishes) trained to perform Sufi music. The passionate voice of the singer has the potential to inspire ecstatic feelings for the *mureeds* of the *tariqat*. With the repetitive sounds and movements of the *zikr* ceremony, the performers experience feelings of joy. The repetition of God's names is performed along with songs about the Prophet, the saints, mystical love and intoxication. The experience of *zikr*, according to a non-dervish participant, was like 'a call to a kind and generous self', an opportunity to 'release worldly needs and desires' and 'seek sensitive emotions'.[27]

On the night of the *zikr* ceremony in which Zeynep, a young female pharmacist, participated, there was one other guest in the *dergah*, who visited the şeyh's room and, along with Zeynep, asked to participate in the ceremony and *sohbets* (talks) of the *şeyh* regularly. The *şeyh* granted their request and invited them to participate in their ritual gatherings every week. According to Zeynep, who had observed ritual performances of alternative spiritual groups in Istanbul (those less guided by Sufi doctrines), having the opportunity to experience and practice *zikr* in a *dergah*, with the presence of a Sufi *şeyh* and his dervishes, motivated her to continue to further seek the Sufi experience as a spiritual practice.

There are also organizations that support the participation of *şeyhs* and dervishes in public settings, rather than trained dancers who perform the whirling ceremony. The designation of *Sema* ceremony as part of World Intangible Cultural Heritage by UNESCO encouraged the Turkish government in 2009 once again to support projects that would include the direct participation of *şeyhs* and dervishes to enact the complete form of the *Sema* ceremony as a tourist attraction. At this point, the Turkish government's commitment to secularism began to change. The Justice and Development Party (AKP), the pro-Islamic conservative political party that promoted itself from its founding in 2001 as the defender of democracy, has been in power since 2002. However, secular intellectuals in Turkey have never stopped either analyzing or cataloguing AKP's undemocratic values and actions such as today's most debated issue: the government's role in improving religious education. As part of the programmes surrounding Istanbul's title of European Capital of Culture for 2010, the government-organized events supported the unlocking of the restored historical Yenikapi Mevlevi Lodge for Mesnevi and Quran lessons, *Sema* trainings, and the enactments of the ceremony.

In September 2010, I had the opportunity to watch a performance of the ceremony in the Yenikapi Mevlevi Lodge, performed in the mystical atmosphere of the restored *semahane* (the space where *zikr* rituals are performed) in the presence of the tombs of old Mevlevi spiritual leaders. Although advertised as a tourist attraction, *Sema* ritual performed by a *şeyh* and his *mureeds* functioned more like a religious ceremony open to a public that consisted of families, lawyers, doctors and businessmen from Europe and the United States. What made the space mystical and the performance more like a religious ceremony was the presence of Sufi *dedes* and dervishes. The day of the enactment, I arrived early at the lodge in order to write in my journal and to have the opportunity to talk to my Sufi friends, whom I have met in Quran and *Mesnevi* (teachings of Rumi) lessons. My friends were performing the *Namaz* (prayer), which is part of the *Sema* ritual sequence. *Namaz* is the form of worship that is a five-times-daily obligation as one of the five pillars of Islam. Aside from the spiritual benefits, *namaz*, with its repeated standing, bending, bowings and preceding sitting or standing up positions, is regarded by Muslims as a healthy form of exercise. After the *namaz*, they came together in front of the *semahane*, and greeted each other using physical gestures specific to the Mevlevi *tariqat*. They held and kissed each other's right hands and saluted with their right hands on their hearts. The sense of simplicity and peace in their actions created an intimate atmosphere for the audience (members of the *tariqat* and group of tourists), as they were about to witness the ceremony. My role in the lodge was more like a guest researcher with intimate relationships with the dervishes. Even though I was there for the purposes of research, the dervishes referred to me as a friend and had me spend time with them before, during and after the ceremony. I was treated as if I was a member of their *tariqat*. They were very respectful and loving to each other and behaved in the same manner to all audience members. As we took our shoes off to enter the *semahane*, the dervishes welcomed us at the door. They were communicating with the guests as they entered the *semahane* one by one, with a calm voice, smiling and answering quick questions. Everyone was also given a booklet that provided an historical overview of Rumi, his work and Mevlevi culture, informing the tourist audience (who were there only to watch the ceremony) that the *Sema* was a religious *zikr* ceremony where the dervishes use whirling to achieve a union with God. We were also asked to be respectful and stay quiet during the ritual. The audience was not permitted to clap during or after the ceremony, to leave their seats, or to take photographs using a flashbulb. In this government-sponsored event at the lodge, the application of rules to peacefully perform the ritual was the affirmation of the respect granted to dervishes. Despite the legal restrictions, the Turkish government's publicizing of Sufi rituals exposed a hidden religious Sufi culture to a public that included both secular and religious tourists from different religious and cultural backgrounds. In this case, in contrast to the exclusion of Mevlevis from *Şeb-i Aruz* celebrations in 1961, the Turkish government today was at least trying to protect Sufi cultural practices as Turkey's cultural heritage.

When *Sema* was enacted in the Yenikapi Mevlevi lodge by the dervishes, the ceremony, including the whirling and the sounds of instruments, was loaded with cultural and religious meaning. The sense of worship served as a form of communicable affect, arising from the way the dervishes saluted each other and walked around the space in silence, their eyes loosely focused on their actions. The dervishes' performance of each gesture was specific in reflecting their desire to beat egotism. Their whirling with their heads slightly bent and their arms raised and open, suggestive of their *naïveté*, represented 'an act and drama of faith'.[28] Each section of the dervishes' whirling was reflective of a high state of peace and joy; however, to them, each section was performed for a different purpose. The first whirling was enacted as the dervish's birth to truth; the second was the witnessing of the magnificence of creation; the third was the transformation of joy into love and, by this means, the sacrifice of mind to love; and the fourth whirling was performed to return to their mission in everyday life.[29] During these sections, they gradually achieved a rhythmic whirling that was accomplished through physical and mental release, and when they completed the sequence and returned back to their mats, they seemed calm and oblivious to worldly passions and desires. Apart from the aesthetic sight of each whirling part, what made the movements of the Mevlevi dervishes inspiring was the visible meditative state and peace that they achieved through the ritual, reminding the audience of an alternative way of human contact that is focused on respect and unity.

In the Yenikapi Mevlevi Lodge, the release achieved through the repetition of ongoing whirling seemed essential to the dervishes and the audience entering a state of joy. The performance of the ceremony was full of regulations to be followed by the *semazens;* however, the sound of musical instruments and chants determined the timing of each action. Therefore, rather than coming across as authoritarian, the *semazens's* physical movements seemed to be unrestricted. As Rumi pointed out, *Sema* was performed 'to discover love, to feel the shudder of the encounter, to take off the veils, and to be in the presence of god'.[30] The performance ended with prayers. The *şeyh* and dervishes left the space quietly and no one clapped.

The audience members watched the ceremony with a sense of amazement. They left the *semahane* curious about Mevlevi culture and the whirling ritual; by the end of the ceremony some of them were chatting about Sufi retreat centres. A group of elderly British audience members who were more familiar with Mevlana's poetry shared their knowledge of his teachings about divine love while others observed the lodge itself, staring at the windows and doors searching for signs of the dervishes's everyday lives.

Conclusion

Habermas opposes the political establishment of religious doctrines because he believes that such doctrines do not provide an acceptably egalitarian basis for political reasoning. However, both within and outside present-day Turkey, there are Sufi *tariqats* that carry democratic values such as diversity and equality and are open to individuals from different religious and cultural backgrounds. The members of such democratic Sufi *tariqats* perform egalitarianism while engaging with the doctrines of religion. The *şeyhs* of such *tariqats* seek to carry on teachings of Sufi mystics such as Rumi, who said:

> Come, come, whoever you are.
> Wanderer, worshipper, lover of living, it doesn't matter
> Ours is not a caravan of despair.
> Come even if you have broken your vow a thousand times,
> Come, yet again, come, come.[31]

During ethnographic research, I had the opportunity to spend four months in a Sufi *tariqat,* which manifested Habermasian democratic values. Its members were drawn from different religious and cultural backgrounds. They even spoke different languages, but were able to live together in the same *dergah* and perform everyday tasks such as meal preparation and cleaning. It is true that there were class differences in the *tariqat* and that *şeyh, dedes* and dervishes had different responsibilities. In addition, the *dedes* and dervishes have great respect for their spiritual guide and they seek to follow their *şeyh's* actions and behaviours. However, because their first aim is to train the *nafs* (ego) and mature with love, they value qualities such as listening and understanding one another.

Sufi rituals performed in various settings and the spinning and positioning of the body in public acts as a memory machine, generating and releasing the historical and current Sufi cultural beliefs and values. As Diana Taylor suggests, performed acts 'generate, record, and transmit knowledge ... they change over time ... but their meaning might very well remain the same'.[32] The contemporary performances of *Sema* are not always created according to the original structure of the ceremony; however, even when enacted by trained non-Sufi dancers in theatres, cultural centres and streets, the rituals can still carry spiritual meaning. It is true that the old Sufi discipline is bewildered by the confines of civilization, although it is quite likely that the *Sema* ceremony and the teachings of Sufi mystics such as Mevlana still speak to a new generation of seekers.

Performance of the *Sema* ceremony is publicized and is at the centre of cultural life in Turkey, reminding people of an alternative religious world that is supportive of a human existence directed with ideas of respect, compassion and unity. Even though the modified enactments of *Sema* such as Azazi's dance performance establish a secular representation of Sufism, they still empower Muslim and non-Muslim individuals through their experience of spirituality. These enactments, as they gain increasing popularity in Turkish cities such as Istanbul, Konya and the Cappadocia region, continue to generate hope for the strengthening of a democratic everyday life in Turkey.

Notes

1. The Arabic word *Sama* (*Sema* in Turkish) means listening. In the Sufi practice, *Sema* is a ceremony that often includes the vocalization of hymns, the playing of instruments, certain movements such as whirling, and the recitation of verses and prayer.
2. Ahmet Yaşar Ocak, *Sufism and Sufis in Ottoman Society* (Ankara: The Turkish Historical Society, 2005), xix.
3. Ocak, *Sufism,* xix–xx.
4. Ocak, *Sufism,* xxi.
5. For more on the inclusion of women in the Sufi rituals, see Shakina Reinhertz's remarks on how Rumi is believed to have taught both male and female students in *Women Called to the Path of Rumi: The Way of the Whirling Dervish* (Prescott, AZ: Hohm Press, 2001).
6. Anne Marie Schimmel, *Mystical Dimensions of Islam* (Chapel Hill, NC: University of North Carolina Press, 1975), 100.
7. Schimmel, *Mystical Dimensions,* 100.
8. Talat Sait Halman and Metin And, *Mevlana Celaleddin Rumi and The Whirling Dervishes* (Istanbul: Dost Yayinlari, 2005), 34.
9. Walter Fedman, 'Structure and Evolution of the Mevlevi Ayin: The Case of the Third Selam', in *Sufism, Music and Society in Turkey and the Middle East,* ed. Anders Hammarlund, Tord Olsson and Elizabeth Ozdalga (Istanbul: Numune Matbassi, 2001), 9–17.
10. Halman and And, *Mevlana Celaleddin Rumi,* 34.
11. Bernard Lewis, *The Emergence of Modern Turkey* (London: Oxford University Press, 1975), 410–11.
12. Schimmel, *Mystical Dimensions,* 240.
13. Schimmel, *Mystical Dimensions,* 240.
14. Lewis, *Modern Turkey,* 410–11.
15. Kudsi Erguner, *Journey of a Sufi Musician* (London: Saqi, 2005), 47.
16. Erguner, *Journey,* 47.
17. More on this discussion can be found in David Smith, 'Networking Real-world Knowledge', *AI & Society,* 21 (2007): 424.
18. UNESCO, 'The Mevlevi Sema Ceremony', http://www.unesco.org/culture/intangible-heritage/39eur_uk.htm, last accessed 23 January 2013.
19. Elif Tunca, 'Reed Flute Players, DJs Perform to Recount Mevlana's Life Story', 19 June 2007, http://www.todayszaman.com/newsDetail_openPrintPage.action?newsId=114331, last accessed 23 January 2013.
20. Roista Boissea, 'Ziya Azazi modernize les Derviches tourneurs', *Le Monde,* 7 October 2009.
21. Halman and And, *Mevlana Celaleddin Rumi,* 31.
22. Nicholas Birch, 'Sufism in Turkey: The Next Big Thing?', 22 June 2010. http://www.eurasianet.org/node/61379, last accessed 23 January 2013.
23. Halman and And, *Mevlana Celaleddin Rumi,* 105.
24. I visited the private homes of Sufi *şeyhs* and dervishes during my fieldwork in Istanbul and had the opportunity to perform everyday tasks with the members of the secret *tariqat.* Spending time with them as a co-performer, I had chance to see how the *şeyh* and other members use their private apartment buildings, flats and houses as a Sufi lodge, or *semahane,* the place where *Sema* or other forms of *zikr* ceremonies are performed.

25. Participant 4. Conversation with the author, 4 January 2012.
26. Participant 4. Conversation with the author, 4 January 2012.
27. Participant 5. Conversation with the author, 6 January 2012.
28. Halman and And, *Mevlana Celaleddin Rumi*, 34.
29. For more information on the spiritual journey that dervishes experience in *Sema* ceremony, see Tugrul Inancer's chapter in Ocak's *Sufism and Sufis in Ottoman Society.*
30. Halman and And, *Mevlana Celaleddin Rumi*, 93.
31. Çıtlak M. Fatih and Bingül Hüseyin, *Rumi and His Sufi Path of Love* (Istanbul: Tughra_Books, 2007), 81.
32. Diana Taylor, *The Archive and the Repertoire* (Durham, NC: Duke University Press, 2003), 20–1.

Works cited

Birch, Nicholas. 'Sufism in Turkey: The Next Big Thing'. Web. 22 June 2010. http://www.eurasianet.org/node/61379. Accessed 23 January 2013.

Boissea, Roista. 'Ziya Azazi modernize les Derviches tourneurs', *Le Monde,* 7 October 2009.

Çıtlak, M. Fatih and Bingül Hüseyin. *Rumi and His Sufi Path of Love.* Istanbul: Tughra Books, 2007.

Erguner, Kudsi. *Journey of a Sufi Musician.* London: Saqi, 2005.

Fedman, Walter. 'Structure and Evolution of the Mevlevi Ayin: The Case of the Third Selam.' In *Sufism Music and Society in Turkey and the Middle East*, edited by Anders Hammarlund, Tord Olsson, and Elizabeth Ozdalga. Istanbul: Numune Matbaasi, 2001.

Halman, Talat Sait and Metin And. *Mevlana Celaleddin Rumi and the Whirling Dervishes.* Istanbul: Dost Yayinlari, 2005.

Lewis, Bernard. *The Emergence of Modern Turkey.* London: Oxford University Press, 1975.

Ocak, Ahmet Yaşar. *Sufism and Sufis in Ottoman Society.* Ankara: The Turkish Historical Society, 2005.

Participant 4. Conversation, 4 January 2012.

Participant 5. Conversation, 6 January 2012.

Reinhertz, Shakina. *Women Called to the Path of Rumi: The Way of the Whirling Dervish.* Prescott, AZ: Hohm Press, 2001.

Schimmel, Anne Marie. *Mystical Dimensions of Islam.* Chapel Hill, NC: University of North Carolina Press, 1975.

Taylor, Diana. *The Archive and the Repertoire.* Durham, NC: Duke University Press, 2003.

Tunca, Elif. 'Reed Flute Players, DJs Perform to Recount Mevlana's Life Story', 19 June 2007. http://www.todayszaman.com/newsDetail_openPrintPage.action?newsId=114331. Last accessed 23 January 2013.

9

From Religion to Culture: The Performative *Pūjā* and Spectacular Religion in India

Saayan Chattopadhyay

The predicament of defining 'religion' is shared by many scholars, who today are cautious about any implication of judgement or prejudice towards a specific point of view concerning the essential nature of religion. Identifying the common markers of religious practice, especially those markers that are not established by the religions themselves, is the foremost difficulty. The issue is significant since it provokes us to consider a larger question: whether or not to categorize as religion those practices whose religious character is more performative than discursive. In other words, a series of acts, reiterations, and citations that are renewed, revised, and consolidated through time constitutes that religious practice in such a way that the construction itself regularly conceals its genesis. I wish to identify and unpack those elements of religious practice that make a religious ceremony into a social phenomenon, based on its customs, motives, and content. If these acts and practices of mediation are accepted as given, it becomes apparent that religions, in one way or another, claim to mediate the transcendental, spiritual, or supernatural and make these accessible for believers.[1] In fact, for religious traditions to continue through history they must be translated, or better, transmediated – put in a new form.[2] This chapter will discuss religion as a practice of mediation, because the forms and practices of mediation that shape religion cannot be ignored.

This chapter will focus on gaining insight into the emergence of new culture industries in India, and the new power structures on which they thrive. The increasing commercialization and liberalization of the media has given rise to new forms of popular culture that involve a repositioning of both the state and the religion they represent.[3] In this context, Habermas's seminal work on religion in the public sphere underlines several issues that illuminate the emerging conditions in which a politics of identity gives rise to specific imaginations of subjectivities and communities. Habermas's work emphasizes the centrality of the capitalist economy for carving out a separate sphere of critique and aesthetic expression, and draws our attention to 'the complicated and dynamic relationship between the spheres of intimacy, the private and the public, implying both the making public of the intimate and private, and the privatization of the public'.[4]

I hasten to add that I use the term public sphere with caution, as the public sphere should not be conceived as a universal notion that inevitably materializes in any part of the world as soon as some minimal provisions are fulfilled. Instead, I assume a rather loose understanding of the public sphere as the space or arena developing in a number of postcolonial societies, like India, in parallel to some degree with political and economic liberalization. I also specifically refer to the neo-liberal public sphere in India that emerged after the deregulation of the market in the late 1980s. Within that context, this chapter will discuss in what way the evident expressions of religion in the public sphere resist the narrative of modernity as defined by the supposed decay of religion's significance in public. This evident resistance demands that we reconsider the role of spectacular religious performances, as they serve a performative function involving the public sphere, the modern citizen-state, and the neo-liberal market – in other words, the basic components of the social imaginary of modernity.

Focusing particularly on the elaborate and grand public worship of the goddess *Dūrgā*, popularly known as *Dūrgā Pūjā* in Bengal, this chapter seeks to understand the ways in which religious performances in India merge with modern urban spaces, utilize global communication networks, follow consumption patterns, employ market rules, operate in secular time, and deploy principles of professionalism and consumerism within neo-liberal conditions. How can one conceptualize the troubled distinctions between public religion and popular culture? Might these emerging circumstances reveal a more nuanced understanding of the public sphere? How are media and religion involved in changing the politics of representation and visibility? Might such changes imply an increased interest in aesthetics instead of ritual efficacy? What forms of mediation are involved in these performative processes, and what are the specific effects on public religious performances when they are deliberately associated with mass culture?

Changing practices of *Dūrgā Pūjā* in Bengal

The *Dūrgā Pūjā* (the Bengali word '*pūjā*' means 'worship') is the most important religious festival among Bengali Hindus. Several thousand large community *pūjās* are organized every year in the city of Kolkata, and hundreds of old family *pūjās* are also celebrated. If one takes into consideration the total number of *pūjās* organized in all the districts of West Bengal then the number would run to hundreds of thousands. In addition, *Dūrgā Pūjā* is celebrated in other states, as well as in other countries by diasporic communities of Hindus. *Dūrgā Pūjā*, celebrated at the beginning of autumn, is the worship of the mythological *Dūrgā*, the ten-armed goddess of fertility. The *pūjā* continues for more than a week; the rituals are elaborate and the preparations start long before.[5] It was during the Mughal era in the seventeenth century that the first recorded *Dūrgā Pūjā* was organized. However, at that time, *Dūrgā Pūjā* was exclusively celebrated by wealthy Bengali Hindu families, who were either landowners or worked for the British colonial regime. During the eighteenth century a new element was added to the festivals when distinguished British officials such as Clive and Hastings were invited to celebrate the *pūjā* with Hindu families. However, the guests took part of the festivities but they were not allowed to enter the sacred space inside the household, the site for the *Dūrgā* idol.[6] Traditional family *pūjā*s are still organized in Kolkata and these family rituals are among the most popular tourist destinations during the *pūjā* festivities, although the grandeur of the family *pūjā* has declined significantly in contrast to the practices of colonial times. *Dūrgā Pūjā* gradually spread from the households of the rural *raja*, or wealthy landlords, to the urban spaces of Kolkata, but nonetheless it was restricted to elite households. The *baroari*, or public worship of the *Dūrgā* goddess, began in the last decade of the eighteenth century when 12 Brahmin men established a committee to organize their own *Dūrgā Pūjā* in Guptipara village in the Nadia district of West Bengal, mainly because some of them had been denied entry into a household celebration. By the first decade of the twentieth century the *baroari pūjā* had become *sarbojanin*, 'for everyone', with the entire *para* (neighbourhood or community) involved. The *sarbojanin Dūrgā Pūjā* had become a *parar pūjā*.[7]

Community *pūjā*s are funded by donations collected from almost every household in the neighbourhood. However, beginning in the early 1990s, the increasing corporatization of the community *pūjā* has facilitated the collection of funds through advertisements and sponsorships. The assistance of political personalities is seen as essential for obtaining advertisements and corporate sponsorships. Local businesspersons as well as well-placed corporate executives have become important conduits for funds supporting community *pūjā*.[8] The budgets for the big community *pūjā* organizers are enormous and can go as high as a few million rupees. There is a competitive attitude among the large community *pūjā*s, and awards, sponsored by large, often multinational corporations, are given in various categories. The design of the *pandal*s, the lighting, the image of the *Dūrgā*, the management of the *pūjā*, and creativity, aesthetics, and ambience are all given awards.[9]

One of the many customs of the almost 24-hour-long *Dūrgā Pūjā* is to visit the grand and elaborate *pandal*s one at a time, a processing which is popularly known as '*pandal* hopping'. Cultural activities play an important part in the *pūjā* celebrations. Almost every publication house, as well as the daily newspapers and weekly magazines, brings out special supplements and anthologies during *pūjā*. From music albums and television shows to films and theatre, all cultural media wait for this very profitable period to release new material. On the last day of the worship a series of grand processions takes place towards the river Ganges for the immersion of the *Dūrgā* idol.

In the last few years, worship of *Dūrgā* based on a particular theme has emerged. A specific concept or idea has come to shape almost all of the organizing facets of the *pūjā* celebration, so that the final outcome will reflect that theme as a particular idea. Often, the conceptualization and execution of the themes is in the hands of established artists such as Bhabatosh Sutar, Sanatan Dinda, Amar Sarkar and Krishnapriya Dasgupta, in collaboration with a number of young art school graduates. Themes can range from natural phenomena such as earthquakes, global warming, and seashells, to cultural activities and events such as origami, cave paintings, Hogwarts Castle, Jurassic Park, Atlantis, and India's World Cup victory, not to mention the replicas of a variety of well-known buildings and structures around the world. The entire arrangement, from designing the *pandal*, the lighting, props, and installations, to marketing and promotion all present that specific theme. However, in an interesting turn of phrase, 'theme-*pūjā*' literally means the worship of themes. Bengalis have often debated this overriding focus on themes. It can be argued that even the first community worship of *Dūrgā* was a themed worship or theme-*pūjā*. During the period of the nationalist movement, community *pūjā*s served an important political role in providing platforms for resistance. For example, in 1926 Shimla Byam Samiti, an association under the patronage of Indian nationalist leader Atindranath Basu, organized a community worship of *Dūrgā*, in which the *Mahisasur* (the buffalo demon) was made up like a British officer, and the goddess *Dūrgā* in Khadi was presented as the *Bharatmata* (mother India) liberating India from colonial rule. The police stopped the *pūjā* procession and the idols were destroyed. As early as 1829 there was a common practice of constructing or presenting a special aspect relating to the *Dūrgā* worship to attract people.[10] However, unlike theme-*pūjā*, the special addition was most often an added attraction and not always entirely integrated with the *Dūrgā* worship.

In the 1980s a new trend arose in which *Dūrgā* idols were made out of unusual materials such as rice, coins, vinyl records, and even vegetables and biscuits, instead of the traditional clay. There was a visible change in the way *pandal*s were designed and in the choice of materials used to construct the *pandal*s. The phrase 'theme-*pūjā*' gradually entered the vernacular in the 1990s. Initiated mainly in the southern part of Kolkata, the arrangement of *Dūrgā* worship centred around a particular theme gradually became more widespread across Kolkata and the suburbs. The changes were not only in the materials and decoration but, more importantly, in the addition of a wider range of cultural practices. The tradition of playing popular commercial Hindi film songs on loudspeakers yielded to alternatives such as the refined songs of Tagore, Indian instrumental music, folk songs, or even the recorded recitation of mantras. The custom of giving awards to the best *pūjā* began in 1985 with the 'Asian Paints Sharad Shamman', as a means of recognizing the best-decorated *pūjā pandal* in Kolkata. A number of well-known companies started giving awards in various categories, and increasingly the winners emerged as those with the most innovative and elaborate themes.

Figure 9.1   Durga Puja street scene

Commercial advertising and brand positioning during the festival has become a major enterprise in itself, and *pūjās* that are able to attract large crowds to their *pandals* become the beneficiaries of this publicity campaign. (Note the advertising in Figure 9.1.) 'Prizes and awards or spectacular displays attract crowds and depending upon the drawing power of particular *pūjās*, advertisers are willing to pay higher rates for having their advertisements and hoardings displayed at the *pūjā*.'[11]

Thus, changes in the public worship of *Dūrgā* have opened sites for new culture industries and the new power structures on which they thrive. Acknowledging the links between religion and the culture industry, especially amid the neo-liberal imperatives set forth by an open market policy, the commodification and proliferation of religion appears as an important aspect of popular mass culture in India. The emerging commercialization and liberalization of the media has given rise to new forms of popular culture that involve a repositioning of both the state and the religion it represents.

The cultural turn of religion

As a culture industry, *Dūrgā Pūjā*, and especially the theme-*pūjā*, makes provision for the wider lifestyle concerns circulating within its socio-cultural environment. Theme-*pūjā* organizers take up specific approaches of 'intentional contemporaneity' to frame their appeal. As I mentioned earlier, over the last two decades the celebration of *Dūrgā Pūjā* has become increasingly corporatized. As one report on theme-*pūjā* remarks candidly, 'the popularity can only be partially attributed to the well-oiled corporate machinery that is employed to endorse the product'.[12] The increasing management of religious symbols is similar to any other kind of brand management, and represents an attempt to capture attention in the middle of an already crowded popular culture, emphasizing the convenience and experiential value of participation. Although religion is typically conceived as a communal affair that incorporates individuals into collectivities, scholars, including Ulrich Beck, Anthony Giddens, and Zygmunt Bauman, argue that late modernity is distinctively centred around the category of the individual, such that in many spheres of action people have 'no choice but to choose'.[13] However, the imperative towards market choice implies discretionary involvement, in the form of a preferred affiliation with particular kinds of ritual, or in the form of a playful alternation between options in the marketplace of pilgrimage. This imperative to choose undermines the strict maintenance of an established tradition. For instance, the custom of *pandal* hopping has a structural affinity with the notion of collective pilgrimage. However, instead of a single destination of pilgrimage, during *Dūrgā Pūjā*, thousands of such spaces/places/destinations jostle for attention, each endorsing, promoting, and advertising to make sure that a large number of visitors come only to their *pandal*. Advertisers are eager to pay higher rates for having their advertisements displayed at the most popular *pūjā*, and also to sponsor them, provided that the *pūjā* with its novel theme can draw a large number of people. The sponsors supporting these performances of public worship spend thousands of rupees to properly market their *pūjā*.

The changes in religious life and the shift in the discourses that enjoin followers to observe piety in their lifestyles are less perceptible than the marked change in their mediation. Market models of religious symbolization and participation have grown together with the awareness that individuals are at liberty to pursue religious meanings in terms that speak to their lifestyles. As Berger noted, some churches adopt marketing-style discourses through which they differentiate their angle on the sacred from others, effectively creating a brand image aimed at informing the choices of potential church-goers.[14] However, in the context of *Dūrgā Pūjā*, what is interesting is that these public worship performances are organized by local clubs, associations, and communities that are almost never religious in nature. Unlike western churches, *Dūrgā* worship is more akin to a cultural practice than a religious practice. The *Dūrgā Pūjā* offers a more literal marketplace of commodified worship that does not essentially require devotion of the kind customarily linked with religious involvement.

It is not difficult show how the 'industry' of *Dūrgā Pūjā* creates cultural goods to be consumed by enthusiasts, as well as by the faithful. (See Figure 9.2.) Viewing the participants in *Dūrgā Pūjā* through the lens of the culture industry construes them as consumers of the products necessitated and produced by that industry. A consumer culture needs objects for the market and uses those

Figure 9.2   Durga Puja – tourist consumers inside a *pandal*

'elements of culture that can most readily be made into discrete elements of exchange'.[15] For *Dūrgā Pūjā*, this entails the commodification of images and objects within a religious context, separating them from their origins in religious tradition, and, hence, shifting them closer to a performative culture. I shall come to the performative aspect in the following sections but here it is important to underline that individuals construct their cultural identities out of this reification: they purchase and consume what is exotic and culturally specific, but not essentially religious or spiritual. In order for a cultural object to be commodified it also must be abstract and nondescript enough (like the 'traditional' Bengali identity) to appeal to a wide range of people. Commodification of religion entails this process of reification and abstraction.[16]

Within the neo-liberal imperatives of the Indian marketplace, Kolkata has become a major retail destination, and in parallel with escalating disposable income among urban professionals in the city, the consumption of lifestyle products has also climbed. All Indian retail chains, as well as multinational branded products, have reported growing sales in Kolkata that explode during *Dūrgā Pūjā*. In 2003 the volume of business during the two months of the festival period was pegged at more than three billion rupees. The practices of giving a *pūjā*-bonus to salaried individuals and offering special retail discount rates encourage everyone to spend. People save during the year to spend before the *pūjās*, since shopping for clothes and other consumer durables is integral to the *pūjā* spirit. The need for these articles of clothing and the significance associated with them has been created by the industry of public worship of *Dūrgā* within a mytho-poetic narrative. There are a number of mythological, folkloric anecdotes, often distorted over time, that endorse receiving and giving new clothes and other such consumables during *Dūrgā Pūjā*. From the perspective of the culture industry, one can see the disappearance of individuality within Bengali Hindu religiosity because the culture has created a standardized way in which a person of faith should behave and act. The apparent distinction between an essential act of religion and an element of Bengali culture has opened the possibility of pursuing apparently religious performance with a more uninhibited involvement.

Similarly, the needs of consumers are met through the media by hundreds of websites focused on *Dūrgā Pūjā*, daily programmes about the *Dūrgā* worship on television, and radio broadcasts. It is worth noting that these programmes and websites rarely highlight the religious or devotional aspect of the event; rather, the tone of such very popular programmes as *Pūjā Parikrama* (Journey during the *Pūjā*) is similar to that of a travel magazine show.[17] In the same way, special programmes on television and radio emphasize the cultural aspect of the *pūjā* with daily variety shows. Even a passing glance at the hundreds of reports, feature stories, and columns published in the daily newspapers and magazines is enough to underscore the fact that there is a deliberate emphasis on the aesthetic rather than the ritual elements of the *pūjā*. The attention of these popular news media publications to the various themes, their artistic inspirations, the involvement of the artists, the many innovative design ideas, and the number and size of the organizations involved draws the focus of the *pūjā* towards its value as a public art event. It is also possible to see a system of reproduction in this culture industry. The local printing press, broadcast media, and even the web media reproduce images, information, and events for mass consumption in order to keep people engaged in the *pūjā* as a series of transactional activities, which ultimately maintains the importance and power of the liberalized market. The continued success of the *pūjā* is contingent upon its effective transition from the religious to the cultural.

Religion of spectacle

It is important to note that religions tend to be rearticulated within globalization, and that public religion has not in fact been relegated as a relic of a premodern past that should ideally be confined to the private sphere. How then can one make sense of this murky line between public religion and popular culture, and what are the implications of this blurring of the relationship between the 'secular' and the 'religious' for the idea of the public sphere? One claim that may lead the way forward is that the cultural turn of religious performance amid the neo-liberal imperatives in India has resulted in a religion of spectacle.

Drawing on Marx's ideas of commodity fetishism and the materialization of rational bureaucracies, social theorists have tried to explore how culture itself has come to be treated as a commodity.[18] While a number of sociologists have expanded Marxian theory into the sphere of religion and identified the ways in which religion has transformed itself into a marketplace, John Drane approaches the issue of consumer religion from a different direction.[19] Drawing from Ritzer's thesis of McDonaldization, he suggests that religion is increasingly being confined in the iron cage of a rational system. Since modern society is governed by rationalized processes, it is only natural that they will affect religious life. 'We love rationalized systems, and try to apply them to everything from our theology to the way we welcome visitors to our Sunday services.'[20] Similarly, in the context of *Dūrgā Pūjā*, the characteristics of McDonaldization can be seen. Efficiency is evident in the ways local *pūjā* authorities take specific measures to handle visitors smoothly and effectively; special maps are distributed for easy navigation around the city; makeshift medical booths, toilets, and firefighting stations are established; the police manage hundreds of thousands of visitors – even in the middle of the night – with commendable precision; even special VIP entrances for the *pūjā* are maintained with the focus on allowing influential, high-ranking visitors to view their *pūjā* as effortlessly and swiftly as possible. These measures mobilize a privileged form of cosmopolitanism, bound up with displays of cultural capital, classes of consumption, and the performance of distinction. Calculability is reflected in the focus on size and quantity among the *pūjā*s. The organizers customarily boast about the size, budget, and massive impact of their *pūjā*s. The daily papers publish the official footfall count of the biggest *pūjā*s every day in the front page. Without any reference to religious motivations or spirituality, the numbers, size, and budgetary expenditure of the *pūjā*s are put forward as measures of success.

The entertainment quotient of religion becomes reinforced when individual visitors are invited to act more like spectators than participants. These dynamics may finally result in the production of a 'Disneyfication' of religious space. Public worship is packaged like an event involving a variety of modes of spectatorial engagement, all planned to produce sensations of pleasure and gratification. The elaborate settings can even create an impression of the shopping mall or an amusement park. Hence, 'the city is transformed into a museum, exhibition or theme-park, where viewing and wonderment seem to entirely supplant worship.'[21] In this sense, following Foucault, *Dūrgā Pūjā* can be thought of as a heterotopic space.[22] Pradip Bose, explaining the almost magical transformation of Kolkata during the *pūjā*, remarks that heterotopia is simultaneously the site of the real and the unreal, the truthful and the false.[23] A space of otherness, an 'elsewhere' space that is characteristically transitory and ephemeral, marked by the gathering of a range of unusual evanescent images, creates a counter-site of the familiar, timeless Kolkata. Indeed, the diverse attractions gathered from all over the world, the Egyptian Sphinx, Angkor Wat, the Taj Mahal, the White House, the Titanic, an alien spaceship, and the captivating exhibition of stories that the lights, props, makeshift structures, electronic gadgets, and even highly-paid celebrities help to tell – all these finally produce a heterotopia of Kolkata. Different segments of time and distinctive spaces remain side by side without the least sense of peculiarity in this heterotopian world. Thus, whether it is the *pandal* made of vinyl records or the wrought iron and mahogany *Dūrgā* idol, every single theme-*pūjā*, as well as the traditional *Dūrgā* worship, becomes an element of this heterotopia. Thousands of individuals of all ages, castes, socioeconomic backgrounds, and even different religions unwaveringly take a proactive part in this world of replication and mimicry. The attraction is only to external appearances, and this heterotopia is created by an assemblage of disparate components in which no single component in particular has greater importance. Spectatorial pleasure takes primacy over the spiritual and the devotional.

Moreover, the theme-*pūjā* often situates the *Dūrgā* idol amid a bizarre collection of other images – the caveman, aliens, characters from popular literary fictions and mythologies, prehistoric animals, robots – all forming a tableau. 'The audience/visitors experience the idol in the middle of a riot of sound, light and colours. It is simply reduced to an exhibit, ready for consumption.'[24] The goddess is centred in an imaginary, almost quixotic ambience, where the audio-visual experience takes primacy.

The performative *pūjā*

Increasingly gravitating towards what can be termed 'Secular Hinduism', spectacular religious performances fulfill a performative function that serves the public sphere, the modern citizen-state, and the neo-liberal market – in other words, the basic components of the social imaginary of modernity. A closer look at these performances would reveal what forms of mediation are involved in their performance processes, and the specific effects they produce on public religious performance when it is deliberately associated with mass culture. I would argue that it is neither the religious representational and ideological function of theme-*pūjā*, nor the notion of space as a mythical/historical idea, that provides this spectacular performance with a definite meaning. Instead I wish to underscore a variety of performative practices, reiterations, and recharacterizations that have come to define the public worship of goddess *Dūrgā*.

Much in the way that 'performativity' describes the constitution of reality or identity through speech or repeated action, the theme-*pūjā*'s performance of discourse produces what it names. The theme-*pūjās* name works of art, but not acts of religion. The theme *pūjās* performatively construct the identity of a particular theme-based public worship of *Dūrgā* by creating and investing it within a predominantly artistic/aesthetic environment. Somewhat paradoxically, theme-*pūjā*'s performative constructions increasingly gravitate towards a more modern, secular identity.

Even in the context of late modernity, it is important to remember, the public sphere is not merely a pre-established field; it is constituted and negotiated through performance. The public sphere provides a discursive arena where members of social groups, even subordinate groups to a certain extent, can invent and circulate 'counterdiscourses' through which to formulate 'oppositional interpretations' of their identities, interests, and needs. As Nancy Fraser emphasizes, 'the concept of a public presupposes a plurality of perspectives among those who participate within it, thereby allowing for internal differences and antagonisms, and likewise discouraging reified blocks'.[25] Hence, the postcolonial, neo-liberal public sphere enables oppositional readings in which the traditional act of worship can be read as a modern practice, customary rituals are essentially assessed through aesthetic parameters, and the performance of religion itself is seen as cultural and thus increasingly secular. Thus, in addition to constructing the public sphere, theme-*pūjā*'s performative practices enact a way of being public. This is what Victor Turner defined in 1986 as 'performative reflexivity':

> A condition in which a sociocultural group, or its most perceptive members acting representatively, turn, bend, or reflect back upon themselves, upon the relations, actions, symbols, meanings, and codes, roles, statuses, social structures, ethical and legal rules, and other sociocultural components which make up their public 'selves.'[26]

In this sense, the codes, acts, and symbols rooted in the religious culture of *Dūrgā* worship are critically, and at times aesthetically, appropriated and thus moved away from their traditional religious culture. Indeed, the practice of theme-*pūjā* reinstates a bond with past traditions and implies the apparent fixity of religion and non-secular time. But through repetition, citation, and performance, the practice of theme-*pūjā* is reproduced and recharacterized again and again, attaining legitimacy and authority, and simultaneously investing in the construction of a modern, globalized, cultured, and, at the same time, pious self. But theme-*pūjā* is not a direct corollary of long-standing cultural habits and pre-established conventions. On the contrary, it assumes a new form, the production of a selective and negotiated field of performance that intensifies and plays up the performative signs of difference.

Theme-*pūjā*'s performative exhibitions involve interactive presentational practices that focus on the staging of mythical, historical, fictional and even fantastical subjects, objects, and narratives, and situating the visitor at the center as consumer. As the exhibition becomes a performative experience, objects take on the role of props in the theatrical staging of a mutual, collective imagination. By surrounding actual or fictional images and objects with interactive settings, lights, music, and evocative imaginary spaces, those images are placed in a broader narrative that has to immerse visitors in times and places they might or might not have visited, or to give visitors insights they did not have before. The performative public worship of *Dūrgā Pūjā* is focused on experiences instead of truths. The visitor is not confronted with one story or narrative that the organizers want to put forward, but multiple stories that criss-cross with each individual's memories, places, images, objects, and so on. These stories can contradict each other, but in a performative context that contradiction is not in fact problematic. After all, performative public worship is not so much about authentically or purely presenting an image, but more about presenting a personal expression, or an artistic impression, and at least implicitly relating it to the custom of *Dūrgā* worship. Hence performativity has an intrinsic connection with making religion public. Religion needs to be repeated and recharacterized not only to reinforce its own authority, but also to establish particular subjective categories like 'modern', 'secular', and 'transnational/global' that may seem to be opposing the very notion of religion itself.

Theme-*pūjā*'s diverse assemblage of images, objects, and narratives can also be read as an excess produced within a broader performative modernity. The manifestations and performances of modernity are sometimes overstated in postcolonial contexts. 'The evolutionary concept of historical change can hardly imagine that there can be a surplus or excess of modernity in some domains of social life in non-Western contexts.'[27] Here, modernity functions as a fetish and the public sphere becomes a site for the circulation of fetishistic modern and secular performances. That is why theme-*pūjā*'s exhaustive processes of building up a communal experience, the collective remembrance of an imagined past, the construction of an ongoing cultural affair, and the public participation of a community are just as important as, if not more important than, the ritual of worship itself. When the performative elements of constructing a modern, secular, global self and community become so overriding, traditional religious practices may take a back seat. Within such performative practices (rituals, customs, and myths), hegemonic narratives of faith are being contested and deconstructed, subsequently resulting in the creation of a distinctive kind of space. This incongruous new space is being constructed out of differences that should be taken into account, not only to recognize the forces that demand its normalization but also, perhaps more importantly, to identify the contradictions at work within it.

Conclusion

In this chapter, I have tried to explore a logic behind the changing mediation of the public worship of *Dūrgā* and to conceptualize the troubled distinctions between public religion and popular culture, and between the secular, the modern, and the religious. Outlining the changing practices of the public worship of goddess *Dūrgā* and the emergence of the theme-*pūjā*, I have attempted to trace the cultural turn of this essentially religious practice. I have argued that this cultural turn, amid the neo-liberal imperatives in post-deregulation India, has resulted in a religion of spectacle. Such spectacular religious performances serve a performative function that involves the basic components of the social imaginary of modernity. This ambivalence regarding the public worship of *Dūrgā* manifests primarily through a multiplicity of positionalities, cultural crossover, and the juxtaposition of different spaces, categories, and memories. However, the juxtapositions, hybridities, and narrativizations, far from being congruent, are carried out in double negation; neither entirely religious nor

wholly secular or modern, they result in specific forms of identity and identification. These citational and liminoid public performances shape new social
imaginaries. The emergence of theme-based public worship of *Dūrgā* offers a
new space in the making of modern social imaginaries, a space in which spectatorial, performative, and ambivalent spatial aspects erect a translucent façade
over religion, devotion, faith, and spirituality.

Notes

1. Jacques Derrida and Gianni Vattimo, eds., *Religion* (Cambridge: Polity, 1998), and
   Hent de Vries, and Samuel Weber, eds., *Religion and Media* (Stanford, CA: Stanford
   University Press, 2001).
2. Lawrence Babb and Susan Wadley, eds., *Media and the Transformation of Religion in
   South Asia* (Philadelphia: University of Pennsylvania Press, 1995).
3. Although, constitutionally, India is proclaimed as a 'sovereign socialist secular
   democratic republic' and does not have any official state religion, Hinduism is
   the principal religion adhered to by more than 80 per cent of the population. In
   the last three decades, Hindu nationalism or *Hindutva* has re-emerged as a popular
   and influential movement, and is part of the new political reality in India.
4. Birgit Meyer and Annelies Moors, eds., *Religion, Media, and the Public Sphere*
   (Bloomington, IN: Indiana University Press, 2006).
5. The Bengali mythology narrates the story of *Dūrgā* as *Uma*, the wife of lord *Shiva*
   living in *Kaliasha*. *Uma* and her children, *Ganesh, Saraswati, Lakshmi* and *Kartik*,
   return to the earth during autumn to visit her parent's home. After four days, she
   returns with her family to her husband *Shiva*. Similarly, Bengali custom prescribes
   that married daughters visit their parents for a few days of the year. However,
   the several versions of the story are interspersed with various different details.
   The image of Goddess *Dūrgā*, which is worshipped by Bengalis, traditionally
   depicts Goddess *Dūrgā* along with her four children on either side and astride a
   lion, equipped with lethal weapons in her ten hands, killing the Buffalo Demon,
   Mahishashur.
6. Kerstin Andersson, 'The Online Durga', *Media Anthropology Network*, 2007, last
   accessed 5 February 2013, http://www.media-anthropology.net/anderson_durga.pdf.
7. Anjan Ghosh, 'Durga Puja: a Consuming Passion', *Seminar* 559 (2006), last
   accessed 5 February 2013, http://www.india-seminar.com/2006/559/559%20
   anjan%20ghosh.htm.
8. Ghosh, 'Durga Puja'.
9. A *pandal* is a makeshift structure usually made of bamboo, planks, and tarpaulin
   as the temporary abode of the *Dūrgā* idol. Traditionally the *pandal* is elaborately
   decorated and lit so that it may attract visitors. There is also a tradition of constructing almost life-size replicas of famous buildings and structures from around
   the world. After the worship is over the *pandals* are dismantled.
10. S. Choudhury, 'Plywood e puraner chon [The Touch of Mythology on Plywood]',
    Robbar, 2 October 2011, 20–2.
11. Ghosh, 'Durga Puja'.
12. Uddalak Mukherjee, 'The Goddess Among the Many Arts', *The Telegraph* (Calcutta),
    6 October 2011, last accessed 5 February 2013, http://www.telegraphindia.com/
    1111006/jsp/opinion/story_14584188.jsp.

13. Michael Bailey and Guy Redden, eds., *Mediating Faiths: Religion and Socio-Cultural Change in the Twenty-First Century* (Burlington,VT: Ashgate, 2011). Also see Ulrich Beck, *Risk Society: Towards a New Modernity* (London: Sage, 1992); Anthony Giddens, *Modernity and Self-Identity: Self and Society in the Late Modern Age* (Stanford, CA: Stanford University Press, 1991); and Zygmunt Bauman, *The Individualised Society* (Cambridge: Polity Press, 2001).
14. Quoted in Bailey and Redden, *Mediating Faiths*, 90.
15. Vincent Miller, *Consuming Religion: Christian Faith and Practice in a Consumer Culture* (New York: Continuum Publishing, 2004), 78.
16. Miller, *Consuming Religion*, 78.
17. Probably the only exception is *Mahisasuramardini*. Originally a live radio programme (later a television programme as well), it is a two-hour audio montage of recitation from the scriptural verses that began in the 1930s. It is aired every year at daybreak on *Mahalaya* to usher in the lunar fortnight and the beginning of *Dūrgā Pūjā*. *Mahisasuramardini* carried an overtly religious approach but it was immensely popular. However, it has lost its former popularity, although different versions of the format are broadcast on radio as well as on television.
18. Colin Campbell, *The Romantic Ethic and the Spirit of Modern Consumerism* (Oxford: Blackwell Publishers, 1989); Guy Debord, *The Society of the Spectacle* (New York: Zone Books, 1994); Frederic Jameson, *Postmodernism or, the Cultural Logic of Late Capitalism* (Durham, NC: Duke University Press, 1997); Jean Baudrillard, *The Consumer Society: Myths and Structures* (London: Sage Publications, 1998); George Ritzer, *The McDonaldization of Society* (Thousand Oaks, CA: Pine Forge Press, 2000). See also Karl Marx, *Capital*, vol. 1, trans. B. Fowkes (New York: Vintage Books, 1977 [1867]).
19. John Drane, *The McDonaldization of the Church: Consumer Culture and the Church's Future* (Macon, GA: Smyth and Helwys Publishing, 2001).
20. Drane, *McDonaldization*, 41.
21. Guha Thakurata, T., 'The Transformed Aesthetics of a Public Festival: Durga Puja in Contemporary Calcutta', *Mohile Parikh Center E-Journal*, 2004, last accessed 5 February 2013, http://mohileparikhcenter.org/site/?q=node/171.
22. Foucault conceptualizes heterotopia in contrast to Utopia. Utopias are sites with no real place that have a general relation of direct or inverted analogy with the real space of society. As Foucault explains, 'There are also, probably in every culture, in every civilization, real places – places that do exist and that are formed in the very founding of society – which are something like counter-sites, a kind of effectively enacted utopia in which the real sites, all the other real sites that can be found within the culture, are simultaneously represented, contested, and inverted. Places of this kind are outside of all places, even though it may be possible to indicate their location in reality. Because these places are absolutely different from all the sites that they reflect and speak about, I shall call them, by way of contrast to utopias, heterotopias.' Michel Foucault, *Des espaces autres*, 1967 lecture translated by Jay Miskowiec. Last accessed 5 February 2013, http://foucault.info/documents/heteroTopia/foucault.heteroTopia.en.html.
23. Pradip Bose, *Samikha O Sandhan: Bhasha, Darshan, Sangeet*, A Collection of Critical Essays on Language, Philosophy and Music (Kolkata: Anushtup, 2005), 103.
24. Bose, *Samikha O Sandhan*, 94.
25. Nancy Fraser, 'Rethinking the Public Sphere: A Contribution to the Critique of Actually Existing Democracy', *Social Text*, 25/26 (1990): 70.
26. Victor Turner, *The Anthropology of Performance* (New York: PAJ Publications, 1986), 24.
27. Nilufer Göle, 'Islam in Public: New Visibilities and New Imaginaries', *Public Culture*, 14(1) (2002): 184.

Works cited

Andersson, Kerstin. 'The Online Durga', *Media Anthropology Network* (2007). Last accessed 5 February 2013. http://www.media-anthropology.net/anderson_durga.pdf.

Babb, Lawrence and Susan Wadley (eds). *Media and the Transformation of Religion in South Asia*. Philadelphia, PA: University of Pennsylvania Press, 1995.

Bailey, Michael and Guy Redden (eds). *Mediating Faiths: Religion and Socio-Cultural Change in the Twenty-First Century*. Burlington, VT: Ashgate, 2011.

Bauman, Zygmut. *The Individualised Society*. Cambridge: Polity Press, 2001.

Baudrillard, Jean. *The Consumer Society: Myths and Structures*. London: Sage Publications, 1998.

Beck, Ulrich. *Risk Society: Towards a New Modernity*. London: Sage, 1992.

Bose, Pradip. *Samikha O Sandhan: Bhasha, Darshan, Sangeet*. A Collection of Critical Essays on Language, Philosophy and Music. Kolkata: Anushtup, 2005.

Campbell, Colin. *The Romantic Ethic and the Spirit of Modern Consumerism*. Oxford: Blackwell Publishers, 1989.

Choudhury, S. 'Plywood e puraner chon [The Touch of Mythology on Plywood]', *Robbar*. 2 October 2011, 20–2.

Debord, Guy. *The Society of the Spectacle*. New York: Zone Books, 1994.

Derrida, Jacques and Gianni Vattimo, eds. *Religion*. Cambridge: Polity, 1998.

Drane, John. *The McDonaldization of the Church: Consumer Culture and the Church's Future*. Macon, GA: Smyth and Helwys Publishing, 2001.

Foucault, Michel. *Des espaces autres*. 1967 lecture translated by Jay Miskowiec. Last accessed 5 February 2013. http://foucault.info/documents/heteroTopia/foucault.heteroTopia.en.html.

Fraser, Nancy. 'Rethinking the Public Sphere: A Contribution to the Critique of Actually Existing Democracy', *Social Text*, 25/26 (1990): 56–80.

Ghosh, Anjan. 'Durga Puja: A Consuming Passion', *Seminar*, 559 (2006). Last accessed 5 February 2013. http://www.india-seminar.com/2006/559/559%20anjan%20ghosh.htm.

Giddens, Anthony. *Modernity and Self-identity: Self and Society in the Late Modern Age*. Stanford, CA: Stanford University Press, 1991.

Göle, Nilufer. 'Islam in Public: New Visibilities and New Imaginaries', *Public Culture*, 14(1) (2002): 173–90.

Guha Thakurata, T. 'The Transformed Aesthetics of a Public Festival: Durga Puja in Contemporary Calcutta', *Mohile Parikh Center E-Journal* (2004). Last accessed 5 February 2013. http://mohileparikhcenter.org/site/?q=node/171.

Jameson, Frederic. *Postmodernism or, the Cultural Logic of Late Capitalism*. Durham, NC: Duke University Press, 1997.

Marx, Karl. *Capital*, vol. 1, trans. B. Fowkes. New York: Vintage Books, 1977 [1867].

Meyer, Birgit, and Annelies Moors, eds. *Religion, Media, and the Public Sphere*. Bloomington, IN: Indiana University Press, 2006.

Miller, Vincent. *Consuming Religion: Christian Faith and Practice in a Consumer Culture*. New York: Continuum Publishing, 2004.

Mukherjee, Uddalak. 'The Goddess Among the Many Arts'. *The Telegraph* (Calcutta), 6 October 2011. Last accessed 5 February 2013. http://www.telegraphindia.com/1111006/jsp/opinion/story_14584188.jsp.

Ritzer, George. *The McDonaldization of Society*. Thousand Oaks, CA: Pine Forge Press, 2000.

Turner, Victor. *The Anthropology of Performance*. New York: PAJ Publications, 1986.

de Vries, Hent and Samuel Weber, eds. *Religion and Media*. Stanford, CA: Stanford University Press, 2001.

Part III Discussion

Esra Çizmeci, Saayan Chattopadhyay, Simon W. du Toit,
Jo Robinson, and Lucie Sutherland

Simon W. du Toit: The work in these three chapters shares a common interest in the question of commodification.

Jo Robinson: There was a kind of sharing of commodified culture operating across nineteenth-century Nottingham; they may have been secular models, but they were also operating in religious cultures at the same time. From looking at the newspapers, one can see that the visual presentation of what was on offer in the churches of the town was very similar to the presentation of what was available to somebody who wanted to go to the theatre or the music halls.

Lucie Sutherland: Focusing on the 1850s and 1860s gave us an opportunity to think about how increasing economic and political liberalization entered the public sphere in a variety of ways. This seems to have a direct relationship to a more secular component in worship, taking worship into secular spaces, and commodifying it in quite particular ways. Our chapters share an interest in the aftermath of those processes of liberalization and what comes next. The idea of secular components to worship was increasing, but not in a straight line. That's what struck me in Esra's work particularly, that for a variety of complex contextual reasons, this process of secularization can take place, but then in certain subtle ways it can recede as well, as particular groups or social actors find their place within the public sphere. It's a process of ebb and flow between increasing secularization, commodification of religion, and of the practice of worship. At the beginning of the twenty-first century, that process is emerging again.

Robinson: There's something quite interesting about the role of performance in that trajectory. In all of the chapters, performance becomes a tool for secularization that can be detached from religion and seen in a different light. At the same time, it also reinforces and returns to spiritual concerns. Performance is a really interesting double-edged tool.

du Toit: Habermas is concerned that religion will so firmly inscribe the boundaries around itself that it will refuse discourse with people outside those boundaries. When religion is connected to a centralized power, it becomes exclusive, along the lines of what was happening during the period of the allegiance between the church and the monarchies. For Habermas the force of the public sphere dislodges that centralization and exclusivity, and perhaps also weakens religious culture. Have you observed efforts to reinscribe some of the boundaries around religious cultures?

Esra Çismeci: When I visited religious orders in Turkey, I heard their fears about how *sema* was being commodified, and was losing its religious value. Sufism was increasingly about popular culture and entertainment. That was disturbing for some of the more fundamentalist *sufis* who live in Istanbul. An alternative side of *sema*, even though it was commodified, was that it also introduced the cultural beliefs and values of the *sufi* order to a secular audience. Young people in Turkey find the material world of modern everyday life confining for their spiritual understanding. *Sema* opens up some inspiration in these young people, but not in relation to *sharia* law. Lucie and Jo were talking about that in relation to the Anglican Church, how the preaching in secular venues gave opportunities to people who would not attend church. The commodification of *sema* performances in secular venues also gave an opportunity to young secular audiences to get to know religion. So there is also a positive value as well as a negative value of bringing the ritual out of the religious context.

Saayan Chattopadhyay: The same kind of thing is happening here in India as well, but there is a much more literal kind of marketplace for commodified worship, and which doesn't really require the devotion of the kind that is generated in religious involvement as such. For the kind of *Durga* worship that I'm talking about there is a large number of advertisers who are eager to pay huge rates to have their advertisements displayed at the most popular worship places, prominently located at the hub of the city and in centralized areas. The advertisers will sponsor the *Durga pūjā*s provided that the *pūjā*s will, with the use of novel themes, draw a large number of people, and become attractive sites to display messages and advertisements. The sponsors of public worship spend thousands of rupees to properly market, and I want to emphasize this word market, these *pūjā*s. The entertainment aspect of religion is reinforced when individual visitors are invited to act more like spectators rather than participants. That is why I have termed them secular Hindus.

du Toit: Was there any resistance to this from a more traditional approach to Hindu worship, one that that would have publicly marked this as somehow excessive?

Chattopadhyay: Even if there was some resistance, it was not powerful or prominent because this worship is being practiced in order to emphasize its cultural and aesthetic aspects. In so doing, it becomes much more inclusive. By making a particular site where there is a homogeneous body of consumers who can consume a range of services, it becomes a cultural practice and not a religious practice. People from different faiths are involved in this, people from different areas who do not actually know about the religious and political aspects of *Durga* worship. They come together and enjoy it as if they were entering a museum, or as if they were entering a kind of nightclub. Museums, nightclubs, these things are used as themes in *Durga* worship, and even the Sufism Esra is discussing is a common theme which has used over and over again in *Durga* worship. The whirling dance is present in *Durga* worship as a popular visual trope, but people don't know the specificities of its tradition or its practices.

du Toit: In the early modern period, the market provided an opportunity for a puritan counterpublic to circulate its discourse, but in so doing the puritans were marked as excessive within the dominant public. The forms of their performances and consumption practices served to mark them as outside the boundaries of what was acceptable.

Sutherland: In the 1830s and 40s, Nottingham had just been through a period that was marked by a range of public and political protests that were overtly linked to movements like Chartism. Throughout the 1850s and 1860s citizens witnessed the expansion of the city, investment in civic pride and identity, and the development of the idea of a coherent and cohesive town. Nottingham could not be called a city until the 1890s, so until then it was a rapidly developing industrial town. In exploring the different denominations and the different religious practices, what we found was rapid development – almost an explosion in the number of sites of worship that people could choose to attend. In the newspaper reports there is little evidence of people, collectives, or organizations working in opposition to those developing practices.

Robinson: In Nottingham, leading up to this period, there was a lack of Anglican dominance. The sphere of religion had always been divided in the town, and fragmented into many different publics. So there isn't a kind of dominant force against which people can compete. When religious services moved out of religious venues and into other places, there was a concern about excess related to religious activity.

du Toit: I appreciated your exploration of the work of Caughey, the American Revival preacher. Towards the end of the chapter you talk about his tour of the British Isles. I found it interesting because of the significance of the Great Revivals in American culture in that period, and their connections with the theatre. It was a strongly performance-oriented tradition, which might have been marked as excessively emotional perhaps, or even excessively physical. It seems to have been a hot commodity.

Robinson: There's a real link between the kind of pleasure that we take from theatre performance and the kind of pleasure that I imagine people were getting from that sort of performance of religion. It was something other, something that was visiting, and something that they weren't going to be regularly exposed to. We can look at it as a performance event as well as a religious event. The pleasures of those experiences are mixed together.

Sutherland: From the newspaper reports you get the sense that it's dangerous. There's a kind of threat inherent to the transience and the spectacular
nature of it as performance.

du Toit: You're proposing a transient public that assembles according to the
dictates of the market.

Çismeci: Resistance was coming from the more religious public in Turkey, the
secular public, and the government. In public perceptions of Sufism, the
word *tariqat* is seen as dangerous. People here still see the performance of
sema as resistant of government secularity. The Sufi order and the practice
of people living together in worship and obeying their *seyh* – their spiritual master – resists secular authority. Religious people who obey *sharia*
law are sometimes in conflict with the Sufi orders, because *sharia* law is
not as important for the Sufi as it is for the fundamentalists in Turkey.
There is a very complex relationship. Resistance comes from the secular
audience and from the fundamentalist audience. There is resistance from
the government, and that is also complex because even though the existence of Sufi orders is not legally permitted, the government, together with
UNESCO, supports commodified performances of *sema*. That's why every
year in Konya, the city where the Sufi order was founded, there's the *Seb-i
Aruz* ceremony, the wedding night of Rumi.

    Seb-i Aruz reminds me of the *pūjā* worship in terms of how much money
is spent, the marketing, and the souvenirs that are produced every year,
and the tourists from all over the world attending. *Seb-i Aruz* shows the
government actually supporting performances of *sema*, even though they
are not religious. So resistance against *sema* performance in Turkey is very
complex. It's never one-sided, and it's multivocal; there's never one idea
of how Sufism actually should exist in Turkey. It's always a struggle for
members of the Sufi orders, especially the sacred ones, whether they can
actually perform outside their *dergahs*. The new members that are practicing *sema* in a more performative tradition – for them it's like practicing
yoga in New York, there's no spiritual value in it.

    Saayan, you suggested that an increasing interest in aesthetics could
allow less religious people to become interested in spirituality. I'm research-
ing the religious charge in the commodified performances of the whirling
dervishes, and I'm interested in analyzing the potential for these less-reli-
gious festivals, events, and ceremonies to awaken the modern secularized
public's need of spirituality. Could the combination of performative and
religious culture allow young seekers to explore their faith? Do you mean
that the *pūjā* moves away from its origin, and is no longer religious? Does
the *pūjā*'s performative construction have spiritual value today?

Chattopadhyay: I'm sceptical about whether the younger generation in India
is looking for a renewed interest in spiritualism.

Robinson: The transferred subliminal relationship between the secular and
the religious marks an interesting connection across these chapters. The

way that transfer can strengthen in both directions is problematic and interesting. The other thing that interested me in Saayan's chapter was the map of the different sites of this activity. Given our concerns about where things take place, does geography and location matter in terms of either commodification or religious ceremony?

Chattopadhyay: The city is transformed into an amusement park. You need a map to get the best of it, and the maps are distributed by the *Durga* committees. The state police distribute the maps, and you require these maps to navigate yourself from one *pandal* to another. There are so many attractions; not only these places of worship, but also the different kinds of decorations and settings for the *pandals* are merged, and the *pandal* map is superimposed on the actual geography. The city becomes a heterotopic place. The overlap creates a different aesthetic experience that is not directly related to religion.

du Toit: Jo and Lucie document a religious performance that was presented in what might have been construed as a secular space, so the space began to affect how the event was read. Are there places within Kolkata that have either stronger religious or secular associations than other places? Is there any difference from one *pandal* to the next? How does the geography affect how the events are read?

Chattopadhyay: The actual religious places, the temples and so forth, lost significance during *Durga* worship. The *pandals* attract the attention of people who have come into the city from different areas, regions, and from other states. Secular places become religious, and the religious places lose their religious significance.

du Toit: So there's a reversal.

Çismeci: A similar reversal occurs during the Sufi performances. There are lodges where *sema* is performed, and then there are concert venues, theatre spaces, and cultural centres where *sema* is performed. When you see *sema* performed in a cultural centre by trained performers who are not dervishes, there is a religious value that comes out of that secular performance. The secular space is transformed into a religious space. There's still some ritual value in the performance. The *Seb-i Aruz* in Konya is becoming more commodified every year, and maybe ten or fifteen years from now it will become more like Kolkata. The experience is going to transform and become even more secular. Perhaps the spirituality will remain, though, in some of the performance venues, or in the *sufi* lodges in Konya.

Sutherland: What struck me in all of our chapters is the increasing capacity for individual agency, among both performers and audience members, within the urban environments, and within these processes of worship. Performance practice co-opts particular environments. Within urban environments, which can also be domestic, intimate, and private, individual groups can inscribe their authority.

Our research marks a process of transition in the twentieth century. In the nineteenth century we're looking at the kinds of choice that are afforded to people within Nottingham. The individual worshipper has to traverse the town and engage with those sites of worship. The fluidity and the options that are presented in the other two chapters show that people have a greater degree of authority through their own practice and engagement.

du Toit: The ways in which patterns of performance, whether religious or secular, serve to inscribe value into a space and create a spatial order is complicated when different kinds of performance transpire within the same spaces, and can occasion some discomfort. Esra, your chapter begins by marking that discomfort, whereas Saayan leads us towards what he calls a heterotopic environment in which there's a complete reversal of the inscriptions on spaces. There's a shift towards playfulness.

Çismeci: Nonconformist denominations, by moving outside the walls of the church, found out what urban people's interests and needs were. That allowed people to improve their subjective identity, and inspired them to discover an alternative way of practicing their faith. They were able to make choices. Secular people in Turkey are stepping forward and starting to research how they will experience their faith in relation to modern everyday life and the confines of the material world. How are they going to find a balance; in what venues will they experience their faith?

du Toit: For Michael Warner, the public is a site for embodied scene making. This question of agency and identity that you have all been pulling at finds its expression in a public or in a counterpublic in that way, and sometimes seems to provide an occasion for resistance as well. In queer counterpublics, individuals hail each other by means of what Warner constructs as flaunting. The counterpublic permits a kind of identity construction that isn't available in other places or in other ways. Those moments of tension and friction are among the reasons why our collaboration on this work is timely. When we look at those moments of tension and friction at their most extreme, when Germany and France and Canada legislate about Muslim women wearing the *hijab*, for example, we can see some real cultural tensions across lines of difference.

Çismeci: We do experience similar dilemmas in Turkey, because now we have a religious political party in power, but we still have some of the qualities of the secularization that came from the founder of Turkey, Ataturk. This is a problem, especially among young people who are trying to discover their identity and how they will practice their faith. Whether they are secular Sufis or in a religious Sufi order, they constantly negotiate these differences that the government imposes on people, whether it is freedom about how to use the headscarf, or freedom about practicing Islamic law. Even though there are differences, there is still opportunity for people to choose how they will practice their faith in relation to their everyday lives. There is a lot more research to be done, because the problems are very complex.

du Toit: A public itself is a complex thing. The questions that draw these chapters together flow out of a common focus on commodification and the market, but the overlap of what is understood as secular and sacred performance has produced some surprising, even contradictory developments. The individual agency available in the marketplace suggests that publics, because they are always in a process of being formed or dissipated, are transient. And transience is a complex state in which to reside.

Thanks for this conversation, and for your work.

Part IV
Ephemeral Publics

10
Coming Out of the (Confessional) Closet: Christian Performatives, Queer Performativities

Stephen D. Seely

In 2007, the Richard Dawkins Society for Reason and Science launched the 'Out Campaign'.[1] In a statement addressing the campaign's purpose, Dawkins claimed that too many atheists remain 'in the closet', and encouraged 'the non-religious to admit it – to themselves, to their families and to the world'.[2] Predictably, the campaign announcement was met with protest from certain religious groups. An article in the *Christian Post*, for example, decided to fight fire with fire and expressed hope that the mass outing of atheists would draw 'believers' out of their own closets into 'the true life of faith'.[3] The decision to frame the campaign in the rhetoric of 'the closet' and 'coming out' prompts immediate associations with queer politics and might seem like a somewhat problematic appropriation. Yet, as a member of the Out Campaign might argue, it is precisely the same hegemonic religious (Christian) forces that work to silence both atheists and queers, effectively pushing both 'communities' out of the public sphere. And it is for this very reason, of course, that both atheists and queers have actively turned to secularization as a crucial political goal. But what is it that makes 'coming out of the closet' such an appealing paradigm for minoritarian populations seeking to increase their public presence and visibility? How did such a paradigm emerge and what are its features? Is there something about the performance of 'coming out' itself that is always already marked by Christianity? Are queerness and religion such natural enemies? And is there a way to think a productive relationship between the two that goes beyond more 'tolerant' religion on the one hand or queer theology on the other?[4]

The Christian epistemology of the closet

In this chapter, I use the paradigm of 'the closet' to explore some of the religious, specifically Christian,[5] structures that lie at the heart of queer performance, politics and identity formation, as well as the religious epistemology that makes something like coming out possible, necessary and coherent. Indeed, more than a simple metaphor for a life of coerced silence and inauthenticity, the contemporary practice of 'coming out of the closet' seems to me to entail three features – *confession, conversion* and *community* formation – all of which are shared with Christianity. Christians, in other words, have been coming out of the closet for centuries, and such a practice is, I want to argue, a fundamentally religious performance. Despite recent attempts to isolate a biological 'cause' for homosexuality, it is in the *conversion*, or coming out narrative itself, that queer (as well as Christian) identity is performatively produced.[6] This coming out process, moreover, not only (re)constitutes one's individual identity, but also brings the very identity categories themselves into being. That is, it is precisely the declaration 'I am Christian' or 'I am gay' that enables the emergence of something like 'Christian' or 'gay' identity that one can then inhabit, come out as, or convert to. The coming out process, then, is necessitated by the fact that these identity categories are formulated primarily through speech acts and other performances rather than in perceived biologicality, and thus, require perpetual re-iteration (that is, *confession*) in order to be made known to others. Because both gay identity and Christianity are conceptualized in terms of interiority or subjectivity, and thus linked to one's private personhood, they must be publicly articulated or performed to be made 'real' to others. These public performances then serve as modes of building and entering '*communities*' that are ultimately based on 'private' subjectivities.

Since the emergence of the contemporary 'gay rights' movement, coming out has become the dominant process by which queer subjects enter the public sphere, a process that has become increasingly globalized. Subsequently, the significance of the practice – both its meaning and its importance – has become self-evident; few sympathetic to queer politics would think to question what it means to come out, or how crucial the practice is. Yet, though the rhetoric of coming out precedes the Stonewall riots[7] and the 'new' forms of queer activism they engendered, the very notion of what the practice entails, the understanding of what it is that one does when one 'comes out', has undergone considerable conceptual modulation. Historian John D'Emilio argues that prior to the Stonewall riots, 'coming out was really more like "coming *into*" a semi-secret world. Coming out *publicly*, as a form of resistance to oppression, was an innovation of Stonewall-era activists...'.[8] Prior to the development and proliferation of liberationist politics, queer subjects would have had no illusions that 'coming out' would alleviate their marginalization in the public sphere. In this period, rather, coming out bore a more literal association to the debutante's coming out ball, signalling one's arrival, or *début*, on the sexual marketplace – a market that, given both the requisite secrecy of the gay social world at the time and the elite sectors of society that participate in debutante balls, would be relatively small and closed.[9] Today, rather than one's coming *into* a 'semi-secret world', coming out tends to be viewed as one's shedding the burden of lies and secrecy, the emergence of one's authentic self in the face of a hostile public premised on the constitutive exclusion of certain types of subjects. In other words, to come out now is to come out *as* a particular kind of person. Thus, whereas coming out once served as something like a rite of passage, a ritual marking one's initiation into a different world, contemporary coming out seems to function more as an individual's public exposure of an identity that always already existed but had to be disguised.

If, as in D'Emilio's account, Stonewall functions (however ceremonially) as a watershed in the practice of coming out, it also represents a more seismic epistemic shift in the conceptualizations of gay identity and politics in general. Prior to the forms of queer activism that emerged in the wake of Stonewall, many gays and lesbians were more concerned with forging spaces of belonging and sexuality and less occupied with the ability to be their 'true' selves (which, of course, still remained effectively impossible in most areas of society).[10] According to D'Emilio, the terms in which queers have conceptualized their sexuality have shifted from an emphasis on a polymorphous fluidity (the notion that all 'categories' of sexuality are inherently oppressive and limiting), through the concepts of 'sexual preference' and 'sexual orientation' to 'sexual identity' (the notion that one's sexuality is innate and immutable).[11] This epistemological evolution, moreover, has been accompanied by a shift in how queer subjects relate to the public sphere and the state: moving from an antagonistic relation to the dominant public, the attempt to construct distinctly queer counterpublics, and the liberation of sexuality and desire on the one hand to contemporary scientific attempts to locate a biological source for sexuality, an increase in positive representations of gays and lesbians as a respectable minority and a high degree of integration into the public sphere on the other.[12] Consequently, there is something about the contemporary closet paradigm that typically links it to secularization, a belief in the biological origins of sexual identity, an increasingly desexualized gay community, and an emphasis on rational self-mastery, truth-telling, and authenticity in a string of thought that might go something like: I was born gay, and so I cannot change my identity and should not be discriminated against; gay people are just like everyone else, it is religion that vilifies us, and we need a secular society where we are free to be publicly who we really are.[13]

The dominance of this orientation in queer politics, as well as the vitriolic anti-gay sentiment expressed by many religious institutions, have often limited the range of possible relations between queerness and Christianity in advance. At best, the relationship between the two is generally one of tolerance: you are entitled to your beliefs or your sexual identity, but they are *private* matters. But is there another way of thinking queerness and Christianity beyond simply privacy and separation? Is there, perhaps, more Christianity inherent in the queer practice of coming out than many would care to acknowledge (especially considering that it is ostensibly the influence of Christian homophobia that necessitates 'the closet' in the first place)?

Is the private sphere the only acceptable zone for religion and queerness in a modern liberal democracy? Is there not, rather, something in both religious and queer performances that have the power to disrupt the public sphere in ways that should be explored and proliferated? And might there even be something to be learned from religion for queer theory? Against nearly all of the assumptions of 'mainstream' queer politics, I want to suggest that we begin not only to understand but also to extract and maximize some of the religious features of queerness. This is in no way a call for the proliferation of so-called 'organized religion', but rather an attempt to explore the *structures* shared between religious and queer performances and the effects these structures could have on the public sphere.

Performing conversion

In *The Hermeneutics of the Subject*, Michel Foucault distinguishes between three types of conversion and lists three features of each. The first, Platonic *epistrophē*, consists of: (1) 'a fundamental opposition between the world down here and the other world'; (2) the 'liberation' of the soul from the body; and (3) the principle that 'to know oneself is to know the true' and that 'to know the true is to free oneself'.[14] The second form is the Hellenistic-Roman practice of *se convertere ad se* (to turn oneself to oneself), which is distinguished from *epistrophē*, by: (1) an opposition not between two worlds but between what we can and cannot 'control'; (2) 'the establishment of a complete, perfect, and adequate relationship of self to self'; and (3) a focus on 'exercise, practice and training' rather than knowledge. Finally, the third form is the Christian practice of *metanoia* which is characterized by: (1) a 'historical and metahistorical event which drastically changes and transforms the subject's mode of being'; (2) a transition from 'one type of being to another'; and (3) 'dying to oneself, and being reborn in a different self and a new form' which has nothing to do with the earlier self. What we typically call 'conversion' today, then, is a complex alloy of both the Platonic and Christian 'technologies of the self'.[15]

The prototypical conversion in the Christian tradition is that of Saul/ Paul of Tarsus. Indeed, while Augustine's *Confessions* is often cited as the first 'western autobiography', some Biblical scholars have positioned Paul as the inaugurator of the conversion narrative as a genre.[16] In his schematization, Foucault situates the emergence of Christian *metanoia* in the third and fourth centuries; however, the conversion of Paul seems already to bear the features of that practice, coupled with Platonic *epistrophē*. Throughout the New Testament, in the Pauline epistles and especially in the *Acts of the Apostles*, Paul's conversion narrative is recounted multiple times. In each re-iteration, one can recognize features of both the Platonic and Christian forms of conversion. As Daniel Boyarin has suggested, Paul's thought is strongly characterized by a neo-Platonic dualist ontology that distinguishes the 'flesh' and the 'spirit', and in which the 'flesh' is significantly devalued.[17] Paul's conversion, then, allows him to transcend the 'flesh', even though he is wont to emphasize his worldly 'righteousness' in his conversion narrative: 'If anyone has reason to be confident in the flesh, I have more. ... Yet whatever gains I had, these I have come to regard as a loss because of Christ' (Phillipians 3:4–7).But Paul's conversion is also *the* exemplar of Christian *metanoia* insofar as it consists of a single event that transforms his entire mode of being, even to the degree that it represents a complete death and rebirth. As he writes in his letter to the Galatians, 'I died to the law [which also signifies the 'flesh'], so that I might live to God [the 'spirit']' (2:19).So much has Paul 'died' to the flesh that after his conversion, he replaces his Hebrew name (Saul) with a Roman one (Paul).

Closely linked to the event of Christian conversion, of course, is the practice of baptism. Indeed, the first action Paul undertakes following his conversion is his baptism (Acts 9:19). In the Pauline epistles, baptism signifies the death and rebirth of the convert: 'Therefore we have been buried with him [Christ] by baptism into death, so that, just as Christ was raised from the dead ... so we too might walk in newness of life' (Romans 6:4).[18] The initial immersion in the water represents the convert's death and burial, and the reemergence represents her rebirth and resurrection.[19] Thus, the baptism functions on two levels: on the one hand it is an outer signification of an 'inner' conversion, a public expression that can 'prove' that something ultimately improvable really did occur; on the other hand, however, it signifies a new birth or 'new creation' (Galatians 6:16). Because the 'content' expressed in a conversion narrative is some type of 'interior' transformation, it requires an outward representation, both in language (the conversion narrative itself) and in other performances (baptism). The public performance of conversion, then, becomes a hermeneutic technology that enables the 'reading' of one's internal or subjective transformation, both by oneself and by others. Jean-François Lyotard makes this point when, in his exegesis of Augustine's *Confessions*, he argues that a conversion narrative is 'only possible if the event doubles up with another meaning, called "allegorical"'.[20] The performance of conversion, in other words, gives one's body and actions a coherent meaning that resides on what Paul would consider the 'spiritual' level, or 'beyond' the 'flesh'.

But if conversion is one of the major logics of the closet, as I want to argue, how is 'coming out' comparable to Christian conversion? Certainly, most gays and lesbians would not consider their sexual identity something to which they have 'converted', as this would imply some degree of 'choice'. Instead of following the reasoning of most mainstream gay rights discourse, which compares homosexuality to race, sex, or other categories of difference that are thought to be 'biological', I want to think of queer identity as it relates to particularly religious modes of subjectivity. Categories such as race and sex are perceived to be fixed (that is, something to which one cannot 'convert'), and are attributed to a subject by others, typically by visual cues. A 'self-ascribed' identity, on the other hand, such as sexuality or religion, must generally be narrated or performed for others to be aware of its existence, which means that queer and Christian identity alike are defined by their very articulations, rather than any 'causes' one might find for them.[21] The 'instability' of these articulated identities compared to 'biological' ones, then, necessitates constant re-iterations of one's conversion narrative. D'Emilio helps illustrate this point as it pertains to gay men: 'As friendship circles form among young gay men, or when middle-aged gay couples begin to socialize together, inevitably they will spend an evening ... exchanging coming out stories. It is a long standing bonding *ritual* among us. As we tell our tales, *coming out becomes the destiny toward which all else in our lives was leading*'.[22] In their continuous repetition, these narratives are public (or semi-public) performances that serve to solidify the narrator's identity as they both render the past leading up to the 'conversion' or 'coming out' less authentic than what follows, as well as assisting in creating bonds among other 'converts'.[23] The constant articulation of one's conversion narrative (as is evidenced in D'Emilio's account of gays bonding by telling coming out stories as well as in the sheer number of Christian 'spiritual autobiographies' that are available) functions to give 'spiritual' or interior transformations some outward representation, without which 'the whole is in danger of simply disappearing'.[24]

It is not, however, only the necessity of narration that links queer coming out to Christian conversion. Indeed, the logic of coming out also bears many of the features that Foucault identifies as characteristic of Platonic *epistrophē* and Christian *metanoia*. The practice of coming out often operates on the epistemological assumption that the truth is to be found within oneself, and that discovering this truth is a means of self-liberation. As Michelangelo Signorile, a popular gay columnist and activist commonly associated with the practice of 'outing' famous 'closeted' homosexuals, writes in *Outing Yourself*, 'Coming out of the closet is a process that gets you in touch with the real you, the person that you were meant to be before you were forced to wear the mask of heterosexuality'.[25] Even more than liberation via self-discovery, however, coming out can also act as a performative death and rebirth. Signorile quotes another author Mark Taylor, who in a remarkably Pauline parlance claims that 'coming out is a death and rebirth experience ... to come out something has to die. ... In a sense, you're killing a former constructed identity and creating a new one.'[26] Bringing together both conversion practices, coming out, according to Signorile, is 'a rebirth', a 'new life' in which one is finally able to live in 'freedom' and 'honesty'.[27] As in Paul's experience, the coming out performance publicly produces the subject's new identity through a symbolic death and rebirth. Likewise, in the case of the queer, then, the coming out process – the 'conversion' – is a performative event that brings one's queer identity itself into being, creates a rupture and reorientation in one's history and temporality, devalues the past in order to legitimate the conversion, and confers what Judith Butler calls a 'binding power' on the narrator through perpetual re-iteration.[28] This binding power is what then consolidates the individual performances into a stable identity, coherent to the subject and to others, making sure that one's 'new' self continues to exist.

Confessions and their vicissitudes

In order to better understand the epistemology of the closet and the relation between queer and Christian performances, it is important to consider the role of the confession. The practice of confession is, today, most closely linked to the Catholic sacrament of penance, in which one reveals one's sins to a confessor and receives absolution. This was not, however, the only, or even the primary meaning of confession in the early church. Augustine, to take the most famous example, often uses the term as a synonym for 'profession' as in a 'confession of faith', or 'I confess your mercies'.[29] In fact, even the *Catechism of the Catholic Church* states that the sacrament of penance 'is also a "confession" – acknowledgment and praise – of the holiness of God and of his mercy toward sinful man'.[30] As is seen in the conversion narratives in the Bible and patristic texts, conversion to Christianity is usually immediately followed by proselytizing and testimony of faith. In this sense, then, the recounting of one's conversion narrative is itself a form of confession, a public performance of one's faith. Thus, confession and conversion are mutually constitutive: what one confesses is one's faith or conversion, but it is this very act of confessing that performatively *produces* that very faith or conversion. As Lyotard points out, Augustine does not confess *because* he has already been converted in the past, but rather that he 'becomes converted or *tries to become converted* while making confession'.[31] Thus, even when a conversion appears to be a single event, it remains necessarily open-ended. Similarly, one does not only come out as gay once, in which that singular event (declaring 'I am gay') constitutes one *as* a 'gay person'; but rather, each time one recounts one's coming out, each time one tells another that one is gay, one confesses oneself, and in that confession contributes to the indefinite process of conversion to that identity.

Foucault's 'turn' to Christianity in his last works complicates the modern sense of 'confession' even more. In 'Christianity and Confession', he argues that it is in Christianity that one finds the emergence of a belief in a truth 'inside oneself', a belief that one *has* a truth distinct from *the* Truth, or 'light'.[32] This interiorization and subjectivization of truth in Christianity led to the development of 'hermeneutics of the self', of which confession is the most significant. According to Foucault, the Catholic sacrament of penance was a 'rather late innovation in Christianity', and to early Christians, 'confession' consisted of two distinct practices. The first, *exomologesis*, was a process of 'publish[ing]' or 'show[ing] oneself'. In this form of 'confession', there was 'no verbal enumeration of sins', but rather 'somatic' and 'symbolic expressions' of one's status as a sinner.[33] In other words, one publicly performed the truth of oneself, rather than speaking it. Significantly, as Foucault argues, this practice of self-publication did not 'obey a truth principle of correspondence between verbal enunciation and reality'.[34] In other words, the subject manifested the truth through corporeal action rather than through speaking – the imperative that one's truth be *spoken* is not operative in this practice. The second form of early Christian confessional practice, on the other hand, was *exagoreusis*, or what Foucault terms 'the permanent verbalization of thoughts'.[35] In this practice, one must continuously analyze and speak one's thoughts; one must discover and verbalize the truth of oneself. Indeed, it is the speaking itself that functions as the hermeneutic device for determining the truth; one can only fully discover the truth by speaking it to another person.[36] The practice of *exagoreusis*, then, is what Foucault calls the 'epistemological temptation of Christianity', insofar as it is oriented towards 'the discursive and permanent analysis of thought', while *exomologesis* is the 'ontological temptation', directed 'toward the manifestation of being'. And, of course, it is, for Foucault, 'permanent verbalization', or 'the epistemological technology of the self' that 'became victorious...[and] is nowadays dominating'.[37]

Foucault's historicization of confessional practices offers two important insights that deserve emphasis here. First, while both forms of confession seek to materialize the inner truth of the subject, *both practices are public performances*. While we tend today to conceive of confession as a 'private' act, one always confesses *to* someone; confession requires an other.[38] Even when the verbal confessions were made in the context of a monastery or church, there was always an audience of at least two: the spiritual advisor and God. Second, it is significant that neither of these forms of confession were directed towards the constitution of a subject or an identity. They were, in fact, quite the opposite. Early Christian practices of confession were actually modes of self-renunciation. Through the performance of *exomologesis*, the subject publicized the death of the subject's penitent status, or, as Foucault phrases it, 'it was the theatrical representation of the sinner as dead or as dying'.[39] The verbal confession, rather, was a way of allowing the truth to transcend the physical body, of externalizing the truth of oneself to an even greater degree. If *exomologesis* externalizes the subject's truth through corporeal performance on the body's surface, *exagoreusis*, or speaking, 'projects' this truth even further from oneself: 'verbalization is a movement toward God...and a renunciation of oneself'.[40] Christian confession, then, is inseparable from self-renunciation. As Foucault puts it, 'truth and sacrifice, the truth about ourselves and the sacrifice of ourselves, are deeply and closely connected'.[41]

It is telling that Foucault's project of writing a history of sexuality led him to examine Christian confession practices at the exact moment when 'coming out' became a common practice of 'gay liberation'. This indicates that there are more than 'merely' structural resonances between Christian confession and queer coming out. In *The History of Sexuality*, Foucault argues that since its invention in early Christianity, the subject's inner truth becomes increasingly reduced to sex; that is, when one tells the truth about oneself, it is increasingly expected that that truth will be of a sexual nature.[42] Moreover, it is precisely in the confession that 'truth and sex are joined' and subjects are compelled, through confession, to 'articulate their sexual peculiarity – no matter how extreme'.[43] Foucault's work also details the 'shifts and transformations' that the confession as a 'form of knowledge-power' has undergone, moving from religious practice to medical and juridical institutions to psychoanalysis and academia.[44] Through this 'incitement to discourse', subjects are driven to articulate our inner thoughts and desires, we are lead to speak our selves (especially our 'sexual' selves) in language so that we can be categorized, studied and regulated by these discursive regimes. Thus, the confession functions to make us coherent not only to *ourselves*, but also to these various disciplines in which we all constantly circulate.

It is within this ritual of confession that I want to locate the coming out practice. In one of his most well-known formulations, Foucault writes of a metamorphosis in which what used to be considered individual acts (for example, sodomy) that were subject to particular laws as such came to be considered constitutive of 'personages' or 'species' (for example, homosexuals) who were then subject to classification and persecution.[45] In other words, at one time an individual 'caught' engaging in anal sex might be guilty of sodomy, but this would not constitute that individual as a particular type of person, except, perhaps, as a criminal or a sinner. At a later historical moment, however, following the emergence of sex as a discursive object, that same action would be 'proof' that that same individual is something called a 'homosexual'. And as 'a homosexual', all types of other information could then be attributed to him. Yet, while the categorizing of homosexuality and myriad other marginal sexualities was largely the domain of medical institutions, Foucault shows that eventually 'homosexuality began to speak on its own behalf'.[46] As a type of 'reverse discourse', homosexuals began to deploy the same categories that had been used to pathologize them in their own self-articulations. Showing the ambivalence of discursive power, homosexuals began to 'come out' in their own name and forge networks with other homosexuals, which eventually led to the emergence of a gay liberation movement and, later, a queer 'community'.[47] Thus, instead of waiting to be studied and categorized as homosexual by medical professionals, queer subjects took the classification into their own hands and insisted on coming out of the closet and speaking their newfound identities publicly.

Yet, even though this 'coming out' functions as a reverse discourse that turns the once-pathologizing dominant discourse back on itself, it is still deeply linked with the tradition of confession. Because individuals had begun to be seen as possessing *a* sexuality, and because this sexuality is largely based on one's interior subjectivity rather than exterior actions, the medical, juridical, and psychiatric institution required individuals to confess and articulate their sexualities. But in coming out on their own behalf, queer subjects are still confessing their sexuality: whether the confession is coerced by a medical professional or whether queers feel as though they want to share it, the effect is largely the same. Indeed Foucault argues that 'the obligation to confess is now relayed through so many different points, is so deeply ingrained in us, that we no longer perceive it as the effect of a power that constrains us; on the contrary, it seems that the truth, lodged in our most secret nature, "demands" to surface'.[48] In other words, the confession ritual is so pervasive that its operations are no longer even perceived. We now feel as though our liberation is thoroughly tied to our ability to speak our sexuality, that if we do not speak it we are repressed.[49] And because of Foucault's 'act-to-identity' formulation, where we once might have felt the need to confess a particular sexual act, a certain 'crime', because it was against our religious codes or laws, for example, we now feel as though we have to confess ourselves in our entirety, *as* a certain *kind* of person who *has* a certain kind of sexuality. This is how coming out functions as a type of confession: we confess because we are (often unconsciously) coerced to speak our sexuality (which queers now do willingly as a type of counter-discourse) using the categories that we have available to do so, and simultaneously the act of confessing performatively constructs a coherent and stable subject who 'is' or 'has' this particular kind of sexuality. The coming out tradition, then, must be seen as part of the incitement to put sex into discourse, to confess it, and to create an intelligible self in the process, one that 'has' a certain kind of sexual identity. And this is why coming out remains a religious performance that will never be heterogeneous to Christian confession and conversion. Indeed, as Jacques Derrida reminds us, confession is inscribed in an 'immense Christian and, above all, Pauline archive'.[50] Coming out, then, is also part of this archive and this is why queer theory and politics cannot abjure all relations to Christianity. This is not something to be overcome, for it is not possible to disentangle coming out from the confession ritual of which it originates, but is only something that can be acknowledged and worked with.

Queerness and religion in the public sphere

If coming out or confession serve to 'liberate' the subject from the burden of secrecy, they just as importantly work to position the subject within a community of other 'converts'. Indeed, as we have seen with both early Christianity and in queer politics, confession marks both one's 'rebirth' as well as one's entry into a community. Thus, coming out is 'public' in two senses: on the one hand, it serves as the public declaration of one's interior or subjective 'truth', and, on the other, it functions to provide a certain group of marginalized subjects with a public presence. These two senses of the public significance of coming out, however, highlight the exceedingly complex position of sexuality vis-à-vis the public/private division. It is the interiorization of the 'truth' of sex, or the belief that sexuality is indicative of the inner essence of one's being, that privatizes it in the first place. Because we view sexuality as something that we 'have', as something definitive, even *constitutive*, of our personhood, and because of the western association of subjectivity and privacy, we feel the need to express ourselves in order to be 'authentic', that if we do not or cannot speak about or sexuality, then it must be 'repressed'. But there is a vast difference between this 'do not' and 'cannot', and thus queer subjects (who, in many cases, cannot share their sexuality publicly) no doubt experience this feeling of sexual repression more acutely than heterosexual subjects (who, in most cases, can if they so choose).

Yet the increasing privatization of sex has been concomitant with its increasing status as a public 'problem'.[51] Sex has become one's most private property: something that belongs intimately to each subject, and something that must be intensely regulated and zoned within the public economy. Being relegated to the 'private sphere', however, does not at all mean that sex is absent from public. On the contrary, the public sphere itself is founded on the constitutive exclusion of certain types of sexuality under the guise that all sex is private, making sex at once what is most private *and* most public in everyday life. The exclusion of queerness from the public sphere under the contention that sexuality is a 'private matter', then, works to render natural and invisible the public sphere's foundational heterosexism; and it is only through this 'privatization' of sex that the public sphere is able to assume the appearance of a purely rational zone, safe from the irrationality of sex.[52]

It is this exclusion of certain subjects from the public sphere, moreover, that has necessitated the creation of so-called 'counterpublics'. For Michael Warner, a counterpublic 'comes into being through an address to indefinite strangers', and constitutes a 'world-making project'.[53] A counterpublic, in other words, emerges through semi-public performances that interpellate some (typically minoritarian) subjects and not others, and that, by definition, would not attempt to address *the* hegemonic public. D'Emilio's distinction between coming out as 'coming into a semi-secret world' and coming out 'publicly' clearly demonstrates the liminality of the counterpublic, located somewhere between private encounters and public modes of address. The use of the word 'world' in both of these descriptions, however, is telling and further illuminates the relation of both queerness and Christianity to the public sphere. In his last lecture series at the Collège de France, Foucault argues that 'one of the master strokes of Christianity, its philosophical significance, consists in it having linked together the theme of an other life (*une vie autre*) as true life and the idea of access to the other world (*l'autre monde*) as access to the truth'.[54] Earlier in the lecture series, he explains that while Platonic philosophy is oriented to 'other world' (that is, the ideal), the Cynics were concerned with the development of an 'other life' within this world. The early Christians, for Foucault, bring these two modes together insofar as they create alternative modes of living ('the other life') *in order to* have access to the other world. What this means is that for early Christians, one could not simply declare one's faith and expect access to the other world without transforming one's fundamental mode of living in 'this' world. Indeed, it is a distinctly Protestant innovation, at least according to Foucault, that one can have access to the other world simply by living the same life as before – that belief is enough in itself. Similarly, the coming out of early queers constituted an attempt to open up another world, a queer world, through the opening up another life, one's queer life. Like Protestant Christianity, however, contemporary queer politics is increasingly oriented towards living the same life as 'everybody else', towards the idea that coming out publicly is the only 'queer' move that one needs to make.[55]

Paradoxically, however, the very mode by which queer subjects have attempted to publicly assert themselves – coming out – has produced an even deeper bifurcation between acts and identities, and driven queer sex and queer modes of living even further from the public sphere. The coming out statement itself ('I am gay') increasingly becomes the sole mode by which queerness is publicly performed within this paradigm, whereas queer acts, or queer attempts to actually restructure relations between subjects, remain relegated to the private sphere. This bifurcation, moreover, works to uphold the foundations of the public sphere as a zone of both heteronormativity and of exclusively 'rational' discourse. A similar orientation can be seen in religion, as religious performances are increasingly pushed out of the public sphere through calls for secularization. Once again, this produces a division between one's actions and one's identity as it is generally acceptable for one to *profess* one's religious faith, while most other religious acts (for example, prayer, chanting, reading a religious text, et cetera) are viewed with suspicion, if not outright hostility when performed in public. Thus, while the public sphere continues to produce itself as heteronormative through the ostensible privatization of sex and the exclusion of queerness, it likewise produces itself as 'secular' through the privatization of religion and the naturalization and exclusion of anything but Protestant Christianity.[56] The very logic that necessitates coming out, then, the logic that renders certain subjects unintelligible or invisible in its very operations is reproduced in the logic that underwrites coming out itself. By reducing queer and religious performances to coming out statements and professions of faith, these subjects continue to be rigidly divided between public and private selves. Consequently, the idea that coming out has made it possible to be one's 'true self' in public is largely an illusion premised on this very bifurcation – one can make brief allusions to that self (that is, the private self) in public but its appearance is endlessly deferred and the organization of the public sphere itself goes unchallenged.

This is, I want to suggest, a valuable site of alliance for queer and religious politics.[57] Performances of both religion and queerness have the power to disrupt the everyday functions of the public sphere, functions that work to exclude or marginalize such subjects. What early Christians and early queers shared is the belief that to have access to the other world they desperately yearned for requires fundamental alterations in one's mode of living in the here and now. Neither early Christians nor early queers could have imagined a hegemonic public sphere in which they would be able to participate, forcing them to create their own counterpublics, their own 'world-making projects', their own ways of (re)imagining relations between strangers. What makes these 'world-making projects' religious is their *faith* in forms of relationality, in modes of being, in futures that do not (yet) concretely 'exist', as well as the perform-ance of that faith in public, or the *conjuring* of these very futures themselves.

This chapter has not at all been a call to dispense with the coming out paradigm, but rather a suggestion of the need to work through the religious epistemology at the heart of one of the most central queer practices. What this epistemology of the closet suggests is that queer and religious politics need not necessarily be opposed, but that there are features within the very genealogy of the practice of coming out itself that could more effectively destabilize both the heteronormativity and the 'rationality' of the public sphere. Instead of a one-time event, for example, we might see coming out as a different kind of conversion, something more akin to the 'lost' practice of *se convertere ad se* – a literal turning, a new mode of caring for the self, an entry into a different way of life. Instead of confession as a mode of liberation or the revelation of an 'authentic' self, coming out could be a profession of faith in new modes of living and being. And instead of automatic entry into an always already existing community, perhaps coming out could be a mode of establishing new relations between strangers, *queerer* worlds in the here and now. Coming out would then no longer be a way of 'showing' the truth, but rather of performing or '*making* the truth' to use the words of Augustine. The 'coming' in coming out would then be a kind of 'becoming' – a way of *becoming out* of ourselves and out of a homophobic society, but also a *becom-ing into* new worlds and new ways of living. This performative becoming would be something that both transforms subjects as well as the very episte-mological and relational foundations of the public sphere itself.

Notes

I would like to thank John D'Emilio, Jennifer Brier, Ed Cohen, Keith Hoffman, Joy Palacios, and Claire Maria Chambers for their insightful comments on various versions of this project. My greatest thanks go to Rachel Havrelock for her faith in this project from its earliest instantiation.

1. See http://www.outcampaign.org/.
2. Richard Dawkins, 'The Out Campaign', 29 July 2007, http://richarddawkins.net/articles/1471. Last accessed 4 February 2013.
3. 'Dawkin's [sic] Call to Atheists "in the Closet" is a Christian Wake-Up Call', *The Christian Post*, 11 August 2007, http://www.christianpost.com/news/dawkin-s-call-to-atheists-in-the-closet-is-a-christian-wake-up-call-28864/. Last accessed 4 February 2013.
4. For important critiques of tolerance as a political goal, see Wendy Brown, *Regulating Aversion: Tolerance in the Age of Identity and Empire* (Princeton, NJ: Princeton University Press, 2006) and Janet R. Jakobsen and Ann Pellegrini, *Love the Sin: Sexual Regulation and the Limits of Religious Tolerance* (New York: New York University Press, 2004). For queer theology, see the excellent collection Gerard Loughlin (ed.), *Queer Theology: Rethinking the Western Body* (Oxford: Blackwell Press, 2007), among many others. This essay does not position itself in any way against queer theology, but rather seeks to think queerness and Christianity together without any particular religious commitment.
5. In this essay I use the term 'Christianity' in a more generalized capacity than any religious studies scholar would be comfortable with. I do not at all intend to homogenize Christianity or Christian practices, but other than the instances where I specifically describe features of early Christianity or Catholic ritual, I refer to a general, mainstream American version of Protestant Christianity.
6. Here I obviously follow Judith Butler's work on the performative production of identity, most famously outlined in *Gender Trouble: Feminism and the Subversion of Identity* (New York: Routledge, 1990), but see also her 'Imitation and Gender Insubordination', in Diana Fuss (ed.), *Inside/Out: Lesbian Theories, Gay Theories* New York and London: Routledge, 1991). For the purposes of this chapter, I take it as axiomatic that identity categories, *though not necessarily differences themselves,* are performative, or produced through their perpetual re-iteration.
7. The Stonewall riots were a series of riots against the ongoing police harassment of patrons at a gay bar, the Stonewall Inn, located in New York City's Greenwich Village in June 1969. The event serves as a watershed in gay history, as the 'birth' of militant anti-homophobic politics, and is commemorated around the world by 'Gay Pride' parades each year.
8. John D'Emilio, *The World Turned: Essays on Gay History, Politics and Culture* (Durham, NC: Duke University Press, 2002), 200.
9. This marketplace, however small or furtive, is neither fully private nor fully public, and constitutes what Michael Warner would call a 'counterpublic'. This transgression of the public/private divide, as well as the notion of counterpublics, will be addressed later in this essay. See Michael Warner, *Publics and Counterpublics* (New York: Zone Books, 2002).
10. For the definitive history of pre-Stonewall gay and lesbian community and political formation in America, see John D'Emilio, *Sexual Politics, Sexual Communities: The Making of a Homosexual Minority in the United States, 1940–1970* (Chicago: The University of Chicago Press, 1983).
11. D'Emilio, *The World Turned,* 155–7.
12. This is not to draw a reductive opposition between 'assimilationist' or 'reformist' gay politics on the one hand and 'transgressive' or 'radical' queer politics on the

other, as has often been done. All periods of queer activism have been marked by both of these strands, which are by no means mutually exclusive. The point here, however, is to show that the change in how gays and lesbians view coming out is indicative of larger shifts in how they think of sexuality and the place of gay subjects in the public sphere more generally.

13. This perspective is one I have rarely encountered in academic queer studies, but nearly everywhere outside of the academy, from blogs and websites to experience in LGBT community activism and among friends. The popular writer Andrew Sullivan's work exemplifies much of this logic, albeit from a classically libertarian position; see his *Virtually Normal* (New York: Vintage Books, 1996). See also Michael Warner's *The Trouble with Normal: Sex, Politics, and the Ethics of Queer Life* (Cambridge, MA: Harvard University Press, 1999), which nicely outlines this line of argumentation in order to critique it.

14. Michel Foucault, *The Hermeneutics of the Subject: Lectures at the Collège de France 1981–1982*, ed. Frederic Gros, trans. Graham Burchell (New York: Picador Press, 2005), 209–15.

15. One of Foucault's interests in *The Hermeneutics of the Subject* is to excavate this second practice of conversion, the turning of the self to the self.

16. See Gabriel Josipovici, *The Book of God: A Response to the Bible* (New Haven: Yale University Press, 1988), esp. 235–53.

17. See Daniel Boyarin, *A Radical Jew: Paul and the Politics of Identity* (Berkeley and Los Angeles: The University of California Press, 1997). Boyarin adds that 'Paul is not quite a Platonist' insofar as 'the morphology of Paul's dualism...does not imply a *rejection* of the body', 59–61.

18. In the letter to the Galatians, Paul also tells the new Christians that after baptism, they become 'children' of God and are born into the new Christian 'family of faith'. See Galatians 3–6, as well as Daniel Boyarin's interpretation of it in *A Radical Jew*, 22–4.

19. See, as only one example, the *Catechism of the Catholic Church*, 1214.

20. Jean-François Lyotard, *The Confession of Augustine*, trans. Richard Beardsworth (Stanford, CA: Stanford University Press, 2000), 72.

21. This is not to say, of course, that others do not *attempt* to ascribe sexual orientation to an individual; however, it is instructive that this is most often done primarily through *gendered* signifiers. In other words, if a man is perceived by others to be gay, it will usually be due to some 'transgression' of masculine norms. Moreover, this is why the terms in which homosexuality is currently articulated are inadequate: locating a biological source for same-sex, or 'queer' desire would only explain the desire itself. Because desire is not something that can be perceived by others without its being expressed, enacted, or articulated, one would still have to put a name to that desire, to speak it into language, to identify oneself (or one's desire) as gay or queer. On the other hand, explaining away homosexuality as a mere 'choice' would also necessitate the putting of that choice into discourse; one would only be aware that one had 'chosen' to 'be' gay if one came out as such. In other words, regardless of how one's impulses or desires originate, to 'be' gay will *always* require the declaration as such, it will always require putting that name on one's feelings or actions.

22. D'Emilio, *The World Turned*, 161. My emphasis.

23. The sharing of these coming out stories among gay men, according to D'Emilio is 'intended to create a bond among individuals' and '[build] ties of community among a group whose links are, frankly, tenuous'. *The World Turned*, 161.

24. Josipovici, *The Book of God*, 243. Here, Josipovici also connects Paul's practice of 'allegorization and internalization' with the necessity and rise of what he terms 'spiritual autobiography', claiming that Paul must constantly tell his conversion story 'not only to explain it to others, but to keep it always before his own eyes, *to make sure it really exists*' (added emphasis).

25. Michelangelo Signorile, *Outing Yourself: How to Come Out as Lesbian or Gay to Your Family, Friends and Coworkers* (New York: Fireside Books, 1995), xxiii. I refer to this text both because of its popularity and because it is representative of the logic of the closet that I am trying to articulate in this essay, not with any assumptions that it is reflective of every individual's experience of coming out.

26. Signorile, *Outing Yourself*, 9.

27. Signorile, *Outing Yourself*, xxx.

28. Judith Butler, *Bodies that Matter: The Discursive Limits of 'Sex'* (New York and London: Routledge, 1993).

29. See countless instances in the *Confessions*, trans. Henry Chadwick (Oxford: Oxford University Press, 2008), especially in Book VIII. See also Chloë Taylor's remarkably helpful *The Culture of Confession from Augustine to Foucault: A Genealogy of the 'Confessing Animal'* (New York: Routledge, 2009), esp. 45.

30. Catholic Church, *Catechism of the Catholic Church*, 2nd edn (Vatican: Libreria Editrice Vaticana, 2000), 1423.

31. Lyotard, *The Confession of Augustine*, 49. Similarly, Foucault argues that 'verbalization is a way for the conversion ... to develop itself and to take effect'. *The Politics of Truth*, ed. Sylvere Lotringer, trans. Lysa Hochroth and Catherine Porter (Los Angeles: Semiotext(e), 2007), 186.

32. Michel Foucault, *The Politics of Truth*, 169–92. See also the first part of this lecture, 'Subjectivity and Truth', in the same volume 147–68.

33. Foucault, *The Politics of Truth*, 175–6.

34. Foucault, *The Politics of Truth*, 175.

35. Foucault, *The Politics of Truth*, 187.

36. Similarly, Signorile argues that if you have 'admit[ted] to yourself that you are gay' but have not told your friends, family *and* coworkers, then 'you are still in the closet'. *Outing Yourself*, ix–x.

37. Foucault, *The Politics of Truth*, 189.

38. Foucault notes that this other can even be a 'virtual presence'. See *The History of Sexuality, vol. 1*, trans. Robert Hurley (New York: Vintage Books, 1978), 61.

39. Foucault, *The Politics of Truth*, 176.

40. Foucault, *The Politics of Truth*, 186.

41. Foucault, *The Politics of Truth*, 187.

42. See, especially, Michel Foucault, *'Scientia Sexualis'* in *The History of Sexuality*, 51–75.

43. Foucault, *The History of Sexuality*, 61.

44. See Foucault, *The History of Sexuality*, 116–18. Derrida likewise calls these institutions 'confession machines'. See Jacques Derrida, *Without Alibi*, trans. Peggy Kamuf (Stanford: Stanford University Press, 2002), 104.

45. Foucault, *The History of Sexuality*, 43.

46. Foucault, *The History of Sexuality*, 101.

47. See David Halperin, *Saint Foucault: Toward a Gay Hagiography* (Oxford: Oxford University Press, 1995) for a history of gay politics and identity vis-à-vis the work of Foucault.

48. Foucault, *The History of Sexuality*, 60.

49. This phenomenon is, of course, an aspect of what Foucault calls the 'repressive hypothesis' in *The History of Sexuality*. The belief in such a hypothesis, moreover, explains the virulence that is often directed by the gay 'community' towards public figures that are perceived to be closeted homosexuals.
50. Jacques Derrida, *Without Alibi*, 97.
51. Foucault, *The History of Sexuality*, 51–74.
52. See Lauren Berlant and Michael Warner's brilliant 'Sex in Public' in Michael Warner, *Publics and Counterpublics*, 187–208. Linking together Habermas and Foucault, Berlant and Warner argue that 'both Jürgen Habermas and Foucault point to the way a hegemonic public has founded itself by the privatization of sex and the sexualization of private personhood'.
53. Warner, *Publics and Counterpublics*, 120–1. See also Nancy Fraser's influential essay, 'Rethinking the Public Sphere: A Contribution to the Critique of Actually Existing Democracy', *Social Text* 25/26 (1990): 56–80.
54. Michel Foucault, *The Courage of Truth: Lectures at the Collège de France 1983–84*, ed. Frederic Gros, trans. Graham Burchell (New York: Palgrave Macmillan, 2011), 319.
55. See, again, Andrew Sullivan's *Virtually Normal* for the argument that queers are, well, virtually normal and should aspire to normal integration into society as it is presently constituted. Lisa Duggan has called this kind of politics 'the new homonormativity'. See her *The Twilight of Equality? Neoliberalism, Cultural Politics and the Attack on Democracy* (Boston, MA: Beacon Press, 2003), esp. 43–66.
56. See Jakobsen and Pellegrini, *Love the Sin*.
57. Jackobsen and Pellegrini have also provocatively called for an alliance between queer and religious politics, arguing that recourse to the freedom of *practice* guaranteed under the First Amendment might be more legally fruitful for queers (and religious minorities) than recourse to privacy rights and calls for secularization. They similarly argue that secularization and privacy leave the heteronormative and Protestant Christian foundations of the public sphere unchallenged and invisible and reduce queer and religious politics to matters of 'debate'. See their *Love the Sin*, with which I am in nearly full agreement.

Works cited

Augustine. *Confessions*, trans. Henry Chadwick. Oxford: Oxford University Press, 2008.

Boyarin, Daniel. *A Radical Jew: Paul and the Politics of Identity*. Berkeley and Los Angeles: The University of California Press, 1997.

Brown, Wendy. *Regulating Aversion: Tolerance in the Age of Identity and Empire*. Princeton, NJ: Princeton University Press, 2006.

Butler, Judith. *Gender Trouble: Feminism and the Subversion of Identity*. New York and London: Routledge, 1990.

———. *Bodies that Matter: The Discursive Limits of 'Sex'*. New York and London: Routledge, 1993.

Catholic Church. *Catechism of the Catholic Church*, 2nd edn. Vatican: Libreria Editrice Vaticana, 2000.

D'Emilio, John. *Sexual Politics, Sexual Communities: The Making of a Homosexual Minority in the United States, 1940–1970*. Chicago: The University of Chicago Press, 1983.

———. *The World Turned: Essays on Gay History, Politics and Culture*. Durham NC: Duke University Press, 2004.

Derrida, Jacques. *Without Allibi*, trans. Peggy Kamuf. Stanford, CA: Stanford University Press, 2002.

Duggan, Lisa. *The Twilight of Equality? Neoliberalism, Cultural Politics and the Attack on Democracy*. Boston, MA: Beacon Press, 2003.

Foucault, Michel. *The History of Sexuality, vol. 1*, trans. Robert Hurley. New York: Vintage Books, 1978.

——. *The Hermeneutics of the Subject: Lectures at the Collège de France 1981–1982*, edited by Frederic Gros. Trans. Graham Burchell. New York: Picador Press, 2005.

——. *The Politics of Truth*, edited by Sylvere Lotringer, trans. Lysa Hochroth and Catherine Porter. Los Angeles: Semiotext(e), 2007.

——. *The Courage of Truth: Lectures at the Collège de France 1983–84*, edited by Frederic Gros, trans. Graham Burchell. New York: Palgrave Macmillan, 2011.

Fraser, Nancy. 'Rethinking the Public Sphere: A Contribution to the Critique of Actually Existing Democracy', *Social Text*, 25/26 (1990): 56–80.

Fuss, Diana (ed.). *Inside/Out: Lesbian Theories, Gay Theories*. New York and London: Routledge, 1991.

Halperin, David. *Saint Foucault: Toward a Gay Hagiography*. Oxford: Oxford University Press, 1995.

Jakobsen, Janet R. and Ann Pellegrini. *Love the Sin: Sexual Regulation and the Limits of Tolerance*. New York: New York University Press, 2004.

Josipovici, Gabriel. *The Book of God: A Response to the Bible*. New Haven, CT: Yale University Press, 1988.

Loughlin, Gerard (ed.). *Queer Theology: Rethinking the Western Body*. Oxford: Blackwell Press, 2007.

Lyotard, Jean-François. *The Confession of Augustine*, trans. Richard Beardsworth. Stanford, CA: Stanford University Press, 2000.

Signorile, Michelangelo. *Outing Yourself: How to Come Out as Lesbian or Gay to Your Family, Friends and Coworkers*. New York: Fireside Books, 1995.

Sullivan, Andrew. *Virtually Normal*. New York: Vintage Books, 1996.

Taylor, Chloë. *The Culture of Confession from Augustine to Foucault: A Genealogy of the 'Confessing Animal'*. New York: Routledge, 2009.

Warner, Michael. *Publics and Counterpublics*. New York: Zone Books, 2002.

11
Performing Jewish Sexuality: *Mikveh* Spaces in Orthodox Jewish Publics

Shira Schwartz

In *The History of Sexuality*, Foucault posits that the more there are laws about sex, the more people speak about sex. He argues that the policing of sex is what allows discourses of sexuality to emerge.[1] This chapter analyzes the ways in which *mikveh* ritual, a monthly ritual bath performed by women after menstruation, and *mikveh* space establish a vocabulary of bodily acts and performance practices that generate communities and sex discourses amongst orthodox Jewish women. This study challenges the Habermasian notion of the public sphere by elaborating one based on privacy, silent prayer, and internal regard for other women, as well as spiritual discipline within a tightly-knit structure of religious commandment. By conflating public and private, *mikveh* ritual practitioners create a community through delineating the private practices of orthodox Jewish women. This 'public of the private' complicates Habermas's ideal public sphere as one created through rational argumentation and debate because it privileges silence, contemplation, practice and the internal spiritual state. Furthermore, the overlap of *mikveh*'s ritual public with other aspects of the orthodox Jewish community (such as the relationship between women and men who are not their husbands) challenges notions that heterosexual practices necessarily lead to heteronormativity. Through first-hand interviews with *mikveh* performers in Toronto, this chapter highlights the concealed yet communal nature of *mikveh* experience/bonding by drawing out a kind of third space that lives between Habermas's model of the Elizabethan coffeehouse[2] and Foucault's notion of sexual regulation as an incitement to discourse.[3]

The *mikveh* is a space that is mediated as a kind of public, but also demands a strong degree of intimacy and privacy. *Mikveh* rituals require performers to (tacitly) commit to confidentiality and discretion. They are highly private ritual acts, requiring nudity, personal prayer, bathing, and performances of a highly intimate nature. Fundamental to *mikveh* space, however, is a community infrastructure. *Mikveh*s are not generally located in individual homes, but rather in synagogues and community centres. It is impossible to perform *mikveh* practices alone. Women congregate in *mikveh* lobbies and waiting rooms before performing the ritual immersion. I argue in this chapter that the *mikveh* inhabits an intermediate space between public and private, one based more on bodies and space than on verbal discourse. This intermediate space can do things that other spaces cannot; it enables the female subject to process her relationship to her husband, her sexuality, and her part in the Jewish community, and, further, it allows for an intimate kind of sharing between orthodox Jewish women that otherwise could not take place. In this way, the *mikveh* acts as a central site of performativity in two ways: one, as a place where ritual happens, and two, as a place where a public is hailed. The counterpublic that *mikveh* spaces generate thus continues to exist when there is no live *mikveh* ritual being performed. *Mikveh* communities exist around and between and through individual *mikveh* practice. The ephemeral nature of this counterpublic challenges the Habermasian ideal of the public as a marketplace or a square for rational debate and the circulation of texts and cultural objects, and, more broadly, of the patriarchal history of publics. The performance practices involved in *mikveh* rituals 'inhabit norms' rather than subvert them, to borrow Saba Mahmood's term,[4] as a way of articulating agency on individual and communal levels. The (anti-)structure of *mikveh* practice thus queers publics by questioning Habermas's coffeehouse model and resisting heteronormative cultural codes.

This chapter roots Jewish performance practices relating to gender and sexuality in Michael Warner's concept of 'text'.[5] Just as Warner describes texts (including his essay 'Publics and Counterpublics') as having a 'kind of public that comes into being ... in relation to texts and their circulation,'[6] the literature pertaining to *mikveh* performance practices, including the corpus of Biblical law, is a text around which the intimate counterpublic of the *mikveh* is formed.

There are two concurrent discourses at play here: (1) narratives and perspectives of orthodox women in contemporary Jewish culture; and (2) rabbinic conversations surrounding Jewish law. Considering the latter for a moment will help flesh out how religious spaces are constructed in Jewish society. Jewish space begins with rituals and speech acts. Material architecture is constructed subsequently surrounding religious conversations and performance practices. The laws of *sukkah*, ritual huts, are perhaps the most illustrative example of this: the law directs the subject to build a hut with a minimum of two and a half walls with any material he or she wishes, in order to house various religious rituals, including the traditional shaking of the *lulav* and *etrog* (objects with symbolic meaning), the recitation of blessings, and several festive meals. Much like the neo-Hindu worship surrounding the Óvila stones, the sanctuary – in this case, the *sukkah* – is constructed to house the act, rather than the other way around. *Yeshiva*s (Jewish study halls) were historically formed in a similar manner.

The rabbinic commentary that the Talmud documents is a formalized discourse that gives rise to a public. In the modern age, groups of men gather daily to read and study Jewish law, thus creating a *yeshiva*, one of the most essential public institutions of contemporary Judaism. Warner's notion of the 'imaginary' is useful here, as some of these conversations begin with the laws that pertain to the Temple ritual, a construct that does not exist today, and address the role of the Temple priesthood, a position of legal authority that has not existed for centuries. Contemporary Jewish law is nevertheless applied during these conversations.

Additionally, it is interesting to note that what is now known as *yeshiva* study (traditionally male scholars congregating in a space to learn Torah) was originally conducted in the marketplace, since the majority of Jews lived in rural areas. The market was the most convenient site for Torah study, so there they congregated for study as well as the *Shabbat Shuva Drasha*, an annual address given by the chief Rabbi to the community. Tractate *Megillah* of the Talmud even states that Torah recitation should be conducted on Mondays and Thursdays[7] specifically (which remains the practice today) because those were generally 'marketplace days'.

The theoretical principle that supports this tradition is a particular philosophy of Jewish space: its sanctity derives from the acts done within it, not vice versa. Jewish space has no intrinsic value (aside from two exceptions, the Holy Temple and the land of Israel, analysis of which would exceed the limitations of this chapter). Jewish oral traditions state that even Mount Sinai, arguably the holiest site in Jewish history, was no longer considered sacred ground for Jewish believers once they vacated. Other rituals involving space also begin from this premise. The traditional *chuppah* (wedding canopy), for example, is a temporary structure constructed around the blessings recited beneath it by bride and groom. Surrounding various rituals and speech acts is a material construct that becomes holy by relation. The *eruv* practice functions in a similar manner. One of the laws of *Shabbat* (Sabbath) and holidays is the prohibition against transferring objects from one domain to another (relating to the principle of rest on *Shabbat*). A ritual enclosure called an *eruv* is thus constructed surrounding an area in order to permit the transference of objects from one domain to another during *Shabbat* and holidays. This enclosure (often made of wire and posts) makes it easier for individuals to congregate during these times. *Eruv* facilitates social life during *Shabbat* and holidays; without this spatial construct, it would be more difficult for individuals to leave their homes, as they would have to ensure that they carried no objects between domains (including prayerbooks, personal belongings, et cetera). It increases mobility, especially for those caring for small children, as it allows for the carrying of these items as well as strollers, diapers, bottles, et cetera.

Mikveh practice marries this Jewish philosophy of space to a cultural context. The (anti)structure of *mikveh* ritual is such that it has no fixed beginning or end. As I hope the ethnographic section of this chapter will illustrate, women who practice *mikveh* law view the ritual bath not as an end, but rather as part of an ongoing ritual of sexual consciousness. The physical space of the *mikveh* thus houses its own ontology, that is, its own sexual consciousness and intimate sharing between subjects in everyday life.

To return now to the first discourse, the narratives and perspectives of orthodox women, there is a similar historic tradition. The only definition in Jewish law of a *Mikveh* space is as a body of 'living water' (usually rainwater). Existing *Mikveh* buildings, however, were constructed to house conversations taking place during *mikveh* practice, to gather women together. The physical structure of the *mikveh* thus exists to hail a counterpublic of *mikveh* practitioners.

In *My Dear Daughter: Rabbi Benjamin Slonik and Education of Jewish Women in Sixteenth-Century Poland*, Edward Fram conducts a genealogy of women's education in Jewish culture, beginning in the 1500s. He writes:

> Twenty-first century women ... have any number of opportunities to familiarize themselves with the laws of niddah [the spiritual state of a woman either when she is menstruating or after, before she immerses herself in the *mikveh*]. If they are not taught in a formal classroom situation, they can easily find this information in books or even on the Internet. How did sixteenth-century women learn all the rules and regulations of such an intimate subject? As in other areas of ritual life that concerned the household, it would seem that their primary source of information was other women, be they mothers, grandmothers, sisters, sister-in-laws, or friends. Since women taught other women the laws of menstruation, when practical questions arose they naturally turned to the same sources for answers.[8]

This oral tradition evolved into what are now known as 'Kallah Classes', designed specifically to teach a new bride (*kallah*) the laws of *mikveh*. Relationships formed as women waited for their turns to bathe, which led to the construction of *mikveh* waiting rooms, which, as my ethnography indicates, are currently significant sites of conversation for orthodox Jewish women. Women wanted to discuss the laws. They wanted to share how they felt, too. From this sprung dialogue and mutual support on emotional and spiritual levels. I suggest that the ontology of Jewish space is thus a kind of 'disappearance', to borrow Peggy Phelan's term.[9] Phelan posits in her book *Unmarked: The Politics of Performance* that '[p]erformance's only life is in the present'.[10] Phelan uses the term disappearance to explain the essential liveness of performance and its irreproducibility. It is precisely the liveness of *mikveh* performances – the ritual at play – that determines its square footage. In a Warnerian sense, the space is imaginary. It exists only in relationship to that which it contains.

If we are to view these conversations as overlapping performance spheres, we may begin to view Warner's description of publics in a different light. He writes:

> For another class of writing context – including literary criticism, journalism, theory, advertising, fiction, drama, most poetry – the available addressees are essentially imaginary, which is not to say unreal: the people, the scholarship, the republic of letters…the brotherhood of all believers, humanity. … These are all publics. They are in principle open-ended. They exist by virtue of their address.[11]

Indeed, the addressees of Talmudic commentary, a writing context that Warner does not mention here, are 'essentially imaginary'. Comparing Warner's example of literary criticism to this kind of public is a fruitful analogy, I believe, since both are considered secondary texts – both discourses revolve around documents preceding them, and yet, paradoxically, hold authority both independently and in relation to their predecessor texts. In a Foucauldian sense, *mikveh* discussion, beginning with the law, is a strand of 'talking sex'[12] that opens up a public based on Jewish sexuality. The laws of *niddah* function as a language with which women can speak about the subject of sex, including sexual desire, that, in the words of Foucault, 'draw[s] from that little piece of ourselves not only pleasure but knowledge, and a whole subtle interchange from one to the other: a knowledge of pleasure, a pleasure that comes of knowing pleasure, a knowledge-pleasure,'[13] in a manner that is considered culturally *kosher*. Using the law as their script, orthodox Jewish women dramaturge the *mikveh* as well as their own sexual desire, while simultaneously negotiating a cultural politic. For example, rabbinic law dictates that husband and wife should ideally have sex the night that the woman returns for the *mikveh* and should not postpone. In the *mikveh* waiting room, when a woman expresses to another woman an urgency she feels to sleep with her husband, her eagerness has a double meaning: it is at once an expression of religious piety and also of sexual desire. In this vein, *mikveh* discourse works as an abstractly-addressed text that creates a society that openly addresses sex, situated within a public (the more general Jewish community) that does not.

In conjunction with Warner and Habermas, this chapter considers Saba Mahmood's position on agency within orthodox Muslim communities (acts of resistance that emerge from *within* existing power structures). She argues that the doing – that is, the mindful enactment – of social norms is what provides the means for its destabilization. This 'productive reiterability' is precisely where agency resides.[14]

Using this theory to read *mikveh* practice sheds light on the meaning behind these performance practices. Orthodox Jewish women utilize *mikveh* spaces to process sexuality, articulate individual agency, establish community, and share experience. *Mikveh* spaces hail their particular (counter)publics through gestural, discursive, bodily acts that simultaneously enact and disrupt fixed notions of gender and sexuality. *Mikveh* creates a space for women to negotiate gender and sexuality from within the law, attending to a kind of nuanced 'doing' of gender (rather than to its undoing). Further, it identifies the ways in which *mikveh* performance practices contest fixed notions of public and private on a social scale, through its nuanced rehearsal process and complex ontological structure: a space that exists only in its doing and in its liveness, in a Phelanian sense, contingent on its contents.

It is important for this analysis that we distinguish between the rituals of the *mikveh* and the public that contains it. *Mikveh* practices – including preparations and bathing – are acts that perform Jewish sexuality amongst orthodox Jewish individuals. In and around these acts is a *mikveh* community based on speech, textual discourse, and a kind of intimate sharing that is formed in Jewish communities. *Mikveh* practice (the ritual) and *mikveh* space (a public) are two distinct elements.

To be clear, the idea of *mikveh* as a kind of counterpublic is not completely consistent with Warner's model. It has no abstract public to which it stands as an alternative. The subversion that this ethnography speaks to is, as Mahmood illustrates, self-contained. It is a subversion from within, produced by its own embodiment and reiteration. While Jewish religion is indeed part of what Habermas calls the 'lifeworld', there is, of course, a gap between the Jewish and non-Jewish world, specifically orthodox Jewish women and non-Jewish women. *Mikveh* waters mark women in a way, insofar as they produce a kind of sexual consciousness distinct from that of secular culture that is ongoing (not merely during *mikveh* practice). Though represented in Jewish women's dress, including hair covering and traditional 'modest' garb, this markedness is symbolic. The intimate sharing that takes place between women in this cohort, and the secrecy of it, binds the cohort together as an intimate public. The performance practices that occur in *mikveh* spaces set these clusters of women apart from an official public, although it does not aim to resist it in a traditional sense. Certain features of this group are consistent with Warner's concept of a counterpublic while others problematize that notion.

The ethnographic material I present below was selected from interviews I conducted with women who practice varying levels of orthodoxy in the Jewish community in Toronto. I have used pseudonyms to preserve confidentiality. First, I will describe the *mikveh* ritual and illustrate the preparatory practices involved in anticipation of the *mikveh* performance, including bodily and spiritual practices. Next, I will explore the ways in which speech and speech acts relate to *mikveh* practice and to the counterpublic formed in the *mikveh* environment, examining how the *mikveh* space acts as a kind of 'secret' that creates key social bonds between women in orthodox Jewish communities.

Mikveh ritual, rehearsal, and performance

According to Jewish law, men and women who are married are obligated to observe a series of highly intricate laws surrounding a woman's menstrual cycle, known as the laws of *taharat mishpacha* or 'family purity'.[15] These laws essentially outline a sexual schedule for married couples, around which *mikveh* performances are based. When a married woman is menstruating, she is in a state of what is called *niddah* in Hebrew, often translated as 'spiritual impurity'.[16]

It is important to note that majority contemporary rabbinic authorities do not translate the term *niddah* in this way. The term 'impurity' has specific negative connotations in English that it does not have in Hebrew. *Niddah* does not mean that the female subject is 'dirty' when she has her period; rather, *niddah* refers to a spiritual state in which an individual is situated if he or she (both men and women can be in *niddah*; a man, for example, after certain seminal emissions ['*zera'*] and other forms of genital discharge ['*ziva'*]) has in some way experienced contact with death (literally or symbolically). This can be either from a physical dead body or its spiritual equivalent. In practice, the laws of *niddah* are often viewed as separate from other forms of *teuma* (which is a larger body of law surrounding ritual impurity, like coming into contact with a dead body). Multiple forms of *teuma* are not usually understood as situated under the umbrella of a singular philosophical principle. Samson Raphael Hirsch, however, joins the two strands together. He defines *teuma* broadly, as a kind of spiritual impurity associated with death or decomposition,[17] as something 'not corresponding to your being'.[18] He states, 'The effect of *teuma* is that *tahara* (purity), i.e. the capacity to live a pure life, disappears, and the Divine Presence is withdrawn'.[19] The connections Hirsch draws between *teuma* and death and *tahara* and life support a reading of *mikveh* as a practice that marks an ontological shift (from death-ness to life-ness), rather than that which merely cleanses the body post-menstruation.

According to Jewish law, physical death occurs when a living, material thing ceases to exist; spiritual death occurs when there is the loss of life potential. Rituals involving spiritual (im)purity steer individuals away from any type of mixture between life and death. In the case of a woman's menstrual cycle, there is a loss of life potential, which means that if the woman were to have sex with her husband, they would be mixing life and death. To avoid this, she immerses herself in the *mikveh*, which brings her from a state of *niddah* into a state of *tahara*, spiritual purity, at which point she is permitted to have intercourse with her husband. The bathing process is symbolic, not literal (it does not physically cleanse the body) yet also functions tangibly as a kind of 'doing' of gender, in a Mahmoodian sense. The ritual purity, though symbolic, is registered on the body through intentionality and embodiment, which effectively marks the body. When a woman prepares for the *mikveh*, for example, she is required to meticulously examine her body; she combs her body hair, washes her body, inspects her fingernails, et cetera. True to form, she dramaturges the ritual, performing a close reading of her body. In effect, symbolic and physical forms of purity work together at the *mikveh* to realize Jewish philosophies of sexuality.

The female subject remains in *niddah* throughout the duration of her cycle, which lasts approximately seven days, and for an additional seven 'clean' (bloodless) days post-menstruation. During this time, husband and wife are not permitted to have sexual intercourse, or, according to mainstream orthodox rabbinic authorities, any physical contact whatsoever. Once the period ceases, the woman immerses her entire body in the *mikveh*, which is technically a body of rainwater but is more often one which is collected in a small pool in a designated room in a synagogue or community centre. Some bathing houses exist on their own, unaffiliated with a synagogue or Jewish organization. At this point she becomes *tahor* (from *tahara*), spiritually pure, once again, and she is ready to have intercourse with her husband for the following two weeks, before she expects her next cycle to begin.[20]

The *mikveh* preparations required of women are extremely thorough. They mostly involve the combing and managing of body and head hair.[21] The first step when preparing for immersion is a thorough cleansing of the body. Then she begins to untangle any knots that exist in her head or body hair. The symbolism behind the rituals of combing and cleansing is that nothing stands between the subject's skin and the *mikveh* water during the immersion.[22] In a sense, the subject stage-manages her body while rehearsing for the *mikveh*, removing anything that can potentially act as a barrier between her flesh and God. This includes tangles in the hair, dead skin, bodily fluid (including wet or dry blood) and other materials that may be present on the body's surface. Once this process is complete, the woman enters the *mikveh* foyer, greeted by a volunteer attendant.

Shoshana, a *mikveh* attendant based in an orthodox Jewish community in midtown Toronto, illustrates some of the specifics regarding the preparatory practices required of the subject prior to entering the *mikveh* site:

> *Before going to the* mikveh *you have to count seven clean days. You have to see no blood whatsoever on the* bedikah *cloth* [a particular fabric designed for vaginal insertion that is used to determine whether or not the subject is still bleeding from her menstrual cycle]. *Then you can begin to prepare for the night of the* mikveh, *which includes a bath beforehand. You have to make sure that all of your body parts and orifices are completely clean. You clean your bellybutton, the insides of your eyes, your ears... The bath has to be at least half an hour long so that you can soak completely. You make sure that your nails*

are cut short and are clean underneath, that there's no dead skin on your feet or hands, that your nail polish is off, that you don't have hang-nails…You make sure your teeth are brushed and they're nothing in between your teeth… Lots of dental floss… and Q-tips for your belly button and your ears and nose. You make sure your hair's all combed out… that it doesn't have any tangles, even under-arm hair and private hair. You don't use conditioner because it doesn't fully wash out… If you have false teeth, you make sure they're in properly… braces too… everything has to be in its right place. For those who are undergoing chemotherapy, and they have a centre line or a pit line, that might be an issue… There are special ways of dealing with that too. You basically have to make your body the cleanest you possibly can be so that nothing can interfere between you and God.

Shoshana explains that the *mikveh* attendant's responsibilities extend beyond her supervision of the subject's physical presence during the dunk. She is trained to observe the individual's demeanour more generally, on an emotional or energetic level. This facet of Shoshana's position stands out as significant, as it is introduces a social dimension to her role. There is a social world being formed here, in addition to the dramaturgy of ritual at work.

The other thing [the attendant will] do is notice if a woman is really agitated. Sorta like, if a she's really not looking forward to going home afterward. A good mikveh-lady will check not only the outside stuff but also the deeper stuff. She'll catch marital issues… signs of abuse. … She'll see how things are really going with the women in her community.

In this passage Shoshana gestures toward a kind of surveillance that *mikveh* spaces provide. On a very basic level, *mikveh*s are places where women get naked; situations of domestic abuse are difficult to cover up when the cuts and bruises are quite literally exposed. On a deeper level, Shoshana is describing an emotional or psychological exposure on the part of the subject that takes place in the *mikveh* room. The very practice of public nakedness that occurs here distinguishes it from other cultural performance spaces in Jewish life. Bodily nakedness seems to cue spiritual nakedness in this environment. Perhaps part of the symbolic cleansing at play in *mikveh* spaces is an element of vulnerability – a kind of purging of emotional toxins in anticipation of intimacy. It is appropriate to note that the timing of *mikveh* ritual is such that it marks the end of a two-week separation period during which husband and wife are not permitted to touch. When a woman immerses in the *mikveh*, she begins a new cycle regarding physical contact with her husband. Jewish law encourages that this new cycle begin with physical intimacy (that is, sexual intercourse) the night she returns from the *mikveh*.

Leah articulates a feeling anticipation – a process of 'counting' – as she describes her *mikveh* experience. She looks forward to her time at the *mikveh* by counting down the days. In this way, Leah actively processes her gender identity during the time that she is not physically present at the *mikveh*.

> *You wait in a process of counting. You're counting those seven days and you're saying: 'OK, I have six days left, I have five days left, I have four days left...'*

The terms 'waiting' and 'counting' are used several times throughout my speaking with Leah, which suggests to me that her preparations for the *mikveh*, her rehearsal, is not simply a physical process – that emotional preparations involved (waiting, counting, anticipating) infuse the laws with spiritual weight. She speaks of the *mikveh* as a milestone, as the climax of her month.

> *The whole day before you go to the* mikveh, *in your head you're mentally preparing – 'How am I gonna do this, how am I gonna have time to prepare, how am I gonna. ...' Because you're gonna make sure that you go.*

For Leah, the *mikveh* is not a monthly ritual; it is, rather, a complex system of laws that generates a consciousness that remains ongoing throughout the month. In light of this, these practices have no beginning or end; they are in constant motion. It also calls into question the locus of the ritual: is the immersive act the heart of the ritual, or is it the waiting and counting that defines the *mikveh* experience? Expanding on Foucault's notion of 'talking sex', I suggest that in addition to a physical space, the *mikveh* is also a construct that occupies a space in Leah's mind. Unlike Habermas's model, this space is not one based on rationality and argumentation; rather, it is an ephemeral space that challenges the norm of the patriarchal intellectual history of the public sphere. This space in Leah's mind houses and permits sexual consciousness, anticipation, and desire. Like the ritual space itself, the (anti)structure of this space is also inherently immaterial. This conceptual space is based upon experience, desire, emotion, inner life, and spirituality. It is contingent upon this content; its borders are not fixed. It exists in relationship to her sexual identity.

There even seems to be a blurring of public and private in this mentality. The laws of *niddah* are ostensibly private, insofar as they involve a woman managing and preparing her naked body. This process, obviously intimate, is performed privately. The dunk itself, however, is performed in the presence of a *mikveh* attendant, who ensures that the dunk has been performed properly and is considered '*kosher*'. Further, due to the complexity and intricate nature of the performance of the laws, women tend to consult rabbinic authorities regularly (usually male rabbis, but sometimes *yoetzet*, women authorities trained in this area) in order to ensure that they are performing the laws correctly. Suddenly, the laws seem far less private, now including the *mikveh* attendant and rabbinic authorities in the process, which ostensibly should pertain solely to husband and wife. The specificity of the law is what gives rise to a public. The instructions for *mikveh* preparation, for example, are so precise that questions invariably arise. This conversation, specifically between a woman, her husband, and her rabbi or *yoetzet* is ongoing; because the performances are monthly, the discourse, like the ritual itself, is cyclical. Every month a different slew of questions are raised and answers are offered in response. A woman also may want to engage in a dialogue about her rabbi's opinion. It may be that she has trouble with his ruling and would like to discuss it. These discourses are not discrete units of time, forming what leans toward (though does not conform to) a more traditional Warnerian public based on discourse, textuality, and rationality.

The laws of *niddah* and their corresponding *mikveh* rituals deeply affect the lives of orthodox Jewish women. *Mikveh* affects a woman's whole life, rather than just one aspect of it, and is thus poiesis – world-making. She performs her Jewish sexuality on a daily basis, not solely when preparing for the *mikveh*, but also when engaging with her children, husband, friends, co-workers, et cetera. The laws create a general sexual consciousness for women in this community because the laws have such a profound effect on their daily lives. The practical implications alone disrupt the quotidian in a major way: if she is in a *niddah* state, every instance that she reaches to touch her husband – even simply to pass him something – is marked with niddah, with sexuality. This creates a charged spiritual reality within orthodox Jewish communities, a concealed yet communal sexual subtext that pulses through the *mikveh* public.

Mikveh publics

Leah, a rebbetzin (female spiritual leader) in her mid-thirties and mother of seven (which is not uncommon in this community), explains how important it is for women to speak about *mikveh* in an open and honest manner. Her approach to *mikveh* as both a physical space and as a special subject for women's discussion supports a view of this structure as a Foucauldian discourse as well as a kind of Habermasian public:

> *You know what: I always tell people that, with* niddah, *I will always be open. When I got married I remember feeling like I was joining a club that I knew nothing about. Even after I took* Kallah Classes, *once I got married it was like, all of a sudden people start talking. I started hearing all these things and I was like, 'Why didn't anybody tell me that* before *I got married?'*

As Leah continues speaking, she attempts to debunk some of the myths about sex generated within orthodox Jewish communities:

> *It's like, you hear, 'It's so beautiful, it's so wonderful, it's the best thing that ever happened to my family'. And it is. But nobody tells you about those frustrating*

times, when you're like, 'I wish I was not in niddah *right now'. There are those times also where it's not fun, and you argue more than you would if you were allowed to touch, and it's definitely not, like, like the most idyllic two weeks, when you're like 'Oh wow!' (Laughs) It's like, a secret. You don't find out these things until you're married. So I always said I was gonna be open with people about it.*

Throughout my research, I found that the concept of *mikveh* as a shared space for women in this community surfaced again and again. In both physical and abstract forms (that is, the physical structure and also the dialogue that it produces), it is a space where women meet on an intimate level. This space has high barriers, however. It is not spoken about with others; it is a kind of secret club or society or, as in Warner's concept, an exclusive and highly marginalized counterpublic. Gaby, also a *rebbetzin* in her mid-twenties, mother of two, recalls several experiences she had during travel when she felt compelled to keep her *mikveh* practice discreet. These experiences highlight the concealed and yet communal nature of this material.

Gaby explains how the *mikveh* is a kind of secret that is only possessed by married women, but one which affects the whole of their public life. She shares with me an experience she had when travelling that manifested this tension:

One time I was traveling to Montreal for work with two hundred teenagers (and mostly male colleagues), and I needed to go to the mikveh. *I just went up to my boss and said, 'I absolutely refuse to go the Saturday night programme and I need the night off!' I have no idea if he ever guessed or not.*

Gaby recalls another travel incident, in Israel this time, when she felt compelled once again to preserve the *mikveh* as a private space.

I had only been married a few months. I was in Jerusalem and I needed to go to the mikveh. *I only told my aunt. I begged her to take me there herself, and I wouldn't let her leave my side. Eventually I had to go in the room alone with the lady who checks you over. She started yelling at me in Hebrew, 'Did you check your feet? Did you check your hands?' Then I think she could tell I was nervous, so she asked me nicely a question in Hebrew, and I didn't understand. So she asked me louder, thinking maybe I was deaf, but that didn't make me understand it any more, so finally I just answered 'yes,' even though I had no idea what the question was. Afterward my aunt told me that the question had been, 'Did you check your earring holes?' Because I didn't have pierced ears at the time, that didn't even occur to me as a question. I never checked my earring holes, because I didn't have earring holes.*

Gaby shared with me that this experience, while unpleasant, was significant to her because it made her feel more connected to her aunt. They were 'in it together', she described. The privacy they shared drew them together.

Michaela, an orthodox woman in her twenties and mother of one, shares with me a similar experience when describing the waiting room at the *mikveh.*

> *When I run into people I'm close to at the* mikveh, *in the waiting room, like my sisters, it's kind of fun. We share more of our private lives with each other than our husbands are comfortable with, so this is sort of a safe space for us to talk about our* mikveh *night. Our husbands can't really fault us for telling each other it's our* mikveh *night if, you know, we see each other at the* mikveh. *You know?*

When asked about the dynamics between women in the waiting room who do not know each other, Michaela explained that there are certain 'rules' of speech in the *mikveh* space. The space has its own set of discursive codes, which attempt to negotiate this combination of intimacy and publicness:

> *When you meet someone you know there, there's sort of a camaraderie. If you talk, it tends to be mundane talk. The kinds of things you would speak about at a grocery store. Sort of on the surface. In a sense, I think you keep it surface to sort of stay away from the fact that something very deep and very personal is about to take place. But if you see the person outside the* mikveh, *you certainly do not mention it. You would never speak about it outside of the* mikveh. *You don't acknowledge it. The* mikveh *is its own reality.*

The sense of privacy described by Gaby seems to resonate with Michaela as well. She understands the privacy as a kind of sanctity that connects directly to the concealed yet communal quality of *mikveh* space. The concealment is important because it preserves what Michaela calls 'the sacredness' of the public that is organically and spontaneously formed.

> *Part of why it's private is because of modesty, but part of it is also about sacredness. Like a secret. Its sacredness – its energy, its power – is preserved by its containment. Just like energy in a tight space. Once you open the space, part of the power is released, and it dissipates.*

Barbara Kirshenblatt-Gimblett's historical analysis of female Jewish performativity helps to contextualize this ethnography on both a religious and a social footing. She links Jewish performativity to Torah ritual and law in her exploration of the Jewish home and charity fairs, Purim balls, and Hanukah pageants.[23] The charity fair in particular, she argues, was a forum through which orthodox Jewish women could engage in a dialogue about their private lives. In 'The Moral Sublime: Jewish Women and Philanthropy in Nineteenth-Century America', Kirshenblatt-Gimblett discusses how the role of the Jewish woman in the public arena has altered, and the ways in which the charity fair was the performative site for this transformation:

> The most powerful fundraising method in the nineteenth-century United States was the charity fair. Organized by women ... the stated purpose of these fairs – to raise money for a good cause – is not the whole story. These events did much more. They shaped public life and placed women at its center, and they did so artfully.[24]

These fairs shaped not only public life for women, but also public identity. By virtue of their public appearance, Purim balls and Hanukkah Pageants constructed a space for women to gather outside of their homes. For the first time, women were performing in public.

Mahmood's unconventional reading of Judith Butler reorients the concept of subversion, rendering it community-specific. She situates resistance from within the law as opposed to against it:

> It is important to note that there are several points on which Butler departs from the notions of agency and resistance that I criticized earlier. ... Butler locates the possibility of agency within structures of power (rather than outside of it) and, more importantly, suggests that the reiterative structure of norms serves not only to *consolidate* a particular regime of discourse/power but also provides the means for its *destabilization*. In other words, there is no possibility of 'undoing' social norms that is independent of the 'doing' of norms; agency resides, therefore, within this productive reiterability.[25]

When speaking about a religious, systematized set of laws, Mahmood believes that it is possible for the female subject to attain power and agency from within. Further, she asserts that under certain conditions the very act of subversion can be misread as an act of submission, if the motivation behind the resistant act is not properly examined:

> [I]f the ability to effect change in the world and in oneself is historically and culturally specific, then the meaning and sense of agency cannot be fixed in advance, but must emerge through an analysis of the particular concepts that enable specific modes of being, responsibility, and effectivity. Viewed in this way, what may appear to be a case of deplorable passivity and docility from a progressivist point of view, may actually be a form of agency – but one that can be understood only from within the discourses and structures of subordination that create the conditions of its enactment. In this sense, agentival capacity is entailed not only in those acts that resist norms but also in multiple ways in which one inhabits norms.[26]

Mahmood identifies the problem of understanding subversion in a simple way. Performance and gender theorists often equate performativity and sub-version with the act of undoing – the conscious deconstruction of gender via performance (for example, parody of gender in drag). In contrast, the ethnography I have conducted with women who speak about *mikveh* and the *mikveh* space explores a second strand of performance theory. Through ges-tural, discursive, bodily acts, *mikveh* creates a 'public of the private', whereas deconstructions of gender in performance might seek to distance a subject's private agency from the control of the public's gaze. When examining acts of cultural subversion it seems equally important to explore acts of doing that exist from within the law as it is to acts of undoing that are in opposition to it. Furthermore, this 'concealed yet communal' practice creates a 'public of the private' where women together seek spiritual succor and support.

Gaby identifies the collapse of private and public when practicing the laws of *niddah*, as she recalls her first experience attending the *mikveh*:

> *We got married two weeks before* Rosh Hashanah. *The first time I went to the* mikveh *after I got married was* Rosh Hashanah. *Which is crazy in itself because the* mikveh *is also supposed to be something that is extremely private, and* Rosh Hashanah *is an extremely public holiday for people to be with their families.*

Gaby draws an interesting comparison between the rituals of Rosh Hashanah, the Jewish New Year, which many would consider public com-mandments, and the *mikveh* ritual, which many would consider private ones. Rosh Hashanah is a holiday that necessitates group congregation and communal prayer. It also requires the gathering of family for a festive meal. These are all public practices, which place Gaby in an uncomfortable posi-tion. In this scenario, she somehow needed to exit her holiday gathering inconspicuously in order to visit the *mikveh*. Further, it would be difficult for Gaby to speak about her situation. Discussing a woman's *mikveh* schedule is considered culturally taboo in many mainstream orthodox communities, as it indicates to the public a precise time of intimacy between husband and wife. Michaela speaks about this taboo when she describes the *mikveh* waiting room.

> *They tell you in* Kallah *classes not to talk about who you see at the* mikveh. *So if you see someone in the waiting room and you want to tell your husband, 'Oh, I saw this person,' you can't. You need to protect their privacy, their* tzniut. *Their modesty. I guess. … In a society where there is no separation [between a time when touch is permitted and a time when it is not], you don't really think about it, the idea that someone might be having sex. But when you have this separation, between times when you're having sex and times when you're not, it's like this monumental moment. And you don't really want to advertise it.*

Michaela later describes a sense of awkwardness that can sometimes arise when, in the waiting room, she begins chatting with another woman, and then one of them is called to proceed to the dunking area.

> *It's always a little bit awkward when one person is leaving and the other wishes them a 'good night'. There's always sort of this subtext. ... Like, 'Have a good niii-ght'. Because, I mean, you both know what's going to happen that night.*

The tension of this intimate-yet-public setting seems to produce a strong sexual consciousness amongst orthodox Jewish women. The women present in this ethnography who practice the laws of *taharat mishpacha* have demonstrated to me a sophisticated sexual consciousness, which includes strong sexual desire and longing for intimacy, heightened awareness of the body, willingness to confront issues pertaining to sexuality, and openness to discussion of sexual experience and expression. In short, while some may view the rituals of orthodox Jewish women as inherently conservative (and even repressive), these are not the voices of subjugated women. They are the voices of women who negotiate their sexualities from within a system rather than positioning themselves as standing against it (the traditional conceit of those who aim to 'subvert' the system).

In the following passage, it is clear that Gaby is taking ownership of her sexuality, negotiating the civics of participation in this public:

> *Everything should be sexual. The way men and women converse with one another should be sexual. I think that the way I talk to other men is a reflection of the way I talk to my husband, and its sex appeal. So I am private about my private life. When I cover my hair, and I make something private between me and my husband – that is our secret. That is our power that we hold together ... I think that it is within everyone's grasp, man, woman, Jew and non-Jew, to bring back their private lives.*

The notion of privacy that Gaby is describing here seems to be insular rather than simply exclusive. By secluding herself from societal expectation, she creates a unique energy between herself and her husband, distinct from her relationships with others. This distinctiveness – her 'secret', as she calls it – is empowering. These moments seem to be powerful for orthodox women; through the (concealment of) the law, women performing Jewishness and sexuality on an ongoing basis.

Lauren Berlant and Michael Warner speak about sex as mediated by publics in their essay 'Sex in Public'.[27] This chapter draws attention to the project of normalization that has made heterosexuality hegemonic. If we are to view *mikveh* practices as a kind of public of the private, a concealed yet communal space between Habermas and Foucault, it seems that the same logic underpinning this project is employed to normalize public acts of intimacy in general. For example, the act of handshaking is considered 'normal' by secular standards, but, according to Gaby, it is a highly sexual act. By refusing to shake the hands of males other than her husband, she subverts hegemonic power structures that dictate this act as mundane, making strange the act of handshaking. This gesture, in turn, becomes a queer act; it disrupts the heteronormative code underneath the handshaking custom and charges this gesture with a religious politic.

Rules like these (limited physical contact between men and women, which specifically reject convention and etiquette laws) exclude orthodox Jewish individuals and families from the kind of 'rightness' Berlant and Warner describe as heteronormative:

> A complex cluster of sexual practices gets confused, in heterosexual culture, with the love plot of intimacy and familialism that signifies belonging to society in a deep and normal way. Community is imagined through scenes of intimacy, coupling, and kinship. ... A whole field of social relations becomes intelligible as heterosexuality, and this privatized sexual culture bestows on its sexual practice a tacit sense of rightness and normalcy. This sense of rightness – embedded in things and not just in sex – is what we call heteronormativity.[28]

On a broader scale, the restrictions pertaining to husbands and wives during *niddah* seem to problematize the same 'field of social relations'[29] as Berlant and Warner's analysis. The signification of the custom that husbands and wives touch in public (handholding or other public displays of affection), and that this is necessarily intimate and familial, is a heteronormative construct. The practice of *niddah* thus queers this dynamic as it extracts orthodox Jewish partnerships from 'belonging to society in a deep and normal way',[30] according to a heteronormative paradigm.

Situating this ethnography in a Habermasian framework and working with Warner's understanding of publics, we can begin to understand *mikveh* ritual as a third space that collapses public and private spheres by drawing out a third space, an ephemeral *mikveh* community, that is concealed yet communal – a 'public of the private'. *Mikveh* space, when understood as both a physical space (a material structure that houses ritual) and also a metaphysical space (communities that exist around and between and through live *mikveh* practice), can be viewed as a quiet queer practice that challenges heteronormativity. The speech acts and discursive, gestural performance practices involved in *mikveh* practice draw attention to sex in a way that is both legible for orthodox Jewish women and also subversive to a secular worldview. The ontology of *mikveh* space (that it 'disappears',[31] existing only in relation to the ritual it contains) queers heteronormative concepts of intimacy and gives rise to a public that negotiates gender and sexuality from within.

Notes

1. Michel Foucault, *The History of Sexuality* (New York: Pantheon Books, 1978), 18.
2. Jürgen Habermas, *The Structural Transformation of the Public Sphere: An Inquiry into a Category of Bourgeois Society*, trans. Thomas Burger (Cambridge, MA: MIT Press, 1989).
3. Michel Foucault, *History of Sexuality*, trans. Robert Hurley (New York, New York: Pantheon Books, 1978), 83.
4. Saba Mahmood, *Politics of Piety: The Islamic Revival and the Feminist Subject* (Princeton: Princeton University Press, 2005), 14–15.
5. Michael Warner, *Publics and Counterpublics* (New York: Zone Books, 2005), 65–6.
6. Warner, *Publics and Counterpublics*, 66.
7. The Schottenstein Edition: *Talmud Bavli,* Tractate *Megilla,* 2a.
8. Edward Fram, *My Dear Daughter: Rabbi Benjamin Slonik and the Education of Jewish Women in Sixteenth-Century Poland* (Cincinnati, OH: Hebrew Union College Press, 2007), xiv.
9. Peggy Phelan, *Unmarked: The Politics of Performance* (New York: Routledge, 1993), 146.
10. Phelan, *Unmarked*, 146.
11. Warner, *Publics and Counterpublics*, 73.
12. Foucault, *The History of Sexuality*, 75.
13. Foucault, *The History of Sexuality*, 75.
14. Mahmood, *Politics of Piety*, 8.
15. Fram, *My Dear Daughter*, 94.
16. Samson Raphael Hirsch, *Horeb: A Philosophy of Jewish Laws and Observations* (London: Soncino Press, 1972).
17. Hirsch, *Horeb,* cxvii.
18. Hirsch, *Horeb*, 317.
19. Hirsch, *Horeb*, 310.
20. Tehilla Abramov, *The Secret of Jewish Femininity: Insights into the Practice of Taharat Mishpachah* (Southfield, Michigan: Targum/ Feldheim, 1988), 50–6.
21. Rabbi Binyomin Forst, *A Woman's Guide to the Laws of Nida* (Brooklyn: Mesorah, 1999), 175–7.
22. Fram, *My Dear Daughter*, 71.
23. Barbara Kirshenblatt-Gimblett, 'The Moral Sublime: Jewish Women and Philanthropy in Nineteenth-Century America', in Barbara Kirshenblatt-Gimblett (ed.), *Writing a Modern Jewish History: Essays in Honor of Salo W. Baron* (New Haven: Yale University Press, 2006), 2.
24. Kirshenblatt-Gimblett, 'The Moral Sublime', 2.
25. Mahmood, *Politics of Piety*, 20.
26. Mahmood, *Politics of Piety*, 14–15.
27. Lauren Berlant and Michael Warner, 'Sex in Public', in Michael Warner, *Publics and Counterpublics* (New York: Zone Books, 2005), 194.
28. Warner, *Publics and Counterpublics*, 194.
29. Warner, *Publics and Counterpublics*, 194.
30. Warner, *Publics and Counterpublics*, 194.
31. Phelan, *Unmarked*, 146.

Works cited

Abramov, Tehilla. *The Secret of Jewish Femininity: Insights into the Practice of Taharat Mishpacha*. Southfield, MI: Targum/ Feldheim, 1988.

Forst, Rabbi Binyomin. *A Woman's Guide to the Laws of Niddah*. Brooklyn, NJ: Mesorah, 1999.

Foucault, Michel. *The History of Sexuality*, trans. Robert Hurley. New York: Pantheon Books, 1978.

Fram, Edward. *My Dear Daughter: Rabbi Benjamin Slonik and the Education of Jewish Women in Sixteenth-Century Poland*. Cincinnati, OH: Hebrew Union College Press, 2007.

Habermas, Jürgen. *The Structural Transformation of the Public Sphere: an Inquiry into a Category of Bourgeois Society*, trans. Thomas Burger. Cambridge, MA: MIT Press, 1989.

Hirsch, Samson Raphael. *Horeb: A Philosophy of Jewish Laws and Observations*. London: Soncino Press, 1972.

Kirshenblatt-Gimblett, Barbara. 'The Moral Sublime: Jewish Women and Philanthropy in Nineteenth-Century America', in Barbara Kirshenblatt-Gimblett (ed.), *Writing a Modern Jewish History: Essays in Honor of Salo W. Baron*. New Haven: Yale University Press, 2006.

Mahmood, Saba. *Politics of Piety: The Islamic Revival and the Feminist Subject*. Princeton, NJ: Princeton University Press, 2005.

Phelan, Peggy. *Unmarked: The Politics of Performance*. New York: Routledge, 1993.

The Schottenstein Edition: Talmud Bavli, Tractate *Megilla*, 2a.

Warner, Michael. *Publics and Counterpublics*. New York: Zone Books, 2005.

12
Busking and the Performance of Generosity: A Political Economy of the Spiritual Gift

Claire Maria Chambers

As Jürgen Habermas imagines it, the public sphere has the potential to be a place for inclusive discussion between equals who are free from the pressures of economy or social status. In this nineteenth-century ideal form of bourgeois public culture, consumption of cultural goods often set the scene for public rational-critical debate. Although cultural goods were marketed and exchanged, the ideas circulated about them remained at the heart of the sphere where private individuals met as 'human beings'. 'Put bluntly: you had to pay for books, theatre, concert, and museum, but not for the conversation about what you had read, heard, and seen and what you might completely absorb only through this conversation.'[1] Habermas's lament in the 1962 publication of *The Structural Transformation of the Public Sphere* seems as appropriate today as it did then: 'Today the conversation itself is administered ... the rational debate of private people becomes one of the production numbers of the stars in radio and television, a salable package ready for the box office.'[2] Does the commodification of opinion cheapen the cultural product itself? Habermas seems to think so: 'the laws of the market have already penetrated into the substance of the works themselves.'[3] This chapter challenges the assumption that cultural goods' being made marketable and exchangeable introduces a flaw into the public circulation of such products. Some cultural goods have for centuries depended upon an economic relationship as the expression of their value and service to a community, such as the music or feats of skill of the street performer or busker. I will argue that the figure of the busker not only challenges the demarcation between state and society and between public and private, but also that the busker helps reimagine the marketplace as a public forum where exchange itself can be valued, escaping the danger of commodification that Habermas fears. It may not be a perfect escape, but the busker's art gestures towards the kind of spontaneous exchange between erstwhile equals that Habermas imagines as the kernel of the relationship between individuals participating in a public sphere. Because busking focuses on a transaction where the display of generosity and the invitation to community is just as important as the living the artist earns or the cultural good the artist proffers, this social drama creates a ritual space where personal relationship – however fleeting – is key. What busking gives is the gift of giving, what one may term a 'spiritual gift' by virtue of its escape from commodification. It lives in human relationship. By taking place on the street corner or in the marketplace, the ritual of giving extends religious sensibility into the public commercial sphere of the contemporary city. Like a liturgy, this 'focused interaction' on the sidewalk creates momentary scenes of sacrifice and sustenance. The exchange of the spiritual gift, the gift of giving, creates a ritual environment that is much like a momentary 'church' – an alternative community created between people liturgically participating in a shared cosmology; a public interaction of the private and the interpersonal that demonstrates the performative construct of the public sphere.

As the following story will illustrate, ritual community may gesture towards an ideal community of equals, but it also serves to underscore present injustice, and the subaltern status the busking 'counterpublic' often occupies. I offer this example because the performative construction of the public sphere necessarily includes disruptions that challenge its continuity. Edward McMichaels, otherwise known as 'The Tuba Man', died as a result of injuries sustained to the head nine days after being beaten by a group of teenagers on the streets of Seattle, Washington, in late October 2008. McMichaels had been a fixture of Seattle downtown street culture and a busking icon. He could be found outside the sports stadiums in the south part of the city, serenading sports fans on their way to the big game with the deep, sonorous notes of his tuba, and taking requests in exchange for a few extra coins in the hat at his feet. Another favourite spot was outside McCaw Hall, home of the Seattle Opera and the Pacific Northwest Ballet, where those familiar with McMichaels noticed that his tuba would complement the music inside.[4] What many did not know about McMichaels was that he was a classically trained musician, proficient on several instruments, and played with the Bellevue Philharmonic as principal tuba player and the Cascade Orchestra, before deciding to hit the streets.[5] What prompted McMichaels's decision to trade stability for the tough life of a busker, working streets and festivals, rain or shine, and dependent on the generosity of his audience, remains a mystery. What is obvious is the impact this lone individual had on the community. People loved his humour, his friendliness, and his music. He lived on their pocket change, and graciously accepted the odd ticket to the ball game or the ballet – tickets he himself could not afford. The public wake at McCaw Hall included scores of musicians, and became a musical celebration of the beloved 'gentle giant', as McMichaels was sometimes called. Articles and websites memorialize him (www.riptubaman.org), and a small group is still trying to raise funds and work with the city to erect a statue in his honour. Public donations were taken through a local bank to pay for his funeral expenses. 'He gave his whole life as a joy and happiness of his fellow man and he gave his highest price in the end', said William Patrick Kiley, his longtime friend.[6] It seems that the city of Seattle responded in kind, returning McMichaels's generosity with their love and support. These actions were also a public outcry against not only the physical but also the economic and cultural violence latent in society. The protest arising from McMichaels's death was a protest against the isolation of an individual whose death was too disconcertingly public, despite the fact that being a public icon was the basis of McMichaels's making a living. McMichaels troubled the distinction between public and private, blurring the borders delineating selves and other selves. This challenge was the gift he offered the Seattle community, but it also put him in the vulnerable position that led to his death.

McMichaels's death can be read as part of the result of the privilege of Cartesian epistemology in the modern tradition and its effect on contemporary political culture. This is the tradition that Habermas promotes when he describes the ideal public sphere as made up of subjects who are autonomous individuals acting to construct their own identities and in their own interests, able to 'bracket' their own participation and objectively judge an outside world. Noelle McAfee suggests applying a Kristevan approach instead, where 'the citizen is always bound up with the political community, never able to completely extricate and separate her judgments from her community', which also resists the notion that the subject is 'a provisional, fragmentary, decentered construction', but could instead be seen as an 'open system'.[7] That is, subjectivity is always under construction in relationship with other selves, and the distinction between self and other blurs in the exchange. The busker blurs the line between public and private by earning and living on the street, and the art of the busker draws others into a ritual transaction where giver, gift and gifting interpenetrate indistinguishably.

What McMichaels gave to the Seattle community could be termed a 'spiritual gift'. Its value could not be contained in an object of exchange, but was present in the relationship between the man and his community. The economy of busking is one that reimagines value as existing in the process of exchange itself.[8] As an example of religion in public, busking's history extends roots not only into the American Protestant traditions of the tithe and charitable giving, but also into the broader Judeo-Christian cultural creed of charity, the Buddhist and Hindu practices of alms-giving, and Native American potlatch. The social drama of generosity is tied into the giving and receiving of *giving itself* as a spiritual gift. Giving is listed by Paul in his letter to the Romans as one of the spiritual gifts attributed to the body of Christ (Romans 12:8). I suggest that 'spiritual gift' can be borrowed from its Christian context to understand the political economy of busking as creating space within secular public culture for the spiritual[9] and communal experience of giving and receiving the gift of giving.

The exchange between buskers and audience can be classed as non-compulsory, but it lies between a donation (which, although a formally voluntary gift, is often tied to a social expectation of return such as prestige or public recognition) and a purchase (a market exchange where a service rendered is paid for according to some standardization of value).[10] The exchange between busker and audience can be neither entirely a donation nor a purchase because the busker has created a social situation in which the audience is already complicit with the performance. One cannot deny one's status and role as audience because one has *already* been included in the performance as soon as one enters the busker's presence. The public square is his stage, and it follows that the public is already his audience. If the exchange were a donation, there would be no expectation of return, but there is indeed a transfer of money for artistic production. If it were simply a market transaction, there would be formally agreed-upon rates, but the money is understood to be generously given according to individual inclination. The whole social drama hinges on the idea that one is not *required* to give, but the lack of that requirement is what actually instantiates its necessity. Because what the busker gives is 'free', the obligation for recompense is more demanding when an audience member explicitly enters into the social relationship of the performance. As one economist notes, '[A]s return becomes more explicit, giving can develop in one direction into exchange, and in the other direction, into compulsory exactions.'[11] What the busker overtly gives is music or a performance for the enjoyment of others, but a great part of the service rendered is that the benefactor has a chance to perform his or her own act of benevolence. Because the 'return' of the busker to his audience is both explicit and vague, the busker creates a social stage for the performance of generosity, where the donor and donee are both involved in the giving of the gift of giving as the creation of an alternative economic and political relationship based on the value of exchange itself.

Where Habermas would argue for the need of a separate place, apart from the market transaction, where the 'cultural good' could be discussed and consumed in order to be fully understood, the busker illustrates that such 'discussion' already happens in the very exchange between artist and consumer. This dialogue may not contain words other than 'thank you', but the exchange is full of viscerally felt meaning. After all, one's dollar dropped into the busker's guitar case is not like inserting coins into a juke box. A seasoned busker continually re-styles his performance to fit an audience, watching and learning from his public as much as it watches him. The exchange creates what Michael Warner calls a counterpublic, and what we might call here a 'counter-economy'; both are defined by their tensions with the normative and offer alternative modes of interaction and self-presentation. Warner even highlights the necessity of economy (exchange) as a feature of the counterpublic: 'A counterpublic, against the background of the public sphere, enables a horizon of opinion and exchange; its exchanges remain distinct from authority and can have a critical relation to power; its extent is, in principle, indefinite, because it is not based on a precise demography but mediated by print, theatre, diffuse networks of talk, commerce, and the like.'[12] Habermas sees a public arising out of discussion about goods that are exchanged (primarily literature). Warner sees counterpublics arising through the valuation of exchange itself, as performances with fluctuating styles. Counterpublics are always counter-economies.

The world of busking itself is a counterpublic, and its history highlights its 'subaltern' status. Culturally, busking is just as easily associated with beggary, knavery, and vagrancy as with the Romantic, idealized bard or minstrel strolling through a wood with a lute slung across his back. Usually in reaction to busking's antiestablishment, sometimes scofflaw nature, such performers are often criminalized or harassed.[13] The god or king disguised as a stranger, who reveals the true nature of the people with whom he interacts, is a myth well-known across cultures, from Zeus's many human disguises, to the angels who visit Abraham, or Jesus on the road to Emmaus. The contemporary busker fits here too as an incarnation of the holy fool, the one whose livelihood is gleaned from between the cracks in society, and whose special status in normative society makes possible a spiritual exchange in a ritualistic setting. It is no surprise, given the love expressed towards a man like McMichaels, his extraordinary ability, and his choice to eschew normative means of disseminating his art, that his friends should seek to memorialize him, and that his talent and personality are now somewhat ensconced in a *mythos*.

That 'mythos' can also be seen through a broader understanding of the busker as a religious-cultural figure. There is a dynamic relationship between a culture's religious history and contemporary secular patterns of philanthropy and altruism; the latter have not evolved out of the former so much as the latter remain informed and inflected by the other. The religious reforms after the end of feudalism in Europe in the fourteenth and fifteenth centuries altered the Church's ability to respond to the needs of the marginalized. Industrialization, accompanied by a rise in poverty, necessitated new structures of care, but where the Renaissance understood the spiritual merit of the mendicant, industrialized Europe increasingly conflated the poor and the criminal, as support for the downcast was increasingly drawn from public institutions since churches were unable to meet the demand. With the modern rise of the welfare state after the Great Depression, responsibility for the well-being of citizens was transferred from hierarchical leadership to a democratic public, which can be read in correspondence with contemporary religious movements that emphasize a socialist perspective, like liberation theology and the social reforms within the Roman Catholic Church as a result of Vatican II.[14] Gifting and donations as part of a public consciousness of support for the dependent have a fluid relationship with this practice's spiritual, religious, and political history, and, as such, a public performance of generosity also performs a religious scenario, inscribing yet again on the palimpsest of public culture the giving of alms, the tithe, the charitable act. The busker is the sacrificial figure who makes this scenario possible.

Furthermore, it is the exchange of money within the scenario that cements the ritual. The performer and audience understand the hat or case to suggest a charitable remuneration is as much a part of the busker's performance as their song, dance or story. Although busking performs itself as 'free', since it does not insist on payment, the most recognizable characteristic of busking is that it draws the responding audience into a communal performance of generosity, opening the playing area into the street itself, where the busker becomes the central character in a social drama of decision – to give or not to give – where what is played out are all the attached implications of that responsive gesture. What this means is that the economy of the gift in busking is about the discovery of identity. The busker gives a gift that, in giving itself, gives oneself to oneself. It is the gift that gives the gift of giving. For example, what the Tuba Man gave his listeners was the opportunity to give back to him, and this giving back gives the giver his or her own fluid sense or understanding of self – both individually and in community, *between* self and other selves, *within* the other, and in constant process. Far from this being a simple scene for unthinking altruism, each exchange with a busker is rife with meaning, as it reimagines the status of the art commodity as about the free flow of a gift in constant consumption, rather than the static objective of possession. It is a spiritual gift because the status of the exchange can no longer be described simply as a 'tithe' or a 'donation', but as an active relationship that creates identity within an immediate community that reflects a ritual cosmological understanding. Who are you and who will you be in relationship to this Other that performs before you, performs *for you, with you, within you*? The gift of giving parallels the subject as constantly in process through relationship with other selves, a constant transaction that is a constant self-discovery.

Some imagine that the transaction between busker and audience creates a political and economic utopia, where all involved are momentarily sustained by the mutual pleasure of an equal exchange (with echoes of Habermas's ideal public sphere). In his study of street theatre, Bim Mason defines entertainers or buskers as 'those with the simple aim of pleasing the audience, either by making them laugh or by impressing them with skills such as juggling, acrobatics or magic. Very little is demanded of the public in terms of participation or thought ... operating on the principle that the more pleasure is received by the public the more money is made.' Mason goes on to reflect that

Apart from the financial considerations there are other benefits to be received from entertaining people. The most obvious one is that of giving pleasure to a large number of people. Most entertainers try to appeal to as wide a range of audience as possible and, outdoors, the performer is much more accessible to the public. This means that they will receive not only direct praise from young and old, but affection too. ... Simply aiming to please is not a high ambition but it lacks the pretensions of other types of performing. It is a joy to create laughter; applause can always be induced and is not necessarily a true response from the audience. Laughter, on the other hand, as a spontaneous expression by the audience, cannot be faked.[15]

I quote Mason at length here because his understanding of street performance is both perceptive and deceptive. Having conducted informal interviews with several Seattle buskers at the famed Pike Place Market, and having sat in on the monthly Seattle Busker's Guild meeting, I might conclude that this kind of performance for the sheer love of it is a strong part of the busker's identity. No one continues to busk as a serious living (and many buskers consider themselves professionals) because they want to 'make it big'. They do it because there is something gained in the art of busking that is not available in traditional musical careers. In fact, several buskers I spoke with have jobs that they understand to support their busking *careers*, instead of careers that support their busking *hobbies*. Todd of the folk duo Pickled Okra, for example, explained to fellow buskers at one meeting how he spends three summer months working at a fishery in Alaska in order to dedicate the rest of the year to his music. MacKenzie and Claire of the Dandelion Junk Queens told me that busking hobbyists do not last long, and they are easy to spot because they go back to their cars when it starts to rain (a frequent occurrence in Seattle). On one very important level, the dedication of these buskers is definitely about the simple giving and receiving of pleasure and happiness in the pursuit of artistic activity these musicians do not desire to live without, and live to share with others. Busking is a lifestyle with a strong spiritual awareness of self-fulfillment and community through art.

However, Mason's definition of street performance as 'simply aiming to please', whether or not it is a 'high ambition', is deceptive because the transaction that takes place between a busker and his audience is far from 'simple'. Professional buskers are intelligent, keen business people. They work very hard, and they understand the incredible political value of community, demonstrated by the creation of an organization like the Seattle Busker's Guild. They have a long tradition of looking out for one another, as described by famous London busker Percy Press in an interview with Brooks McNamara about his early life as a Punch and Judy showman: 'There was a kind of bond, a freemasonry, on the streets then, because the life was so hard. Buskers would always tell each other where the good pitches were, for example, though if someone had a recognized pitch you wouldn't trespass on it.'[16] Furthermore, buskers know that their presence on the street has political significance. The definition of street entertainment as 'simply aiming to please' needs stronger political reinforcement. Bradford Martin's more recent study of public performance helps with that revision: '"Public performance" can be defined as a self-conscious, stylized tactic of staging songs, plays, parades, protests, and other spectacles in public places where no admission is charged and spectators are often invited to participate, and it conveys symbolic messages about social and political issues to audiences who might not have encountered them in traditional venues.'[17] Busking at the Pike Place Market is a political activity that reconceptualizes the artist's relationship to the public sphere and the institutionalization of artistic and political legitimacy. Authentic political, artistic, and economic activity can take place outside of established institutions, peripherally to them, or move in and out of them. '[R]adical artistic expressions and cultural forms serve not merely as rehearsals for politics but rather amount to a form of 'counterculture' or 'oppositional stance,' contesting mainstream values and society.'[18] Busking creates an economy that reimagines what work and labour look like, and how the artist integrates into the fabric of society. Busking, in its reconfiguration of community for even a short time, argues for the revolutionary transformation of art-as-commodity into art-as-gift, exiting a capitalistic model of wealth as owned by individuals and creating an alternative economy where wealth exists in the free flow of the exchange itself. 'It is in giving that you might receive' is a phrase from the popular spiritual consciousness that describes this exchange.[19] It manifests the spiritual gift of giving when art-as-gift makes possible giving-as-gift.

Anyone who has spent time in a major city knows the basic 'social drama' of busking. That I use anthropologist Victor Turner's well-known concept to describe the relatively peaceful interactions of busker and audience may seem strange to those familiar with Turner's work, since by his definition the social drama begins with (step one) the breach of a norm, or 'the infraction of a rule of morality, law, custom or etiquette in some public arena', which then (step two) becomes a conflict or a crisis.[20] But this is exactly why I invoke Turner's terminology. Busking indeed exposes the crisis of the artist in the economic system in which they refuse to participate by setting up on the street and gathering a crowd, rather than working through other traditional venues. In step three of Turner's social drama, 'sides are taken, factions are formed', and in step four, these sides either reintegrate into society or recognize a schism. For Turner, the social drama represents a unit of social process that is a fact of everyone's experience in every human society. He is concerned with the more stable structures that they reveal: 'The phase of crisis exposes the pattern of current factional struggle within the relevant social group, be it village or world community; and beneath it there becomes slowly visible the less plastic, more durable, but nevertheless gradually changing social structure, made up of relations which are relatively constant and consistent.'[21] The social drama of busking is a soft breach in propriety. The busker sets up her act on a public thoroughfare, co-opting space for alternative use, demanding attention and diverting traffic in places where it may or may not be legal to do so. They may have to negotiate with police and shopowners to stand their ground (crisis). A group like the Seattle Busker's Guild at the Pike Place Market represents a faction that has embraced busking as a legitimate art form, and integrated it into the culture of the Market and the city. The culture of busking is a direct challenge to the orthodoxy of capitalism, and that it has found strong footholds in places like the Pike Place Market speaks to the 'gradually changing social structure' of the artist in relationship to society that the busker works to continue. The busker is the overt sign of such covert challenge and change. As with other kinds of revolutionaries – heretics, radicals, mystics – buskers inhabit a fluid social status where they are both revered by fans and followers but also somewhat despised by the ideological apparatus within which they create their alternative economies and communities. Again, theirs is a sacrificial role, because their willingness to put their livelihoods on the line for their art, to live and work in the margin, makes possible the social imaginary of an alternative economy and politics.

Before this possible romanticization and spiritualization of the busker goes too far, let us remember that the fleeting experience of an alternative community and economy is exactly what buskers know how to exploit, because it is good for business. The good feeling derived from giving is a product just as much as the performance. Popular literature abounds with articles on the benefits of giving. A recent *Newsweek* article by Peter Singer, the ethicist and charitable giving advocate behind the website *thelifeyoucansave.com*, addresses the psychology behind generosity, pointing out contradictions between ethical imperatives and how people actually behave when faced with an opportunity to sacrifice time, energy or money on behalf of a needy other. 'Futility thinking' discourages potential donors when they think their contribution would just be a 'drop in the ocean' in the face of an over-whelming problem like world poverty. But when presented with specific details and evidence of the change their money could make, giving becomes a more attractive option. The unspoken subtext is that giving is in fact a kind of getting: charity is never freely given; it is investment and exchange. After arguing that American citizens could give enough to cut world poverty in half without any noticeable sacrifice, Singer ends his article with one last plug for giving on the basis of what you can get: 'The good person is also – typically – a happy person. A survey of 30,000 American households found that those who gave to charity were 43 percent more likely to say they were "very happy" about their lives than those who did not give. [...] Many people find that when they begin to give, they free themselves from the acquisitive treadmill and find new meaning and fulfillment in their lives.'[22] What Singer does not mention is that freedom from the 'acquisitive treadmill' is itself an acquisition. This model certainly informs the busker's performance, because the ownership model of wealth could pertain to an interaction between busker and audience member just as easily as the model of 'spiritual gift'. Still, however the busker may exploit charitable feelings, they can also invite a continuation of the flow of the commodity between producer and receiver that Singer's model does not include. Again, it is in the exchange itself that value lies, not in the product or the producer.

The Seattle Buskers' Guild has institutionalized a culture of generosity by creating a permanent home for buskers in and around the Pike Place Market. In 2004, the Seattle City Council proclaimed a 'Seattle Busker's Week', which celebrates busking city-wide, culminating every year with the Busker's Festival at the Pike Place Market, which serves not only to display and celebrate busking as an important part of Seattle's art life but also to celebrate the practice of busking around the rest of the Pacific Northwest and indeed the world. The guild is unique in that it has given a home to a performance culture that identifies with the wanderer and the vagabond, giving a kind of legitimacy to the proudly 'illegitimate', offering mediation between buskers and the Market, and promoting busking in general. Busking, through creating communal performances of generosity, peddles more than music, laughter or feats of skill: it offers the gift of giving outside an economy of ownership. Because the busker performs on the street, does not sell tickets, does not have a contract with advertisers or a manager or a production company, the performance depends on spontaneous interactions with the public that flow freely between audience and artist.

The busker works against the understanding of 'gift' as something that must entirely exit an economy in order to be 'freely given'. The idea that there are 'no free gifts' has been a strong claim among anthropologists since Marcel Mauss published his influential essay on the subject in 1950. As Mary Douglas writes in her introduction to Mauss's *The Gift*, 'If we persist in thinking that gifts ought to be free and pure, we will always fail to recognize our own grand cycles of exchanges, which categories get to be included and which get to be excluded from our hospitality.'[23] She emphasizes that Mauss's landmark study reveals the gift as an index of the cultural transactions that define a society. Mauss understands the gift not in terms of abstract value as attached to things, but in terms of personal characteristics. The gift demands reciprocity through obligation because it gives the giver as much as it gives the object of the gift: 'Souls are mixed with things; things with souls. Lives are mingled together, and this is how, among persons and things so intermingled, each emerges from their own sphere and mixes together. This is precisely what contract and exchange are.'[24] In Mauss's understanding of Malinowski's study of the Kula gift exchanges around the islands of Papua New Guinea, the gift itself is ownership and possession – this is what it *confers upon* the giver and receiver, such as status or notoriety. More generally speaking, in the exchange of gifts, the personality of the clan or tribe expresses itself through the self-expression of individual givers who give personally planned gifts. '[B]y giving one is giving *oneself*, and if one gives *oneself*, it is because one 'owes' *oneself* – one's person and one's goods – to others.'[25] The social drama of generosity performed by buskers can be read as a ritual transaction that draws the casual passer-by into an alternative social set-up that insists on the responsibility of one for all others. By extending the gift of music out into the public sphere for enjoyment, the busker demands attention, as if to say, 'You are already receiving my gift of music ... should you not already be giving something in return?' The person who turns their head to listen has already acknowledged their participation in a kind of exchange process where the gift is already in the process of being given.

If the gift is not 'free', is it still a gift? It seems that this is a question that would trouble a society where value is placed on ownership more than a society where value is regarded as living within exchange itself. Some suggest that in order for the gift to revise capitalistic expenditure and ownership, it should be defined as only a one-sided transaction. For example, Jacques Derrida argues that a true gift is always 'deferred' from the grasp of actuality because in order for there to be a gift 'there must be no reciprocity, return, exchange, counter gift or debt. If the other gives me back or owes me or has to give me back what I give him or her, there will not have been a gift.'[26] According to Derrida, any kind of necessity for exchange or restitution would annul the gift. In another work, Derrida characterizes the act of hospitality in a similar vein. In order to open the door to the stranger, the host must enact what disallows him to be a good host: the very act of opening up his home to the perfect stranger, which makes his home now subject to a flow of traffic from the outside, and no longer a refuge whose safety he can offer in confidence. The act or gift of hospitality turns back and destroys itself within the action of the offer. But Derrida does not allow that the gift or hospitality remain simply unattainable. Rather, he works through a way to think of them as instantiating themselves through the very perversion of their own laws:

> It wouldn't be effectively unconditional, the law [that is, the ultimate law of hospitality to give freely to the stranger], if it didn't *have to become* effective, concrete, determined, if that were not its being as having-to-be. It would risk being abstract, utopian, illusory, and so turning over into its opposite. In order to be what it is, *the* law thus needs the laws, which however, deny it, or at any rate threaten it, sometimes corrupt or pervert it. And must always be able to do this.[27]

To turn back to the example of the gift as always caught up in the momentum of reciprocity, we can understand the gift to depend upon the law of reciprocity as both a 'perversion' of the 'pure gift' *and* what makes it possible. *The* law (singular) of the exchange is that the moment of giving must be a spontaneous offer, but the *laws* (plural) of gifting stipulate that this spontaneous offer performs a social structure that only lives through its continuous transaction. The source of value is not contained in the ritual action but in the exchange itself, as Arjun Appadurai argues by way of George Simmel: 'the economy of a particular social form "consists not only in exchanging *values* but in the *exchange* of values"'.[28] The active, living relationship between gifter and giftee describes Appadurai's 'commodity situation', where exchangeability is the socially relevant factor. What busking performs is a social situation where the gift, through acts of generosity, is not only in the exchange itself, but in the gift of giving – so that one may identify oneself with the 'spiritual gift' of giving.

Lewis Hyde writes, in *The Gift*, his classic essay on the role of the artist in the modern world, that the gift lives not in things, but in consumption. '[A] gift is consumed when it moves from one hand to another with no assurance of anything in return. There is little difference, therefore, between its consumption and its movement. A market exchange has an equilibrium or stasis: you pay to balance the scale. But when you give a gift there is momentum, and the weight shifts from body to body.'[29] In Hyde's thought on consumption we can grasp a consummation between the idea of a 'free gift' – that is, one that is given without the desire for return – and the necessity for the momentum of giving and receiving within a social structure. A gift is completely consumed when it is freely given, which in turn is what assures its flow within the economy of exchange. This would be 'a gift that is its giving'.

In addition to a gift that is its giving, the social drama of generosity allows for the spiritual gift of giving. The nuanced difference between 'a gift that is its giving' and the 'spiritual gift of giving' is that the first describes the fluid exchange *relationship* between gifter and giftee in the creation of an alternative economy. The second describes an alternative, process-oriented *identity* as a giver in a community of givers in the creation of an alternative politics. By creating a social drama that instantiates the two together, buskers and their audience participate in the political economy of the spiritual gift. In my interactions with buskers in the Market, the gift of my interest in their art and their life stories (as well as my dollar bills and coins) prompted hours of conversation and storytelling – gifts which I treasured in the moment and, through this chapter, seek to give away again. In the moment of the shared connection over an artist's passion for his music, there is a shared joy and excitement that is erotic and highly pleasurable. This eroticism describes the interpenetration of the economic and the political in the spiritual gift. As Hyde further writes,

> [L]ibido is not lost when it is given away. Eros never wastes his lovers. When we give ourselves in the spirit of that god, he does not leave off his attentions; it is only when we fall to calculation that he remains hidden

and no body will satisfy. Satisfaction derives not merely from being filled but from being filled with a current that will not cease. With the gift, as in love, our satisfaction sets us at ease because we know that somehow its use at once assures its plenty.[30]

Sometimes I never knew what word or phrase would pique a busker's interest and tip us into a long, unprecedented conversation. After a guild meeting, after asking every question I could think of, I was walking back out to the street with busker Ronn Benway of 'Raw Corn', and commented off-hand that busking was such an interesting 'subculture'. This particular turn of phrase unleashed a passionate oration from Ronn, who told me that he would never give up busking because street performance is 'totally different' from every other kind of performance in the world. 'You touch so many people' he said, 'and it's just you and the instrument in your hands'. He spoke with the conviction of a religious convert, which underscored my strong impression that the lifestyle of busking itself, to those who practice it faithfully, is the community and the purpose that they serve with their lives. In a long conversation with Reggie Miles, a blues musician who plays the saw and steel guitar and is a regular fixture at the Market and many festivals around the Pacific Northwest, the phrase I heard him most often repeat was, 'Even though I didn't make any money ...'. Even though he didn't make any money playing this or that festival, or if he just made enough to cover his fuel and dinner for the night, he considered opportunities to perform well worth the time, because it allowed him to witness 'the most beautiful things I've even seen', and often resulted in other opportunities he could not have predicted. One of his favorite stories is about how he ended up in the *Wall Street Journal* because someone who wrote for the newspaper happened to hear his original song 'Wall Street Bailout Blues', and decided to write an article about how musicians have been commenting on the recession in the United States.[31] This seemed to impress upon Miles the conviction that his music has a life of its own for which he serves as a medium. Both Benway and Miles expressed their commitment to busking as participating in a purpose larger than themselves. In these reflections I do not intend to make out buskers as mendicant saints, but to suggest that because busking and street performance both challenge the normative structure of society and seek to gradually change it, buskers might experience their performance as momentous and meaningful, taking great joy in the unprecedented and unexpected. As they described it, busking seemed a spiritual discipline.

Popular culture often connects busking to begging and panhandling, things that make people uncomfortable because they expose social disunity and economic violence, as did the death of McMichaels. We suffer when we see the suffering of others, and buskers remind us of that when they suffer us to enjoy their work. Lewis Hyde describes the experience of receiving a gift as 'suffering gratitude', because to receive the gift affects the receiver deeply when it prompts his or her own response:

> The labor of gratitude is the middle term in the passage of a gift. It is wholly different from the 'obligation' we feel when we accept something we don't really want. (An obligation may be discharged by an act of will.) A gift that has the power to change us awakens a part of the soul. But we cannot receive the gift until we can meet it as an equal. We therefore submit ourselves to the labor of becoming like the gift. Giving a return gift is the final act in the labor of gratitude, and it is also, therefore, the true acceptance of the original gift.[32]

The way a society treats its commodities speaks volumes about how that society understands itself interpersonally. An economy that values things for the way they can be manipulated, controlled, collected, or thrown away reveals a society that treats people in the same manner. The economy of busking emphasizes vulnerability, which is why the busker and the vagrant may often be conflated in the popular imagination, and why the tragic death of someone like the Tuba Man needs to be recognized as a symptom of a society's inability to become like the gift that the artist offers, one that is the giving itself, one that gives the gift of giving in process with other selves, rather than a commodity that can be bought, stored, circulated.

Street artists often have to deal with stigmatization, lack of rights, and voicelessness when in conflict with the law, despite often being sponsored by cities or private organizations, such as parks, recreation centres, and festivals. The fact that buskers self-select as workers is part of the difficulty – no agency represents them. As far as I know, the high level of organization of the Seattle Busker's Guild is unique and unusual, since busking as a culture is rather anarchic. The buskers of the Pike Place Market, while acknowledged as a trademark of the popular tourist destination and as an indispensable part of the 'local colour' that draws customers to the Seattle waterfront district, often deal with restrictions to their movement and freedom in their performance choices (such as volume and content), harassment and a lower social status, all the while working to maintain a high degree of professionalism. At a monthly Buskers' Guild meeting in the Market held in December 2010, a great portion of the meeting was dedicated to a discussion of the conflicts often encountered with the Market vendors, who sometimes complain to Market authorities that buskers interfere with sales. The Market board responds by tightening regulations for buskers, such as shortening time limits spent at one location, and stipulating that busking can only happen at certain designated corners, marked by the familiar numbered music note painted on the pavement (see Figure 12.1). (Due to recent renovations in the Market, several of these spots have been eliminated but not replaced, another source of consternation for regular buskers who depend

Figure 12.1   One of the numbered music notes painted on the Market sidewalk to indicate an official busking spot, December 2010. Photo by the author

on the Market venue for their livelihood.)[33] It is a complicated relationship, because while the Pike Place Market seems to want to make a legitimate place for the celebration and appreciation of busking, especially considering its sponsorship of the annual Busker's Festival, it also seems wary of allowing the freelancing enterprise of busking its own self-regulation.

Nevertheless, the Pike Place buskers do self-regulate among their own in-group. In my informal interviews with musicians in the Market, several people pointed out that although busking is traditionally a 'laid-back' and informal enterprise, eschewing formal organizational structures, they respond effectively to needs in their own time and on their own terms. For example, they ensure that whoever is at the Market during the course of a day gets to circulate to the prime performance spots. They openly admit that they sometimes encounter conflict amongst themselves, but for the most part they operate within an open economy of sharing, understanding that co-opting a resource for one artist at the expense of another (such as staying in a prime performance spot for too long) stops the flow of exchange between musicians and their audiences, and so is good for nobody. Buskers use materials at hand to communicate with one another, creating a scheduling system with recycled cardboard, pens, thumb tacks, and masking tape. As buskers circulate throughout the Market, they read the impromptu signs tacked up next to the busking spots upon which other buskers have written their projected timeslots and reservations. As I walked through the Market on several occasions, I noticed that these timelines were revised throughout the day, with crossings-out and insertions. This low-tech yet highly proficient method allows for movement and change throughout the day. The communication is effective even while the buskers are dispersed throughout the Market or moving back and forth from the Market to other places in the city.

Self-regulation is an integral aspect of an exchange if a gift is to be its giving. When an outside 'regulator' imposes a structure on the exchange, the gift can no longer give itself, but is beholden to an external monitor. The scheduling system is one example of self-regulation that arises within the busking community, but busking can also create spontaneous, momentary communities of self-regulation. The encounters between buskers and their audiences fit Erving Goffman's descriptions of focused interactions – 'public gatherings that bridge the gap between urban anonymity and private relationships'.[34] '[A]n exceptional amount of cooperation and self-regulation, even feelings of community, are generated in the audience circles. Moreover, these instances of focused interaction cut across ethnic and racial lines in ways that attest to the cultural complexity and sophistication of their participants.'[35] An 'unfocused interaction' describes something like pedestrian traffic: 'When we walk in public thoroughfares, we exchange multiple subtle cues with people on either side of us and with those approaching from the opposite direction. [...] Although not always executed with the utmost grace, this coordination helps to prevent the collisions that would otherwise constantly occur.' 'Focused interaction' refers to situations in which a group of people relate to each other through focus on a central organizing activity. 'Rules of transformation tell the players how the real world will be modified inside the encounter. With the outside world held at bay, players create a new world within. A kind of membrane forms around them. They often experience a sense of intimacy, the closeness of sharing a world apart,' giving the audience 'permission to play'.[36] Although it does not exclude the possibility that there are unspoken rules that reflect internal organization, the social drama of busking creates a focused interaction where the exchange of music, money, and enjoyment can circulate without the distraction of outside regulation. This is an important aspect of its creation of a ritual environment in which the spiritual gift of giving becomes operative.

In another conversation with gregarious storyteller Reggie Miles, I asked him to describe a favourite moment from his career. He followed with a touching story about how on a warm spring day, a 'beautiful little girl' in a flowing dress began to dance to his music, all of her own accord. Soon, another little girl joined her, and a crowd began to gather to witness the dance. The bearded Miles, in his signature rugged denim jeans, flannel shirt, heavy boots and red suspenders, was more than likely a gruff counterpart to the dancing children, the juxtaposition forming something of the charm for the gathering audience. What Miles emphasized in his story was that while the dancers and the audience were responding to his music, he was no longer the star act, but instead an instigator of an event that they all created together – a 'focused interaction,' in Goffman's sense, a ritual community in process through the exchange. He was additionally pleased that several people pulled out cameras and camcorders, which meant his music was being recorded and distributed out into the world. The performance was out of his hands, but also giving back to him in many ways (on more than one occasion, he told me, someone has recognized his act from a YouTube video, which often results in a tip, and reinforces his belief that anyone recording him live in the Market is good promotion). Never satisfied with only one example, Miles then launched into a related tale about a Christmastime ferry ride across the Puget Sound, when buskers used to be allowed to play in the passenger cabin as the ferry made its crossing. Miles had taken out his saw, and with his bow coaxed from it a soulful rendition of 'Silent Night.' A woman and her daughter began to sing along. Then, another musician, unknown to Miles, stepped up and took out a mandolin. Soon, others gathered around, rounding out the impromptu chorus with harmonies. Miles told me that what impressed him most about his profession is that it always brings strangers together and creates spontaneous communities based solely on the love of the music. 'What an incredible moment,' he said.

Miles smiled broadly at me all during that conversation, obviously enjoying it, and I realized we'd been talking late into the evening as the Market vendors began shutting up their stalls. I smiled back. I expressed my gratitude to him for his time, and my apologies that I had no more change to put in his guitar case, especially since I noticed his saw leaning against his chair, and had hoped to hear him play. With the utmost in graciousness, Miles took up his saw, and I knelt to listen. 'Greensleeves' hauntingly echoed down the tiled walkways (Figure 12.2). I realized later that Miles, as a busker, would never have refused my request, because he understood that busking depends on the continuation of the exchange between artist and audience. Once that flow is stopped for whatever reason, busking stops being the art that it is and turns into a musical commodity. In our conversation and with 'Greensleeves', Miles gave me a gift that, in giving itself, gave me to myself. I experienced my economic relationship and my political identity with this person in a way that took us out of the normative exchange of money for services and created something different, where the mutual exchange reimagined the status of the art commodity as about the free flow of a gift in constant consumption, rather than performing hierarchical relationships of possession and ownership, and reimagined the gift itself as about an identity with the gift of giving, rather than wholly caught up in the exchange itself. This gave me to myself, as in process with other selves, between and within

Figure 12.2 Blues musician Reggie Miles plays his saw and sings for an audience of one, December 2010. Photo by the author

other selves, as free to wander within that reciprocal exchange that treads a shifting pathway between the private, the interpersonal, and the public; free to explore the spirituality of a political economy, and the political economy of a spiritual gift.

In the spirit of the busker's tireless promotion of her fellow artists, I end this chapter by asking readers to please support their local buskers, and refer to the websites below for music samples and more information about the performers mentioned above:

More information about busking at the Pike Place Market: www.pikeplace market.org
Reggie Miles: http://www.myspace.com/reggiemiles
Ronn Benway of 'Raw Corn': http://www.myspace.com/ronnbenway
The Dandelion Junk Queens: http://www.freewebs.com/dandelionjunkqueens
Pickled Okra: http://www.myspace.com/pickledokrabluegrass
The Gloria Darlings: http://www.myspace.com/gloriadarlings
Emery Carl, a.k.a. the 'Busker King': http://www.thetroubadourshow.com/ EmeryCarl.html

Notes

Research and writing for this chapter was supported by the Sogang University Research Grant of 2012. Many thanks to Joshua Edelman, Simon W. du Toit, and Carolyn Roark for feedback on earlier versions of the chapter.

1. Jürgen Habermas, *The Structural Transformation of the Public Sphere: An Inquiry into a Category of Bourgeois Society,* trans. Thomas Burger (Cambridge, MA: MIT Press, 1991), 164.
2. Habermas, *The Structural Transformation,* 164.
3. Habermas, *The Structural Transformation,* 165.
4. Brad Wong, 'Remembering Seattle's Tuba Man with Music,' *The Seattle Post-Intelligencer,* 8 November 2008, http://www.seattlepi.com/local/387071_ tubaman09.html, last accessed 4 February 2013.
5. Lornet Turnbull, 'Seattle's Tuba Man Dies from Beating Injuries', *The Seattle Times,* 5 November 2008, http://seattletimes.nwsource.com/html/localnews/2008352227_ tubaman05m.html, last accessed 4 February 2013.
6. Matt Markovitch, 'Local Musicians Sound Final Note for Tuba Man', *Komo News,* 8 November 2008, http://www.komonews.com/news/local/34150519.html, last accessed 4 February 2013.
7. Noelle McAfee, *Habermas, Kristeva, and Citizenship* (Ithaca, NY and London: Cornell University Press, 2000), 15–16.
8. That value lies in exchange itself and not the objects of exchange has been promoted by scholars such as Arjun Appardurai and Lewis Hyde, as discussed below.
9. 'Spiritual' is a multivalent term. For the purposes of this article, by 'spiritual' I mean an inclusive sense of participating in a community or a cosmos larger than the self. I do not intend to uphold any particular religious tradition over another when referring to a human regard for spiritual life, even though my examples will stem mostly from my training in Christian Biblical theology.
10. I am taking my vocabulary here from S. Rhani Bhatnagar, 'From Charity to Taxes: Observations on the Sociology of Religious and Secular Giving', *Journal for the Scientific Study of Religion,* 9(3) (Autumn 1970): 209–18.
11. Bhatnagar, 'From Charity to Taxes', 214.
12. Michael Warner, *Publics and Counterpublics* (New York: Zone Books, 2005), 56.
13. Published in 1997, Parita Mukta's article 'On Beggars, the Homeless, and the Poor', *Economic and Political Weekly,* 32(24) (14–20 June 1997): 1387–8, remains a clarion call to societies whose efforts at globalization may in many ways remain blind to the needs and deaf to the political voices of the socially marginalized. Mukta critiques the campaign rhetoric of Blair's Labour Party for exactly this reason.
14. For a more complete picture of the religious history of the tithe in the United States, see James Hudnut-Beumler's *In Pursuit of the Almighty's Dollar: A History of Money and American Protestantism* (Chapel Hill, NC: University of North Carolina Press, 2007).
15. Bim Mason, *Street Theatre and Other Outdoor Performance* (London and New York: Routledge, 1992), 30.
16. Percy Press and Brooks McNamara, 'An Interview with Percy Press and a Portfolio of Buskers', *Educational Theatre Journal,* 27(3) (October 1975): 316.
17. Bradford D. Martin, *The Theatre Is in the Street: Politics and Public Performance in Sixties America* (Amherst and Boston: University of Massachusetts Press, 2004), 4.

18. Martin, *The Theatre Is in the Street*, 19.
19. The phrase comes from the *Prayer of St Francis* by an anonymous author. There are several popular renditions in English. The full line is 'O Divine Master, grant that I may not so much seek to be consoled as to console, to be understood, as to understand; to be loved, as to love. For it is in giving that we receive, it is in pardoning that we are pardoned, and it is in dying that we are born to eternal life.' It is a quite efficient summation of a basic Christian theological tenet (reflected especially in the asceticism of the lifestyle promoted by the historical Francis of Assisi) that, paradoxically, through a perceived negation, the believer actually finds grace, salvation, eternal life, comfort, et cetera.
20. Victor Turner, *From Ritual to Theatre: The Human Seriousness of Play* (New York: PAJ Publications, 1982), 69–70.
21. Turner, *From Ritual to Theatre*, 70.
22. Peter Singer, 'The Science Behind our Generosity: How Psychology Affects What We Give Charities', *Newsweek*, 28 February 2009, http://www.newsweek.com/2009/02/27/the-science-behind-our-generosity.html, last accessed 4 February 2013.
23. Mary Douglas, 'Foreword: No Free Gifts', in Marcel Mauss, *The Gift: The Form and Reason for Exchange in Archaic Societies*, trans. W.D. Halls (New York and London: W.W. Norton, 1990), xv.
24. Marcel Mauss, *The Gift: The Form and Reason for Exchange in Archaic Societies*, trans. W.D. Halls (New York and London: W.W. Norton, 1990), 20.
25. Mauss, *The Gift*, 46. Emphasis in original.
26. Jacques Derrida, *Given Time: I. Counterfeit Money*, trans. Peggy Kamuf (Chicago: University of Chicago Press, 1992), 11.
27. Jacques Derrida, *Of Hospitality,* trans. Rachel Bowlby (Stanford: Stanford University Press, 2000), 79.
28. Arjun Appadurai, 'Introduction: Commodities and Politics of Value', in Arjun Appadurai (ed.), *The Social Life of Things: Commodities in Cultural Perspective* (Cambridge: Cambridge University Press, 1986), 4.
29. Lewis Hyde, *The Gift: Creativity and the Artist in the Modern World* (New York: Vintage Books, 2007), 11.
30. Hyde, *The Gift*, 27.
31. Robert Tomsho, 'No Dough in the Do-Re-Mi: Songwriters Take On the Recession. Instead of "Brother, Can You Spare a Dime?" It's "Buddy, Can You Spare a Trillion Dollars?"', *The Wall Street Journal*, 6 February 2009, http://online.wsj.com/article/SB123387724064054525.html, last accessed 4 February 2013.
32. Hyde, *The Gift*, 65.
33. Seattle is not the only city whose street musicians and artists are simultaneously revered and somewhat despised. Susie J. Tanenbaum's ethnographic study of the New York City subway system as an underground community and venue for art, music, vending and other activities that have very little to do with transit also notes subway musicians' difficulty in maintaining professional legitimacy and freedom while at the same time working with city authorities. The Music Under New York (MUNY) programme sponsored by the Metropolitan Transit Authority (MTA) creates a programme of subway music throughout the year, with free tokens and a stipend for those who make it through rigorous auditions. 'The MUNY frame establishes a power structure that often severely constrains musicians' patterns of use of subway space and complicates their relationships to one another.' Susie J. Tanenbaum, *Underground Harmonies: Music and Politics*

in the Subways of New York (New York: Cornell University Press, 1995), 132. The question is whether the MTA has accepted freelance subway musicians as part of subway culture, or appropriated them for control. The same can be asked of the Pike Place buskers' relationship with the Market.

34. Quoted in Tanenbaum, *Underground Harmonies*, 97.

35. Tanenbaum, *Underground Harmonies*, 97.

36. Tanenbaum, *Underground Harmonies*, 98.

Works cited

Appadurai, Arjun. 'Introduction: Commodities and Politics of Value', in Arjun Appadurai (ed.), *The Social Life of Things: Commodities in Cultural Perspective*. Cambridge: Cambridge University Press, 1986.

Bhatnagar, Rhani. 'From Charity to Taxes: Observations on the Sociology of Religious and Secular Giving'. *Journal for the Scientific Study of Religion*, 9(3) (Autumn 1970): 209–18.

Derrida, Jacques. *Given Time: I. Counterfeit Money*, trans. Peggy Kamuf. Chicago: University of Chicago Press, 1992.

——. *Of Hospitality*, trans. Rachel Bowlby. Stanford: Stanford University Press, 2000.

Habermas, Jürgen. *The Structural Transformation of the Public Sphere: An Inquiry into a Category of Bourgeois Society*, trans. Thomas Burger. Cambridge, MA: MIT Press, 1991.

Hyde, Lewis. *The Gift: Creativity and the Artist in the Modern World*. New York: Vintage Books, 2007.

Markovitch, Matt. 'Local Musicians Sound Final Note for "Tuba Man"', *Komo News*, 8 November 2008. http://www.komonews.com/news/local/34150519.html. Last accessed 4 February 2013.

Martin, Bradford D. *The Theatre Is in the Street: Politics and Public Performance in Sixties America*. Amherst and Boston: University of Massachusetts Press, 2004.

Mason, Bim. *Street Theatre and Other Outdoor Performance*. London and New York: Routledge, 1992.

Mauss, Marcel. *The Gift: The Form and Reason for Exchange in Archaic Societies*, trans. W.D. Halls, foreword by Mary Douglas. New York, London: W.W. Norton, 1990.

McAfee, Noelle. *Habermas, Kristeva, and Citizenship*. Ithaca and London: Cornell University Press, 2000.

Mukta, Parita. 'On Beggars, the Homeless, and the Poor', *Economic and Political Weekly*, 32(24) (14–20 June 1997): 1387–8.

Press, Percy and Brooks McNamara. 'An Interview with Percy Press and a Portfolio of Buskers', *Educational Theatre Journal*, 27(3) (October 1975): 313–22.

Singer, Peter. 'The Science Behind our Generosity: How Psychology Affects What We Give Charities', *Newsweek* 28 February 2009. http://www.newsweek.com/2009/02/27/the-science-behind-our-generosity.html. Last accessed 4 February 2013.

Tanenbaum, Susie J. *Underground Harmonies: Music and Politics in the Subways of New York*. New York: Cornell University Press, 1995.

Tomsho, Robert. 'No Dough in the Do-Re-Mi: Songwriters Take On the Recession. Instead of "Brother, Can You Spare a Dime?" It's "Buddy, Can You Spare a Trillion Dollars?"', *The Wall Street Journal*, 6 February 2009. http://online.wsj.com/article/SB123387724064054525.html. Last accessed 4 February 2013.

Turnbull, Lornet. 'Seattle's Tuba Man Dies from Beating Injuries', *The Seattle Times*, 5 November 2008. http://seattletimes.nwsource.com/html/localnews/2008352227_tubaman05m.html. Last accessed 4 February 2013.

Turner, Victor. *From Ritual to Theatre: The Human Seriousness of Play.* New York: PAJ Publications, 1982.

Warner, Michael. *Publics and Counterpublics.* New York: Zone Books, 2005.

Wong, Brad. 'Remembering Seattle's Tuba Man with Music', *The Seattle Post-Intelligencer.* 8 November 2008. http://www.seattlepi.com/local/387071_tubaman09.html. Last accessed 4 February 2013.

Part IV Discussion

Claire Chambers, Shira Schwartz, and Stephen D. Seely

Shira Schwartz: Regarding the question, 'Do our examples describe "ephemeral publics"?' I would say yes. The discourses that emerge both within and outside the typical bathing house are ongoing and hail an ephemeral public that continues to exist where there is no live *mikveh* ritual at play. So *mikveh* communities exist around and between and through individual *mikveh* practice, and so in this way I would call them ephemeral.

Stephen Seely: I too would say what I try to describe is ephemeral. The coming out ritual or performance began as much more ephemeral but then moved towards a kind of ontologized identity in which queerness is not thought of as ephemeral, but actually as the opposite, as an identity with which one is born. My chapter argues for a movement 'back' – for lack of a better word – to that kind of ephemerality as a productive site of queer possibility. I'm specifically challenging the subordination of ephemeral practices or rituals to a logic of identity.

Claire Chambers: Stephen, later in your chapter you talk about going against the grain of the 'virtually normal', making a compelling connection between that demand you read in queer politics that the statement 'I am gay' qualifies someone for that identity, and a mainstream protestant Christian worldview where belief assures salvation, as opposed to a life that integrates faith and practice. I like the recognition that there's a difference between a declaration of identity in order to solidify a political presence versus a declaration that has more to do with an interior understanding of selfhood.

Schwartz: I thought that was particularly evident when Stephen spoke about performatives as a way of becoming. The language is not constative, not merely reflective of an authentic self, but an iteration, a becoming into a new queerness that is constructive and creative.

Seely: I see a parallel between all three chapters in that public space is constructed around practices. In mainstream protestant Christianity and also in identitarian queer politics, it seems that ritual is subordinate to the idea that we are here because we are queer *already* or Christian *already*, which becomes more important than any ritual activity. But ritual can actually *constitute* the public. In that sense, the practice itself is far more important than the identity with which one enters the space.

Chambers: With the busking example, I'm not really interested in the conceptual space of the participants of the ritual, but about the external form of the space and practice itself. For example, I talk about Goffman's 'focused interaction' and the spontaneous creation of that ritual space, whereas you both think about shared conceptual space, really trying to understand the dynamic of shared imagined communities. I'm interested in how form itself exists alongside the imagined communities or spaces, and how formal ritual can challenge the invisible norms of such communities.

Schwartz: Claire, although I'm speaking more about the conceptual space and you're speaking more about the form, we share an interest in Derrida's theory that the act of following *a law* by enacting the *laws* of the ritual may actually subvert that first law. When I think about applying these terms to the *mikveh* space I wonder how the performance of *mikveh* discourses, like discussions about sexuality between women using the vocabulary of *nidah*, disrupts the law of *mikveh* practice, which is that of an individual, personal, private act between a woman and God. But the laws (plural) of a *mikveh* public require a *mikveh* attendant and a communal structure, which subverts the law of complete privacy. It seems both our examples show a formal structure that is subverted by its own ritualized performance. I think that kind of undoing comes up a lot – the undoing from within; there's *a law* in place, but then the *laws* necessary to carry it out undo that original law.

Chambers: I'm thinking about the *how* and the *what*. There's the material life of the ritual in which the laws are embedded that are important to the upkeep of the community – so that's the 'what'. But then the 'how' is like the life of that 'what' –

Schwartz: The spirit of it.

Chambers: Yes. So that transition between the 'how' and the 'what' really interests me in buskers' practice. The normal market focuses on the 'what', the good that the artist produces and offers for sale, but the busker is focusing on the 'how' of the interaction between the audience and the performer, sometimes working to break that barrier, and that breakage is often what justifies the performance.

Seely: Shira, I like your discussion of Mahmood's *The Politics of Piety* and her re-reading of Foucault, especially in terms of his reception in queer theory that says we are always already resistant, or else we're normative – I think she blows all of that apart. With the buskers, you can't say that it is outright resistance to capitalism, but it opens a different kind of economy from within those spaces. With the *mikveh*, you can't just say that it is anti-patriarchal. There could be feminists who look at it and see the subjugation of women, but it opens up a completely different space from within the inhabitation of those norms. For me, I'm taking on the normativity of gay identity. I have a problem with queer politics that sees itself as always already subversive and therefore resistant to religion.

Schwartz: Stephen, you didn't directly quote Mahmood, but the way that you bring together the structure of the confession, as a very organized religious practice, with the coming out process, and the way you think about a productive relationship between the two that goes beyond tolerance, questions whether or not queerness and religion are natural enemies. I think that's really the spirit of Mahmood as well – that there's a relationship here that is not merely oppositional, and that defining that kind of opposition in advance gets us into trouble, because that only highlights one's own subject position, and is not a productive way to engage these two forces. There is a relationship and an entanglement there, and even more so, similarities in their forms.

Seely: I really like the word entanglement. As Mahmood points out in *The Politics of Piety*, it's scary for people to think about the entanglements of religious practices and structures of resistance. While some people want to just write off religion as patriarchal or homophobic or normative in advance, she shows how we are always already caught up in those practices. Similarly, my chapter tries to force you to sit with the discomfort that comes from an entanglement of queerness and Christianity.

Chambers: So what's the relationship between resisting being '*already* resistant' and what Mahmood is saying about that entanglement *already* being in place? I'm trying to understand these different 'alreadys'.

Seely: Mahmood's point is about the Mosque movement in Egypt, which some feminists would write off as patriarchal, asking why these women would engage in their own subjugation. Mahmood says it's a fantasy of leftist feminists or queer theorists or activists, to think that we can identify the terms of resistance in advance, that we would call any practice simply normative or oppressive. We are ignoring that we generally live in proximity to norms, and very rarely are we in a space of outright resistance. She reads Foucault and points out that he's saying we can't step outside those terms to know the stakes in advance. My piece challenges queer politics that want to abjure all relationships to Christianity in advance, or that see Christianity precisely as what generates the forces of homophobia and normativity. We are already bound up in the relationship between Christianity and queerness. The idea that we must always already be resisting Christianity or religion is always oppressive to us: it's a fantasy, a delusion. I think we can find a different way to negotiate that entanglement, because it's not the case that queer people who are religious are somehow 'confused'.

Schwartz: There are Orthodox Jewish queer individuals who have come out, speak about being gay, and are living embodiments of the entanglement.

They cannot erase the text – the laws, the Jewish scripture – but their identity is as a practicing Jew, so they embrace that entanglement.

Chambers: Can we talk about the relationships between texts and the ephemeral publics we are addressing? For Shira, the Talmudic texts play a significant role in these women's lives.

Schwartz: For sure. The way that text is thought about in Jewish practice is that it cannot be left on its own – it cannot exist without the reader or the interpreter. For instance, the Torah is actually like lecture notes, and needs the oral tradition complementing it. This performative principle necessitates liveness – texts need the commentary of human beings. In *mikveh* ritual there is a tension between the text's demands and actual practice. But the very stringency of the text allows discourses to emerge because when you have a question, you ask a rabbi or a female authority, a conversation takes place, and a public is hailed. This is a touchy subject, but one of the things women have trouble with is that sometimes it's unclear physiologically when a women is at the end of her cycle and can start to count her clean days before she can enter the *mikveh*. Some women even consult rabbis when examining spotting in their underwear: What is this? Is this blood? What colour? Does this count? Some women are very comfortable doing this, and others less so. It's very political! This would never happen if the text was not so strict.

Chambers: There's this very interesting relationship between the explicit or voiced, and the implicit or the silent. It seems the *not said* constitutes this counterpublic of the private, but then again discourse is generated by the specificity of the texts. Where does this public exist for these women? I'm just curious about the interaction between the voiced and the tacit.

Schwartz: Two main publics are formed here: practitioners and authorities. The authorities proclaim the rabbinic rulings about women's menstrual cycles. But another public is formed in the practice of the laws, the sharing between women, and the spirituality of it. A lot of the time that public is coded because women use the vocabulary of *mikveh* and *nidah* to voice their emotions. A woman may speak about the urgency she feels to go to the *mikveh* from a pious perspective, but the double meaning is that she's saying, I am anxious to sleep with my husband because I haven't touched him for two weeks.

Chambers: Stephen, could you also speak to this relationship between the voiced and not voiced? Ostensibly, confession is all about what is being said. But there's a lot in your chapter about what is implied in the participation in that confession.

Seely: I'm trying to challenge that only the spoken constitutes a public act, and the reduction of all queerness to one public statement. So much is unacknowledged. And then there is often virulence directed against people who do not make that declaration. We saw this just recently with Jodie Foster at the Golden Globes. So many of my queer friends reacted by saying that she has a 'responsibility' to make that public declaration, and that if she doesn't, she's a traitor to the queer community. She should clearly say 'I am gay', otherwise it's a betrayal.

Chambers: Which invites the question: how can we possibly regulate such a thing? How can we talk about the overlap between these internal conceptual spaces and the lived practice of public space? How can we say that because of someone's internal conviction, or spiritual experience, or private sexual identity, they belong to or participate in a kind of public space? It seems contradictory – the contradiction between wanting to respect the privacy of someone like Foster and her decision, and the difficulty of needing that shared interior experience to use as material to create the environment for that public.

Seely: For me it brings up the impossibility of creating any kind of prescription. If we were actually able to challenge the foundational heteronormativity of the public sphere, then we wouldn't have the idea that if you didn't speak publicly about your queer sexuality that you are a traitor. The point is that the declaration *doesn't* actually challenge the heteronormativity of the public sphere, but reinforces that bifurcation between the public self, which is the speaking self, and the private self, which is having whatever kind of sex you have at home.

Schwartz: So if the queer project is successful, the speech act of coming out would not be necessary?

Seely: Right. Maybe it's a kind of utopian ideal.

Schwartz: Your chapter uses the speech act of coming out to challenge the idea that there's a contest between a person's biological make-up and the heteronormative expectations of society. You speak about how queerness is always performative – not a collision of a biological fact with a social force, but a constant relationship with society, so much so that it is indistinguishable. This essentialist idea of the collision of inside and outside is an illusion; it's also about space and disappearance. Queer space doesn't have borders because it is constantly becoming; there is no containment of it. The containment of the speech act of coming out – that's not real.

Seely: And I think that this lack of containment goes through all our chapters. These publics are ephemeral because they are porous, temporally and spatially dispersed, they last longer than the ritual encounters themselves.

Chambers: I think this ties back into the discussion about the circulation of texts as constituting a public. When I started to talk with buskers, a surprising discovery was the importance of media in how they understood the effectiveness of their performances – especially photography, journalism, and videos that people might put up online. They seemed to understand the capture of their image or music or art and its circulation, beyond their control, as a really positive thing that would circle back to them, expanding the purview of their art. And often it would be anonymous. So being unnamed but still having influence was a strong idea – their presence created a 'text' for circulation that had significance beyond themselves. They almost became their own texts for circulation that created the counter-economy in which they worked.

Another point of contact I wanted to bring up is the issue of audience. Shira, in the ethnography section of your chapter you discuss the importance of the figure of the *mikveh* attendant; does she act as a kind of audience for the women? Stephen, you discuss how conversion/confession depends on the presence of an other to function, because you're always confessing *to* someone. My chapter also deals with the possibility that there could be a conversion of identity from audience member to performer. Might these theatrical terms give you a different perspective into your chapter?

Schwartz: What is important about *mikveh* ritual is that it does contain that audience member. Locating myself now within the orthodox community, I believe that for every law there is a spiritual component and a social component. The audience is an important part of that sociological level. For example, if there is physical evidence that a woman is being abused (because there is domestic abuse in the Orthodox Jewish community as there is in every community), the *mikveh* attendant would take notice. Attendants are trained to note any sign of abuse and approach women in a non-threatening way and offer help. That's an extreme example of the therapeutic aspect of *mikveh*. On a less extreme level in the relationship between a woman and the *mikveh* attendant there is an emotional vulnerability that takes place. It's a doorway to talk about the husband–wife relationship more broadly, and also the details of a relationship. The audience member is a key role in terms of the social dynamic of this public, the way that the *mikveh* is meaningful on a practical and personal level.

Seely: Actually this question kind of stumps me, perhaps because I don't often work in performance studies. I do talk about how the confession requires an audience of at least two, or as Foucault says at least a virtual audience.

Schwartz: In your chapter, Stephen, I was struck by the phenomenon of recalling coming out stories to one another. I imagine that in that situation the role of the audience is important, because the reaction of your audience might figure into how you tell that story in the future. So what your audience finds funny, interesting, sad, compelling, or tragic about the coming out story is going to influence not only how you re-tell it, but also the way you conceptualize that experience for yourself. The theatricality of that situation is very interesting to me.

Seely: D'Emilio, from whom I take that quote, emphasizes the community formation aspects of the audience. We often think of coming out as only the transformation of the individual – you are now liberated, because you have come out! Yes, you've come 'out of the closet', but what has actually happened is that you have entered *into* a relationality with your audience. It breaks down the idea of the audience as a passive observer, which emphasizes the importance of the world-making project, and not just the act of individual liberation.

Chambers: Something I really enjoyed discovering in interviewing the Seattle buskers is that there's almost this paratheatrical attitude toward their performance. I'm taking that term 'paratheatrical' from Grotowski – meaning theatre practice without an audience, or theatrical activity focusing on the community of the performers themselves. In my experience with paratheatrical training, you reach a point where the performance for one another becomes also a performance for oneself, which results in the creation of a tightly knit, small, momentary society, an alternative community. For the buskers, they are not so much working to break apart the strictures of the audience–performer duality, but are very open to that possibility, which I think also speaks to their social function as a group who often exist alongside or even outside the law and the rules of the 'normal' economy. It's very much an alternative world-making, but at the same time one almost has to be looking for that in order to recognize it. In terms of ephemerality, that fluidity between performer and audience, or at least between speaker and receiver, is definitely an important component of our conversation.

Schwartz: For Jewish Orthodox practice, there is always an audience because the performance of ritual is always in the presence of God. From hand-washing in the morning to saying blessings over food, wearing *tzitzit* [knotted fringes on garments] if you are a man – there are so many rituals that no one else 'sees', but you do it for yourself and God. There is this idea of performance as always paratheatrical in a way for yourself. A lot of people would say that it should never be for show. Even though communities perform rituals together, the intentionality is always that it's about me and God, and that's it.

Chambers: In contemporary society, religions are conceived as existing as *other* from society, which would demarcate a boundary between a performer – for example, the religion – and an audience – for example, society at large. What you are talking about, Shira, challenges a secular person, or anyone outside of that particular religious setting, to think through what it would be like to comprehend the world in a different way, what it's like to regard the world as a religious world, rather than saying, 'This is my religion within these confines, which exist within the world'. This is a very different view from someone who says, 'I belong to the world *through* the practice of my faith'.

Seely: About the lack of a sense of privacy, Shira – it is also a transformation of consciousness, which is what I also find productive about rethinking queerness. It's a kind of psychic public rather than a private identity – something that you carry with you conceptually, and you might not need to share it verbally, but it's not necessarily only your private identity, either.

Schwartz: The question of 'bad faith' is important here too. In a religious context there are two dimensions of performance: one is actually performing the law and the other is the theatricality of going through the motions. Let's say a woman has been counting the days to determine when she can go to the *mikveh*. It's not uncommon that although a woman has been clean for a few days, she might suddenly experience spotting. She is then faced with a choice: do I start counting again, or do I overlook the spotting? At the end of the day, the woman is the one upholding the laws for herself and her family, responsible for the quote–unquote 'authenticity' of it.

Seely: I think 'ephemeral publics' is an appropriate heading for all three chapters because they are contesting the rigid division between public and private in the first place, and the spillage of private acts into public spaces and vice versa, both temporally and spatially.

Chambers: Thank you both for your insight. I am sure this conversation will continue in the larger debate about the place of religion in the public sphere.

Index

Note: 'n' after a page reference denotes a note number on that page.

adiaphora 28, 43n7
aesthetic 5, 139, 185, 194–6, 212
affect 5, 92, 118–21, 134
affections 29–30, 37–8, 52, 60
Al-insan-al-kamil 180
alms 258, 261
Al-wallaya 180
altruism 260–1
Agnew, Jean-Christophe 31, 41
antitheatricality 27, 41, 94
Asad, Talal 11–12
Austin, J.L. 40, 93
amusement park 202, 213
Anatolia 180
And, Metin 182, 187
Andersson, Kerstin 206n6
Anglicanism 74, 98, 107–10, 155,
    166–7, 173–6, 210–1
    The Book of Homilies 39, 93
anti-Christ 144
apocalypse 134, 142
Appadurai, Arjun 267
Arnold, Matthew 102
'Asmodeus' 174
Atatürk, Mustafa Kemal 182–4
Augustine 97, 222–5
awkwardness 121, 127–30, 252
Aylmer, Bishop John 33
Azazi, Ziya 186–7, 191

ballet 100–6, 154, 157
Bauman, Zygmunt 199
Bailey, Adrian R. 173
Bailey, Peter 166
Beck, Ulrich 199
Bengal 195–7, 200–1
Berger, John 199
Berlant, Lauren 252–3
binarization 4, 14–15
Blayney, Peter 34
Book of Common Prayer 101
Booth, Michael 165

Boyarin, Daniel 222
Bose, Pradip 202
'bracket' 7–8, 258
Bradlaugh, Charles 107–8
Brown, Wendy 232n4
Butler, Judith 11, 14, 37, 225, 232n6,
    250

Cameron, Kirk 124–6
capitalism 37, 76, 78, 91, 99, 196, 199,
    264, 267, 279, *see also Marketplace*
Carroll, Noel 144
Cartesian epistemology 258
Catholic 27–8, 35, 51, 71–7, 101, 225
Caughey, James 175–6
Çelebi, Adel 182
charisma 125, 128, 181
Christian identity 134–6, 140, 147
Christian Socialism 98, 100, 111n9, 159
church
    as community 98–9, 109–10
    early practice 225–6
    of England, *see Anglicanism*
    as figurative space 98, 103, 15
Church and Stage Guild 97–8
Church Missionary Society, The 7
Church Reformer 103, 106–7
the closet 219–21
Collinson, Patrick 29, 36
Colosseum Music Hall 174
Comfort, Roy 123–6
commodification 18, 27, 201, 209–10,
    256, 269, 272
communication 8, 10, 57, 90, 141
community 2, 10, 57–63
confession 119, 225–8
conversion 121, 223–5
Cooper Union discussion 11
Cornick, David 166, 172, 176
cosmopolitanism 202
counterpublic 8–9, 40–1, 75, 93–94,
    214, 229, 238, 242, 259–60

culture industry 198–201
Cvetkovich, Ann 121

dance 97–8, 179, 186–7, 271–2 *see also*
 ballet
Dasgupta, Krishnapriya 197
Davies, Horton 169, 175
de Certeau, Michel 9, 121
D'Emilio, John 220–1, 224
demons 81, 142–6, 156
Derrida, Jacques 131n29, 228, 266, 279
de Tocqueville, Alexis 121
devotion 2–3, 49, 52–3, 57–8, 61–2
dévots 91
dichotimization 2
Dinda, Sanatan 197
discourse, circulation of 28, 33, 41, 91,
 117
Disneyfication 202
divine beauty 105, 155, 157
donation 196, 259–61
Douglas, Mary 141, 265–6
Drane, John 202
Drury Lane 104, 107
Dūrgā Pūjā 195–205

East End 100
economics 99, 169, 256–9, 263–7
Elizabeth I of England 35–9, 88
embodied, embodiment 8–9, 29, 37,
 42, 126, 135, 150,
Enlightenment rationality 15, 71
Enoch Arden 168
entextualizing 98–100, 103
ephemeral 202, 253, 278–84
epistemology, performative 13, 16
Erdoğan, Yılmaz 185–6
Erguner, Kudsi 182, 184
erotic 104, 267
Ersig, Patrick 127–8
ethnography 191, 239–42, 251–3
evangelical 76, 99, 103, 118–20, 136,
 154
excess 153, 205, 211

Fish, Stanley 10–12
Fletcher, John 125, 131n27
Foley Sherman, Jon 126
Foucault, Michel 14, 38, 202, 207n22,
 222–30, 237, 246

fracture 98–9, 103, 108
France 49–51, 62–3, 91
Freedom from Religion
 Foundation 147–8
Fraser, Nancy 7, 204
The Function of the Stage (Headlam) 100

Gates, Henry Louis 125
gender 12, 157, 238–44
generosity 127, 183, 256–61
gesture 55, 129, 147, 153, 155, 189–90,
 242, 253, 256
Gharavi, Lance 17
Giddens, Anthony 199
globalization 201, 204
Goffman, Erving 271–2, 279
Grammar of Assent (Newman) 100–1
Greenham, Rev Richard 28–30
Guild of St Matthew 109

Habermas, Jürgen 5–12, 50, 117–29,
 135, 190–1, 194, 237–8, 252–3,
 256
An Awareness of What is Missing
 (2007) 9
'bourgeois public sphere' 5–7
coffeehouses 17, 27, 124, 237–8
democracy 5–7, 9–11
*The Structural Transformation of the
 Public Sphere* (1962) 5, 135, 256
'translation' of the religious
 argument 6, 15
hailing 36, 93–4, 117–18, 153, 278
Halperin, David 234n47
happiness 257, 262
Harvey, David C. 173
Harwood, George 167, 170
Headlam, Stuart Duckworth 97–119
hegemonic 14–15, 79, 125, 205,
 229–31, 252–3
heterotopia 202–3, 214
hijab 1, 214
Hindu 2, 74–5, 195–6, 210
Hirschkop, Ken 5
holy fool 260
horror 134, 144, 153–8
hospitality 183, 265–6
Hudgins, Tom 136–7
humoral physiology 29–30, 38
Hyde, Lewis 267–8

illative sense   102
intimacy   119, 126–8, 189, 195,
      237–42, 252–3
irony   75, 108, 158

Jasper, David   98–9
Jewish law   238–40, 243–5
Jonson, Ben   29
Judgement House   134–40

Kadiri   182
Kershaw, Baz   17, 139
Kierkegaard, Søren   126, 128
kingdom of heaven   105, 109
Kirby, Torrance   27, 29, 38
Kolkata   195–202
Kong, Lily   164–5, 174
Kristeva, Julia   258

Lancasterian School Room
      (Nottingham)   172
legitimation   87–94
Levinasian 'face'   126, 131n31
LGBT, *see queer*
liberalization   194–5, 201, 209
liturgy   51, 101, 257
Living Waters   123
Lyotard, Jean-François   223, 225

Mahmood, Saba   12, 23, 238, 241–2,
      250–1, 278–80
Making Publics project   27, 42n4
'Mapping Performance Culture:
      Nottingham 1857–1867'   165
marketplace   29, 31–2, 121, 126,
      199–200, 210, 238–9, 256–7
Marshfield, Wisconsin   145–9
Martin, Bradford   263
Marx, Karl   201–2
Mason, Bim   261–2
mass   51–5, 88–91, 159
Maurice, F.D.   102, 105
Mauss, Marcel   265
McAfee, Noelle   258
McDonaldization   202
McKenzie, John   17
McNamara, Brooks   262
Meisel, Joseph   169
metatopos   20
Methodism   167–74

Mevlana   182, 187, 190–1
Mevlevi   182–90
Mikveh   237–53
modernity   120, 153, 182, 195, 205
Molière   91–2
Montgomery, Walter   168
Morrell, Jesse   119–25
mythos   260

neo-liberal public sphere   195, 200–1
Nafs   187, 191
Namaz   189
Newman, John Henry Card   101–3,
      106
Nightmare (performance)   145–9
Tulsa, Oklahoma   151n17
Nonconformism   166–70
North American Mission Board   120
Nottingham (nineteenth-century
      town)   163–76
Nottingham Arboretum   173
Nottingham Journal   163–4, 170–5
Nottingham Mechanics' Institute   173
Nottingham Telegraph   174

Ocak, Ahmet Yaşar   180
Olier, Jean-Jacques   51, 55–6
Open Air Outreach   119
Orr, Captain   164

P-Nasty   125, 157
Pandal   196–200
Parody   156
Paul of Tarsus   122, 222–4
Paul's Cross   28–34, 41
Park Row Chapel (Nottingham)
      178n32
Pellegrini, Ann   134–5
performance   3–4, 13–18, 27–34,
      41–2, 62, 87–90, 126–8, 139–41,
      150, 165–6, 184–8, 203–5, 211–14,
      237–8, 259–65
   and civic order   27, 39
   and government   87–9, 93–4
   and place   89–90
performance studies (field)   4, 13–17,
      111n15, 118, 126
performative speech   8, 21, 28, 31–2,
      36–7, 41, 92–3, 282, *see also*
      J.L. Austin

performative 1–17, 28, 31, 93–4, 125,
134–5, 194–5, 203–5, 224–5, 231,
257, 281–2
public sphere as 7, 10, 13–15
religion as 1–2, 8, 12
performativity 111n15, 203, 208, 238,
249–51
Perkins, William 38
personal, the 1, 37, 49–50, 56, 83, 121,
126–7, 134–141, 154, 249, 265–6,
279
Phelan, Peggy 14, 240
phenomenology 15–16, 131n31
philanthropy 249, 259–61
playfulness/playlessness 125, 199, 214
pilgrimage 199
Pir 181
pleasure 100, 105, 155, 159, 211, 241,
261–2
Poole, Kristen 37
poesis (world-making) 9, 119–20, 139
'poetry of motion' 97, 100–1, 106
Polytechnic Hall (Nottingham), *see*
Coliseum Music Hall
prayer 30, 49–63, 137
Prayer Walking 120
preaching 8, 28–42
and hailing 35–6
and performance 28–33
and Protestant tradition 8
Priestnall, Gary 165
private religion 121
prophetic speech 29–31, 38–41, 78,
92–4, 139
Protestant 8, 32–3, 38, 74–6, 122–3,
230, 258, 278
public 1–9, 14–15, 27–8, 30–3, 36–42,
134–7, 147–8 *et passim*
publics 3, 6–9, 27, 50, 56–7, 87, 93–4,
103, 118–19, 126–8, 164, 170, 211,
215, 238–42, 281–2
counterpublics 8–9, 27–8, 40–1, 75,
93–4, 117–18, 170, 214, 229, 231,
238–42, 259–60, 281
and cultural commodity 2, 18, 261
depersonalization 37, 50, 56, 117,
126
and discursive circulation 9, 28, 39,
54, 59–62, 75, 91, 117, 141, 238,
282–3

how characterized 62, 117–18, 125
ideal 20, 258, 261
intolerable 118, 125
spatial metaphor 2, 98, 126, 138,
214, 218
as performative event 7, 13–7
and private 1–2, 8–11, 27–9, 37,
49–51, 75, 121, 148, 179, 187, 195,
229–32, 237–8, 246, 251–3, 256–8,
281–4
public sphere 1–20, 42, 83, 117–21,
138, 154–6, 194–5, 203–5, 219–22,
228–31, 237, 257–9
Pūjā Parikrama 201
Pūjā, Themed 198, 203–5
Puritan 27–42, 89–90, 93–4, 121
and performance 29–30
prophesyings 38, 43n11
Vestiarian Controversy 28

queer 219–31, 238, 253, 278–82
Quran 181–2, 187–9

rabbi, rabbinic 81, 238–9, 246–7, 281
Rawls, John 6
regulation 190, 237, 269
self-regulation 270–1
Religious Census (1851) 166–7, 172,
175
religious practice(s) 49–53, 60
Rhymers Club 107
Richard Dawkins Society 219
Rifai 182
ritual 16–7, 30, 42, 75, 90, 153,
184–7, 201, 228, 237–40, 244–5,
257–8
Temple ritual 239
Ritzer, George 202
Rumi 182–5
Ruskin, John 99, 101, 155

sacrifice 154–5, 226, 257, 264
sacramental socialism 98
sacred vocation 50–1, 105
Şalliel, Orhan 185
Sarkar, Amar 197
Saul of Tarsus, *see Paul of Tarsus*
Schechner, Richard 16
Schimmel, Anne Marie 183
Schmitt, Carl 5

Seb-i Aruz 183–4, 189, 212–13
secular 2–12, 172–6, 182–8, 203–6
Sema 181–91, 210–12
Seminary, Saint-Sulpice 49–54
Seminary, Saint-Nicolas-du-
    Chardonnet 49–50, 53, 62–3
sermon-tasting 169
sexuality 121, 221–9, 237–8,
    242, *see also Foucault and
    Mikveh*
Shakespeare, William 27–8
Sharia 210–12
shopping 200
Signorile, Michelangelo 224
Singer, Peter 264–5
Smith, David 185
spectacle 77, 143, 158, 201
spiritual gift 256–67
Spufford, Margaret 32
Spurgeon, Charles 122
Stockwood, Rev John 28–42
Skinners Company 33
street preaching 117–28
Stonewall riots 220–1
subculture 268
Sufism 179–81, 185–7, 210–12
Sutar, Bhabatosh 197

Talmud 238–41, 281
Tariqat 180–3, 189–2, 212
Tartuffe 91
Taylor, Charles 11
Taylor, Diana 13, 191
Tawhid 180
Tennyson, Alfred (Lord) 168
textuality 8–9, 32
theatre performance 27, 31, 94,
    100–4, 163–5
Theatre Royal Nottingham (New)
    168
Theatre Royal Nottingham (Old)
    173
Thomas Road Baptist Church
    120
tithe 261
Tonbridge School 33
Torah 239, 249, 281
total depravity 123
Tribulation Trail 141–5
Tunca, Elif 186

Turner, Victor 15, 27, 128, 204,
    263
Communitas 128
liminality 41, 229
social drama 27, 263

Ulema 179, 181
UNESCO 184–5
untranslatability 13–7

Veled, Sultan 182
Venerable English College, Rome 154
Victoria, Queen 166
visceral 140, 150, 154–9, 259
voluntarism 118, 259
vulnerability 127–8, 245, 269

Warner, Michael 7–9, 19, 29, 38–42, 50,
    54–9, 75, 90–4, 118–20, 128, 170–1,
    214, 229, 238–42, 253, 259–60
alternative poetic world 31
counterpublics 8–9, 27–31, 41,
    75, 87–9, 94, 117–18, 121, 170,
    214, 229–32, 238–42, 257–60
embodied sociability 29
Monsters of Impudence 36
Publics and Counterpublics 8, 238
stranger sociability 8, 31–3, 54–6,
    60–2, 94
world-making 9, 39, 117–20, 139,
    229, 231, 247, 284
Watt, Tessa 32
Way of the Master 124, 131n27
wedding 184, 212, 239
Welch, Gina 120
West Bengal 195–6
West, Cornel 8, 11
Whately, Richard 97, 101–2
Whitgift, Bishop John 36
Wilde, Oscar 97
Wilson, Robert 185
Wittenberg, David 126
Witwatersrand, University of 92
Wolterstorff, Nicholas 10

Yachnin, Paul 27–8, 50, 56
YouTube 119, 125, 272

Zikr 181–2, 187–9
Žižek, Slavoj 121

Printed and bound by CPI Group (UK) Ltd, Croydon, CR0 4YY